ADVANCING THE METHOD AND PRACTICE OF TRANSNATIONAL LAW

This book adopts a transnational methodology to reflect on the legalisation of international economic relations. A Liber Amicorum for Professor Francis Snyder, it outlines the ways in which legal scholarship has taken his legacy further in relation to the concept of transnational law, the 'law in context' method, and the evolution of sustainability law. The lens is both theoretical and practical, delving into international investment law, financial/monetary law, free trade agreements, indigenous rights and food law, and covering case studies from EU law, WTO law, American law, Chinese law and Indonesian law.

The chapters explore how Snyder's ideas have advanced legal research and determined change in regulation, impacting trade relationships worldwide. Part I of the book gives an overview of the actors, the norms and the processes of transnational economic law, discussing sites of governance, legal pluralism and soft law. Part II takes stock of the 'law in context' research method, looking not only at the way in which it can be refined and used by academics, but also at the practical implications of such a method to improve regulatory settings and promote social and policy goals (including the emerging generation of FTAs, such as TPP, TTIP and RCEP). Part III focuses on sustainability law, assessing Snyder's contribution to systemic changes and reforms in China and the Asia Pacific region.

The book is a must-have for any academic or practitioner interested in an up-to-date account of the recent developments in transnational trade law research.

Advancing the Method and Practice of Transnational Law

Building Bridges Across Disciplines

Edited by
Julien Chaisse
and
Oana Ştefan

•HART•
OXFORD • LONDON • NEW YORK • NEW DELHI • SYDNEY

HART PUBLISHING

Bloomsbury Publishing Plc

Kemp House, Chawley Park, Cumnor Hill, Oxford, OX2 9PH, UK

1385 Broadway, New York, NY 10018, USA

29 Earlsfort Terrace, Dublin 2, Ireland

HART PUBLISHING, the Hart/Stag logo, BLOOMSBURY and the Diana logo are trademarks of Bloomsbury Publishing Plc

First published in Great Britain 2023

A catalogue record for this book is available from the British Library.

A catalogue record for this book is available from the Library of Congress.

Library of Congress Control Number: 2023939201

ISBN: HB: 978-1-50996-449-9
ePDF: 978-1-50996-451-2
ePub: 978-1-50996-450-5

Typeset by Compuscript Ltd, Shannon

FOREWORD

More than a major work, it is a pathway.

Liber amicorum is a harmonious Latin phrase that is a delight to utter. It is irrefutably a manifestation of the affection you can have for someone to whom you owe so much. This spark of humanity is admirable within the academic realm that is so often permeated with rivalries and resentment.

By sheer coincidence, Francis Snyder holds dual distinctions as both an eminent colleague and a precious friend. His frank expression, his smile and firm handshake, all bear witness to his honest character. But one must go beyond that to measure the mark left by this outstanding scholar.

This book will, I am sure, give you a sweeping view of the countless fields that Francis Snyder fertilised. For my part, I shall only allude to a select few moments from our two decades of academic companionship – mainly in Aix-en-Provence and occasionally in Shenzhen. I will not detail how globalisation was explained to the layperson by analysing, in an iconoclastic way, the distribution channel of Chinese bicycles. A paragon of pedagogy! More than any other person, Francis has led me to consider how demanding thorough legal research is. With him, the scientific nature of law is not a matter of debate, it is self-evident. He has chosen to reinstate law in its context and to reconnect it to *praxis*. The paramount challenge lies in successfully defining the 'truth' of law by transcending the opposition between those who stick to the knowledge of normative content and those who prefer to immerse it within the field of collective practices and social customs at the risk of making it invisible.

Contemporary societies are changing, and the methods of legal regulation are evolving in consonance. The creation of standards is part of a now polycentric environment in which the public authorities are being overtaken by other actors. More than ever, globalisation imposes the idea of legal pluralism, as evidenced by the diversification of sources as well as the actors involved in their production. In a plural world, it is indeed illusory to imagine that the strength and legitimacy of law should depend on its unity. If the *imperium* remains, it is altered by the increasing fluidity of forms and the frequent volatility of norms. Moreover, law is being transformed as the sites of governance multiply (a concept coined by Francis). The formation of law is no longer the sole concern of states or public institutions, but involves other actors whose intervention inevitably influences the form as well as the substance of the norm. The adaptation of the modes of government to the requirements of open governance inevitably impact on the system of sources itself. Thus, including the intended recipients of the norm in its elaboration profoundly modifies the content of the rules adopted after a confrontation between inherently contradictory interests. The balance of power becomes creative because it is tempered by being included in an institutional logic. It is no longer heretical to consider that the norm must result from the involvement of all the parties involved (however great the tensions that weigh upon it) rather than from an act of unilateral will.

Francis was keen to build an explanatory theory that would account for these upheavals, and he blurred the boundary that artificially separates fundamental research from applied research. Proceeding from a 'policy-oriented approach', applied research is less concerned with building theoretical models than with proposing concrete solutions to prosaic problems through a casuistic approach. Conversely, fundamental research, which does not take social, economic and political contexts into account, is more 'contemplative'. The dichotomy is not convincing because it seems at odds with more nuanced realities. Indeed, legal research has both fundamental and applied dimensions. If some research, for example, is developed with practical considerations in mind or targets a wider audience than mere academic readers, it does not necessarily alter its scientific character. Above all, it requires going beyond epistemological thresholds and taking an interdisciplinary and holistic approach whenever relevant.

Francis Snyder helped me to push open all these doors. Ultimately, he has not only imparted upon us a seminal work, but has also cleared a pathway along which successive generations of researchers will test their aptitude for innovation and marvel.

Rostane Mehdi
Professor of European law
Director of Sciences Po Aix
Visiting Professor at College of Europe
Chaire Jean Monnet ad Personam

ACKNOWLEDGEMENTS

We would first like to extend our heartfelt thanks to Professor Francis Snyder, who has been a persistent fountain of inspiration and direction throughout our academic and professional pursuits. His teachings and scholarship have served as a foundational springboard for numerous lines of inquiry that we have chosen to pursue as academics, in an ongoing effort to harness the multiplicity of sources, contexts and transnationality within the law, towards fostering the growth and development of policy, economics and society. Given the numerous global crises that we currently face, it is clear that Francis' work and methodology are indispensable. We are deeply grateful for his unwavering support and wisdom, and for the profound impact it has had on our personal and professional growth as scholars.

Julien was fortunate enough to have Professor Snyder as his mentor during his studies at the Faculty of Law in Aix-en-Provence and the Academy of International Trade Law in Macau during the early 2000s. He quickly became an avid reader of Francis' works, which greatly shaped his intellectual framework. He was particularly struck by the approach of viewing law in context and Francis' early focus on the role of sustainability which influenced Julien's work on water regulation. Over the years, Julien and Francis have collaborated on several projects, including food and wine law, the global shift towards the Asia-Pacific region, and the development of economic integration.

Also during the early 2000s, Oana met Professor Snyder at the College of Europe, in Natolin, and followed his class on World Trade Organization (WTO) law as a teaching assistant, at a time when she was toying with the idea of a career in academia. Whilst the course was an eye-opener as to the law in context methodology, it was Francis' chapter on 'Soft Law and Institutional Practice in the European Community' that inspired her further work on soft law. Francis was generous to offer comments on the very first drafts of her PhD proposal and, months later, to forward casually an advert for a PhD position at University College Dublin with the then recently appointed Professor Imelda Maher. Oana is also a direct beneficiary of several editions of WISH workshops, which have supplied a solid base for her academic network and an inexhaustible source of friends. Years later, she was fortunate to collaborate with Francis on a project on the reception of EU soft law in the national legal orders.

We would also like to extend our gratitude to our many colleagues who have made invaluable contributions to this project through writing chapters or offering their support and expertise. Their friendship for Francis and their dedication and passion for our field have immeasurably enriched this book, and we are honoured to have had the opportunity to collaborate with such knowledgeable and talented individuals.

Professor Snyder and Richard Hart had a long-standing relationship, having met when Hart was establishing himself as a publisher and publishing numerous books together. It was therefore a natural fit for this project to be realised through Hart Publishing. We are deeply appreciative of Hart's support. Special recognition goes to Sinead Moloney (Editorial Director), Roberta Bassi (Senior Commissioning Editor) and Verity Stuart (Assistant Editor) for their exceptional contributions throughout the process. Their unwavering commitment to quality and excellence shines through in every page of this book, which serves as a tribute to Professor Snyder. It is a great privilege to be associated with such a reputable academic publishing house.

We trust that this book will provide valuable insights and inspiration to those who read it and we are humbled to have been a part of this project.

Julien Chaisse and Oana Ştefan
Hong Kong and London, February 2023

CONTENTS

NOTES ON CONTRIBUTORS

Alberto Alemanno is Jean Monnet Professor in EU Law and one of the leading voices on the democratisation of the EU. His research focuses on how the law may be used to improve people's lives, in particular through the adoption of power-shifting reforms countering social, economic, and political inequalities within European societies and beyond. He is the author of more than 40 scientific articles and several academic books. He is also the founder and editor-in-chief of the *European Journal of Risk Regulation* and the *Revue européenne du droit*, and a member of the Editorial Committee of the *Journal of Consumer Policy*.

Paulo Canelas de Castro is Jean Monnet Chair in EU Law at the University of Macau, where he is also the Coordinator of the Master's programme in European Union Law, International Law and Comparative Law. He also serves as President of EUSA-Macau and has been a lecturer for the Academy of International Trade Law. His research focuses on water law issues and he has written several books, chapters and articles on the subject. His publications include *Recent Developments in Water Law. Principles and Comparative Cases* (2006) and *The European Union at 50: Assessing the Past, Looking Ahead* (2010).

Julien Chaisse is a professor at the City University of Hong Kong (CityU), School of Law. He specialises in international economic law (trade, investment and tax), cyber-law, vitivinicultural law and dispute resolution. He is the co-Editor-in-Chief of the *Journal of World Investment & Trade* and Editor-in-Chief of the *Asia Pacific Law Review*, and is on the editorial boards of several top academic journals.

Mark Feldman is Professor of Law at the Peking University School of Transnational Law. His research areas include multinational enterprises, international investment and dispute resolution, and China as a rule maker and institution builder.

Henry Gao is a professor at Singapore Management University. His papers have appeared in many journals, including the *International and Comparative Law Quarterly*, *Journal of International Economic Law*, *World Trade Review*, *Harvard International Law Journal* and *Journal of World Trade*. He is also an editorial board member of the *Journal of International Economic Law* and *Journal of Financial Regulation*, His current research focuses on issues relating to digital trade, the World Trade Organization (WTO) and China, and WTO reform.

Carol Harlow is Emerita Professor of Law at the London School of Economics and Political Science. She has made significant contributions to the literature in tort law, some with a public law flavour. Her publications include *Law and Administration*

(1984), which is regarded as a seminal book in the area, *Pressure through Law* (1992) and *Process and Procedure in EU Administration* (2014) (all co-authored with Richard Rawlings).

Imelda Maher is the inaugural Sutherland Full Professor of European Law and the former Dean of Law (2017–21) at UCD Sutherland School of Law and Dublin European Institute. Her research focuses on the relationship between law and governance and she has published extensively on competition law and EU governance.

Agustín José Menéndez is Associate Professor of Political Philosophy at Universidad Complutense de Madrid. He is the author of *Justifying Taxes*, *The Constitution's Gift* (with JE Fossum), *Challenging European Citizenship* (with ED Olsen) and *Costituzionalismo Europeo* (with M Dani). He is currently writing (together with M Dani) a monograph on the constitutional theory of European integration. He was Editor-in-Chief of the *European Law Journal* from 2013 to 2018, and is one of the founding managing editors of the *European Law Open.*

Leone Niglia is Jean Monnet Chair Professor at the Faculty of Law, Sapienza University of Rome. He is author and editor of numerous articles and books, including *The Structural Transformation of European Private Law: A Critique of Juridical Hermeneutics* (2023); *The Struggle for European Private Law: A Critique of Codification* (2015); and *Pluralism and European Private Law* (2013).

Federico Ortino is Associate Director of Centre for International Governance and Dispute Resolution (CIGAD), and Professor of International Economic Law at the Dickson Poon School of Law, King's College London. He is an editorial board member of the *Journal of International Economic Law*, *Yearbook on International Investment Law and Policy*, *Journal of International Dispute Settlement* and *Journal of World Investment and Trade.* His current research focuses on the origin and evolution of international treaty standards as well as the legitimacy challenges faced by the emerging system of international investment law.

M Sornarajah is CJ Koh Professor at the Faculty of Law, National University of Singapore. He is also Visiting Professor at the Centre for Human Rights, London School of Economics. He is the author of numerous works, including *The Pursuit of Nationalized Property* (1986); *International Commercial Arbitration* (1992); *The Law of International Joint Ventures* (1994); *The International Law on Foreign Investment* (1996; 4th edn published in 2015); *The Settlement of Foreign Investment Disputes* (2001); and *Resistance and Change in the International Law on Foreign Investment* (2015).

Ying Song is Associate Professor of Law at Peking University Law School. Her research interests include environmental law, international law, and law and public policy, with a specific focus on the insights gained from the law of the EU.

Oana Ştefan is a Reader at the Dickson Poon School of Law, which she joined in 2013. She research focuses on EU law, in particular energy law, competition and state aid, and constitutional and administrative law. Her most recent work combines socio-legal and doctrinal analysis, quantitative and qualitative methods, while exploring the legitimacy and effectiveness of EU soft law. In 2021, after EU-funded research, she co-edited *EU Soft Law in the Member States*. She is also the author of *Soft Law in Court*, a book that analyses the ways in which the Court of Justice of the European Union deals with soft law.

Keebet von Benda-Beckmann († 2022) was Professor Emeritus and associate of the Department of Law and Anthropology at the Max Planck Institute for Social Anthropology. Her publications included the co-edited *Rules of Law and Laws of Ruling: On the Governance of Law* (2009) and the co-authored *Political and Legal Transformations of an Indonesian Polity* (2013).

Qianlan Wu is an assistant professor at the School of Law, University of Nottingham. Her main research interests lie in international competition law and competition regulation in China and Chinese law and market governance.

Jin Zining is Research Fellow with Peking University School of Law and a scholar of Chinese administrative law and risk regulation, with a special emphasis on environmental risk regulation. She is the author of such books as *Reconsidering the Public/Private Law Distinction* (2007) and *Administrative Law at Risks* (2014), of more than 30 journal articles.

Advancing the Method and the Practice of Transnational Law

An Introduction

JULIEN CHAISSE AND OANA ŞTEFAN

I. Introduction

As the authors of this book were sending in the final versions of their chapters, China was ending its COVID-19 restrictions, whilst war continued raging in Ukraine, pushing supply chains to the limit, wreaking havoc with praised European energy transitions and causing sky-rocketing food insecurity in Africa. This is far from the idyllic picture of the US packaged Barbie doll 'Made in China', albeit wearing Japanese nylon locks and a Taiwanese plastic body, who famously featured in Francis Snyder's writings and teaching of global economic networks and global legal pluralism some 20 years ago. Yet, the underlying storyline is still the same: transnational law plays a major role in constructing or deconstructing economic relations worldwide. The challenge to strengthen global governance without leaving out entire regions or communities is still there. Scholars and policy makers are called to continue the work started by Snyder to identify and put in practice the best governance configurations that would help carve out the most sustainable future. This book is a celebration of Snyder's work as an academic and educator impacting policies and the law from Europe to Asia and Africa. It is also an open invitation to take this work further in order to answer to the current economic governance problems faced by today's world. In this vein, it formulates reflection points and ideas for further research that scholars might want to embark upon.

Francis Snyder's work and career are difficult to summarise in a few words, or even to structure in separate, clear-cut streams. Such exercise would be counterproductive since, as admitted by Snyder already in the 1990s: 'Logic, in this post-modern age, is problematic. Theories of linear development are even more suspect.'[1] An excursus could, however, be made into the depth and breadth of research coverage, blending law, anthropology and economics, and relying not

[1] F Snyder, '"Out on the Weekend": Reflections on European Union Law in Context' EUI Working Paper Law No 94/11, https://cadmus.eui.eu/handle/1814/115.

only on doctrinal study, but also on field research and archival historical research. Such richness is complemented by the vastness of topics covered. Research on political parties in Mali and Senegal led to a PhD and a decade of empirical work on legal and economic anthropology,[2] and a focus on change and comparison through time and across space. This crystallised in an interest on development and underdevelopment,[3] and a long-standing research agenda on food and agriculture. Food and agriculture have been a constant in Snyder's work, illustrating the:

> [C]oncern for roots in the historical sense, a method of analysis that gave special attention to *filières* or networks of economic relations, a sensitivity to the interconnections between aspects of life, often in different parts of the globe, simply because they occurred at the same time: in other words, the diverse themes which development theorists have sometimes identified as relations between centre and periphery, sociologists have approached in terms of systems theory or functionalism, and Jung called synchronicity.[4]

The interest in the Common Agricultural Policy of the European Union (EU) is thus unsurprising, with Snyder authoring seminal work in this area,[5] whilst reinventing the methodology of EU law. The Law in Context approach is a methodology that seeks to go beyond a strictly doctrinal comprehension of law and take into account the wider societal consequences of legal regulations and procedures. Snyder's initiative inspired a movement that encouraged scholars to scrutinise EU law from social, economic and political perspectives, deviating from a narrow doctrinal inquiry. It stood at the foundations of various publications, including one major outlet, the *European Law Journal*, focusing not only on method, but also on constitutional and institutional reforms of the EU.[6] Expanding the research interests outside of the EU was unavoidable, and, as announced in his European University Institute (EUI) Working Paper in 1994, Snyder did venture into EU–China relations, becoming the expert not only of these aspects, but also of World Trade Organisation (WTO) law[7] and China's food safety law.[8] His impactful work led to important amendments to the Chinese Food Safety Law, passed in 2015, as well as to a China Friendship Award (中华人民共和国友谊奖, the People's Republic of China's highest award for 'foreign experts who have made outstanding contributions to the country's economic and social progress').

[2] F Snyder, *Capitalism and Legal Change: An African Transformation* (New York, Academic Press, 1981).

[3] F Snyder, 'Law and Development in the Light of Dependency Theory' (1981) 14 *Law and Society Review* 723.

[4] Snyder (n 1).

[5] F Snyder, *Law of the Common Agricultural Policy* (London, Sweet & Maxwell, 1985).

[6] F Snyder, *New Directions in European Community Law* (London, Weidenfeld & Nicolson, 1990).

[7] See, for instance, F Snyder, *The EU, the WTO and China: Legal Pluralism and International Trade Regulation* (Oxford, Hart Publishing, 2010).

[8] See, for instance, F Snyder, *Food Safety Law in China: Making Transnational Law* (Leiden, Brill, 2016).

What emerges from the rich picture sketched above is an everlasting endeavour to use the law, in its plurality of sources, contexts and transnationality, to fuel an efficient development of policy, economics and society. Endeavouring to follow the same path, this book collects together a series of essays which analyse the evolution and the current challenges faced by the international economic governance, whilst focusing loosely on three themes. Part I provides a comprehensive and critical analysis of Snyder's understanding of the law, whilst delving into the consequences of his work for the development of the area of legal studies. Part II has a methodological focus, exploring Snyder's preferred methodology of law in context. Accordingly, studying the legal frameworks in their political, economic or social context is essential for the development of the law itself. Part III focuses on sustainability law, a field to which Snyder has contributed enormously, having a solid impact on both scholarship and policy making.

II. Part I: Governance and the Law

The reforms in the legal system and the developing global order have complemented each other in the past. With the advent of new advanced technology, the coming of modern companies, the different nature of work accompanying new factors in the domestic and the international scenario, economic globalisation has also roped in legal transformation on a transnational scale. The main cornerstones of globalisation and law encompass the fields of sociology of law, the political economy of law and international relations. Whilst working at the interface between all of these areas, Snyder has made valuable contributions to the field of transnational governance, which have often had a concrete impact on the law in different jurisdictions.

Governance is a concept that refers to the institutions and procedures that are intended to provide accountability, transparency, responsiveness, rule of law, stability, equality and inclusivity, empowerment and broad-based involvement. These characteristics should be provided by the institutions and procedures. These qualities are often present in effective governmental administration. In addition, governance is the administration of public affairs in a manner that is responsive, participatory, inclusive and transparent. These principles, norms and regulations governing the process are commonly known as the 'rules of the game'. As a result, governance may be nuanced and might not always be easy to see. In legal terms, governance can be defined as the establishment and implementation of a set of rules to ensure an element of accountability and transparency over the governing entity, barring which legal and constitutional sanctions could be attracted. The early legal reforms and regimes of the twenty-first century had disparate natures and contents, extents and forms of execution. Unlike the past system of state-based governance, the reforms varied to a striking extent. As concluded by Snyder, 'a multiplicity of other sites of governance complement, supplement, or compete with the State, hence the term "governance" instead of "government"'.[9]

Many thinkers and theories have emerged from the interface between globalisation and the law. The first one remains the concept of social fields, developed by Bourdieu. This concept reflected the way in which the 'new transnational and global economic and political processes and political trends changed the role of lawyers, the logic of legal practices and the nature of legal field'.[10] The external factors started influencing the legal and political environment by affecting the 'background assumptions, actors and orientation'.[11] Furthermore, the national decisions were apparently international-oriented, as they were carved in such a way as to complement the transnational legal regimes. This led to the enhancement of the standard and position of international players and of the states with respect to other states as well.[12] Sassen's research revolves around the complex and intertwined link between domestic and international rules, norms and guidelines.[13] In such a situation, it is not possible to separate the national and the international in a distinctive manner.[14] However, the origin, content and reason behind the interpretation and application of the domestic norms are very closely related to international, transnational or intergovernmental institutions, norms and dispute resolution processes. This is evident from the fact that regional (*sui generis*) organisations such as the EU are based on international norms, including the WTO international trade rules, code of conduct and standards, or the results of international dispute settlement processes. In another instance, Santos differentiated between globalised localism and localised globalism.[15] Globalised localism can be defined as the process by which the local processes are globalised, whilst localised globalism signifies the impact of transnational practices on local conditions. The localisms most frequently globalised in the legal world have been American. The WTO Agreement on Trade-Related Aspects of Intellectual Property (TRIPS) is reflective of how the US remains influenced by the 'external' or 'international' reforms.

The research that Snyder has done on extraterritoriality and transnational governance may be understood better by placing it within this context. Importantly,

[9] F Snyder, 'Economic Globalisation and the Law in the 21st Century' in A Sarat (ed), *The Blackwell Companion to Law and Society* (Oxford, Blackwell) 624–40.

[10] ibid.

[11] ibid.

[12] E Wibbels, 'Dependency Revisited: International Markets, Business Cycles, and Social Spending in the Developing World' (2006) 60(2) *International Organization* 433.

[13] S Sassen, *A Sociology of Globalization* (New York, WW Norton, 2007).

[14] J Chaisse and G Dimitropoulos, 'Domestic Investment Laws and International Economic Law in the Liberal International Order' (2023) 22(1) *World Trade Review* 1. See also S Chaudoin, HV Milner and X Pang, 'International Systems and Domestic Politics: Linking Complex Interactions with Empirical Models in International Relations' (2015) 69 *Princeton University Department of Politics Methodology* 275; A Adsera and C Boix, 'Trade, Democracy, and the Size of the Public Sector: The Political Underpinnings of Openness' (2002) 56(2) *International Organization* 229.

[15] B de Sousa Santos, 'Globalizations' (2006), 23(2–3) *Theory, Culture & Society* 393.

Snyder has developed a conceptual framework that is constructed around the five primary sites of governance in order to comprehend the issues that arise as a result of economic globalisation and to provide potential answers to these issues.[16] The first is the Contract, the second is Hierarchy, the third is Networks, the fourth is *Lex Mercatoria* and the fifth is 'Sites of Global Pluralism'. Although they often overlap, the origin, structure and relevance of these many sites of governance are all very distinct from one another, despite the fact that they frequently overlap.

First, contract as a site of governance is a bilateral or multilateral agreement between two or more equal parties which may be states, companies, or even individuals. For instance, the Organisation for Economic Co-operation and Development (OECD) Convention on Combating Bribery of 1997 requires countries to ratify their membership by signing the Convention.[17] Second, hierarchy represents governance at multiple levels. Such levels of governance coordinate and work together on the same or different subject matters. It is the common goal that brings coherence to the hierarchical system. Third, transnational networks can be public, private or a mix of both. Transnational public networks, according to Snyder, 'offer the world a blueprint for the international architecture of the 21st century'.[18] The presence of transgovernmental networks helps judges to derive references and benefits from the expertise of foreign governments and non-state actors. At the same time, private networks encompass alliances, cartels and business associations involving private regimes and informal practices.[19] The study of private governance has further delved into corporate control and accountability, with hybrid networks improving relations between regimes such as the US and the EU. Fourth, *Lex Mercatoria* or the 'law of the merchant' is used by private actors to settle disputes related to businesses[20] and, applying Teubner's reflexive law approach, could be regarded as a model of new global law.[21] According to Snyder, *Lex Mercatoria* has been shaped as a contemporary law with its relevance reaching out to 'allocating risks, regulating market access and linking local and global domains'.[22] Fifth, the sites of global pluralism incorporate 'public, private

[16] In one of his writings 'EU, China, and Technical Standards in BRI: Extraterritoriality or Transitional Governance', Snyder address the interconnections between social and legal fields, standards, and soft law in the BRI. See F Snyder, 'EU, China, and Technical Standards in the Belt and Road Initiative (BRI): Extraterritoriality or Transnational Governance?' in N Cunha Rodrigues (ed), *Extraterritoriality of EU Economic Law: European Union and its Neighbours in a Globalized World*, vol 4 (Cham, Springer, 2021),.

[17] Convention on Combating Bribery of Foreign Public Officials in International Business Transactions 1997, art 14.

[18] Snyder (n 9).

[19] K Raustiala, 'The Architecture of International Cooperation: Transgovernmental Networks and the Future of International Law' (2002) 43 *Virginia Journal of International Law* 1.

[20] RJ Howarth, '*Lex Mercatoria*: Can General Principles of Law Govern International Commercial Contracts?' (2004) 10 *Canterbury Law Review* 36.

[21] R Michaels, 'The True *Lex Mercatoria*: Law beyond the State' (2007) 14(2) *Indiana Journal of Global Legal Studies* 447.

[22] F Snyder, 'Governing Economic Globalisation: Global Legal Pluralism and European Law' (1999) 5(4) *European Law Journal* 334.

and hybrid forms of governance with an emphasis on strategic action'.[23] Sites can be divided into public, private or mixed and can further be divided into market-based or polity-based, with each having structural or relational aspects.

According to Snyder, 'globalization is governed by the totality of strategically determined, situationally specific and often episodic conjunctions of a multiplicity of sites throughout the world.[24] These sites have institutional, normative and processual characteristics. The totality of these sites represents a new global form of legal pluralism'.[25] Sites can be divided into public, private or mixed and can further be divided into market-based or polity-based, with each having structural or relational aspects. Snyder regards legal pluralism as involving disparate institutions, norms and dispute resolution processes situated at varying structured sites around the globe. These structured sites include US law, EU law, codes of conduct of corporations, conventions, WTO law etc. The judicial and legal characteristics are embodied in a site during its development which is influenced by strategic actors such as companies, governments and non-governmental organisations. Sites may be interlinked – ie, they might possess relational aspects. For instance, the internationalisation of human rights is a pure example of the synergy developed through common norms amongst several sites.[26] On the contrary, structural aspects include 'institutions, norms and dispute resolution processes'.

A common pedestal upon which the global economic networks are placed and operated is provided by global legal pluralism. These sites may not differ from each other; however, when taken together, their internal background and features constitute global legal pluralism. In the words of Snyder: 'Global legal pluralism does more, however, than simply provide the rules of the game. It also constitutes the game itself, including the players.'[27] In his some of his latest work, Snyder provides a map of the interaction between European legal pluralism and BRI soft law and contractual arrangements.[28] Altogether, he worked on many different facets of law, such as legal rechannelling, legal and medical pluralism, global food safety law, soft law and governance, as well as a specific focus on economic globalisation and transitional governance.

According to Snyder, soft law can be defined as 'rules of conduct which in principle are not legally binding but which nevertheless have practical and

[23] G de Burca, RO Keohane and C Sabel, 'New Modes of Global Governance' (2013) 45 *International Law and Politics* 723.
[24] Snyder (n 22).
[25] ibid.
[26] J Coatsworth, 'Internationalizing Human Rights: A Look at the Americas' (2003) III(1) *ReVista Harvard Review of Latin America*, https://revista.drclas.harvard.edu/internationalizing-human-rights.
[27] R Robertson, *Globalization: Social Theory and Global Culture*' (London, SAGE Publications, 1992); P Hirst and G Thompson, *Globalization in Question: The International Economy and the Possibilities of Governance*, 2nd edn (Cambridge, Polity Press, 2000); A Giddens, *The Consequences of Modernity* (Cambridge, Polity Press, 1990); JF Lechner and J Boli (eds), *The Globalization Reader*, 3rd edn (Oxford, Blackwell Publishing, 2008) 501; Snyder (n 9).
[28] F Snyder, 'The BRI Kaleidoscope: European Legal Pluralism and BRI Soft Law' in V Ntousas and S Minas (eds), *The European Union and China's Belt and Road* (Abingdon, Routledge, 2021) 67.

even legal effects'.[29] Unlike hard law, it can be better adapted to conditions of uncertainty and has lower contracting and sovereignty costs. Soft law plays an instrumental role in the governance of sensitive issues by bringing different-minded governments and companies to the same table and in agreement, and has played a crucial role in the effectiveness of transnational legal orders such as the EU. Examples of soft law include economic, environmental, social and human rights areas like the General Assembly resolutions, declarations (the Universal Declaration of Human Rights), codes of conduct, guidelines, programmes of action and documents resulting from international conferences. The debate about the legality and efficiency of such norms remains in question. This also concerns an eclectic range of standards set up by international standard institutions like the International Organization for Standardization (ISO). For example: International Accounting Standards Committee (IASC) 'currently includes 153 professional accounting bodies in 112 countries and is responsible for developing and approving international accounting standards. IASC standards are not legally binding, so they act as "strategic networker" to convince governmental actors to adopt and give legal force to its voluntary standards'.[30]

Part I of this book looks at the actors, the norms and the processes of transnational economic law. The chapters in this part draw on various themes and theories central to Francis Snyder's work on governance and the law, such as sites of governance, legal pluralism and soft law. This part spreads out various policy areas, such as international investment law and free trade agreements, also covering case studies from EU law, US law and Chinese law. Canelas de Castro reconceptualises the notion of legal personality in an increasingly interdependent world, pleading for more work to be done to address a mismatch between international legal doctrine and reality.[31] Reflecting on the norms of transnational law, Maher reflects on Snyder's contribution to the definition of soft law, and the place of soft law in the hybrid transnational regulatory landscape. Zooming in on the Asian Infrastructure Investment Bank, Feldman shows how interactions between public and private actors contribute to the development of global and regional norms. Alemanno looks at the actors of EU governance and suggests improvements to the ethics system, further developing the work of Snyder on EU constitutional law, including his research on inter-institutional agreements. Sornarajah discusses a failure of transnationalisation, taking as a case study foreign direct investment (FDI) contracts made with a state and assessing how the various systems of norms put in place have not led to satisfactory outcomes.

[29] F Snyder, 'The Effectiveness of European Community Law: Institutions, Processes, Tools and Techniques', (1993) 56 *MLR* 19, 32.

[30] Snyder (n 9).

[31] M Longo, Michael 'Reconceptualising Public International Law: Convergence with the European Union Model?' (2002) 25(1) *UNSW Law Journal* 71.

III. Part II: Law in Context

A recent trend among academic legal scholars has been to develop a holistic understanding of law rather than binding it to its literal interpretation.[32] The field of legal studies has seen a drastic shift of focal point towards studying the context behind the law rather than studying the law in isolation. This methodology was propagated by Snyder, who was a staunch advocate of studies involving the interface between law and other fields like society, culture etc.[33] This methodology departs from the assumption that, in order to have a deeper yet clearer understanding of law, we as lawyers and/or legal scholars must look at law and how it governs the society, but also at how the society functions in accordance with those laws and legal principles. We must take into consideration the historical and political events and perspectives which led to the emergence of legal principles and traditions. The law in context methodology postulates that law is not a concept that can be understood in its individuality. Rather, the understanding of legal principles should be done by utilising a multidisciplinary approach and law should be studied while intertwined along with historical, political principles and events, whilst also taking into consideration various other disciplines like sociology, public administration, criminology, and also various legal and philosophical aspects.

The law in context as an approach 'started to gain recognition since [the] 1960s when a need was felt to diverge from the normal approach of seeking law in the strictly embodied self-sustained legal principles laid down through various judgments and statutes also known as the "black-letter law"'[34] and shifted focus towards various societal problems, altering the normative structure along with it. As times changed, it became clear that law can only present a part of the solution and, in order to resolve these problems completely, certain non-legal disciplines such as political and social sciences needed to be relied upon.[35] Soon enough, the *Law in Context* book series was launched in the 1970s[36] to critically analyse legal phenomena in their cultural, social, political, technological, environmental and economic contexts.

Pure doctrinal analysis has come under fire in recent years from a number of writers for being 'intellectually rigid, inflexible, and inward-looking' in how it approaches understanding law and how the legal system functions.[37] 'The perspective of law in context may be summarised as follows: either law is viewed from the standpoint of other disciplines, using their theories and modes of analysis;

[32] Congressional Research Service, 'Statutory Interpretation: Theories, Tools, and Trends' (18 May 2022), https://crsreports.congress.gov/product/pdf/R/R45153.
[33] Snyder (n 6).
[34] EL Rubin, 'Law and the Methodology of Law' (1997) 1997 *Wisconsin Law Review* 525.
[35] M McConville and W Hong Chui, *Research Methods for Law*, 2nd edn (Edinburgh, Edinburgh University Press, 2007) 1.
[36] W Twining explains in his book *Jurist in Context* (Oxford, Oxford University Press, 2019), 91 how this idea came about following his interactions with students in Dar es Salaam.
[37] DW Vick, 'Interdisciplinary and the Discipline of Law' (2004) 31 *Journal of Law and Society* 164.

or law provides the starting point, but is situated in a broader context, whether social, economic, political or cultural. Both strands ultimately aim to contribute to a social theory of law'.[38]

Applying and promoting the law in context approach to EU studies, Snyder observed that the law of the European Community, which is now known as EU law, was frequently seen as 'a highly technical set of rules, a dense doctrinal thicket into which only the ignorant or the foolish would "jump in and scratch out their eyes", still less try to understand in terms of social theories of law'.[39] In his classes at Warwick Law School, Snyder always emphasised the need of putting legal principles in their proper perspective. It was therefore paramount to focus on the relationships that exist between different types of institutions, norms, ideologies and procedures in EU law. Snyder saw European law as 'a complex web of politics, economics, and law', which demanded to be investigated and comprehended via 'a political economy of law or an interdisciplinary, contextual, or critical approach'. Yet, while he advocated for the introduction of novel approaches to legal education and research in Europe, he was adamant that this should not be done at the expense of the continent's long-established tradition of 'highly sophisticated scholarship concerning legal doctrine' in areas such as institutions, procedures and competition law.[40]

Snyder not only advocated for the law in context methodology, but also relied on it extensively in his work. For instance, with regard to the Common Agricultural Policy,[41] he emphasised the concepts such as 'interest' and 'interest representation', which according to him formed the basis of any study of law of society. This eventually served as the foundation for a study of European law making aimed at anthropologists and was initially 'published in a book about the anthropology of law'.[42] Snyder asked for a new agenda suggesting that European law was in need both of 'a social theory of law' and studies from the 'perspective of critical theory'.[43]

A significant contribution by Snyder to the legal scholarship was the founding in 1995 of the *European Law Journal* (*ELJ*). Snyder served as the founding editor-in-chief of the *ELJ*, tagged as a 'Review of the Law in Context'. Its mandate was to 'articulate and deepen the study and understanding of European law in its social, cultural, political, and economic aspects'.

The impact of Snyder's writings was also evident in the US.[44] In the UK, the year 1996 saw a distinct collection of writings entitled *The New Legal Dynamics*

[38] F Snyder, 'Soft Law and Institutional Practice in European Community' (1993) European University Institute 93/5.

[39] Snyder (n 6).

[40] ibid.

[41] F Snyder, *Law of the Common Agricultural Policy* (London, Sweet & Maxwell, 1985).

[42] F Snyder, 'Thinking about "Interests": Legislative Process in the European Community' in J Starr and JF Collier (eds), *History and Power in the Study of Law* (New York, Cornell University Press, 1989) 168–98.

[43] ibid 169. See also Harlow, ch 6 in this volume.

[44] Harlow (n 43).

of European Union[45] being published. These articles were written along the same lines as those that can be found in Snyder's work entitled *New Directions*, and their purpose was to 'further contribute to the expanding of scope of legal study towards a new approach in European legal studies'.[46] Legal scholars who, according to the definition provided in *New Directions*, already included socio-legal studies, postmodern theory, critical legal studies, law in context and other disciplines would be equipped with the tools of interdisciplinary scholarship as a result. Some examples of this type of scholarship include comparative politics, international relations, public policy analysis and theories of institutional behaviour.[47]

Against this background, Part II of this volume critically takes stock of the progress made so far with law in context, showing avenues for future development and refinement. The chapters in this part look not only at the way in which the method can be refined and used by academics, but also at the practical implications of such a method in improving regulatory settings and promoting important social and policy goals. Harlow reflects on the development of the law in context methodology at the beginning of a new era, marked by a new, open-source journal, *The European Law Open*. Menéndez shows that the law in context methodology has not been fully exploited in EU scholarship, which remained largely faithful to linear and uncritical accounts of European integration through law. He thus pleads for a renewed agenda, which would need to challenge and reconsider established concepts of EU law. Already answering this call, Niglia proposes shifting the focus of academic investigation from constitutional doctrines and the role of courts to the actors' substantive choices regarding the distribution of powers between the EU and the Member States. The fields chosen resonate with Snyder's work, with Niglia delving into sectors such as agriculture or competition. Snyder's contribution to researching transnational legal processes is relied upon by Gao in his chapter looking at the EU–China Comprehensive Agreement on Investment.

IV. Part III: Sustainability Law

Sustainability law has been high on Snyder's research agenda, from his early contributions to transnational agricultural law to recent research which has informed the reform of food law in China. The notion of sustainability refers to anything that can be maintained over time.[48] This implies that an unsustainable society

[45] J Shaw and G More, *The New Legal Dynamics of European Union* (Oxford, Clarendon Press, 1995).
[46] J Shaw, 'Introduction' in ibid 1–14.
[47] See J Shaw, 'European Union Studies in Crisis? Towards a New Dynamic' (1996) 16 *OJLS* 231. See also Shaw (n 46) 1–3.
[48] R Heinberg, 'What is Sustainability?' (*Post Carbon Reader*), https://mycourses.aalto.fi/pluginfile.php/1159956/mod_page/content/9/Heinberg_WhatIsSustainability.pdf.

can never be maintained for very long and eventually disintegrates. The idea of sustainability as a concept first appeared in the Brundtland Report of 1987.[49] Sustainable development was defined as development that 'meets the needs of the present generation without compromising the ability of future generations to meet their own needs'.[50] This notion of sustainability continues to be extensively utilised and has proven to be rather influential.

The complex and unique nature of numerous environmental issues often leads people to worry about the future of the planet. The vast majority of people, however, are of the opinion that the most important thing to keep in mind while trying to achieve sustainability is the legacy that we leave for the generations that come after us. There are a great number of people and organisations that are dedicated to the concept of sustainability, and they show their devotion to this value by the policies they create, the activities they engage in on a daily basis and the routines they follow. The present generation as well as the generations that will follow after it will need to adapt to sustainable living. Sustainability improves the quality of life for the generation that is now alive by increasing the likelihood that future generations will survive and providing those generations with more self-assurance to cope with the world they will pass on to subsequent generations. In addition, it is commonly known that the rate of social change is speeding up to levels that have never been seen before. It is projected that the boundary-breaking capabilities of globalised markets and newly developed technologies may soon eradicate pre-existing social and political fault lines. This rate of change has a significant impact on the survival of human civilisation over the long run, and the transition to a society that is more environmentally responsible may prove to be the most challenging challenge that humankind has ever encountered.

Sustainability is typically supported by three fundamental components: the economy, society and the environment.[51] In this sense, the term 'sustainability' has been widely used to describe improvements in areas such as the overuse of natural resources, manufacturing processes (including their energy use and polluting byproducts), linear product consumption, investment direction, citizen lifestyles, consumer purchasing habits, technological advancements, or business and broader institutional changes.[52]

It follows that such a multifaceted subject cannot be treated in a basic and simple manner, particularly in light of the fact that sustainability is a process rather

[49] T Kuhlman and J Farrington, 'What is Sustainability?' (2010) 2(11) *Sustainability*, https://doi.org/10.3390/su2113436.

[50] United Nations World Commission on Environment and Development, *Our Common Future* (Oxford, Oxford University Press, 1987).

[51] L Allen, 'What are the Three Pillars of Sustainability?' (*Treehugger*, 7 August 2021), https://www.treehugger.com/what-are-the-three-pillars-of-sustainability-5189295.

[52] 'Sustainability – What is it? Definition, Principles and Examples' (*You Matter*, 18 June 2021), https://youmatter.world/en/definition/definitions-sustainability-definition-examples-principles.

than an end in itself.[53] The only way to achieve fundamental economic change necessary for sustainable development is to invest in new technologies for resource extraction, manufacturing, transportation and energy generation.[54] Therefore, advancing sustainable development ultimately entails advancing investments that enhance sustainability and advance fair social and economic growth.[55]

The first steps in the direction of sustainability in international law have been made through soft law. Non-binding declarations, such as the Rio Declaration, the Brundtland Report,[56] the Millennium Development Goals and the Stockholm Declaration, have had a significant impact on the way in which the law and legal institutions approach issues relating to sustainability. Once again, lax legal requirements are the driving force behind the current trend. The initiative known as the Sustainable Development Goals (SDGs), which has been led by Member States of the United Nations, including members of civil society, provides a chance to further strengthen the legal dimensions of sustainable development. The SDGs, also known as the Global Goals for Sustainable Development, are more political ideals than legally enforced requirements and can qualify as soft law. This is because of the nature of what they represent and the way in which they were developed. In addition, the process of promoting sustainability involves the development of international harder norms concerning the environment. These norms include the polluter pays principle, the right of access to environmental information, intergenerational equity, common but differentiated responsibilities, precautionary decision making and the right of access to environmental information. As a consequence of these ever-evolving environmental norms, our understanding of human rights, such as the right to life, health and culture, has definitely advanced in recent years.[22] In addition to these norms, multinational or bilateral agreements have also had a significant economic impact on sustainability transitions according to the International Institute for Sustainable Development.[57] For example, actors such as the EU or the US can expand their sustainability policy beyond their national boundaries by governing through trade.[58] Most observers believe that new regulations and modifications to current laws are essential for sustainability.

However, it is less frequently acknowledged that sustainability may be attained by simply applying current rules to new issues or by making incremental changes

[53] United Nations Economic Commission for Latin America and the Caribbean, *Sustainable Development: Changing Production Patterns, Social Equity and the Environment* (Santiago: United Nations, 1991) 146.

[54] ibid.

[55] C Bellmann and AV Tipping, 'The Role of Trade and Trade Policy in Advancing the 2030 Development Agenda' [2015] *International Development Policy* 124. See also J Chaisse, 'Promises and Pitfalls of the European Union Policy on Foreign Investment: How Will the New EU Competence on FDI Affect the Emerging Global Regime?' (2012) 15(1) *Journal of International Economic Law* 51.

[56] GH Brundtland, *Our Common Future: Report of the World Commission on Environment and Development. Geneva*, UN-Document A/42/427, 1987.

[57] A Lahteenmaki-Uutela et al, 'Legal Rights of Private Property Owners vs Sustainability Transitions?' (2021) 323 *Journal of Cleaner Production* 129.

[58] ibid.

to old laws.[59] There are several laws that serve as foundations for sustainability and many of them are not environmental laws.[60] For instance, a regulation passed in Cuba in 1994 made it simpler for city dwellers to cultivate and sell food on vacant property.[27] Since then, the government has supported this type of agriculture with financial, technical and marketing support. All important components of a food security programme have been witnessed in the programme, including more organic and sustainable food production and employment creation.

The rules for adjudicating disputes in matters pertaining to sustainability may need to be reviewed. It is crucial to consider issues of the burden of proof and decision making when there is scientific uncertainty. The threshold of evidence in classic *quiatimet* lawsuits, where the plaintiff is seeking to prevent anticipated injury, is tremendously high – ie, either a substantial possibility of irreparable harm or almost certain harm.[61] Legislative reform is required if the common law cannot address scientific uncertainty effectively. For instance, in *Palmer v Nova Scotia Forest Industries*,[62] the court dismissed a *quiatimet* request for an injunction against aerial pesticide spraying of a Nova Scotia forest even after carefully examining voluminous scientific data. At least in civil cases, lawyers and scientists speak a different language about probability: lawyers base their decisions on a balance of probabilities while scientists need a 95 per cent confidence threshold.[63] As a result, more effort has to be made to create an acceptable legal response to scientific uncertainty, risk analysis, epidemiological inference and other statistical inference, and new laws regarding shifting the burden of evidence in such areas may be proposed.

According to Snyder, supporting the transition process towards the sustainability of the economic and social reforms will facilitate the integration of the global community and the global economy.[64] Therefore, the difficulty is in pursuing economic transformation while also incorporating sustainability into economic growth and avoiding social unrest. Due to these intertwined economic and legal systems, food safety standards, amongst other issues, are becoming an issue of concern on a global scale.

The trend of globalisation has led to major changes in many different elements of food safety. The Slow Food Movement (SFM), which began in Italy in 1986 and has now extended across the rest of the globe, is something that has piqued

[59] JC Dernbach and JA Mintz, 'Environmental Laws and Sustainability: An Introduction' (2011) 3 *Widener Law School Legal Studies Research Paper* 11.

[60] ibid; M Goepel, 'Formulating Future Just Policies: Applying the Delhi Sustainable Development Law Principles' (2010) 2(6) *Sustainability* 1; X Qian, 'Rethinking Investment Treaties for Sustainable Development: From the "New Delhi Declaration" Principles to Modern Investment Law and Policy' (2022) 17(2) *Asian Journal of WTO & International Health Law and Policy* 405.

[61] PS Elder, 'Sustainability' (1991) 36 *McGill Law Journal* 831.

[62] *Palmer v Nova Scotia Forest Industries* 1983 Can LII 2898 (NSSC).

[63] Elder (n 61).

[64] F Snyder (ed), *The European Union and China, 1949–2008: Basic Documents and Commentary* (London, Bloomsbury Publishing, 2009).

Snyder's curiosity.[65] The SFM promotes a cultural movement away from the quick, commercial and global industrialisation of food in favour of 'good, clean, and fair' food. The SFM, which has millions of members in over 160 countries, has made a commitment to preserve regional and historic cuisines, guarantee the safety and quality of food, and advance ecologically responsible and sustainable forms of economic growth. It also encourages people to consume food that is seasonal and local because it is founded on the belief that the decisions we make as a society in relation to our food will have an effect on how food is grown, produced and distributed, which will eventually lead to a change in the world. This belief motivates the SFM's promotion of seasonal and local food consumption.

Another long-term focus of Snyder's work is public health in China, which has been at risk from the hazardous pesticides utilised in agricultural production.[66] The Chinese government, which now chairs the Codex Alimentarius Committee on Pesticide Residues and actively participates in international standards organisations, intends to achieve rapid progress in the regulation of harmful pesticides. Evidently its policies acknowledge the close connection between agricultural use of pesticides and the presence of pesticide residues in food – that is, between domestic public health policy and international trade.

More generally, Snyder shows how in contemporary societies and trade relations, product standards are pervasive.[67] The gradual positioning of domestic standards with international standards, state governments' negotiation of new bilateral agreements and the government's backing for a small group of elite export enterprises will all contribute to the opening up of significant new markets for businesses.[68] Thus, the move towards sustainability is double-edged – that is, it ensures public health and at the same time determines market access.

Part III unpacks sustainability from different perspectives rooted in Snyder's work. Von Benda-Beckmann shows how exploring the language of the law is crucial not only for legal research purposes, but also for the promotion of indigenous rights in the context of decolonisation. Sustainable development is explored by Song, who offers a case study of the legal incorporation of this principle in China. Ortino looks at social sustainability, in particular the trade and labour links in free trade agreements (FTAs). With regard to food safety, Zining looks at the precautionary principle and its application in the regulation of genetically modified organisms (GMOs) in China, as compared to the US and EU approaches.

[65] F Snyder, Z Hu and X Zheng, 'Slow Food in Europe, the USA and China: A Comparative Perspective' (2018), Peking University School of Transnational Law (STL) Research Paper No 18-6, http://dx.doi.org/10.2139/ssrn.3167906.

[66] F Snyder and L Ni, 'A Tale of Eight Pesticides: Risk Regulation and Public Health in China' (2017) 8 *European Journal* of *Risk Regulation* 469.

[67] F Snyder, 'The EU, China and Product Standards' (2016) Peking University School of Transnational Law Research Paper No 16-9, https://ssrn.com/abstract=2843008.

[68] F Snyder and L Ni, 'Chinese Apples and the Emerging World Food Trade Order: Food Safety, International Trade and Regulatory Collaboration between China and the European Union' (2018) *Chinese Journal of Comparative Law*, https://ssrn.com/abstract=3101626.

Sustainability in the digital world is explored by Wu, who reflects on how China could influence new norms for the global data trade.

V. Concluding Remarks

As has been shown in this introduction and announced right at the outset, this book takes the good advice to reject 'suspect' linear approaches to transnational legal studies. It uses the vast, varied body of work of Francis Snyder as a starting point for future reflections on many distinct, sometimes intertwined, lines of inquiry that academics may choose to pursue. Given the numerous crises that our globe is experiencing today, there is no question that this research is required now more than ever.

An academic career, however, is not just about one's publications and courses (and, may we add, policy impact), but also about one's 'colleagues, publishers, and particularly one's students', as Snyder puts it so eloquently and accurately.[69] This book highlights not just the work of the academics, but also the communities that he influenced, beginning with his colleagues from numerous universities, such as Aix-en-Provence, Warwick, University College London (UCL), the London School of Economics and Political Science (LSE), Peking University, the EUI, Macau, the College of Europe and a large number of other institutions. Ex-students who are now pursuing professions in academia or practise in various parts of the globe have also submitted chapters demonstrating how they have been influenced by the work of their former professor and how they continue his work. Snyder, a matchmaker extraordinaire, has had the ability throughout the years to create the circumstances for unexpected meetings that lead to long-term, solid partnerships. As a result, these communities are characterised above all else by a strong sense of camaraderie. The International Workshop for Young Scholars (WISH), convened by Snyder for many years, has launched careers and established tightly knit academic networks. At the workshop, which was organised on topics as diverse as Snyder's interests, early career researchers and PhD students presented papers and established academics served as discussants and, later, as mentors and friends. This offered PhD students the once-in-a-lifetime chance to have their work published early in respected outlets and have their voices heard before ever completing their dissertations. In addition to the thought-provoking topics, ideas and methodology, the body of work that Snyder has produced over the course of his professional life offers as an illustrative model for how to cultivate talent and advance future research and academic careers. After all, it is the process of handing down great ideas from one generation to the next, always with the intention of improving society as a whole, which embodies both logic and linearity.

[69] Snyder (n 1).

PART 1

Governance and the Law

1

The *Dramatis Personae* of International Law in the Era of Globalisation

Rethinking International Legal Personality

PAULO CANELAS DE CASTRO

I. Introduction

The historical period in which contemporary international law finds itself is by many dubbed as the era of globalisation. All known difficulties in identifying dates or moments of rupture in the flow of time notwithstanding,[1] it can be said to have begun with the end of the Cold War associated with the fall of the Berlin Wall. It has been a period of profound revision of balances of the structural notes characteristic of the international system[2] and of the international law governing it. These transformations are so numerous and have such significant impacts that they may be equated with true paradigm shifts[3] in the way in which the international system and international law are structured. The era of globalisation may therefore be seen as a new moment in the course of history in general, and in the history of the international system and international law in particular.[4]

[1] R Aron, 'Evidence and Inference in History' (1958) 87(4) *Daedalus* 11.

[2] S Hoffmann, 'International Systems and International Law' (1961) 14 (1) *World Politics* 205.

[3] T Kuhn, *The Structure of Scientific Revolutions* 3rd edn (Chicago, University of Chicago Press, 1996).

[4] I have previously looked into aspects of the subject: P Canelas de Castro, 'Globalisation and its Impact on International Law: Towards an International Rule of Law?' (2005) 20(9) *Boletim da Faculdade de Direito da Universidade de Macau* 223; P Canelas de Castro, 'Globalização e Direito Internacional: Rumo ao Estado de Direito nas Relações Internacionais?' in Faculdade de Direito da Universidade de Coimbra, *Nos 20 Anos do Código das Sociedades Comerciais. Homenagem aos Profs. Doutores A. Ferrer Correia, Orlando de Carvalho e Vasco Lobo Xavier*, vol III (Coimbra, Coimbra Editora, 2007) 759–824; P Canelas de Castro, 'Direito Internacional na Era da Globalização: Mudanças de Paradigmas no Sistema Internacional e na Ordem Jurídica Internacional' in AC Nascimento Gomes, B Albergaria and M Rodrigues Canotilho (eds), *Direito Constitucional. Diálogos em Homenagem ao 80º. Aniversário de J.J. Gomes Canotilho* (Belo Horizonte, Forum, 2021) 929–1014.

The purpose of this chapter is to identify some of the most important changes experienced in international law regarding the international system that it governs, particularly the actors recognised to stand as legal subjects in the domain – the *dramatis personae* of the international legal order – and to reflect on their significance.

Naturally, transformations of the magnitude that we associate with this era of globalisation are not unprecedented, and they gain greater clarity, in terms of both content and meaning, when contrasted with other profound changes that have taken place in periods of humanity's journey, in which the end of one era and the beginning of another have also been registered.

This was notably the case with the end of the Thirty Years' War in 1648 through the conclusion of the Peace Treaties of Münster and Osnabrück.[5] These established the international system dubbed the Westphalia Model.[6] This was also the case with the Congress of Vienna in 1815.[7] This event not only sealed the failed attempt by Napoleon I to establish an international order based on new legitimacies and the hegemonic power of France, but also opened up a new international system in which, increasingly and structurally, international cooperation between sovereign states gradually took root and sometimes even began to appear in the institutionalised form. This was also the case again in the twentieth century, first with the impetus provided by the establishment of the League of Nations.[8] In an era of 'great expectations', the first signs of a new world were established, particularly because the relationship between individual state initiatives and the representative organisation of all states was altered, and also because a world less resigned to the fate of conflicts and wars was envisaged, albeit in an unrealistic way.[9] This cardinal change culminated later with the order established after the Second World War and the constitution of the United Nations (UN).[10] Thereafter, states took up a fundamental obligation to conduct non-violent international relations, committing to positive cooperative, peaceful and secure relations for the well-being of their peoples and individuals. Moreover, they have done so in

[5] A Hobza, 'Questions de droit international concernant les religions' (1924) 4(5) *Recueil des Cours* 377, 379; L Gross, 'The Peace of Westphalia' (1948) 42 *AJIL* 20, 41; A Nussbaum, *A Concise History of the Law of Nations* (New York, Macmillian Company, 1954).

[6] J Delbrück and R Wolfrum, *Völkerrecht*, vol I/1, 2nd edn (Berlin, Walter de Gruyter, 1989) 2–21; WG Grewe, *The Epochs of International Law* (Berlin, Walter de Gruyter, 2000).

[7] C Webster, *The Congress of Vienna, 1814–1815* (London, Bells & Son, 1950); F Münch, 'Vienna Congress' (2000) IV *Encyclopedia of Public International Law* 1286, 1289.

[8] P Gerbet, VY Ghebali and MR Mouton, *Société des Nations et Organisation des Nations Unies* (Paris, Richelieu, 1973); C Parry, 'League of Nations' (1997) III *Encyclopedia of Public International Law* 177, 186.

[9] R Bernhardt, WK Geck, G Jaenicke and H Steinberger, *Völkerrecht als Rechtsordnung, Internationale Gerichtsbarkeit, Menschensrechte. Festschrift für Hermann Mosler* (Berlin, Springer, 1983); H-U Scupin, 'History of the Law of Nations: 1815 to World War I' (1999) II *Encyclopedia of Public International Law* 767, 793.

[10] C Tomuschat (ed), *The United Nations at Age Fifty: A Legal Perspective* (Leiden, Brill, 1995); JA Frowein, 'United Nations' (2000) IV *Encyclopedia of Public International Law* 1027, 1043.

an increasingly institutionalised way, epitomised by the constitution of the UN. It is this order that is fundamentally constitutive of another model of the organisation of the international society, as an alternative to the Westphalian Model,[11] and that, in the wake of the work other authors, can be called[12] the Model of the Charter of the United Nations,[13] we see 'deepening' and even gaining new structural features with the movements that have been taking place since the final decade of the twentieth century. Unlike the previous processes of transformation of the international system, those of the present era of globalisation are now more generally and immediately visible, making the world 'shrink' into the form of a global village,[14] perhaps because this is also the era of the omnipresence of new information and digital technologies[15] which allow for assessments of reality in real time across all spaces. The impacts of globalisation are also very tangible on the international system and on the law that is dedicated to it, particularly by transforming the role and status of the traditional actor in the international system – that is, the state.[16]

This chapter draws on the law in context approach and the attention paid to the new actors and forms of global governance resulting from globalisation, including the identification of and interplay between the different sites of governance that

[11] P Canelas de Castro, *Mutações e Constâncias do Direito da Neutralidade* (Coimbra, Universidade de Coimbra, 1994) 198; P Canelas de Castro, 'De quantas Cartas se faz a paz internacional?' in Antunes Varela, D Freitas do Amaral, J Miranda and JJ Gomes Canotilho (eds), *Ab Uno Ad Omnes, 75 Anos da Coimbra Editora* (Coimbra, Coimbra Editora, 1999).

[12] Canelas de Castro, *Mutações* (n 11); A Cassese, *International Law*, 2nd edn (Oxford, Oxford University Press, 2005).

[13] Tellingly, the Charter shall be qualified by some as the constitution of the contemporary international community. *cf* C Tomuschat, 'Obligations Arising for States without or against Their Will' (1993) 241(IV) *Recueil des Cours* 217; P-M Dupuy, 'The Constitutional Dimension of the Charter of the United Nations Revisited' (1997) 1 *Max Planck Yearbook of United Nations Law* 1; R St J Macdonald, 'The Charter of the United Nations as a World Constitution' in MN Schmitt (ed), *International Law across the Spectrum of Conflict: Essays in Honour of Professor LC Green on the Occasion of His Eightieth Birthday* (Newport, RI, US Naval War College, 2000) 263–300; P-M Dupuy, 'Ultimes remarques sur la "constitutionalité" de la Charte des Nations Unies' in R Chemain and A Pellet (eds), *La Charte des Nations Unies, constitution mondiale?* (Paris, Pédone, 2006).

[14] A notion coined by Marshall McLuhan, *The Gutenberg Galaxy: The Making of Typographic Man* (Toronto, University of Toronto Press, 1962) 31; M McLuhan, *Understanding Media: The Extensions of Man* (New York, McGraw-Hill, 1964).

[15] See M McLuhan, *The Medium is the Message: An Inventory of Effects* (New York, Bantam, 1967). For the projection of these suggestions into the digital revolution (the World Wide Web only appeared three decades after McLuhan's first works), see P Levinson, *Digital McLuhan: A Guide to the Information Millenium* (London, Routledge, 1999); P Pernthaler, 'Die Globalisierung als Herausforderung an eine modern Staatslehre' in H Schäfer (ed), *Staat, Verfassung, und Verwaltung. Festschrift anläßlich des 65. Geburtstages von Prof. Dr.Dr.h.c. Friedrich Koja* (Vienna, Springer, 1998) 69; P Dicken, *Global Shift: Transforming the World Economy*, 3rd edn (London, Guilford Press, 1998) 141; C Engel, 'Das Internet und der Nationalstaat' in K Dicke (ed), *Völkerrecht und internationales Privatrecht in einem sich globalisierenden internationalen System- und Auswirkungen der Entstaatlichung transnationaler Rechtsbeziehungen* (Heidelberg, CF Müller, 2000) 325–425.

[16] Reflection on the mutations of the state – the main legal subject of this order – and beyond the scope of this chapter, is addressed in the works listed in n 4 above.

Francis Snyder, to whom this study is dedicated, so proficiently pursued.[17] The identification of the distinctive features of globalisation constitutes a key step in this study. We will then analyse and evaluate the fundamental changes and structural impacts of globalisation on international law in relation to that core issue of any legal order which pertains to the subjects whose legal personality it recognises. Finally, we will make some considerations about the significance of these shifts in the context of an international legal order in a state of flux.

II. Globalisation: A Brief Characterisation of the Contemporary Horizon

Globalisation begins by differentiating itself from the important transformations that took place after the Second World War. While signifying a closer relationship between various agents of international relations, and primarily states, these can still be reduced almost exclusively to forms of internationalisation.[18] It is a reinforced internationalisation, more intense, even institutionalised, but still internationalisation, since it remains fundamentally based on the relationship between the dominant state structures, or those international organisations (IOs) that have the states as their members, establish relations with them or regulate them. Internationalisation concerns cooperative activities between state actors on a level that transcends state borders, but that are ultimately still fundamentally under their control.[19] This can still be said to occur with IOs, where states pursue their goals and functions together.[20] In contrast, globalisation is linked not only to states' relations, but also to the numerous relationships established by, fundamentally, individuals and groups of individuals – ie, non-state actors. The concept seeks to capture, in addition to relations between states which remain predominant, all those variegated, polygonal relations between individuals or human groups, which

[17] Amongst the rich bibliography by Professor Francis Snyder over decades of illuminating and impactful scholarship, see, early on, F Snyder, 'The Effectiveness of European Community Law: Institutions, Processes, Tools and Techniques' (1993) 56 *MLR* 19; F Snyder, 'The Gatekeepers: The European Courts and WTO Law' (2003) 40 Common Market Law Review 313; 'Gouverner la mondialisation économique' (2003) 54 *Droit et Société* 435; F Snyder, 'Economic Globalisation and the Law in the 21st Century' in A Sarat (ed), *The Blackwell Companion to Law and Society* (New York, Blackwell, 2004); F Snyder, 'L'Union européenne et la gouvernance de la mondialisation: La traduction du droit de l'OMC en droit communautaire' in *L'intégration européenne au XXIème siècle* (Brussels, Bruylant, 2004); F Snyder, 'Les sites de gouvernance' in L Boisson de Chazournes and R Medhi (eds), *Une société internationale en mutation: quels acteurs pour une nouvelle gouvernance?* (Brussels, Bruylant, 2005) 299; and F Snyder, *The EU, the WTO and China: Legal Pluralism and International Trade Regulation* (Oxford, Hart Publishing, 2010).

[18] U Hingst, *Auswirkungen der Globalisierung auf das Recht der völkerrechtlichen Verträge* (Berlin, Duncker & Humblot, 2001); J Delbrück, 'Das Staatsbild im Zeitalter wirtschaftsrechtlicher Globalisierung' (2002) 11, https://opendata.uni-halle.de/bitstream/1981185920/76441/1/BeitraegeTWR_3.pdf.

[19] J Delbrück, 'Globalisation of Law, Politics, and Markets: Implications for Domestic Law – A European Perspective' (1993) 1 *Indiana Journal of Global Legal Studies* 10, 11.

[20] A Emmerich-Fritsche, *Vom Völkerrecht zum Weltrecht* (Berlin, Duncker & Humblot, 2007).

are interwoven independently of those that occur within the state framework or between states. These relations may be of an economic or cultural nature, they may concern information or products, they may relate to damages to the environment, as well as they may result from the flows throughout the world of people, goods, services, capital, ideas and even pathogens and diseases.[21]

From this departing point derives that the definition of globalisation is not easy. This is partly because globalisation is a multifaceted, hybrid phenomenon, which makes it somewhat elusive for integration into well-defined taxonomic categories. Even only one manifestation of globalisation, political globalisation (albeit a central one),[22] is itself an expression of this multiplicity: it denotes the evolution of the ordering of human communities, previously almost exclusively a result of the state, towards a much more multifaceted process, comprising other levels of public authority (eg, IOs) and in which other actors, which were traditionally seen as private and lacking intervention in the governance procedures of communities, ultimately also interact in the pursuit of public objectives and the fulfilment of public tasks.[23] It therefore appears wiser to approximate this complex reality by attempting *ab initio* to seek a pluri-comprehensive, all-embracing, holistic concept.[24] Any notion of globalisation will certainly have to refer to a set of processes. Some of these processes – eg, mass migrations, global terrorism, climate change, depletion of the ozone layer, global diseases and pandemics[25] – can be considered objective, while others have a more pronounced subjective nature.

From another angle, globalisation is not only an objective phenomenon of the global interconnection of various areas of life, with a growing number of non-state actors, with the concurrent growing political and economic power of cross-border influence and profound changes in social and political integration, but is also a volitional act. It can also be understood as a politically determined process, as a

[21] E Richter, *Zerfall der Welteinheit: Vernunft und Globalisierung in der Moderne* (*Theorie und Gesellschaft*) (Frankfurt am Main, Campus, 1992); W Weidenfeld, 'Abschied von der alten Ordnung, Europa im Umbruch' in O Kimminich, A Klose and L Neuhold (eds), *Mit Realismus und Leidenschaft, Ethik im Dienst einer humanen Welt, Festschrift für Valentin Zsifkovits zum 60, Geburtstag* (Graz, Schnider, 1993); W Schäfer, 'Globalisierung: Entmonopolisierung des Nationalen?' in H Berg (ed), *Globalisierung der Wirtschaft: Ursachen – Formen – Konsequenzen* (Berlin, Duncker & Humblot, 1999) 9; W Bonß, 'Globalisierung unter soziologischen Perspektiven' in R Voigt (ed), *Globalisierung des Rechts* (Baden-Baden, Nomos, 1999/2000) 39; U Hingst, *Auswirkungen der Globalisierung auf das Recht der völkerrechtlichen Verträge* (Berlin, Duncker & Humblot, 2001) 106ff. See also J Habermas, 'Die postnationale Konstellation und die Zukunft der Demokratie' in J Habermas, *Die postnationale Konstellation. Politische Essays* (Frankfurt am Main, Surkamp, 1998) 101.

[22] Other manifestations can be aggregated conceptually into clusters, making it possible to also speak of economic globalisation, social globalisation, cultural globalisation and ecological globalisation. See D Held, A McGrew, D Goldblatt and J Perraton (eds), *Global Transformations: Politics, Economics and Culture* (Stanford, Stanford University Press, 1999); MB Steger, *Globalisation: A Very Short Introduction* (Oxford, Oxford University Press, 2003).

[23] J Delbrück, 'Transnational Federalism: Problems and Prospects of Allocating Public Authority beyond the State' (2004) 11(1) *Indiana Journal of Global Legal Studies* 33.

[24] Gomes Canotilho, 'Principios y "nuevos constitucionalismos": el problema de los nuevos principios' (2010) (7)(14) *Revista de Derecho Constitucional Europeo* 324, 329.

[25] Emmerich-Fritsche (n 20).

deliberate rather than organic strategy[26] of governmental and non-governmental actors. This is particularly so in economic globalisation, where its agents appear committed to the results of liberalisation, privatisation and deregulation of markets, to various degrees.[27] Even though such efforts have also been pursued in other times, contemporary globalised transnational relations, particularly in the commercial or financial fields, are qualitatively different for taking place in minimal time and without state borders appearing to matter. In particular, it can be seen that, in this context, multinational companies play a decisive role, as they seem to be able to relocate their industrial units in jurisdictions that offer them the best operating environment because they have more favourable tax burdens, or because production costs are lower, or because there are other advantages that make the investments of these companies more profitable. Financial transactions can also be made expeditiously. In the same way, the effects of any economic crisis can be immediately felt, also allowing for quick reactions.[28] For their part, state governments see the effective possibility of controlling these multinational companies' operations or these financial flows as being greatly reduced.[29]

Additionally, globalisation is a subjective phenomenon, a perception that political, economic, social, cultural and ecological processes are less rooted in states. In this way of perceiving the contemporary world, globalisation introduces a difference in relation to the previous experience of international cooperation: in the latter, the perception was that IOs were still a kind of *longa manus* of the states, an extension to solve problems or find ways of responding to radical state aspirations. International dynamics were still pursued on behalf of states and in order to respond to their interests. Today, however, in the era of globalisation, when phenomena like global warming, climate change and environmental crises are in play, the perceived need is for responses in accordance with common values or options, a common interest of humankind. Even when rooted in a particular space, political, economic, social, cultural, environmental and legal dynamics often share so many common elements with identical processes in other spaces that it is possible that may be seen as not specific to a territory, but instead as requiring the mobilisation of other (non-state) actors and means. The process of responding to such political challenges corresponds to the concept of global governance,[30]

[26] O Höffe, *Demokratie im Zeitalter der Globalisierung* (Munich, CH Beck, 1999) 9.

[27] This is what is generically blamed on certain leading states, such as the US, and international financial organisations (the International Monetary Fund and the World Bank), with the 'Washington Consensus' (*cf* J Williamson, 'What Washington Means by Policy Reform' in J Frieden et al (eds), *Modern Political Economy and Latin America* (London, Routledge, 2000)) as well as powerful multinationals.

[28] D Held, A. McGrew, D Goldblatt and J Perraton, *Global Transformations: Politics, Economics and Culture* (Stanford, Stanford University Press, 1999) 149.

[29] P Canelas de Castro, 'Empresas multinacionais e Direito Internacional – notas introdutórias sobre um regime emergente' in IC Tong et al (eds), *Estudos em Homenagem ao Professor Doutor Augusto Teixeira Garcia* (Coimbra, Almedina, 2023).

[30] B Zangl and M Zürn, 'Make Law, Not War: Internationale und transnationale Verrechtlichung als Baustein für Global Governance' in B Zangl and M Zürn (eds), *Verrechtlichung. Baustein für Global Governance*? (Bonn, Dietz, 2004) 15 represent this by the formula 'governance by, governance with, and governance without government'.

multilayered governance, or governance in network,[31] in a more inclusive process of decision-making not only of states and states within multilateral institutions, but also one in which precisely non-state actors at a global scale or scope of action often play a relevant role.

Globalisation can thus be broadly understood as the process or processes of 'deterritorialisation' of a myriad of political, economic and social relationships involving national and international actors, both public and private, including individuals, in a global interrelationship of such actors in space and time, in which a common good or public interest of humankind is recognised and sometimes pursued. From another perspective, one can speak of denationalisation or destatisation[32] in relation to the control over a whole range of relations that it no longer mediates or ensures. In such a context, by contrast, the individual will no longer be understood as an element of a state,[33] but rather as a 'global being', a member of a heterogeneous world society.[34]

By contrast, it is also important to note that globalisation does not imply a world government, a world state superpower. Nor does it imply the corresponding transformation of international law into a law of the world or a cosmopolitan law of global citizenship[35] with Kantian resonances,[36] as has been more recently projected by Jürgen Habermas. Nor does globalisation always have to be perceived as a (uniformly) universal phenomenon; rather, it is recognised that the processes of

[31] EO Czempiel, 'Governance and Democratization' in JN Rosenau and EO Czempiel (eds), *Governance without Government* (Cambridge, Cambridge University Press, 1992) 250; JN Rosenau, 'Governance, Order, and Change in World Politics' in JN Rosenau and EO Czempiel (eds), *Governance without Government* (Cambridge, Cambridge University Press, 1992) 1ff; B Kohler-Koch, 'Die Welt regieren ohne Weltregierung' in C Böhret and G Wewer (eds), *Regieren im 21. Jahrhundert zwischen Globalisierung und Regionalisierung* (Wiesbaden, Springer, 1993) 121ff; D Held, *Democracy and the Global Order: From the Modern State to Cosmopolitan Governance* (Stanford, Stanford University Press, 1995) 73ff; JCV de Roberts, 'Governance: An Opportunity?' in EE Harris and JA Yunker (eds), *Toward Genuine Global Governance: Critical Reactions to 'Our Global Neighborhood'* (Westport, Praeger, 1999) 35ff; B Zangl and M Zürn, 'Make Law, Not War: Internationale und transnationale Verrechtlichung als Baustein für Global Governance' in Zangl and Zürn (eds) (n 30) 12ff; Emmerich-Fritsche (n 20).

[32] In German literature, the concept of *Entstaatlichung* is used for phenomena that transcend the framework of the hitherto dominant state order. See J Delbrück, 'Zur Entwicklung der internationalen Rechtsordnung' (1998) 16(2) *Sicherheit und Frieden* 67.

[33] S Strange, *The Retreat of the State: The Diffusion of Power in the World Economy* (Cambridge, Cambridge University Press, 1996); AK Lindblom, *Non-governmental Organisations in International Law* (Cambridge, Cambridge University Press, 2005) 12, who speaks of the 'diffusion of state power'. Both underline a trend towards a gradual (relative) decline in the capacity and status of states, namely in the supply of the public goods necessary for meeting the challenges of the present time, such as human rights, the environment, and instruments of global governance.

[34] See T Wobbe, 'Konzepte der Weltgesellschaft' in T Wobbe, *Weltgesellschaft* (Bielefeld, Transcript, 2000) 9ff; R Stichweh, *Die Weltgesellschaft: Soziologische Analysen* (Frankfurt am Main, Suhrkamp, 2000), 7ff; N Luhmann, *Die Gesellschaft der Gesellschaft* (Frankfurt am Main, Suhrkamp, 2002).

[35] On this tradition in international law and its ethical-philosophical and jusnaturalist origins, as well as its refraction in contractualist, rationalist theories and Habermasian discourse ethics, see Emmerich-Fritsche (n 20).

[36] Immanuel Kant, *Zum ewigen Frieden. Ein philosophischer Entwurf* (Darmstadt, Königsberg, F Nicolovius, 1983); *Die Metaphysik der Sitten. Rechtslehre* (Darmstadt, Weischedel, 1983) 7, especially 475ff.

globalisation have different expressions, intensities and impacts in different regions of the world, as they do in different human universes and fields of human activity.

Regardless of the difficulties in characterising such a plural and complex set of phenomena, what seems relevant is that globalisation affects the contemporary international system, the actors therein and even the structure, lending them new characteristics. Likewise, globalisation imports profound, intense and extensive impacts on the normative structure of international law. In particular, it seems to imply profound changes with regard to the seat and forms of use of public authority and the capacity to provide public goods for the various social and human groupings, so much so that the traditional contrasts between the national and international domains sometimes no longer seem appropriate. Several authors[37] suggest that this new constellation of post-national forms[38] of exercising authority and guaranteeing public goods requires a new type of regulation, a new kind of international law. The different social context to some extent seems to call for a substantive constitutional inspiration and meaning, with (constitutional) multi-level expression and involving 'constitutional' or 'constitutional substitutes' of contents and forms. Generally speaking, globalisation thus calls for a reconstruction of international law that no longer roots it (or grounds it only) in equating the state as the sole authority or legal subject and in the subsequent traditional and rigid boundaries between the 'domestic' domain of the state and the domain of the international,[39] where international law, fundamentally or even exclusively, appears as the space of relations between states. In using constitutional language and constitutional dogmatic tools, and integrating the functions proper to a public authority, such globally 'constitutionalised'[40] international law would become capable of better 'apprehending' this new contextual reality, namely by denoting it in other normative terms. A starting point in such a reconstruction of international law pertains to the central question of the recognition of the actors of the system, with their universe becoming more plural and complex.

III. The Impact of Globalisation on the Core Issue of Legal Subjectivity in International Law: The Recognition of New Subjects of International Law

Globalisation thus affects a very broad spectrum of political, economic, social and cultural activities at the international, transnational and supranational levels, as well as at the domestic, national level. It also affects international law. One of its

[37] Emmerich-Fritsche (n 20) 1062.

[38] J Habermas, 'Hat die Konstitutionalisierung des Völkerrechts noch eine Chance?' in J Habermas (ed), *Der gespaltene Westen* (Frankfurt am Main, Suhrkamp, 2004).

[39] D Anzilotti, *Corso di Diritto Internazionale Lezioni Tenute Nell'universita di Roma Nell'anno Scolastico 1922–23* (*Introduzione-I Soggetti-Gli Organi*), 3rd edn (Rome, Atheneum, 1929).

[40] See section IV below.

most important impacts on the international legal order pertains to the core issue of subjectivity, ie, who is recognised to have legal personality.

It is symptomatic that, faced with globalisation, international legal doctrine, although with initial resistance and certainly some 'delay' in relation to the reality of an international system that had visibly become more plural and richer as to the participation therein, has felt the need to revisit the perennial question[41] of international legal personality. The driver was to determine whether other actors, in addition to the 'consecrated' ones, should be recognised and whether they ascended to the status of subjects within the international legal order.[42]

A subject of law is opposed to an object of law,[43] primarily because it has international legal personality and the aptitude or ownership of rights and obligations in the respective legal order. This, in our understanding, necessarily implies the relativity of the subjects of international law to the concrete terms of the international legal order. The ensuing problem of including new subjects in the normative system is therefore answered in historically situated terms, in relation to the concrete stage of development of this legal order, itself a function of the normative expectations, needs and consensus obtained in the particular human community.[44] We understand that the International Court of Justice (ICJ) has authoritatively sustained a similar conclusion when, in its Opinion of 1949 on the question of *Reparations for Injuries Suffered in Service of the United Nations* (*Reparations for Injuries*), it stated that 'the subjects of law in any legal system are not necessarily identical in their nature or in the extent of their rights and their nature depends upon the needs of the community'.[45]

[41] This alleged historical omnipresence derives from the centrality of the problem in the international legal order. See M Cosnard, 'Rapport introductif' in SFDI, *Le sujet en droit international, Colloque du Mans* (Paris, Pédone, 2005) 3.

[42] There is no necessary coincidence between the question of legal personality (a person has legal personality if he or she is the holder of rights and the addressee of duties in international law: *cf* A Verdross and B Simma, *Universelles Völkerrecht. Theorie und Praxis*, 3rd edn (Berlin, Duncker & Humbolt, 1984) 221–22; K Hailbronner, 'Der Staat und das Einzelne als Völkerrechtssubjekte' in WG Vizthum (ed), *Völkerrecht* (Berlin, De Gruyter, 1997) 180) and the question of legal subjectivity, but the notions are related. If the condition of subject supposes personality, the reverse does not seem to be true: personality is the aptitude to be a subject of law. This doctrine is, however, contested by some, who instead sustain that the notions respect the same reality and that the terms are synonymous and can be used interchangeably; see, eg, C Dominicé, 'La personnalité juridique dans le système du droit des gens' in J Makarczyk (ed), *Essays in Honour of Krzystof Skubiszewski: Theory of International Law at the Threshold of the 21st Century* (Dordrecht, Kluwer, 1996) 148. The problem becomes even more complex when these notions are related to that of international legal capacity, as is partly the case in the historic *dictum* of the ICJ in its 1949 advisory opinion on the issue of *Reparations for Injuries Suffered in the Service of the United Nations* (1949) ICJ Rep 179.

[43] In the positivist, orthodox doctrine of international law, in which this law is of states and for states, individuals, by contrast, appear as the *object* of international law. See G Manner, 'The Object Theory of the Individual in International Law' (1952) 46 *AJIL* 428.

[44] JE Nijman, *The Concept of International Legal Personality: An Inquiry into the History and Theory of International Law* (The Hague, TMC Press, 2004).

[45] *Reparations for Injuries* (1949) ICJ Rep 179.

In practice, the question only arises with regard to secondary subjects of law,[46] since the state has been and remains the uncontested primary subject[47] from the origins of international law.[48] However, since the international legal order does not provide a uniform normative answer to this issue, since it does not contain a list of subjects who possess international legal personality, the concrete responses will be determined in accordance with the theoretical perspective on international law that is adhered to[49] and the concrete content taken from readings of positive law at any given time. Although not resolving the issue once and for all, the ICJ's case law contributes to this in the historic *Reparations for Injuries* advisory opinion by highlighting the criteria of the titularity of rights and obligations and the capacity to avail oneself of these rights by way of international proceedings as relevant indicators. The doctrine, although divided, seems to equally point to several vectors: the subject of international law is the addressee of the norms which enshrine rights or obligations in accordance with the international legal source.[50] To the preceding criterion, the requirements of the capacity to exercise rights and fulfil obligations are sometimes also added;[51] namely the capacity to create norms of international law[52] and to submit claims to adjudicatory bodies. There even seems to be a tendency, of a more liberal and 'gradualist' nature,[53] to equate diverse forms of participation in the construction or even application of the international legal order, namely in legal proceedings, with the qualification as a subject of international law.

[46] H Mosler, 'Subjects of International Law', (1988) VIII *Encyclopedia of Public International Law* 442.

[47] The dogma of the state as the subject of international law, unceasingly proclaimed by doctrine, has also been affirmed by international jurisprudence. Thus, the Permanent Court of International Justice (PCIJ) in the judgment of the *Lotus* case stated that 'international law governs relations between independent States'. Case Series A no 10 *France v Turkey* (the case of the *S.S. 'Lotus'*) [1927] PCIJ 18.

[48] Hence, Cosnard suggests that the question of international legal subjectivity only really emerged at the beginning of the twentieth century, when the exclusivity of the state started to be challenged: Cosnard (n 41).

[49] A-LVaurs-Chaumette, *Les sujets du droit international pénal: vers une nouvelle définition de la personnalité juridique internationale?* (Paris, Pédone, 2009) 2.

[50] M Siotto Pintor, 'Les sujets du droit international autres que les Etats' (1932) 41 *Recueil des Cours* 278, 279; D Anzilotti, *Cours de droit international public* (Paris, LGDJ, 1999); J Combacau and S Sur, *Droit international public*, 8th edn (Paris, Montchrestien, 2008) 316.

[51] CT Eustathiades, 'Les sujets du droit international et la responsabilité internationale – nouvelles tendances' (1953) 84(3) *Recueil des Cours* 414; F Sudre, *Droit international et droit européen des droits de l'homme*, 8th edn (Paris, Presses Universitaires de France, 2006); P-M Dupuy and Y Kerbrat, *Droit international public*, 11th edn (Paris, Dalloz, 2012).

[52] P Weil, 'Le droit international en quête de son identité' (1992) 237 *Recueil des Cours* 122; C Dominicé, 'La personnalité juridique dans le système du droit des gens' in J Makarczyk (ed), *Essays in Honour of Krzystof Skubiszewski: Theory of International Law at the Threshold of the 21st Century* (The Hague, Kluwer, 1996) 171; G Distefano, 'Observations éparses sur les caractères de la personnalité juridique internationale' (2007) *Annuaire français de Droit international* 117.

[53] R Higgins, *Problems and Process: International Law and How We Use it* (Oxford, Oxford University Press, 1994) 5; I Rossi, *Legal Status of Non-governmental Organisations in International Law* (Leuven, Lirias, 2009) 369–370.

A. International Organisations

At the start of the era of globalisation, it is safe to say that, in addition to sovereign states[54] and a few more traditionally recognised subjects of international law, such as the Holy See[55] and the Order of Malta,[56] IOs were also already firmly entrenched[57] as subjects of international law.[58]

However, they have a different status from that of the state: they appear as derived and functional subjects of international law.[59] The recognition of these new, derived and functional actors of international law finds its sociological foundation in the fact that intergovernmental IOs have become institutionalised and independent, relatively stable centres of international policy making.[60] Naturally, in terms of their origin, IOs are the product of the creation of states, resulting from their individual political will. In particular, it is the states that in the IO's founding treaty, define its goals and powers. This fact, hyperbolised by the realist school of international relations, even led it to deny that IOs may constitute independent political actors. In this line of thought, IOs are instead presented as mere instruments of powerful states, which, by this means, pursue their national

[54] Brierly, one of the best-known jusinternationalists for generations of students of international law, still defined international law as 'the body of rules and principles of action which bind civilised states in their relations with other states'. *cf* J-L Brierly, *The Law of Nations*, 6th edn (Oxford, Oxford University Press, 1963). The criteria set out above for identifying the condition of subject of international law also seems to be based on the state, as if reserving the condition of subject to the state. Hence, many say that it has full legal personality (see, for example, P-M Dupuy and Y Kerbrat, *Droit international public*, 11th edn (Paris, Dalloz, 2012) 233). Others present it as an original and primary subject, connatural or innate to the law system (see C Dominicé, 'La personnalité juridique dans le système du droit des gens' in J Makarczyk (ed), *Essays in Honour of Krzystof Skubiszewski: Theory of International Law at the Threshold of the 21st Century* (The Hague, Kluwer, 1996) 171). However, it should be noted that this 'favouring' of the state also implicitly opens up the possibility that other actors may have a personality (albeit minor) and so they also stand as subjects of law, albeit secondary subjects.

[55] HF Köck, 'Holy See' (1995) II *Encyclopedia of Public International Law* 866–69.

[56] J Cremona, 'Malta, Order of' (1999) III *Encyclopedia of Public International Law* 280.

[57] T Marguerite and R Prouvèze, 'Le droit international et la doctrine saisis par le fait: la diversification des sujets du droit international sous l'effet de la pratique' (2016) *Revue québécoise de droit international* 163 argue that there is 'almost unanimity' in affirming the personality of IOs, attributing it to the fact that IOs derive from the will of the states, thus not calling into question sovereignty as the traditional foundation of international law.

[58] However, this does not imply that in contemporary international law there are no grey areas regarding the status of IOs. Instead, these uncertainties may be illustrated by the works of the International Law Commission (ILC) on the international responsibility of IOs. *cf* (2011) II *Yearbook of the International Law Commission* 2. Similarly, inconsistencies in their treatment as subjects of international law by international judicial bodies may be noted – for example, by the European Court of Human Rights in *Behrami and Behrami v France* and *Germany and Norway* App Nos 71412/01 and 78166/01 (decision of the Grand Chamber, 2 May 2007).

[59] R Bindschedler, 'International Organisations, General Aspects' (1995) II *Encyclopedia of Public International Law* 1299.

[60] F Seyersted, *Objective International Personality of Intergovernmental Organisations: Do Their Capacities Really Depend upon Their Constitutions?* (Copenhagen, Krohns Bog Trykkeri, 1963).

power interests.[61] In reality, however, through the action of their organs, IOs gradually asserted themselves as autonomous centres of deliberation and independent decision making. In the actual dynamics of life, IOs thus take part in modern international relations, asserting themselves vis-a-vis individual member states. This equally became a fact in legal terms, as, for instance, the ICJ's Advisory Opinions *Reparations for Injuries* and *Legality of the Threat or Use of Nuclear Weapons* denote, explicitly recognising IOs as subjects of international law.[62] IOs' decisions are not merely the sum of the member states' acts of will; they constitute autonomous legal acts directly attributable to the organisations as institutionalised entities.[63] These acts, which often translate into law making at the international level,[64] may be binding on all IO member states[65] and even on those which did not contribute to their adoption.[66]

B. Individuals

Naturally, already before individuals came to be widely recognised as legal subjects of international law prior to and as a result of globalisation, some internationalists at the theoretic-dogmatic level had been exploring avenues contrary to the dominant paradigm of state-centred legal subjectivity. In their works, it is the individual who is the main subject of international law. This was the case, in particular, with the sociological school of international law, of Nicolas Politis and Georges Scelle,[67] in the period between the two World Wars. Subsequently, after the Second World War, this trend is also visible in Hersch Lauterpacht's works[68] and, following the same basic idea that international legal rules and international institutions are deeply rooted in the particular socio-cultural characteristics of certain communities, those

[61] HJ Morgenthau, *Politics among Nations: The Struggle for Power and Peace* (New York, Knopf, 1948); HJ Morgenthau, 'Political Limitations of the United Nations' in GA Lipsky (ed), *Law and Politics in the World Community* (Berkeley, University of California Press, 1953) 150; W Link, *Die Neuordnung der Weltpolitik. Grundprobleme globaler Politik an der Schwelle zum 21. Jahrhundert* (Munich, CH Beck 1998) 114.

[62] *Reparations for Injuries* (1949) ICJ Rep 179; *Legality of the Threat or Use of Nuclear Weapons* (1996) ICJ Rep 226.

[63] C Tietje, 'The Changing Legal Structure of International Treaties as an Aspect of an Emerging Global Governance Architecture' (1999) 42 *German Yearbook of International Law* 35ff; E Klein, 'Die Internationalen und supranationalen Organisationen' in WG Vitzthum (ed), *Völkerrecht*, 3rd edn (Berlin, De Gruyter, 2004) 281ff.

[64] JE Alvarez, *International Organisations as Law-Makers* (Oxford, Oxford University Press, 2005); J Alvarez, 'The New Treaty Makers' (2012) 25 *Boston College International and Comparative Law Review* 218ff.

[65] A Reinisch, 'Sources of International Organisations' Law: Why Custom and General Principles are Crucial' in S Besson and J d'Aspremont (eds), *The Oxford Handbook of the Sources of International Law* (Oxford, Oxford University Press, 2017) 1143–63; J Klabbers, *An Introduction to International Organisations Law*, 3rd edn (Cambridge, Cambridge University Press, 2015) ch 8, 158ff.

[66] On the impact of IOs on international law in general, see JE Alvarez, *The Impact of International Organisations on International Law* (Leiden, Brill, 2016).

[67] See, respectively, N Politis, *Les nouvelles tendances du droit international* (Paris, Hachette, 1927) 64–66; G Scelle, *Précis de droit des gens* (Paris, Recueil Sirey, 1932).

[68] H Lauterpacht, *International Law and Human Rights* (London, Stevens, 1950).

of Julius Stone,[69] Wilfred Jenks,[70] Bartholmeus Landheer[71] and Richard Falk.[72] The common denominator of these doctrinal works that contributed to the advancement of the recognition of legal personality to individuals is the detachment from the dominant idea of a law of a society of states towards one in which the legal order is based instead on an international community in which individuals are endowed with legal entitlements and play a role as (main) subjects of international law.[73]

The eventual effective recognition of individuals as subjects of international law has its sociological roots in the fact that the vast majority of states and their people accept the normative and heuristic notion of human rights.[74] Similarly, most human communities see the protection of individuals and their legal entitlement as indispensable in contemporary relations. This is documented, for instance, in such normative references as the Preamble to and Articles 1(3) and 55(c) of the United Nations Charter, Article 1 of the Universal Declaration of Human Rights, and the preambles to the International Covenants on Human Rights of 1966, setting out a general imperative for universal respect for human rights and fundamental freedoms for all human beings without distinction.[75] Moreover, it is maintained that this necessity sometimes stands independently of the will of states, and even against the state of nationality.[76] This evolution is often attributed to a genuine revolution in mentalities brought about by the tragic, humanity-destroying acts committed during the Second World War. These facts

[69] J Stone, 'Problems Confronting Sociological Enquiries Concerning International Law' (1956) 89 *Recueil des Cours* 73–74; J Stone, 'A Sociological Perspective on International Law' in R St J Macdonald and DM Johnston (eds), *The Structure and Process of International Law: Essays in Legal Philosophy, Doctrine and Theory* (The Hague, Martinus Nijhoff, 1983) 263ff.

[70] CW Jenks, *The Common Law of Mankind* (New York, Frederick A Praeger, 1958) 14–18.

[71] B Landheer, *On the Sociology of International Law and International Society* (The Hague, Martinus Nijhoff, 1966) 56–64, 108–13.

[72] RA Falk, 'The Adequacy of Contemporary Theories of International Law: Gaps in Legal Thinking' (1964) 40 *Virginia Law Review* 247–49; 'A New Paradigm for International Legal Studies: Prospects and Proposals' (1975) 84(5) *Yale Law Review* 973–79.

[73] On these moments of theoretical development, see A Bianchi, *Theory and Philosophy of International Law* (Oxford, Oxford University Press, 2016) 246–57; M Hirsch, 'The Sociological Perspective on International Law' (2019) Hebrew University of Jerusalem Legal Studies Research Paper Series n 19-01.

[74] P Häberle, 'Die Menschenwürde als Grundlage der staatlichen Gemeinschaft' in *Handbuch des Staatsrechts der Bundesrepublik Deutschlands*, vol I (Heidelberg, CF Müller, 1995) 815ff; M Kotzur, 'Wechselwirkungen zwischen Europäischer Verfassungs- und Völkerrechtslehre' in A Blankennagel, I Pernice and H Schulze-Fielitz (eds), *Verfassung im Diskurs der Welt: Liber Amicorum für Peter Häberle zum siebzigsten Geburtstag* (Tübingen, Mohr Siebeck, 2004) 289ff.

[75] K Stern, 'Idee der Menschenrechte' in *Handbuch des Staatsrechts der Bundesrepublik Deutschlands* V (Heidelberg, CF Müller, 1992) 108; W von der Wense, *Der UN-Menschenrechtsausschuß und sein Beitrag zum universellen Schutz der Menschenrechte* (Berlin, Springer, 1999) 15; P Mastronardi, 'Menschenwürde und kulturelle Bedingheit des Rechts' in T Marauhn (ed), *Die Rechtsstellung des Menschen im Völkerrecht. Entwicklungen und Perspektiven* (Tübingen, Mohr, 2003) 59ff.

[76] K Dicke, 'Die der Person innewohnende Würde und die Frage der Universalität der Menschenrechte' in H Bielefeldt, W Brugger and K Dicke (eds), *Würde und Recht des Menschen – Festschrift für Johannes Schwartländer zum 70 Geburtstag* (Würzburg, Könighausen und Neumann, 1992) 165ff; J Delbrück, 'Die Universalisierung des Menschenrechtsschutzes: Aspekte der Begründung und Durchsetzbarkeit' in A Zunker (ed), *Weltordnung oder Chaos? Beiträge zur internationalen Politik: Festschrift zum 65. Geburtstag von Professor Dr. Klaus Ritter (Internationale Politik und Sicherheit)* (Baden-Baden, Nomos, 1993) 551–66.

demonstrated the vacuity of the state mediation theory of international law norms and the danger that the state – even the state of nationality of those individuals – can pose for individuals.[77] It is this vision of things and of what international normativity should be or become – arguably reflected in the objectives of the international community, namely the inclusion of the objective of the promotion and protection of human rights in Article 1(3) of the UN Charter – that would make it possible to overcome the classic doctrine that persistently denied the quality of subject of law to individuals.

In the traditional doctrine of subjects of international law, the law is equated with the law of states. Individuals are instead the mere object of international law.[78] In the same general sense, and with the same foundation in a vision rooted in an inflated perspective of state sovereignty, the theory of the mediation of individuals by states makes the latter the immediate addressees of international legal norms: states are the holders of rights and obligations. Consequently, it falls to states to mediate these provisions or reflect them on individuals and for their benefit – that is, if the state incorporates them into its domestic law. This doctrine finds expression in the Opinion of the Permanent Court of International Justice (PCIJ) regarding the question of the competence of the Danzig courts, in which the PCIJ pronounced the *dictum* that 'an agreement cannot, as such, create rights and obligations for individuals', although it simultaneously recognised that the object of the agreement may be to create rights and obligations for individuals that can be enforced by national jurisdictions.[79] In the same vein, the institute of diplomatic protection was and remains a purely interstate liability mechanism, in which the individual is undeniably the subject of litigation. Tellingly, even today, as evidenced by the codifying efforts of the ILC, any compensation that results from such diplomatic protection is titled and administered by the state.[80] According to this approach, even though some norms of international law deal with the condition of individuals, this is without prejudice to the holder of rights and obligations remaining the state of the nationality of the individual. Another example is the right to immunities. In this context, individuals can only indirectly be considered as benefiting; in reality, these are state prerogatives.[81]

[77] See, eg, C Dubost, 'Les crimes des États et la coutume pénale internationale' (1946) 11(6) *Politique étrangère* 553.

[78] The theory of individuals as objects of international law, often associated with dualist postulates, is a *vexata quaestio* that has been debated since at least G Jellinek, *System der Subjektiven öffentlichen Rechte* (Tübingen, Mohr, 1905). *cf* A Peters, 'Das subjektive internationale Recht' (2011) 59 *Jahrbuch des öffentlichen Rechts der Gegenwart* 439.

[79] *Jurisdiction of the Courts of Danzig*, PCIJ, Serial B, n 15 (1928) 17–18. See also *La Grand, Germany v United States of America* (2001) ICJ Rep 77, 89.

[80] 'Draft Articles on Diplomatic Protection with Commentaries' (2006) 2(2) *Yearbook of the International Law Commission* 97ff.

[81] C Dominicé, J Belhumeur and L Condorelli, 'L'individu, la coutume internationale et le juge national' in *L'ordre juridique international entre tradition et innovation* (Geneva, Graduate Institute Publications, 1997) paras 35, 40.

The recognition of a legal status for individuals instead derives from the waves of consecration of human rights following the Second World War. These human rights contribute to rendering individuals the status of subject of law. Individuals directly benefit from this condition and it is this one which allows them to pursue their specific fundamental rights.[82] The significance of this move in the contemporary international legal order, following the Second World War,[83] will be enhanced by the very consolidation and profound normative development of the branches of international law devoted to guaranteeing and protecting the rights of individuals, from the outset (but not only) against states,[84] that globalisation will facilitate.

International human rights law, just like international humanitarian law and international criminal law, which have the same foundations in common and pursue the same objectives, definitively set aside the classic treatment of international law regarding individuals, opening up the path of legal subjectivity to them. This makes individuals holders of international rights and obligations of human protection in international law.[85] At a material level, these bodies of law confer rights upon individuals that are enforceable against states. Or, from another angle, they prescribe obligations to states for the direct benefit of individuals. They also impose on states the obligation to guarantee the enjoyment by individuals of their rights by acting against interferences by other individuals or other agents, according to the theory of positive obligations, an element of the 'respect-protect-fulfil' triptych[86] constituted by the practice of the committees mandated to monitor and ensure compliance with the International Covenants on Human Rights.

[82] A Emmerich-Fritsche, *Vom Völkerrecht zum Weltrecht* (Berlin, Duncker & Humblot, 2007) 459–572.

[83] H Lauterpacht, *International Law and Human Rights* (Hamden, Archon Books, 1968); LB Sohn and T Buergenthal, *The International Protection of Human Rights* (New York, Bobbs-Merrill Company, 1973); K Vasak (ed), *Les dimensions internationales des droits de l'homme* (Paris, UNESCO, 1978).

[84] This is certainly the case with international criminal law, particularly after the adoption of the Statute of the International Criminal Court (ICC).

[85] The international law of human rights and international humanitarian law share both values and foundations. The fundamental difference between them concerns the condition of application, since international humanitarian law applies in a context of armed conflict, while human rights apply in principle at any time, although with particularities in the case of armed conflict. In this sense, see ICJ Opinion, *Question Concerning the Legal Consequences of the Construction of a Wall in the Occupied Palestinian Territory* (2004) ICJ Rep 106; and C Droege, 'Droits de l'homme et droit humanitaire: des affinités électives?' (2008) *Revue internationale de la Croix-Rouge* 871.

[86] The triptych concerns obligations or duties for states, corresponding to the human rights of individuals or groups. The obligation to respect means that states must refrain from interfering with or impairing the enjoyment of human rights. The obligation to protect means that states must protect individuals or groups against violations of their human rights. The obligation to fulfil means that states have to undertake positive action for the effective enjoyment of human rights. The concept of this threefold obligation was first formulated by H Shue, *Basic Rights: Subsistence, Affluence and US Foreign Policy* (Princeton, Princeton University Press, 1980) and has been adopted by the Committee on Economic, Social and Cultural Rights, which uses it repeatedly in its documents.

The great difference in the era of globalisation results from the fact that another constituent element of this common international law of human protection,[87] international criminal law, a branch of international law that since the era of globalisation has strongly developed, imposes a broad set of international obligations directly on individuals. Individuals are thereby also transformed into passive subjects of international law. International criminal law regulates not only the rights of states, but also the rights of individuals on a universal scale, using the common means of international law. It is this international law that directly incriminates,[88] as it is in the forms provided for by international law that international criminal responsibility is implemented.[89] International law thus increasingly creates and develops obligations for individuals, while at the same time granting them new rights. Moreover, in the new international criminal law, individuals also appear as the beneficiaries of the rules contained in this branch of international law. This is the case, in particular, with a set of rights of a procedural nature, which, although inspired by the general right to a fair trial of international human rights law – namely Article 14 of the International Covenant on Civil and Political Rights (ICCPR) – have come to be specifically rooted in the special framework of the statutes of the various international criminal jurisdictions.[90] The individual is the passive subject of immediate obligations that protect the fundamental rights of other individuals, the disrespect of which implies that individual's criminal responsibility. Importantly, the source of this responsibility, whether ascertained in domestic jurisdictions or in international jurisdictions, is international. It follows that in contemporary international criminal law the individual is clearly the holder of international rights and obligations.[91] Thus, the first criterion set out by the ICJ for the qualification as a subject of international law is fulfilled.

The same may be concluded regarding the second criterion of international legal personality: the capacity of individuals to assert their rights in international justice.[92] Contemporary international law in fact includes international mechanisms that allow individuals to enforce their rights or verify their responsibility. On a par with the development of globalisation, the international legal order, especially from the 1990s onwards, has created various ad hoc, hybrid

[87] Thus, see O de Frouville, *Droit international pénal: Sources, incriminations, responsabilité* (Paris, Pédone, 2012) 8–9.

[88] C Dominicé, J Belhumeur and L Condorelli, 'L'individu, la coutume internationale et le juge national' in *L'ordre juridique international entre tradition et innovation* (Geneva, Graduate Institute Publications, 1997) 93–107.

[89] B Simma and A Paulus, 'Sources du droit international pénal' in H Ascensio (ed), *Droit international pénal* (Paris, Pédone, 2012) 79.

[90] In this, international criminal law may appear as a guarantee of the efficacy of the two other branches of this common law of human protection: human rights and international humanitarian law.

[91] A-L Vaurs-Chaumette, *Les sujets du droit international pénal: vers une nouvelle définition de la personnalité juridique internationale?* (Paris, Pédone, 2009) 16.

[92] Cançado Trindade is of the opinion that this capacity does not stand as a constitutive element of the condition as a subject, but rather as its consequence, as a characterising trait as legal subject. See AA Cançado Trindade, 'L'humanité comme sujet du droit international: nouvelles réflexions' (2012) 61 *Revista da Faculdade de Direito da Universidade Federal de Minas Gerais* 81ff.

and internationalised criminal jurisdictions. This process of the progressive institutionalisation of this law culminated with the adoption of the Rome Statute in 1998 and the establishment of the International Criminal Court (ICC). Simultaneously, the international community had also been consolidating and developing multiple jurisdictions and bodies for the protection of human rights. Since the general mission of these bodies is to ensure that human rights treaties are well implemented by states parties, a concomitant trend is developing for the corresponding jurisdictions to open to individuals, the raison d'être of these human protection regimes. An example of this trend is Protocol I to the ICCPR. Together, these mechanisms guarantee individuals access to the courts, to both international jurisdictions specialising in human rights, as well as international jurisdictions committed to the prosecution of international crimes.[93] In the latter, even when individuals do not appear as plaintiffs, they can participate in the proceedings under the special status of victims and as witnesses for the prosecution. Moreover, in these jurisdictions, the accused individual is already indisputably and fully a passive subject of law. It is in these jurisdictions that the criminal consequences of the actions of accused individuals are determined, as it is in these bodies that individuals can ascertain their rights and even obtain compensation for damages that they may have suffered in the event of, for example, a miscarriage of justice.[94] Furthermore, individuals enjoy important procedural rights within these instances. This is the case, for example, in the context of the ICC, with refusal proceedings, incidental proceedings or the right of appeal.[95]

Conversely, regarding the criterion of participation in law making, the status of the individual remains unchanged: in general, individuals are deemed incapable of producing international legal acts.[96]

C. Other Private Subjects

However, the analysis of the international legal order in the era of globalisation shows that the diversification of actors entitled to act and maintain a 'voice'[97] goes much further than IOs and individuals, contributing to constituting or reinforcing

[93] A Cassese and M Delmas-Marty (eds), *Crimes internationaux et jurisdictions internationales* (Paris, PUF, 2002) 71; T Margueritte, 'International Criminal Law and Human Rights' in W Shabas and N Bernaz (eds), *Routledge Handbook of International Criminal Law* (New York, Routledge, 2011) 436ff.

[94] Thus, the jurisprudence that has been affirmed by international criminal tribunals in cases such as *Nahimana, Barayagwiza and Ngeze*, ICTR-99-52-T (before the ICC in Rwanda, 3 December 2003) paras 1106–07. This determination was then substantially reiterated in *Lubanga* ICC01/04-01/06-772 (OA4) (before the ICC, 14 December 2006) para 37. See also art 85 of the Statute of the ICC. In the doctrine, see T Margueritte, 'International Criminal Law and Human Rights' in Shabas and Bernaz (n 93) 445ff.

[95] Marguerite and Prouvèze (n 57) 171.

[96] See, however, the discussion below on international contracts under international investment law.

[97] J Nijman, *The Concept of International Legal Personality: An Inquiry into the History and Theory of International Law* (The Hague, TMC Asser Press, 2004) 9.

a more diversified and complex international community, including and recognising the growing role of non-state actors.[98] This presence of private non-state actors in contemporary international and global relations is so striking that some go so far as to characterise the present day as the age of non-state actors.[99]

Yet, it is interesting to note that the generic term 'non-state actor' used to designate these other participants in the (new) international legal system, such as multinational companies and non-governmental organisations (NGOs),[100] cannot but be deemed problematic, as it determines the essence of these actors by what they are not (ie, they are not states). Philip Alston rightly notes that this definition can only have been 'intentionally adopted in order to reinforce the assumption that the state is not only the central actor, but also the indispensable and central one around which all other entities gravitate'.[101] Such a definition also connotes or reinforces the view of that legal doctrine that resists accepting the legal personality of non-state legal persons[102] and instead insists on affirming the state as the sole participant in the creation of law.[103]

D. Multinational Enterprises

The global system will also reach those actors so relevant to globalisation: multinational enterprises. In spite of some attempts,[104] international law does not contain an established definition of a multinational enterprise. However, it may be defined as 'a group of enterprises of different nationality that are united by

[98] D Narayan, R Patel, K Sghafft, A Rademacher and S Koch-Shulte (eds), *Voices of the Poor: Crying out for Change* (Washington DC, World Bank, 2000). In a sociological observation, they note that, for most individuals, their factual relationship with the international legal system is precisely through these actors and not through 'distant' states.

[99] JT Mathews, 'Power Shift' (1997) 76(1) *Foreign Affairs* 50.

[100] A Bianchi, *Non-state Actors and International Law* (Aldershot, Ashgate, 2009); J d'Aspremont, *Participants in the International Legal System: Multiple Perspectives on Non-state Actors in International Law* (Routledge, London, 2011); M Noortmann, A Reinisch and C Ryngaert (eds), *Non-state Actors in International Law* (Oxford, Hart Publishing, 2015).

[101] P Alston, 'The "Not-a-Cat" Syndrome: Can the International Human Rights Regime accommodate Non-state Actors?' in P Alston (ed), *Non-state Actors and Human Rights* (Oxford, Oxford University Press, 2005) 3.

[102] See, eg, A Mahiou, 'Le droit international ou la dialectique de la rigueur et de la fléxibilité: cours général de droit international' (2009) 337 *Recueil des Cours* 265. Pellet also attributes 'timidity' to the doctrine, 'including the most open', noting the difference with which it looks at individuals and other private persons: A Pellet, 'Le droit international à l'aube du XXIème siècle (La société internationale contemporaine – Permanences et tendances nouvelles)' (1997) I *Cours euro-méditerranéens Bancaja de droit international* 98. Margueritte and Prouvèze (n 57) 173–74 wonder if these actors will be the last bastion of this resistance or even outright dogmatic rejection vis-à-vis the recognition of international legal personality beyond States (and, as seen, with time, International Organisations, even individuals), and ultimately resistance towards integrating into the plan of international legal dogmatics the developments that the reality of international and global relations already insinuate.

[103] D Josselin and W Wallace (eds), *Non-state Actors in World Politics* (Basingstoke, Palgrave, 2001).

[104] P Fischer, 'Transnational Enterprises' (1985) VIII *Encyclopedia of Public International Law* 921–22.

common ownership ties and respond to a common management strategy'.[105] Their subsidiaries are located in several host states and are subject to the instructions of a parent enterprise, which is located in one of the states.[106] From a legal point of view, multinational enterprises are not international enterprises, but national enterprises belonging to one jurisdiction, as determined by their act of incorporation or seat. In this link with a national legal order, they immediately differ from IOs, whose specific governing legal order is international law.[107]

Multinational enterprises can be considered the main protagonists of economic globalisation and are powerful actors. Their turnover sometimes far exceeds the budget of many a state.[108] Equally, their effective overall power is sometimes greater than that of many states. This power derives from the influence that they can exert on the states that host their investments and the fact that states usually find it difficult, if not impossible, to control these enterprises in their life dynamics.[109]

Multinational enterprises have long been present and interacting with the international system as well as with international law.[110] Some proclaim them 'invisible' to international law, in the sense that it is national law that characteristically regulates them immediately. This only underlines the fact that while multinational enterprises are originally creatures of national law, their business operations are focused on a wider space than the territorial state space, and that they formulate international policies in their goal of profit making; in short, there is a discrepancy between their (initial) de iure national status and their de facto impact in the international framework, as it equally points to the relevance of the question about their international (possible) status.[111] However, although for several decades now, a few international law scholars such as Wolfgang Friedmann have suggested that multinational enterprises can be considered participants in the evolution of modern international law,[112] the classical opinion, which is still largely dominant among scholars (even those who usually defend progressive

[105] S Joseph, 'Taming the Leviathan: Multinational Entreprises and Human Rights' (1999) 46 *Netherlands International Law Review*.172.

[106] PN Doremus et al, *The Myth of Global Corporation* (Princeton, Princeton University Press, 1998). See also Resolution 3 on 'Multinational Enterprises' from the Institut de Droit International (1978) 57(2) *Annuaire de l'Institut de Droit International* 339.

[107] B Großfeld, 'Multinationale Unternehmen und nationale Souveränität' (1978) *Juristische Schulung* 73; R Higgins, 'A Multinational Corporation or an International Organization' in R Morgan et al (eds), *New Diplomacy in the Post-Cold War: Essays for Susan Strange* (London, Macmillan, 1993) 187.

[108] Fischer (n 104) 926.

[109] P Vellas, 'Les entreprises multinationales et les organisations non gouvernementales, sujets du droit international' in *Mélanges offerts à Paul Couzinet* (Toulouse, Université de Toulouse, 1974) 773–94.

[110] S Tully, *Corporations and International Lawmaking* (London, LSEPS, 2004) 68–73; PT Muchlinski, *Multinational Entreprises and the Law*, 2nd edn (Oxford, Oxford University Press, 2007) 5ff.

[111] F Johns, 'The Invisibility of the Transnational Corporation: An Analysis of International Law and Legal Theory' (1994) 19 *Melbourne University Law Review* 922.

[112] W Friedmann, *The Changing Structure of International Law* (New York, Columbia University Press, 1964) 230.

positions, such as Antonio Cassese) is instead that they have no rights or obligations, stressing that states, regardless of their ideological orientation, are reluctant to give enterprises international legal personality.[113]

Today, however, it seems more appropriate to recognise that multinational companies contribute, directly or indirectly, to the making of international rules,[114] which should be taken as the first indicator and justification for recognising their international legal personality.[115] An important element in this respect of overall international law reconstruction is the fact that, for a long time now, multinational enterprises have also been concluding contracts or agreements with host states in order to host their investments and foster the development sought by these states. These contracts and agreements and the relationship between many previously reticent states and multinational enterprises will become much more numerous and intense with the evolution of the global context brought about by globalisation. Mahiou, for instance, points to the dissolution of the international bloc of socialist states, the triumph of the liberal model of development and the weakening of solidarity between the member states of the Group of 77 as important factors in this evolution, and highlights the effect of so many developing countries, once reluctant to deal with multinational companies, now frequently doing so through these contracts or agreements.[116] Some doctrines even recognise these contracts or agreements, which are at the direct origin of a form of international law that has no direct raison d'etre other than these transnational companies, to be integrated into the categories of sources of international law.[117]

Multinational enterprises also participate in the drafting of international treaties. The negotiation and even drafting of major international economic treaties are, in actual fact, often done at the instigation and with the support or direct involvement of these companies; as was seen in the Agreement on Trade-Related Aspects of Intellectual Property Rights, Including Trade in Counterfeit Goods.[118]

More recently, the contribution of multinational enterprises to the construction of international law can be further illustrated by examples of self-regulation, with the production of the 'soft law' rules[119] of the codes of conduct that multinational

[113] A Cassese, *International Law in a Divided World* (Oxford, Clarendon Press, 1986) 103.

[114] This was also denied by the more politically and socially oriented 'New Haven School': while it accepts that corporations are powerful independent actors, it considers that they are not competent to make international law. *cf* M McDougal, H Lasswell and M Reisman, 'The World Constitutive Process of Authoritative Decision' (1996) 19 *Journal of Legal Education* 403.

[115] JI Charney, 'Transnational Corporations and Developing Public International Law' (1983) *Duke Law Journal* 748ff.

[116] Mahiou (n 102) 271.

[117] ibid.

[118] 186 *UNTS* 299ff.

[119] On the concept of soft law, see R Baxter, 'International Law in "Her Infinite Variety"' (1980) 29 *ICLQ* 549; R Ida, 'Formation des normes internationales dans un monde en mutation: Critique de la notion de soft law' in *Le droit international au service de la paix, de la justice et du développement, Mélanges Michel Virally* (Paris, Pédone, 1991) 333; U Fastenrath, 'Normativity in International Law' (1993) 4 *European Journal of International Law* 305.

enterprises voluntarily adopt or accept to affect them. An example of these is the OECD Guidelines for Multinational Enterprises adopted in 2011.[120,121]

There is also a growing consensus in international society, as in the more plural international community, that multinational enterprises should be subject to certain obligations to respect fundamental human rights and fundamental elements or standards of social and environmental responsibility.[122] The United Nations Global Compact was created under the auspices of the World Organisation as a step in this direction.[123] It is still a non-binding 'pact' on human rights, labour, environment and anti-corruption[124] that encourages companies globally to adopt sustainable practices and policies, and to comply with the Decalogue of Principles.[125] Other international legal rules proposed or drafted to hold these companies accountable and ensure respect for human rights, labour law and environmental law included the Norms on the Responsibilities of Transnational Corporations and Other Business Enterprises with Regard to Human Rights,[126] approved in 2003 by the Sub-Commission on the Promotion and Protection of Human Rights of the Economic and Social Council (ECOSOC).[127] The Commission on Human Rights did not approve the draft, but rather called for the appointment of a special representative on the issue. The appointment of John Ruggie, the special representative on the issue of human rights and transnational corporations and other business enterprises, took place in 2005. Among the resulting works are the Guiding Principles on Business and Human Rights that seek to translate the Commission's framework of the threefold obligation to respect, protect and fulfil into this area. The draft was adopted by the Human Rights Council in 2011 and has been developed by other projects of the Special Rapporteur.[128]

[120] www.oecd.org.

[121] NMCP Jägers, *Corporate Human Rights Obligations: In Search of Accountability* (Cambridge, Intersentia, 2002), 19–35; JL Dunoff, SR Ratner and D Wippman, *International Law Norms, Actors, Process: A Problem Oriented Approach*, 2nd edn (Boston, Aspen Publishers, 2006) 216–34.

[122] A Clapham, *Human Rights Obligations of Non-state Actors* (Oxford, Oxford University Press, 2006) 79ff.

[123] www.unglobalcompact.org.

[124] *Guide to Corporate Sustainability: Shaping a Sustainable Future*, www.globalcompact.org https://d306pr3pise04h.cloudfront.net/docs/publications%2FUN_Global_Compact_Guide_to_Corporate_Sustainability.pdf.

[125] SV Schorlemmer, 'Der "Global Compact" der Vereinten Nationen – ein Faust'scher Pakt mit der Wirtschaftswelt?' in SV Schorlemmer (ed), *Praxishandbuch UNO: Die Vereinten Nationen im Lichte globaler Herausforderungen* (Heidelberg, Springer, 2003) 507.

[126] United Nations, 'Norms on the Responsibilities of Transnational Corporations and Other Business Enterprises with Regard to Human Rights' (2013) UN Doc E/CN.4/Sub.2/2003/12/Rev.2 (26 August 2003).

[127] In the doctrine, highlighting other normative initiatives, see Tully (n 110) 418; Dunoff, Ratner and Wippman (n 121); E Duruigbo, 'Corporate Accountability and Liability for International Human Rights Abuses: Recent Changes and Recurring Challenges' (2008) 6 *New Wales University Journal of Human Rights* 222; LC Backer, 'The United Nations' "Protect-Respect-Remedy" Project: Operationalizing a Global Human Rights Based Framework for the Regulation of Transnational Corporations' (2011) 9 *Santa Clara Journal of International Law* 37; MT Kamminga and S Zia-Zarifi (eds), *Liability of Multinational Corporations under International Law* (Leiden, Brill, 2021).

[128] JG Ruggie, *Just Business: Multinational Corporations and Human Rights* (New York, Norton, 2013); JG Ruggie, 'Multinationals as Global Institutions: Power, Authority, and Relative Autonomy' (2017) 12(3) *Regulation & Governance* 317.

To these other indicators of an emerging international legal personality for multinational enterprises, it should be added that international economic law (covering investment, trade and international financial operations law) currently provides a set of legal mechanisms by which companies can bring claims against states before various international bodies, whether non-judicial or judicial.[129] Such mechanisms include recourse to institutional bodies (both treaty-based and non-treaty-based) with defined procedures for hearing complaints, legally binding decision-making bodies and enforcement procedures.[130]

This participation of multinational companies in the mechanisms for ensuring compliance with international economic law may be direct or indirect. This indirect participation in jurisdictional mechanisms occurs, for example, within the framework of the dispute settlement system (DSS) of the World Trade Organization (WTO).[131] Thus, many of the international economic disputes formally brought by states before specialised tribunals are in fact undertaken, sponsored and supported by the companies affected by the commercial action that is the subject of the complaint.[132] That this is so is understandable, as these enterprises are the most interested parties in the case. They are the ones which know the market and are therefore in the best position to assess the effective (non-)compliance with the rules governing it, thus contributing with their testimonies to the proper establishment of the relevant facts.[133] There are also cases of direct participation. This is exemplified by the special dispute settlement mechanisms[134] within the framework of international investment law, namely through investor-host state arbitration[135] resorting to the International Centre

[129] C McLachlan, L Shore and M Weiniger, *International Investment Arbitration: Substantive Principles* (Oxford, Oxford University Press, 2008); R Dolzer and C Schreuer, *Principles of International Investment Law*, 2nd edn (Oxford, Oxford University Press, 2012).

[130] M Sornarajah, 'Power and Justice in Foreign Investment Arbitration' (1997) 14 *Journal of International Arbitration* 103. Within the European Union (EU), companies can bring actions directly before the Court of Justice of the European Union for violations of EU law. See M Horspool and M Humphreys, *European Union Law*, 8th edn (Oxford, Oxford University Press, 2014).

[131] The relationship between the de facto propelling company and agent defending violated rights and the state that formally initiates and sustains the proceedings before the WTO DSS is particularly evident in the case of *Korea – Anti-dumping Duties on Imports of Certain Papers from Indonesia*, WT/DS312/R, 28 October 2005 (Panel Report).

[132] S-P Croley and JK Jackson, 'WTO Dispute Procedures, Standard of Review and Deference to National Governments' (1996) 90 *AJIL* 193; S Charnovitz, 'Economic and Social Actors in the World Trade Organization' (2001) 7 *ILSA Journal of International and Comparative Law* 259.

[133] Ph Maddalon, 'Les rapports des groupes spéciaux et de l'organe d'appel de l'OMC' (2005) 51(1) *Annuaire français de Droit international* 629.

[134] Fischer (n 104) 925.

[135] G van Harten and M. Loughlin, 'Investment Treaty Arbitration as a Species of Global Administrative Law' (2006) 17 *European Journal of International Law* 121; AS Alexandroff and IA Laird, 'Compliance and Enforcement' in P Muchlinski, F Ortino, and C Schreuer (eds), *The Oxford Handbook of International Investment Law* (New York, Oxford University Press, 2008) 1171; B Kingsbury and S Schill, 'Investor-State Arbitration as Governance: Fair and Equitable Treatment, Proportionality, and the Emerging Global Administrative Law' in B Kingsbury, A Gorgillo and RB Stewart (eds), *El Nuevo Derecho Administrativo Global en América latina* (New York, Institute for International Law and Justice, 2009).

for Settlement of Investment Disputes (ICSID) set up by the 1965 Washington Convention.[136] In this particular context, which is as unique as it is remarkable, multinational enterprises have access to the arbitral courts under exactly the same conditions as states.[137] It should also be noted that even when multinational companies do not have *ius standi* next to some of these judicial bodies – ie, the right to bring actions themselves – and instead have to resort to state mediation through diplomatic protection, like in the DSS of the WTO, they have been granted the right to participate in proceedings, for example, as amicus curiae.[138]

In addition to these manifestations of action, presence and participation in the international workings of globalisation, and even rights and obligations that are legally relevant in contemporary life, there are, in the practice of UN sanctions, examples of situations in which some multinational enterprises have been directly subject to such punitive measures for violating the rules on economic embargoes previously laid down by the UN Security Council and the UN General Assembly.[139] This was the case with the inclusion in blacklists and, even more specifically, with the concrete denunciation of the actions of tankers owned by international oil companies, consisting in the transportation of oil by these vessels to the Republic of South Africa, in violation of the embargo previously decreed by the Security Council as an enforcement measure in the fight against the apartheid regime in South Africa. What those sanctions implicitly meant was that the multinational companies owning those ships were deemed direct holders of obligations under international law within the framework of the sanctions regime established. The UN, by defining such a regime and acting accordingly in the face of acts perceived to violate that regime, took the non-state actor international company to be a legal entity, capable of and effectively standing as a holder of international legal obligations.[140]

[136] D Carreau and P Julliard, *Droit international économique*, 4th edn (Paris, Dalloz, 2010) 19.

[137] Article 25 of the Washington Convention, or Convention for the Settlement of Investment Disputes between States and Nationals of Other States (1966) 575 *UNTS* 175.

[138] Article 13, para 1 of the Memorandum of Agreement on Dispute Settlement, annexed to the Agreement establishing the World Trade Organization (Annex 2), which enshrines this option for cases brought before the panels or working groups. The Appellate Body within the WTO DSS has extended this option to the appeal process, albeit prudently. Examples of the use of this option can be seen in *United States – Import Ban on Certain Shrimp and Shrimp-Based Products*, WT/DS58/R, 15 May 1998 (Working Group report) and WT/DS58/AB/R, 12 October 1998 (Appellate Body report); *Canada – Final Determination on Countervailing Duties on Certain Hardwood Lumber from Canada, WT/DS257/AB/R of 19 January 2004* (Appellate Body report); *European Communities – Measures Affecting Asbestos and Asbestos-Containing Products*, WT/DS135/AB/R, 12 March 2001 (Appellate Body report).

[139] C Langenfeld, 'Embargo' (1999) II *Encyclopedia of Public International Law* 62, 66; Tully (n 110) 172.

[140] ES Schmidt, 'United Nations Sanctions and South Africa: Lessons from the Case of Southern Rhodesia' in United Nations, *Sanctions against South Africa* (New York, United Nations, 1987) 21; T Stoll, 'Rhodesien/Zimbabwe; Konflikte, Südafrika' in R Wolfrum (ed), *Handbuch Vereinte Nationen* (Munich, CH Beck, 1991) 501.

E. NGOs

International NGOs[141] will also begin to be recognised as having limited international legal status.

As with multinational enterprises, international law does not contain an established definition of NGOs, although Resolution 1996/31 of the UN Economic and Social Council identifies the attributes of NGOs.[142] However, the international legal doctrine points to certain constituent elements: these are private associations created by natural or legal persons on the basis of a private law contract; they pursue objectives (normally non-profit making) at the national or cross-border level; they have an institutional structure and a permanent headquarters for this purpose; and they are subject to state law, even when they act at the international level.[143] Regardless of their legal personality, subject to the laws of a specific state,[144] the existence and effectiveness of NGOs increasingly occur at the global international level. Their large number,[145] their vigorous presence in decisive fora of deliberation on global governance, their well-established international practice of networking, their systematic use of the internet for communication,[146] the skills that they display and, even more specifically, their political capacity to influence decision makers not only make NGOs a remarkable, unavoidable element of the international and transnational relations of the global era[147] and of contemporary global governance, in the context of a generic transformation of humanity into a global civil society,[148] but also increasingly raise the question of their international

[141] More broadly, in 'Cooperation between the UN and All Relevant Partners, in Particular the Private Sector', UN Doc A/56/323 (2001), para 6 and Annex 1, the UN Secretary-General refers to the 'private sector', where enterprises are also included. In the doctrine, T Princen and M. Finger (eds), *Environmental NGOs in World Politics* (London, Routledge, 1994) 6 define NGOs as associations of individuals representing elements of public opinion, established under domestic law, with a permanent (ideally democratic and transparent) organisation or governance structure, and possessing specialised skills or knowledge capabilities.

[142] Previously, Resolution 288 (X) of 27 February 1950 merely stated that it was 'any international organisation which is not founded by a treaty'.

[143] O Kimminich and S Hobe, *Einführung in das Völkerrecht*, 6th edn (Tübingen, Francke, 1997) 149; J Delbrück, 'Nichtregierungsinstitutionen. Geschichte – Bedeutung – Rechtsstatus' (2003) 13 *Rechtspolitisches Forum* 3.

[144] Based on the criterion of the headquarters or the constitutive act, it is national law that governs NGOs. See G Kegel, *Internationales Privatrecht, Ein Studienbuch* (Munich, CH Beck, 1995) 413; D Thürer, 'The Emergence of Non-governmental Organisations and Transnational Enterprises and the Changing Role of the State' in R Hoffmann (ed), *Non-state Actors as New Subjects of International Law* (Berlin, Duncker & Humblot, 1999) 45; K Doehring, *Völkerrecht. Ein Lehrbuch* (Heidelberg, CF Müller, 1999) 84.

[145] Tully (n 110) 46.

[146] See J Neyer, *Postnationale politische Herrschaft: Vergesellschaftung und Verrechtlichung jenseits des Staates* (Baden-Baden, Nomos, 2004) 85, with examples.

[147] R Falk, 'The Nuclear Weapons Advisory Opinion and the New Jurisprudence of Global Civil Society' (1997) 7 *Transnational Law and Contemporary Problems* 333.

[148] If the concept of civil society were limited to its private dimension, based on the theory that distinguishes state and society (*cf* EW Böckenförde, *Die verfassungstheoretische Unterscheidung von Staat und Gesellschaft als Bedingung der individuellen Freiheit* (Wiesbaden, Springer, 1973); HH Rupp,

legal status. In fact, the problem of recognising such a status thus arises from the acceptance of the contemporary transformation of the traditional international system into a different, global international system comprising transnational vectors.[149] To date, no such status enabling NGOs to be generically recognised and ensured protection exists.[150] A larger part of international legal doctrine also makes many objections to a generic international personality resulting from the mere participation in international relations.[151]

Regardless of this lack of general status of NGOs, nothing seems to prevent the recognition of the legal personality of at least some NGOs. This certainly implies that there is no legal necessity for legal policy to sustain a *numerus clausus* in relation to international legal subjectivity. As seen with regard to IOs, there is no kind of a priori impediment to international law attributing personality to other actors in international life besides states. Although such a restriction may be alleged,[152] in the end, nothing seems to impose it.

Acceptance of the reality of international practice and the important role that this effectively plays in the current global system instead seems to abound in the sense that the international legal community resulting from globalisation is open to at least the most important non-governmental actors being included in the universe of functional limited subjects. What is decisive, it seems, is to verify if international law itself contains positive normative responses that effectively extend international legal subjectivity to these actors typical of globalisation, and if it contains rules that make these actors holders of rights and even obligations

'Die Unterscheidung von Staat und Gesellschaft' in J Isensee and P. Kirchhof (eds), *Handbuch des Staatsrechts der Bundesrepublik Deutschlands* II, 3rd edn (Heidelberg, CF Müller, 2004) 879), it would be devoid of political content. It is not this 'bourgeois' notion that is embraced here or that permeates studies on globalisation and its legal regulation. Rather, it is a politically charged or significant concept, in which the members of civil society perceive themselves as citizens involved in defining the destinies of the *polis*. This notion of *citizenship* in the global space is reminiscent of the one that Habermas presents, eg, in *Faktizität und Geltung, Beiträge zur Diskurstheorie des Rechts und des demokratischen Rechtsstaats*, 4th edn (Frankfurt am Main,Suhrkamp, 1994) 443. On the other hand, it is a notion analogous to that which, in the international normative context, results from the Civil Society Declaration issued by the Global People's Forum at the Johannesburg Summit on Sustainable Development in 2002.

[149] PC Jessup, *Transnational Law* (New Haven, Yale University Press, 1956) 106. While 'international' describes interactions between states, 'transnational' refers to cross-border transactions that also involve non-state actors. See T Risse-Kappen, 'Introduction' in T Risse-Kappen (ed) *Non-state Actors: Domestic Structures and International Institutions* (Cambridge, Cambridge University Press, 1995) 3.

[150] S Hobe, 'Der Rechtsstatus der Nichtregierungsorganisationen nach geltendem Völkerrecht' (1999) 37 *Archiv des Völkerrechts* 152; A Emmerich-Fritsche, *Vom Völkerrecht zum Weltrecht* (Berlin, Duncker & Humblot, 2007) 854. It should be noted that even within the already limited European framework and with an equally limited thematic scope, the European Convention on the Recognition of the Legal Personality of International Non-governmental Organisations of 24 April 1986 requires prior verification of a national legal subjectivity and includes numerous exceptions.

[151] H Mosler, 'Die Erweiterung des Kreises der Völkerrechtssubjekte' (1962) 22 *Zeitschrift für ausländisches öffentliches Recht und Völkerrecht* 1; S Hobe, 'Völkerrecht im Zeitalter der Globalisierung' (1999) 37 *Archiv des Völkerrechts* 152; U Hingst, *Auswirkungen der Globalisierung auf das Recht der völkerrechtlichen Verträge* (Berlin, Dunker & Humbolt, 2001) 154.

[152] For instance, it is still invoked by I Brownlie, *Principles of Public International Law*, 4th edn (Oxford, Oxford University Press, 1995) 58.

that are directly attributable to these rules. Similarly, these NGOs will become legal subjects if rules of international law empower them to enforce these titles in accordance with international law. When this is the case, regardless of whether these titles result from the recognition of faculties to perhaps even participate in the increasingly complex process of developing international law or whether they appear as effective substantive rights and obligations, or procedural rights relating to the process of the jurisdictional application of the law, it seems necessary to conclude that at least some NGOs acquire international legal personality.

In contemporary international law, there are in fact increasing elements of positive law which corroborate this conclusion.

First, there is the experience of institutionalising the participation of NGOs in the creation of international law specific to labour relations, within the unique but also limited framework of the ILO, where both employers' and workers' organisations have a common seat within the tripartite mode of working of this particular IO. Also noteworthy is the fact that international NGOs participate as observers in the work of IOs of the UN family, and that NGOs are given a legal status therein under the secondary rules of international law created by the organs of these IOs. This is the case, for example, with procedural rules enacted by the IO in the exercise of the competencies recognised as belonging to it in its primary law, especially the constituent treaty of that organisation. The practice of the UN illustrates such a trend.[153] On the basis of Article 71 of the UN Charter, the ECOSOC has reached agreements setting out ways of consulting with NGOs.[154] The status thus defined comprises three categories: general consultative status; special consultative status; and the status for other NGOs that do not enjoy the first two. Under this differentiated consultative status, qualified NGOs may contribute their views and address UN bodies, in addition to being able to request the inclusion of issues of their interest on the agenda.[155] Similar rights and observer status are also foreseen by Article V(2) of the WTO Agreement. Additionally, the possibility of consulting NGOs has been exercised by the WTO Secretariat, which invites NGOs on a thematic basis. The practice of the WTO also comprehends the possibility for NGOs to contribute position documents by electronic means. However, they are excluded from participating in meetings of the WTO bodies.[156]

[153] FW Stoecker, *NGOs und die UNO. Die Einbindung Nichtregierungsorganisationen (NGOs) in die Strukturen der Vereinten Nationen* (Frankfurt am Main, Peter Lang, 2000) 90.

[154] R Lagoni and Chaitidou, 'Article 71' in B Simma et al (eds), *The Charter of the United Nations: A Commentary*, vol II, 2nd edn (Oxford, Oxford University Press, 2002) 1068.

[155] UN ECOSOC Resolution 1296/XLIV of 23 May 1998. In the literature, see O Kimminich and S Hobe, *Einführung in das Völkerrecht* (Tübingen, UTB, 2008) 149; Hobe (n 150); V Epping, 'Völkerrechtssubjekte' in K Ipsen (ed), *Völkerrecht. Ein Studienbuch*, 4th edn (Munich, CH Beck, 1999) 78; I Seidl-Hohenveldern and G Loibl, *Das Recht der internationalen Organisationen, einschießlich der Supranationalen Gemeinschaften*, 7th edn (Cologne, Carl Heymanns, 2000) 4.

[156] J Neyer, *Postnationale politische Herrschaft: Vergesellschaftung und Verrechtlichung jenseits des Staates* (Baden-Baden, Nomos, 2004) 55; A. Emmerich-Fritsche, *Vom Völkerrecht zum Weltrecht* (Berlin, Duncker & Humblot, 2007) 855.

In addition to these rights, it is worth highlighting the capacity of NGOs to influence the formation of decision making and their contributions to shaping international public opinion and even the formation of rules in law making. This has been particularly seen in their participation in the areas of human rights protection and the international protection of the environment. While this practice does not amount to NGOs being given a general faculty to contribute their views directly to the deliberations of IOs and or a right to vote, it does signify that there is a freedom for them to make proposals under observer status and, in some cases, to participate in special working groups together with state representatives. This may be seen, for example, in relation to the Washington Agreement on the Protection of Endangered Species[157] and the participatory rights of NGOs in the implementation of the Convention on Desertification.[158]

Furthermore, NGOs are involved in the production of standards, contributing to their definition as well as contributing knowledge, awareness raising and pressure, which are particularly relevant in their implementation.[159] This has been documented in the fields of international environmental law,[160] international humanitarian law, the international law of the sea[161] and human rights law. Some international treaties, in particular, are known to have been strongly influenced in terms of their content and general sense by the contributions made by NGOs in the process of their adoption.[162] Such was the case, for example, with the 1973 Treaty on Trade in Endangered Species of Wild Flora and Fauna,[163] the 1989 Convention on the Rights of the Child,[164] the 1997 Treaty on the Prohibition of

[157] Article XI, para 7. See also S Oberthür, 'Auf dem Weg zum Weltumweltrecht? Tendenzen und Wirkungen der Verrechtlichung der internationalen Umweltpolitik' in B Zangl and M Zürn (eds), *Verrechtlichung. Baustein für Global Governance*? (Bonn, Dietz, 2004) 119.

[158] UN Convention to Combat Desertification in Those Countries Experiencing Serious Drought and/or Desertification, Particularly in Africa, UN Doc.A/AaC.241/27 (1994) 33(5) ILM 1328. See also KW Danish, 'International Environmental Law and the "Bottom-up" Approach: A Review of the Desertification Convention' (1995) 3(1) *Indiana Journal of Global Legal Studies* 133.

[159] T van Boven, 'The Role of Non-governmental Organisations in International Human Rights Standard-Setting: A Prerequisite for Democracy' (1990) 20 *California Western International Law Journal* 207; P-M Dupuy and L Vierucci (eds), *NGOs in International Law: Efficiency in Flexibility?* (Cheltenham, Edward Elgar, 2008).

[160] P Canelas de Castro, 'Mutações e Constâncias do Direito Internacional do Ambiente' (1994) 2 *Revista jurídica do urbanismo e do ambiente* 145, 183; J Gupta, 'The Role of Non-state Actors in International Environmental Affairs' (2003) 63 *Zeitschrift für ausländisches öffentliches Recht und Völkerrecht* 463.

[161] S Hobe, 'Global Challenges to Statehood: The Increasingly Important Role of International Nongovernmental Organisations' (1997) 5 *Indiana Journal of Global Legal Studies* 1919; J Delbrück, 'Laws in the Public Interest' – Some Observations on the Foundations and Identification of *Erga Omnes* Norms in International Law' in V Götz et al (eds), *Liber Amicorum Günther Jaenicke – Zum 85. Geburtstag* (Berlin, Springer, 1998) 26; U Beyerlin and M Reichard, 'The Johannesburg Summit: Outcome and Overall Assessment' (2003) 63 *Zeitschrift für ausländisches öffentliches Recht und Völkerrecht* 226.

[162] Hobe (n 151); U Hingst, *Auswirkungen der Globalisierung auf das Recht der völkerrechtlichen Verträge* (Berlin, Duncker & Humblot, 2001) 49; Gupta (n 160).

[163] (1973) 12 *ILM* 1055.

[164] S Detrick (ed), *The United Nations Convention on the Rights of the Child: A Guide to the 'Travaux Préparatoires'* (Dordrecht, Martinus Nijhoff, 1992).

the Use, Stockpiling, Production and Transfer of Anti-personnel Mines and on Their Destruction[165] and the 1998 Statute of the ICC.[166] Similarly, it is generally acknowledged that, through their participation, NGOs contributed powerfully to shaping the will of the Conferences on Environment and Development in Rio de Janeiro in 1992,[167] on Human Rights in Vienna in 1993, on Women's Rights in Beijing in 1997, on the Statute of the ICC in Rome in 1998 and on Sustainable Development in Johannesburg in 2002.[168]

Besides their growing participation in the drafting of international law, international NGOs have also played an important role in its application. They contribute to the implementation of some of the instruments of international law, in particular by monitoring compliance, in a watchdog role that is recognised or assigned to them in part by the bodies of institutions linked to those instruments.[169]

To this first level of analysis and detection of international law rules enabling the international legal capacity of NGOs, a second level should be added: primary international law also contains instruments and rules that directly confer rights upon these actors, which are directly exercisable by them. These rules of primary IO law also sustain the limited international legal personality of NGOs. This is the case, for example, when certain international treaties directly attribute substantive rights to international NGOs, like the right to freedom of assembly and association held by NGOs under Article 11 of the European Convention on Human Rights.[170] NGOs may also be granted procedural rights, as foreseen by the Aarhus Convention.[171]

The other element identified by the ICJ in 1949 as an important vector for defining international legal personality consists of the recognition of the right of action before international courts or tribunals or before non-judicial monitoring bodies created by certain conventions. This may be evidenced in particular by instruments for the protection and promotion of human rights, which also define the framework of competence of these bodies, whether jurisdictional or non-jurisdictional. Examples include the 1503 procedure before the Economic, Social and Cultural Rights Committee, the complaint procedure under the United Nations Educational, Scientific and Cultural Organization (UNESCO), and the

[165] United Nations, 'Conference on Disarmament' (CD/1487, United Nations, 1997).

[166] Marguerrite and Prouvèze (n 57) 184.

[167] NGOs are said to be important players in the discipline adopted in 10 of the 42 chapters that make up Agenda 21. See Report of the United Nations Conference on Environment and Development, United Nations General (4) Assembly, A/Conf.151/26.

[168] Beyerlin and Reichard (n 161). On this modality of the contribution of NGOs to the process of defining international law, through their participation in summit conferences, with various examples, see also R Wedgwood, 'Legal Personality and the Role of Non-governmental Organisations and Non-state Political Entities in the United Nations System' in R Hoffmann (ed), *Non-state Actors as New Subjects of International Law* (Berlin, Duncker & Humblot, 1999) 20; Thürer (n 144) 37.

[169] Canelas de Castro (n 160) 183.

[170] M Hempel, *Die Völkerrechtssubjektivität internationaler nichtstaatlicher* Organisationen (Berlin, Duncker & Humbolt, 1999) 88.

[171] United Nations Economic Commission for Europe, *The Aarhus Convention: An Implementation Guide*, 2nd edn (New York, UNECE, 2014).

complaint procedure in the case of consistent patterns of gross and credible violations of human rights and fundamental freedoms before the current Human Rights Council.[172] This is especially the case with regional conventional law, whether it be the American Convention on Human Rights and its corresponding Commission,[173] the European Convention on Human Rights and Fundamental Freedoms and the European Court of Human Rights,[174] or the African Charter on Human and Peoples' Rights and its Court on Human and Peoples' Rights.[175] There are, however, some restrictions on the exercise of this right of action, such as the fact that collective interest actions (*actio popularis*) cannot be filed in the absence of a direct interest of the holder of the right, distinct from that of the NGO members.[176] In criminal matters, the involvement of NGOs is even more restricted, being limited to the possibility of transmitting information to the Prosecutor of the ICC, who opens an investigation on their own initiative.[177]

Another means for NGOs to participate in international court proceedings is their intervention as amicus curiae. This procedure, while not making NGOs parties to the proceedings, enables them to submit written communications on the factual and legal aspects of the case. However, while not generally available in all international jurisdictions, this is the case in jurisdictions dealing with litigation pertaining to the protection of human rights and international humanitarian law. NGOs are also recognised as having rights to intervene as amicus curiae before the international criminal justice system[178] or before the WTO Dispute Settlement System[179] and in arbitration proceedings within the framework of international investment law.[180]

Finally, reference should be made to the Council of Europe European Convention on the Recognition of the Legal Personality of International

[172] See www.ohchr.org/EN/HRBodies/HRC/ComplaintProcedure/Pages/HRCComplaintProcedureIndex.aspx. In the doctrine, see M Hempel, *Die Völkerrechtssubjektivität internationaler nichtstaatlicher Organisationen* (Berlin, Duncker & Humblot, 1999) 127.

[173] Article 44 of the 1969 Convention. *cf UNTS*, v 1144.

[174] Article 34 of the 1950 Convention. *cf UNTS*, v 213.

[175] Article 3 of the 1998 Protocol to the African Charter on Human and Peoples' Rights establishing an African Court on Human and Peoples' Rights. The Court may be called to act among other subjects by NGOs which have obtained observer status from the Commission. It is also necessary that the state of nationality of such NGOs has accepted this procedure by special declaration.

[176] See, eg, Case C-321/959 *Greenpeace v Commission* [1998] ECR I-01651 and, in the doctrine, Y Winisdoerffer, 'La jurisprudence de la Cour européenne des droits de l'homme et l'environnement' (2003) 2 *Revue Juridique de l'Environnement* 213.

[177] Article 15 of the Rome Statute.

[178] Article 74 of the Rules of the Criminal Court for the former Yugoslavia and Article 103 of the Rules of the ICC.

[179] Article 13, para 1 of the Understanding on Rules and Procedures for the Settlement of Disputes, Annex 2 to the Marrakesh Agreement.

[180] *cf* the examples of recent cases in which problems of international water law intersect with problems of international investment law, all concerning cases brought before international arbitration bodies under investor-host state dispute settlement mechanisms, making use of the resources of the ICSID, such as the *Aguas del Tunari v Republic of Bolivia* [2005] ICSID Case No ARB/02/3; *Biwater Gauff (Tanzania) Ltd v United Republic of Tanzania* [2008] ICSID Case No ARB/05/22 or *Suez v Argentine Republic* ICSID Case Nos ARB/03/17 and ARB/03/19. These examples are the more

Non-governmental Organisations of 24 April 1986, which directly tackles the issue of the legal personality of NGOs, enshrining the principle of recognition by all states parties of such legal personality when obtained by an NGO under the law of another state party.[181]

From all these developments, the conclusion seems to follow that at least some NGOs have acquired international legal personality.

F. Minorities and Indigenous Peoples

After a period of somewhat less visibility, minorities and Indigenous peoples are also acquiring through globalisation a new prominence in the international legal framework. In fact, from a historical perspective, this is a legal re-emergence, particularly in comparison with the pattern of international legal protection that had been established in the eighteenth and nineteenth centuries, a period in which, for example, the Indians of North America were granted a limited status of legal protection, whereby they were accepted as contracting parties to conventions between state governments and Indian tribes. Subsequently, although the question of defining legal regimes for the special protection of minorities still figured prominently in the age of the League of Nations, with the 1919 Paris Peace Treaty giving rise to a set of treaties for the protection of European minorities and elevating them to the status of an international issue, the normative strategy of minority protection was virtually abandoned in the immediate post-the Second World War era. In the second half of the twentieth century, it was argued that the previously enacted special status of protection of minorities had resulted in the aggravation of ethnic conflicts in several states and that these conflicts had contributed to the outbreak of the Second World War. The international legal strategy that was subsequently advocated as a result instead involved ensuring the protection of the human rights of all people, without discrimination on the basis of race, ethnicity, religion or any other grounds. This newly advocated strategy would also guarantee the protection of minorities, although through the protection of each individual member.

However, in more recent decades in the era of globalisation, with the end of the Cold War, a number of developments, both factual and normative, are going to lead to a new change of direction and the adoption of another approach. Amongst

significant as they involved an important shift in international jurisprudence and led to the revision of international treaties and pertinent provisions (such as the Washington Convention and the 2006 ICSID Arbitration Rules) to accommodate this participation by NGOs. See P Canelas de Castro, *Mutações e Constâncias do Direito Internacional da Água. Mudanças de Paradigmas* (Coimbra, Universidade de Coimbra, 2016) 336; P Canelas de Castro, 'Towards the Harmonization of the Human Right to Water with the Protection of International Investments in the Context of the Processes of Privatization of Water Services?' (2016) 13(1) *Soochow Law Journal* 43, 57.

[181] MO Wiederkehr, 'La Convention du Conseil de l'Europe sur le statut des organisations non-gouvernementales' (1987) 33(1) *Annuaire français de Droit international* 749.

these factors are: the reconceptualisation of national security issues, now also including a human security vector; focusing on infra- and supra-state entities; the accentuation of ethnic conflicts, immediately within the European framework of the Balkans; the phenomena of reconstitution of political spaces, which also start to comprise an alternative to inclusion in the whole state via the means of 'looser' regional integration; and the very success of the human rights movement and the processes of decolonisation and self-determination of non-self-governing peoples.[182]

Within the framework of international law, this redefinition of the status of *minorities* in the more favourable context of globalisation[183] is notably expressed in the adoption of the 1992 UN Declaration on the Rights of Persons Belonging to National or Ethnic, Religious and Linguistic Minorities.[184] This instrument builds on the normative basis of the ICCPR and, in particular, the core provision of Article 27, which serves as direct inspiration to the Declaration, as the latter expressly acknowledges. It is equally influenced by the first post-Second World War international treaty designed to protect minorities from the greatest threat to their existence, the 1948 Convention on the Prevention and Punishment of the Crime of Genocide. However, it is not a mere reflection of these instruments, but rather complements or goes beyond their normative content, especially by enshrining a new or strengthened set of minority rights.

The rights of ethnic, religious or linguistic minorities and Indigenous peoples are an integral part of international human rights law. Like the rights of the child, women's rights and refugee rights, minority rights are a legal framework designed to ensure that a particular group, which is a minority in a state framework and is therefore in a vulnerable, disadvantaged or marginalised position in society, is able to achieve substantive equality and is protected from persecution.

[182] On the latter, see M Galvão Teles and P Canelas de Castro, 'Portugal and the Right of Peoples to Self-Determination' (1996) 34(1) *Archiv des Völkerrechts* 2, 46.

[183] P Thornberry, *International Law and the Rights of Minorities* (Oxford, Clarendon Press, 1991); G Alfredsson, 'Indigenous Populations, Protection' (1995) II *Encyclopedia of Public International Law* 946, 951; G Gilbert, 'The Council of Europe and Minority Rights' (1996) 18 *Human Rights Quarterly* 160; JJ Preece, *National Minorities and the European Nation-States System* (Oxford, Clarendon Press, 1998); K Henrard, *Devising an Adequate System of Minority Protection: Individual Human Rights, Minority Rights, and the Right to Self-Determination* (Leiden, Nijhoff, 2000); R Hoffmann, 'Protecting the Rights of National Minorities in Europe' (2001) 44 *German Yearbook of International Law* 237; G Pentassuglia, *Minorities in International Law: An Introductory Study* (Strasbourg, Council of Europe, 2002); JJ Preece, *Minority Rights: Between Diversity and Community* (Cambridge, Polity, 2005); TH Malloy, *National Minority Rights in Europe* (Oxford, Oxford University Press, 2005); M Weller, *The Rights of Minorities in Europe: A Commentary on the European Framework Convention for the Protection of National Minorities* (Oxford, Oxford University Press, 2006); D Šmihula, 'National Minorities in the Law of the EC/EU' (2008) 8(3) *Romanian Journal of European Affairs* 51, 81; M Weller, D Blacklock and K Nobbs (eds), *The Protection of Minorities in the Wider Europe* (Basingstoke, Palgrave, 2008); P Macklem, 'Minority Rights in International Law' (2008) 6(3)(4) *International Journal of Constitutional Law* 531, 552.

[184] General Assembly, 'Declaration on the Rights of Persons belonging to National or Ethnic, Religious and Linguistic Minorities: Resolution', United Nations Digital Library, UN Doc A/RES/47/135 https://digitallibrary.un.org/record/158458?ln=en.

General Comment No 23 on the rights of minorities of the Human Rights Committee,[185] which gives an authoritative interpretation of Article 27 of the Covenant, states that 'this article establishes and recognises a right which is conferred on individuals belonging to minority groups and which is distinct from and additional to all the other rights which, as individuals, and in common with all others, they already hold and are entitled to enjoy under the Covenant'. Article 27 thus constitutes autonomous rights under the Covenant. The interpretation of its scope by the Human Rights Committee has had the effect of ensuring the recognition of the existence of diverse groups within a State, of the fact that decisions making such recognition are not the exclusive competence of the State, and that States are obliged to take positive measures 'necessary to protect the identity of a minority and the rights of its members to enjoy and develop their culture and language and to practice their religion, in community with other members of the group'. More specifically, the rights of minorities under the Declaration are the right to protection by states of their existence and their national or ethnic, cultural, religious and linguistic identity; the right to enjoy their own culture, to profess and practise their religion, and to use their own language in private and in public; the right to participate effectively in cultural, religious, social, economic activities and public life; the right to participate effectively in decisions affecting minorities at the national and regional levels; the right to establish and maintain associations of minorities; the right to establish and maintain peaceful contacts with other members of their group and with persons belonging to other minorities, both within their state and beyond state boundaries; and the freedom to exercise their rights, both individually and in community with other members of their group, without discrimination. These rights correspond to the obligations of states to take steps to protect and promote the rights of members of minorities, and of the specialised agencies and other international organisations of the UN family to assist in the realisation of those rights.[186]

This overall global movement of growth and densification of the protective normative content of a law dedicated to minorities is also discernible at a regional level. Thus, in particular, in the European framework,[187] after the events in the Balkans after 1989, with the adoption of two treaties within the framework of the Council of Europe (the European Charter for Regional or Minority Languages

[185] Human Rights Committee, *General Comment No 23: Article 27*, 1994.

[186] In 2005, the Working Group on Minorities adopted a commentary to guide the interpretation and application of the UN Declaration on Minorities. See Secretary-General, 'Commentary of the Working Group on Minorities to the United Nations Declaration on the Rights of Persons belonging to National or Ethnic, Religious and Linguistic Minorities', United Nations Digital Library, UN Doc E/CN.4/Sub.2/AC.5/2005/2.

[187] Besides the works of Preece (n 183), Malloy (n 183), Weller (n 183), and Šmihula (n 183), see T Orlin, 'Minorities and Human Rights Education. Human Rights Law as a Paradigm for the Protection and Advancement of Minority Education in Europe', in C Mahler et al (eds), *The United Nations Decade for Human Rights Education and the Inclusion of National Minorities*, (Frankfurt am Main, Peter Lang, 2009), 159–69.

of 1992[188] and the Framework Convention for the Protection of National Minorities of 1995),[189] the Copenhagen Document of 1990 of the Organisation for Security and Cooperation in Europe (OSCE) and the particular regime of minorities in the framework of the Charter of Fundamental Rights of the EU. The concern that a lack of minority protection undermines international and regional stability also informs the criteria for membership in the EU and the North Atlantic Treaty Organization (NATO). The candidate countries must comply with the Copenhagen Agreement on criteria for admission to the EU which were laid down by the European Council in 1993. These criteria include the requirement that candidate states demonstrate 'stability of institutions guaranteeing democracy, the rule of law, human rights and respect for and protection of minorities'. A democratic political system and functioning, including respect for persons belonging to minorities in accordance with OSCE standards, is also one of the criteria for NATO membership.

In addition to substantive rights,[190] the instruments adopted in this area in the era of globalisation strengthen and perfect mechanisms for the participation of minorities and their representatives in the application and development of these regimes and in verifying the progress of states in complying with the obligations enshrined therein. This web of mechanisms, instruments and institutions is now very complex and includes, first and foremost, the conventional human rights bodies, including not only the committees mandated to monitor compliance with the ICCPR and the ICESCR, but also the bodies with the same mission established under other conventions protecting the rights of vulnerable groups or combating discrimination (children, women, migrant workers, people with disabilities and racial discrimination). They act on the basis of reports which give rise to recommendations in the form of 'Concluding Observations'. Early warning mechanisms and urgent procedures have also been put in place to prevent and respond to crises of respect for the rights of minorities. In addition, there are also special human rights procedures established under the current Human Rights Council, which deal with special issues or the special situations of particular states. These special procedures include the intervention of the Independent Expert on minority issues, established in 2005, whose mandate is to promote the implementation of the 1992 Declaration by making enquiries on national or thematic issues, the results of which give rise to reports and dialogue with states, the Forum on Minority Issues, in which international and global actors of various kinds participate to list issues affecting minorities and adopt recommendations to improve their lot, and other special procedures with 'state mandates' or 'thematic mandates'.[191] Also of relevance are

[188] European Charter for Regional or Minority Languages (148) *CETS*.

[189] Framework Convention for the Protection of National Minorities (157) *CETS*. See G Gilbert, 'The Council of Europe and Minority Rights' (1996) 18 *Human Rights Quarterly* 160.

[190] For other sources of minority rights, see Human Rights Office of the High Commissioner, *Minority Rights: International Standards and Guidance for Implementation* (New York, United Nations, 2010) 17.

[191] ibid 23.

the mechanisms of the Human Rights Council, under which, in accordance with the procedure established by UN General Assembly Resolution 60/251 of 2006, there is a periodic universal review of compliance by all states every four years, on the basis of reports submitted not only by state governments but also by other organisations, which may include contributions from interested parties. There are also more specific procedures within the framework of the ILO and UNESCO.[192] In several of these mechanisms and procedures and before the various bodies involved, minorities have the opportunity or are called upon to actively provide information and report experiences relevant to the evaluation of the respect of their rights and the formulation of policies or new instruments that strengthen or develop these rights.

In addition to minorities, *Indigenous peoples* will also find their own rights in the era of globalisation. International law does not provide an unambiguous definition of Indigenous peoples. In particular, the main normative text concerning Indigenous peoples, the UN Declaration of 2007 on the Rights of Indigenous Peoples, contains no definition. Articles 9 and 33 state that Indigenous peoples and individuals have the right to belong to an indigenous community or nation in accordance with the traditions and customs of the community or nation concerned, and that they have the right to determine their own identity.[193] For its part, the ILO, in another legal instrument dedicated to Indigenous peoples, the Convention on Indigenous and Tribal Peoples in Independent Countries (No 169), distinguishes between indigenous and tribal peoples. In Articles 1 and 2, the ILO Convention highlights the importance of self-identification of Indigenous peoples.

Today, the rights of Indigenous peoples derive in particular from these two international instruments: the 2007 UN Declaration and, in a more restricted context, the 1989 ILO Convention 169. Among the rights of Indigenous peoples that are recognised, the right to self-determination stands out, which is closely related to their other political rights and, in particular, the right to participate in decision making regarding issues that affect their rights and through their representative institutions. These political rights of indigenous peoples correspond to the duties of states to consult and cooperate with these peoples – in particular, to obtain their free, prior and informed consent before adopting and implementing legislative or administrative measures that may affect them.[194] Indigenous

[192] ibid 19.

[193] In JM Cobo, 'Study of the Problem of Discrimination against Indigenous Populations', United Nations Digital Library, https://www.un.org/development/desa/indigenouspeoples/publications/martinez-cobo-study.html, a broader list of identifying criteria is given, but self-identification is relevant. In addition to the more common criteria of the conventional instruments, the UN Permanent Forum on Indigenous Peoples adds an emphasis on the elements of a strong connection with surrounding territories and natural resources, distinct social, economic and political systems, and distinct language, culture and beliefs.

[194] The UN Specialized Mechanism on the Rights of Indigenous Peoples, which from 2009 to 2011 carried out a detailed study on Indigenous peoples and their right to participate in decision making, and the Special Rapporteur on the rights of Indigenous peoples, through reports on thematic issues and country issues, has focused on the issue of Indigenous peoples' participation rights, reinforcing

peoples are also recognised as having rights to their lands, territories and natural resources,[195] various economic, social and cultural rights,[196] innovative collective rights in good measure,[197] rights to equality and non-discrimination, and rights in relation to treaties, agreements and other arrangements between indigenous peoples and states.[198] Some of these rights are the same as those enjoyed by minorities under more recent international law, which is because indigenous peoples are often also in a minority in the states in which they reside. However, the UN Declaration on the Rights of Indigenous Peoples has a more comprehensive protective content than that of the international legal instruments associated with minorities.[199]

To these must be added other legal developments, especially at the regional level.[200] Of particular note in this respect is the jurisprudence of the Inter-American Court of Human Rights and decisions of the African Commission on Human and Peoples' Rights. This jurisprudence,[201] concerning core issues relating to this

important jurisprudential developments, both by the Human Rights Committee and the Inter-American Court and Commission on Human Rights, to ensure that the participation of Indigenous peoples implies special care in obtaining their prior, free and informed consent in relation to activities that have an impact on these peoples, their lands, territories and natural resources. See 'Expert Mechanism on the Rights of Indigenous Peoples, Advice n. 2: Indigenous Peoples and the Right to Participate in Decision-Making' (2018) United Nations Digital Library, UN Doc A/HRC/18/42.

[195] See the corresponding jurisprudence in *Mayagna (Sumo) Awas Twingni Community v Nicaragua* [2001] IACHR 9, IHRL 1462.

[196] Human Rights Committee, *General Comment No 23*, 1994; and Committee on Economic, Social and Cultural Rights, *General Comment No 21*, 2009 on the right to participate in cultural life. Also of note is *Massacre of the Plan de Sanchez v Guatemala* [2004] IACHR 12, IHRL 1499.

[197] With the exception of the right to self-determination, group rights were virtually unknown in international human rights law.

[198] MA Martínez, 'Study on Treaties, Agreements and Other Constructive Arrangements between States and Indigenous Populations' (1999) United Nations Digital Library, https://digitallibrary.un.org/record/276353?ln=en.

[199] Among the main differences between minorities and Indigenous peoples is the fact that minorities do not necessarily have the long-standing, traditional and spiritual connection to their lands and territories that is usually associated with the self-identification of Indigenous peoples. Furthermore, the 2007 UN Declaration on the Rights of Indigenous Peoples requires states to consult and cooperate with Indigenous peoples to obtain their free, prior and informed consent before undertaking development activities that may have an impact on these peoples, while the 1992 UN Declaration on Minorities provides a more general right to participation in decision making and requires that the legitimate interests of persons belonging to minorities be taken into account in national planning and programmes. Similarly, see Office of the High Commissioner, *Indigenous Peoples and Human Rights. The United Nations Human Rights System: Fact Sheet n. 9/Rev.2* (New York, United Nations, 2013) 5.

[200] Recently, see R Pereira, 'Public Participation, Indigenous Peoples' Land Rights and Major Infrastructure Projects in the Amazon: The Case for a Human Rights Assessment Framework' (2021) 30 *Review of European, Comparative & International Environmental Law* 184, 196.

[201] This jurisprudence consists, in particular, of decisions in leading cases of the Inter-American Court of Human Rights, such as the case *Mary and Carrie Dann v USA* [2002] 470 US 39, 7502, Inter-American Court of Human Rights 11(140); *Mayagna Awas Twingi Community v Nicaragua Yaxye Axa Indigenous Community* [2001] IACHR 9, IHRL 1462; *Saramaka People v Suriname* IACHR Series C no 172, IHRL 3046; *Sarayka v Ecuador* [2012] IACtHR Series C No 245; or the African Commission on Human and Peoples' Rights in *Endorois – Centre for Minority Rights Development (Kenya) and Minority Rights Group International (on Behalf of Endorois Welfare Council) v Kenya* [2009] communication no 276/03.

status – such as the question on the need for economic development projects to obtain the free, prior and informed consent of indigenous peoples or the question of what constitutes sufficient consultation – has made it possible to argue, in a globally progressive sense, that the rights of Indigenous peoples to their lands, territories and resources,[202] as well as the principle of their free, prior and informed consent,[203] are now part of the *corpus iuris* of binding human rights.

In addition to these substantive rights, indigenous peoples have the right to participate in the intricate institutional system of the UN family that applies and enforces the complex normative framework of human rights. Indigenous peoples have acquired unprecedented access to the system, especially to those bodies whose action specifically addresses indigenous peoples' issues, such as the Permanent Forum and the Specialised Mechanism.

In particular, this can be seen in the practice of enabling the representative organisations of Indigenous peoples to participate in UN human rights events and mechanisms without requiring them to be accredited before the ECOSOC, an accreditation that is required of other non-state actors. The extent of such participation at the UN is clearly visible in the annual sessions of the Permanent Forum and the Expert Mechanism. During these sessions, Indigenous peoples also have the opportunity to meet with the Special Rapporteur to report on the rights compliance issues they are facing.[204]

IV. Conclusion

The effects of globalisation on the international system led international law to rethink its traditional approach to the core issue of legal subjects, ie, of those entities or actors whom the international legal order recognises to have legal rights for participating in its workings. Today, the problem focuses in particular on the question of the legal status granted to non-state actors. One line of response to this problem continues to proclaim, in a somewhat mechanical and viciously circular reiteration, that international law is the law between states, at most also including IOs, so that non-state actors do not have legal personality.[205] Other authors

[202] In the doctrine, see L Rodríguez Pinero, 'The Inter-American System and the UN Declaration on the Rights of Indigenous Peoples: Mutual Reinforcement' in S Allen and A Xanthaki (eds) *Reflections on the UN Declaration on the Rights of Indigenous Peoples* (Oxford, Hart Publishing, 2011). For examples in the increasingly contentious area of international water law, see Canelas de Castro (n 180).

[203] On this particular right, its application and the case law to which it has given rise, see J Anaya, *International Human Rights and Indigenous Peoples* (New York, Kluwer, 2009); RB Lillich, H Hannum, SJ Anaya and D Shelton, *International Human Rights: Documentary, Supplement* (Austin, Kluwer, 2009); JS Phillips, 'The Rights of Indigenous Peoples under International Law' (2015) 26(2) *Global Bioethics* 120, 127.

[204] See www.ohchr.org/EN/Issues/IPeoples/SRIndigenous Peoples/Pages/SRIPeoplesIndex.aspx.

[205] See, eg, K Doehring, *Völkerrecht. Ein Lehrbuch* (Heidelberg, CF Müller, 1999) 196, who categorically rejects the possibility of NGOs being subjects of international law, holding that the very nature of private entities by definition excludes them from the spectrum of entities capable of attaining the status

maintain that there would be no advantage in recognising the legal status of NGOs and other non-state actors and that, on the contrary, the absence of such a status allows them to play a useful independent and critical role vis-à-vis states, the dominant subjects within the system, one that allows them to reflect public opinion, defend collective interests and enrich international public discourse, as well as helping to achieve the desired common good.[206] Both positions appear to us to be flawed, fundamentally because they do not question what the effective normative response of a continuously developing international law itself is today regarding the problem of legal personality or subjectivity. If the definition of international legal personality remains that it is the capacity to hold rights and obligations under international law, the developments in international law have mapped out evidence that the contemporary international community has effectively created rules that integrate a wider universe of actors and extend international legal subjectivity to entities other than states.[207] In particular, some NGOs and some multinational enterprises, as well as other groups and individuals have achieved the condition of international legal subjects, although their personality is functional, because it is related to certain community purposes that are relevant in the framework of contemporary international law, and is also limited in its character. This is in line with the ICJ's *dictum* in its *Reparations for Injuries* Opinion that 'the subjects of law, in a legal system, are not necessarily identical as regards their nature and the extent of their rights'.[208] This is also a welcome development whereby the more 'abstract', almost 'nominalistic' issue of the personality of certain actors imperceptibly shifts towards the more normatively 'dense', 'operational' query about what is the specific legal capacity to act in certain, specific international law relations.[209] Moreover, this is in harmony with the (at least partial) tendency for an overall movement of a growing international law, in its 'post-ontological hour',[210] to transform itself from a merely interstate order into a legal order which henceforth also contains elements of transnationality,[211] in correspondence with the confirmed

of subjects of international law. In his general course at the Academy of International Law, Crawford, in a more dogmatically elaborated position, put forward four fundamental arguments for reaching a fundamentally similar result of rejection of recognition of the international legal personality, in particular of multinational enterprises: the entities are the creation of states; a lack of international obligations on those entities; a lack of legal capacity in the international context; and a lack of horizontal application of international law between private persons. See J Crawford, 'Chance, Order, Change: The Course of International Law' (2013) 35 *Recueil des Cours* 249.

[206] S Riedinger, *Die Rolle nichtstaatlicher Organisationen bei der Entwicklung und Durchsetzung internationalen Umweltrechts* (Berlin, Duncker & Humblot, 2001); Mahiou (n 102) 265.

[207] K Ipsen (ed), *Völkerrecht. Ein Studienbuch*, 4th edn (Munich, CH Beck, 1999) para 20, who then argued that states were free to give international legal personality to NGOs and do so by treaty, illustrating that this had already occurred with the International Committee of the Red Cross.

[208] (1949) ICJ Rep 178.

[209] See also C Walter, 'Subjects of International Law' (2013), https://hoclv.com/wp-content/uploads/2017/11/2.-subjects-of-international-law.pdf, para 30.

[210] T Franck, *Fairness in International Law and Institutitons* (Oxford, Oxford University Press, 1995) 5.

[211] A constant theme of Francis Snyder's here honoured – as evidenced, for example, in the titles of publications such as F Snyder and L Yi, 'Transnational Law and the European Union: Reflections from WISH in China' (2013) 19(6) *European Law Journal* 1; F Snyder, *Food Safety in China: Making*

existence today of a globalised international system and in response to the latter's more plural and complex needs, concerns and expectations. The usefulness of recognising the international legal personality of these other actors, the reason for proceeding with this pathway of inclusion which makes international law appear more integrative of reality and its 'living forces', is precisely that it contributes to the consolidation of an international law that is more capable of fulfilling the normative project that it contains. Furthermore, only thus will it be able to fully honour the ('constitutional') axiological and teleological determinations that underpin positive international law, reflected in its general principles as well as in its *erga omnes* and *ius cogens* provisions, and to enhance the sense of international law as a truly international legal *order*, where rights are taken seriously[212] and the legal *system* appears, both substantively and procedurally, to be endowed with fairness and legitimacy.[213]

Transnational Law (Leiden, Brill, 2015); F Snyder, *The Future of Transnational Law: EU, USA, China and the BRICS* (Brussels, Bruylant, 2015).

[212] R Dworkin, *Taking Rights Seriously*, 8th edn (London, Duckworth Overlook, 1996); JJ Gomes Canotilho, 'Tomemos a sério os direitos económicos, sociais e culturais' in *Estudos sobre direitos fundamentais*, 2nd edn (Coimbra, Coimbra Editora, 2008), 35–68.

[213] T Franck, 'Legitimacy in the International System' (1988) 82(4) *AJIL* 705, 759; T Franck, *The Power of Legitimacy Among Nations* (New York, Oxford University Press, 1990); T Franck, *Fairness in International Law and Institutions* (Oxford, Oxford University Press, 1995) 5–6.

2

EU Governance and Soft Law

The Bamboo and the Oak

IMELDA MAHER*

I. Introduction

This chapter is a reflection on and response to Francis Snyder's opening chapter for the 2022 handbook on soft law.[1] In this tour de force, Snyder comes to the startling conclusion that the term 'soft law' should be jettisoned. Given that his definition of soft law is one of the most widely quoted in EU law scholarship,[2] it is important to explore his analysis and why he has come to this conclusion. The key to understanding Snyder's chapter is the significance he gives to normative hybridity in providing the necessary governance tools for a sustainable future. This present chapter approaches the development of Snyder's thinking of soft law by taking the two bookends of his work on soft law – his seminal 1993 *Modern Law Review* article[3] and his 2022 book chapter – to reflect on his contribution to soft law scholarship. The primary focus is EU law. Having outlined the nature of soft law in the EU, the chapter then turns to an analysis of Snyder's two papers, starting with his 1993 article before turning to the 2002 chapter and providing some concluding thoughts.

* Thanks to Colin Scott, Julien Chaisse, and Oana Ştefan for their comments. All errors remain my own.

[1] F Snyder, 'Bamboo, or Governance through Soft Law: Hybridity, Legitimacy, and Sustainability' in M Eliantonio, E Korkea-aho and U Mörth (eds), *Edward Elgar Research Handbook on Soft Law* (Cheltenham, Edward Elgar, 2022).

[2] A total of 3.52 cites a year according to AW Harzing, 'Publish or Perish' (2007), available from https://harzing.com/resources/publish-or-perish, with Google scholar listing 753 citations as of August 2022.

[3] F Snyder, 'The Effectiveness of European Community Law: Institutions, Processes, Tools and Techniques', (1993) 56 *MLR* 19.

II. Defining Soft Law

Soft law is 'rules of conduct which, in principle, have no legally binding force but which nevertheless may have practical effects'.[4] This is the widely accepted definition that Snyder provided in his 1993 article. It is a testament to the lucidity of his writing that this definition has remained a constant in the burgeoning literature on soft law, especially in EU legal scholarship.[5] It has provided a key reference point, despite the slippery nature of soft law in national,[6] EU[7] and international law.[8] He has introduced only one modification to that definition, adding that soft law may have legal as well as practical effects.[9] This modification points to refinements in the discussion of soft law in both international law and EU law scholarship.[10]

The conceptual connection between soft law in international and EU law is well established, with Snyder pointing to Borchardt and Wellens in their seminal 1989 article on soft law in what was then the European Economic Community (EEC).[11] They trace the emergence of the soft law concept to the 1970s, although they also note how Baxter[12] referred to political treaties as soft law in international law, with the post-Second World War Yalta agreement being given as an example.[13] Terpan draws on the influential discussion of legalisation in international relations by Abbott and Snidal in his analysis and categorisation of the many different forms of soft law in the EU.[14] He argues that it is best to view norms on a continuum from

[4] ibid 32.

[5] O Ştefan, M Avbelj, M Eliantonio, M Hartlapp, E Korkea-aho and N Rubio, 'EU Soft Law in the EU Legal Order: A Literature Review', King's College London Law School Research Paper (4 March 2019), https://ssrn.com/abstract=3346629 or http://dx.doi.org/10.2139/ssrn.3346629. The authors note that Snyder's is the most quoted definition of soft law when they discuss EU soft law (at 10).

[6] M Eliantonio, E Korkea-Aho and O Ştefan (eds), *EU Soft Law in the Member States* (Oxford, Hart Publishing, 2021), which contains chapters on soft law in nine EU Member States, the UK and China.

[7] For EU soft law, 'the vast array of shapes and forms that EU soft law documents take renders automatic coding impossible'. It is also noted that the variety of soft law acts is much greater than hard law: see B Cappellina, A Ausfelder, A Eick, R Mespoulet, M Hartlapp, S Saurugger and F Terpan, 'Ever More Soft Law? A Dataset to Compare Binding and Non-binding EU Law across Policy Areas and over Time (2004–2019)' (2022) 23 *European Union Politics* 1, at 5 and 10.

[8] For an overview, see A Boyle, 'Soft Law in International Law-making' in MD Evans (ed), *International Law*, 5th edn (Oxford, Oxford University Press, 2018).

[9] Snyder first raised this modification at the Jean Monnet 6th International Workshop for Young Scholars, UCD, November 2007. See also O Ştefan, 'European Competition Soft Law in European Courts: A Matter of Hard Principles' (2008) 14 *European Law Journal* 753, 756. Senden also includes 'certain (indirect) legal effects' in the definition of soft law. See L Senden, *Soft Law in European Community Law* (Oxford, Hart Publishing, 2004) 112.

[10] These are well rehearsed in the Ştefan et al (n 5).

[11] Snyder (n 1) 2; KC Wellens and GM Borchardt, 'Soft Law in European Community law' (1989) 14(5) *EL Rev* 267, 278.

[12] RR Baxter, 'International Law in "Her Infinite Variety"' (1980) 29(4) *ICLQ* 549, 550.

[13] Yalta Conference Agreement, Declaration of a Liberated Europe, 11 February 1945, History and Public Policy Program Digital Archive, National Archives, http://digitalarchive.wilsoncenter.org/document/116176.

[14] F Terpan, 'Soft Law in the European Union: The Changing Nature of EU Law' (2015) 19(1) *European Law Journal* 58, 70.

binding hard law to soft law to non-legal social norms with varying degrees of legal relevance. In doing so, he modifies the Abbott and Snidal continuum of legalisation which has three elements: obligation, precision and delegation.[15] He sees precision as something that goes to the degree of obligation and – perhaps unsurprisingly for a lawyer – he replaces delegation with enforcement. Enforcement is a major consideration in the debate of soft law, particularly in relation to the European and national courts.[16] Soft law as a norm and the analysis of soft law in the EU thus shares and owes its roots to norms and debates in the international law and international relations domains, but, as Terpan shows, it has become an important and distinct feature of the EU legal order.

While the term 'soft law' may have emerged in the 1970s, non-binding norms have been a constant feature of the EU Treaties since the 1957 Treaty of Rome, with recommendations and opinions expressly listed as legal acts of the EU that have no binding force.[17] And as measures without binding legal force, the Treaties have always excluded them from judicial review.[18] The range of non-binding soft law measures in the EU now extends far beyond these two forms. In fact, the first soft law measures, which date from 1962, were Notices issued on competition law by the European Commission.[19] Guidelines and notices have since become a very well-established feature of EU competition law. There have been various attempts to categorise, count and establish whether the amount of soft law has grown in the EU, but the range of instruments makes it difficult if not impossible to be definitive on this.[20] Recommendations and opinions account for 2.7 per cent in the Directory of Legislation in Force,[21] compared to a figure of 5 per cent in 1997.[22] Hofmann suggests this apparent diminution in recommendations and opinions can be explained in part by an increase in non-Treaty soft law measures

[15] KW Abbott and D Snidel, 'Hard and Soft Law in International Relations' (2000) 54(3) *International Organization* 421. For a critique of their constructivist approach, see M Finnemore and SJ Toope, 'Alternatives to "Legalization": Richer Views of Law and Politics' (2001) 55(3) *International Organization* 743.

[16] For contrasting views, see O Ştefan, 'Helping Loose Ends Meet? The Judicial Acknowledgement of Soft Law as a Tool of Multi-level Governance' (2014) 21(2) *Maastricht Journal of European and Comparative Law* 359; J Scott, 'In Legal Limbo: Post-legislative Guidance as a Challenge for European Administrative Law' (2011) 48 *CML Rev* 329.

[17] Article 288 TFEU. The wording as it relates to recommendations and opinions has not changed. The terminology in the European Coal and Steel Community Treaty of Paris 1951 was different, but nonetheless, Article 14 ECSC expressly mentions opinions as having no binding force.

[18] Article 263 TFEU.

[19] The measures were known as the Christmas Notices and dealt with exclusive dealing with commercial agents and patent licences; see [1962] OJ 139/2921 and [1962] OJ 139/2922. See also L Senden and S Prechal, 'Differentiation in and through Community Soft Law' in B de Witte, D Hanf and E Vos (eds), *The Many Faces of Differentiation in EU Law* (Antwerp, Intersentia, 2001).

[20] Snyder also notes the difficulties of categorising and containing soft law in China; see F. Snyder, 'Three Worlds of Chinese Soft Law' in Eliantonio, Korkea-Aho and Ştefan (n 6) 267.

[21] The Directory lists all EU legislation in force at a particular date; see https://eur-lex.europa.eu/browse/directories/legislation.html.

[22] A von Bogdandy, F Arndt and J Bast, 'Legal Instruments in European Union Law and Their Reform: A Systematic Approach on an Empirical Basis' (2004) 23 *Yearbook of European Law* 91.

such as guidelines and notices.[23] The fluidity of classification can be seen in one Commission measure which has Communication, Notice and Guidelines in its title.[24] While the greater awareness of soft law instruments and efforts to classify them means it is unlikely that a similar heading would be used now, it nonetheless highlights how fluid soft law can be. This is not to suggest that the nature of EU soft law is chaotic;[25] instead, it is complex. However, concerns have rightly been raised as to its transparency, which is particularly concerning given that one of the prized functions of soft law in the EU is its ability to improve transparency between the Union and the Member States and citizens.[26] Thus, soft law in its many forms has been part of EU law since the early 1960s and remains an important governance tool within the EU legal order, albeit a controversial one.[27] Through an exploration of Snyder's work, we will see how the context and debates around soft law have changed in the intervening period and what that augurs for EU governance – of which soft law is part – in the future.

III. 1993: An Early Reflection on EEC Soft Law

A. Effectiveness

In his 1993 article, Snyder gave an early exegesis on the importance of soft law for the then EEC.[28] He was concerned with the effectiveness of EU law, seeing effectiveness as including but not limited to 'implementation, enforcement, impact and compliance'[29] and with the legal and institutional preconditions for effectiveness. Taking a law in context[30] approach – ie, treating 'law and legal phenomena critically in their cultural, social, political, technological, environmental and

[23] A Hofmann, 'Types of EU Soft Law and Their National Impact' in Eliantonio, Korkea-Aho and Ştefan (n 6).

[24] Communication from the Commission – Notice – Guidelines on the application of Article 81(3) of the Treaty [2004] OJ C101/97. See O Ştefan, 'European Competition Soft Law in European Courts: A Matter of Hard Principles?' (2008) 14(6) *European Law Journal* 753.

[25] Von Bogdandy et al (n 22) 92. In fact, Mörth notes that in the EU, the alternative to soft law in some policy fields is not hard law, but uncoordinated national action (at 348).

[26] O Ştefan, 'Soft Law and the Promise of Transparency in the Member States' in Eliantonio, Korkea-Aho and Ştefan (n 6).

[27] See, eg, J Klabbers, 'The Undesirability of Soft Law' (1998) 67 *Nordic Journal of International Law* 381.

[28] For ease of reference, the Community and Community law will be referred to as EU and EU law hereinafter.

[29] Snyder (n 3) 19. Later in the article (at 25), he identifies seven different forms of effectiveness in the Community: enactment; application of regulations by the Member States; transposition of Directives; implementation of the transposed laws or secondary Community law by national civil servants; use of Community law by economic and other actors as they orientate their behaviour according to law; recourse to litigation; and enforcement of law by courts.

[30] Snyder published the first book in EU law in the groundbreaking *Law in Context* series (now published by Cambridge University Press).

economic contexts'[31] – the article explores administrative and judicial responses to non-compliance with EU law by the European Commission and the Court of Justice of the European Union (CJEU) providing systemic comparison of institutions, processes, tools and techniques.[32] Writing after the signing of the Maastricht Treaty[33] and the completion of the 1992 programme – the much-heralded deadline for the completion of the single market – the article also explores more normative questions, including the future vision of the Community. Taking this abstract question, Snyder grounds it in a consideration of whether there are even the criteria and processes to help make choices about the future, thereby linking purposes, rules, processes and institutions of the then Community.

The article sees implementation as negotiation: recursive, continuous and circular in nature, with compliance by national bureaucracies being critical, and such compliance involving legal and political processes leading to organisational change. It is in the context of this wider conceptual framing of effectiveness of law that the discussion of soft law emerges, with Snyder identifying it as one of three techniques used by the Commission to secure effectiveness of Community law.[34] The landmark definition – rules of conduct which, in principle, have no legally binding force, but which nevertheless may have practical effect – is provided 15 pages into the article.[35] Thus, the main and perhaps unexpected impact of the article is not the rich conceptual and law in context discussion of effectiveness, but the definition of a concept that is only one technique analysed in the piece and an analysis expressly limited to one actor: the Commission.

B. Soft Law and the European Commission

The discussion of soft law in the article is framed in functional terms. In Snyder's view, the limited competence of the Commission to use the command of (hard) law to secure compliance necessitated recourse to other means, with soft law being

[31] Harlow quotes with approval the definition of law in context provided by the *Law in Context* series, which goes on to state a 'contextual approach involves treating legal subjects broadly, using materials from other humanities and social sciences, and from any other discipline that helps to explain the operation in practice of the particular legal field or legal phenomena under investigation'. See C Harlow, 'The EU and Law in Context: The Context' (2022) 1 *European Law Open* 209 at 13 and ch 6 in this volume.

[32] In doing so, the title of the article echoes the subtitles of the seminal *Integration through Law* studies cited by Snyder in fn 18 of his article. See M Cappelletti, M Secombe and JHH Weiler (eds), *Integration through Law, Volume 1: Methods, Tools and Institutions, Book 2: Political Organs, Integration Techniques and Judicial Process* (Berlin, Walter de Gruyter, 1986).

[33] The Treaty is referred to in the introduction. The article was published in January 1993. The Treaty was signed in February 1992 and came into effect on 1 November 1993: see F Laursen, 'The Treaty of Maastricht' in E Jones, A Menon and S Weatherill (eds), *Oxford Handbook of European Studies* (Oxford, Oxford University Press, 2012).

[34] Snyder (n 3) 27. The other two techniques were litigation and structural reform involving national administrations.

[35] ibid 32.

the most important of these.[36] Recommendations are given as an example, with the thorny obligation of national courts to take recommendations into consideration being mentioned, without discussion of the fuzziness of this requirement and how it differs from a duty of application.[37] Snyder sees the Commission practice following national administrative practice.[38] There is no discussion of the practice and influence of public international law, (which has since become the dominant narrative and is discussed by Snyder in his 2022 chapter). He provides as an example one of the most famous and influential pieces of soft law: the Commission communication setting out guidelines for mutual recognition published following the *Cassis de Dijon* case.[39] He discusses the Commission view of the legal base for the Communication: Articles 5 and 155 of the EC Treaty,[40] both of which have been repealed.[41] The very broad obligation in Article 5 on all the institutions to exercise their powers under the conditions and for the purposes of the Treaty has been partially replaced by Article 13(2) of the Treaty on European Union (TEU), which arguably limits the institutions to the powers conferred by the Treaties.[42] Similarly, Article 155 EC has been partially replaced by Article 17(1) TEU.[43] The broad sweep of Article 155 inter alia expressly gave the Commission power to formulate recommendations or deliver opinions on Treaty matters, where the Commission thought it necessary to ensure the proper functioning and development of the Common Market. Article 17(1) TEU, on the other hand, requires the Commission to promote the general interest of the EU and take appropriate initiatives to that end. The language is open-ended, but perhaps one of the reasons for the reduction of recommendations and opinions noted by Hofmann[44] may be due in part to this change in the Treaty.

Snyder proceeds to analyse only one form of soft law, the Commission communication, identifying three types: information, declaratory and interpretive. He notes their benefits: systematic; more like legislation than litigation; under the

[36] ibid 31–36.

[37] Case C-322/88 *Grimaldi v Fonds des Maladies Professionnelles* [1989] ECR 4402. For a discussion of the challenges it poses, see PL Láncos, 'A Hard Core under the Soft Shell: How Binding is Union Soft Law for Member States?' (2018) 24(4) *European Public Law* 755, 760ff.

[38] Citing English, French and Italian academic sources without giving specific examples.

[39] Communication from the Commission concerning the consequences of the judgment given by the Court of Justice on 20 February 1979 in Case 120/78 ('Cassis de Dijon') [1980] OJ C256, 3 October, 2–3; Case 120/78 *Rewe-Zentral AG v Bundesmonopolverqaltung für Brantweinn ('Cassis de Dijon')* [1979] ECR 649. For a discussion of the importance of the Communication, see KJ Alter, S Meunier-Aitsahalia, 'Judicial Politics in the European Community: European Integration and the Pathbreaking *Cassis de Dijon* Decision' (1994) 26(4) *Comparative Political Studies* 535.

[40] He correctly notes that Article 5 EC could not impose new legal obligations on the Member States; see Case 229/86 *Brother Industries v Commission* [1987] ECR 3757.

[41] In fact, in the conclusions, Snyder warned of the increasingly extensive interpretation of Article 5 EC.

[42] P Craig and G de Búrca, *EU Law: Text, Cases and Materials*, 5th edn (Oxford, Oxford University Press, 2011) clvii.

[43] ibid clxxi.

[44] A Hofmann, 'Types of EU Soft Law and Their National Impact' in Eliantonio, Korkea-Aho and Ştefan (n 6).

control of the Commission; and proactive. They define what is settled and in dispute, circumscribe the arena for debate, and define the agenda for negotiation and litigation.[45] These characteristics in his view mean that they provide guidelines for negotiating the effectiveness of EU law. This functional analysis ultimately sees the communications of the Commission advancing its agenda-setting role.[46]

C. Soft Law and the Courts

Snyder's article foreshadows case law about how soft law is treated before the CJEU,[47] noting how Commission measures (instructions and codes) designed to supplement anti-fraud legislation were reviewed by the Court and in both instances annulled on the basis that the measures had legal effects and went beyond simple clarification of the underlying regulations imposing additional obligations on the Member States, which the Commission did not have the power to do.[48] However, these early cases did not presage the unsystematic approach of the CJEU to reviewing soft law measures, where practice seems to vary depending on the policy field.[49] What the cases discussed by Snyder signified and what is a focus of his 2022 chapter is the extent to which Commission soft law operates in the shadow of hard law. This is the hybridity of soft law in the EU.[50] Snyder notes a key tension for soft law: the more formalised the measure, the greater the chance that it will be effective. This in turn risks the measure crossing the boundary between what he terms negotiation and legislation, and being subject to judicial review.[51] The advantages of the measure – communication over which the Commission has control – would

[45] Snyder (n 3) 33.

[46] For a recent analysis of the Commission's agenda-setting role, see B Oztas and A Kreppel, 'Power or Luck? The Limitations of the European Commission's Agenda Setting Power and Autonomous Policy Influence' (2022) 60(2) *Journal of Common Market Studies* 408.

[47] For a detailed discussion of Case 310/85 *Deufil* [1987] ECR 901 concerning state aid codes, see F Snyder, 'Soft Law and Institutional Practice in the European Community' in S Martin (ed), *The Construction of Europe* (Dordrecht, Springer, 1994). The iterative relationship between the Commission and the Court concerning soft law has been more recently explored in Ştefan (n 16).

[48] Case C-303/90 *France v Commission* [1991] ECR I-5315. In both instances the measures challenged were published in the C series, where non-binding measures are found, but this did not preclude review by the Court. See also Case C-325/91 *France v Commission* ECLI:EU:C:1993:245, where a communication from the Commission imposing additional reporting obligations on Member States in relation to public undertakings was annulled for going beyond the requirements imposed by the relevant directive; and Case C-327/91 *France v Commission* ECLI:EU:C:1994:305, where the EEC/US competition cooperation agreement was annulled, as the competence to enter into international agreements resided with the Council and not the Commission.

[49] M Eliantonio and O Ştefan, 'Soft Law before the European Courts: Discovering a "Common Pattern"?' (2018) 37 *Yearbook of European Law* 457, 459.

[50] See N Jääskinen, 'Final Thoughts' in Eliantonio, Korkea-Aho and Ştefan (n 6) 360: 'we are rarely dealing with purified forms of soft law or hard law, but rather some sort of a hybrid of both'. See also the discussion below.

[51] On measures having legal effects and hence subject to review, see Case 22/70 *Commission v Council* [1971] ECR 263 (the ERTA case).

be lost. This functional focus does not address the problem of transgressive law making and the concerns to which this gives rise in relation to the legitimacy and democratic nature of the EU.

D. National Administrations and Commission Negotiations: Whither Soft Law?

Snyder explores structural reform – reshaping or reforming legal economic and political structures as another means of possibly increasing effectiveness of Community law. In exploring such reforms among bureaucracies, one example is interorganisational exchanges between the Commission and national administrations or non-governmental organisations (NGOs). All such negotiation and reshaping have to take place within the legal competences of the Commission. The boundaries here between these negotiations with national administrations and measures constituting soft law are at best fuzzy. This can be seen in the discussion of the *Commission v France* case already analysed in his article in relation to soft law.[52] Snyder notes that there, the CJEU had rejected the Commission argument that it was entitled to take informal measures having no legal force determining the scope of a law within the framework of partnership with national administrations. The Commission argued that such arrangements made through consensus gave legal certainty and did not affect third parties. This discussion shows the difficulties of categorising soft law. It also implicitly highlights the need for flexibility and coordination in bureaucratic governance on the one hand, and the need for accountability and transparency on the other.[53] Snyder rightly points to how effectiveness of Community law can drive what is perhaps best described as the Europeanisation of national administrations,[54] whereby national policies and laws are changed incrementally and functionally.[55] In the latter sections of the article, he discusses the development of direct effect, state liability and the principle of equivalence of remedy by the CJEU as a means of ensuring the effectiveness of EU law. He notes the impact it has on national judicial practices, implicitly pointing to the Europeanisation of national courts and their procedures.[56]

[52] C-303/90 *France v Commission* ECLI:EU:C:1991:424.

[53] See U Mörth, 'The National Politics of EU Soft Law: Sweden and the Balancing Act between Output and Input Legitimacy' in Eliantonio, Korkea-Aho and Ştefan (n 6).

[54] Europeanisation is a contested term; see S Saurugger, 'Europeanisation in Times of Crisis' (2014) 12 *Political Studies Review* 181.

[55] H Kassim, The National Co-ordination of EU Policy: Confronting the Challenge' in H Kassim, G Peters and V Wright (eds), *The National Co-ordination of EU Policy: The Domestic Level* (Oxford, Oxford University Press, 2000) 235–64.

[56] See, eg, L Conant, 'Europeanisation and the Courts: Variable Patterns of Adaptation across National Judiciaries' in M Green Cowles, J Caporaso and T Risse (eds), *Transforming Europe: Europeanisation and Domestic Change* (Ithaca, Cornell University Press, 2001).

E. Soft Law: A Small Part of Effective EEC Law?

Snyder's article is primarily concerned with the effectiveness of EU law, seeing all the Commission tools as forms of negotiation and implying overlap between them. If soft law is seen as a form of negotiation, then if we return to the idea of a law spectrum, we can see it as running from open to closed, where closure marks the point where negotiation has ended and resulted in a binding hard law, with the openness of the negotiations increasing as the actors move away from that point. It is striking that in his conclusion, Snyder sees structural reform as by far the most important tool of the Commission when dealing with recalcitrant Member States and devotes little discussion to soft law.[57] Nonetheless, his concerns about structural reform and the administrative negotiation within it resonate with soft law. There is the risk that only limited interests will be represented (even though there is potential for a broad range of interests); like soft law, the aim can be to go beyond legal doctrine to achieve broader social political and economic aims, and the risks are lack of transparency, ambiguity and uncertainty. He also warns of the risk of policy-making-by-administration. Despite these concerns, he does not jettison any of the tools identified, instead raising what he regards as the basic question: which policies, issues and participants are more suitable to each institution, process, tool and technique? He notes that negotiation and adjudication alone are insufficient for the effectiveness of the law and other tools may be required, most notably effective political institutions at the EU level. Hence, in this article, soft law represents one, but not the most important, tool to improve the effectiveness of EU law at a time when this was a serious concern due to administrative incapacity or recalcitrance by Member States, especially in relation to single market legislation.

The question of effectiveness remains, but on a much more fundamental level now in relation to the rule of law and specifically the ability of national courts to give effect to EU law without political interference.[58] This was not envisaged in 1992, though some of the concerns raised by Snyder remain, pointing to core elements of the rule of law; in particular, how we understand legality and transparency remains of concern. Reflecting 15 years after the *Modern Law Review* article on soft law and the rule of law, Dawson noted how the debate over soft law continued to 'rage'.[59] Thus, it is perhaps unsurprising that Snyder starts his 2022 chapter by asking: can soft law really govern? And is the rule of law dead?

[57] For a more detailed treatment by Snyder of soft law at that time, see F Snyder, 'Soft Law and Institutional Practice in the European Community' in S Martin (ed), *The Construction of Europe* (Dordrecht, Kluwer, 1994).

[58] Case C-156/21 *Hungary v Parliament and Council* EU:C:2022:97; Case C-157/21 *Poland v Parliament and Council* EU:C:2022:98 (both full court rulings); Case C-430/21 *RS* ECLI:EU:C:2022:99 (on the principle of primacy and national courts). See generally L Pech, 'The Rule of Law as a Well-Established and Well-Defined Principle of EU Law' (2022) *Hague Journal of International Law*, https://doi.org/10.1007/s40803-022-00176-8 9.

[59] M Dawson, 'Soft Law and the Rule of Law in the European Union: Revision or Redundancy?', EUI Working Paper RSCAS 2009/24 at 14.

IV. 2022: Revisiting Governance Through Soft Law

A. Soft Law, State Law and Executive Management

By posing such stark questions at the start of the chapter, Snyder immediately locates the discussion in the context of current concerns about the rule of law.[60] He also refers to his 1993 article by asking what institutions, processes, tools and techniques are required for a post-COVID-19 sustainable future. His 2022 chapter argues that soft law is a key part of legal pluralism and is at pains to point out that soft law is not a phenomenon restricted to Western liberal democracies, but is found throughout the world and across time, thereby expanding the canvas for analysis well beyond the geographical scope of the 1993 article, while retaining the EU as the key focus of analysis.

The 2022 chapter explores how soft law contrasts with two other normative forms – state law and executive management – where the latter is concerned with the contractualisation of governance. The 1993 article did not discuss executive management, instead emphasising how the Commission techniques were centred on negotiation with national administrations and Member States. Despite or perhaps because of the focus on EU law in the 1993 article, there was little focus on state law, save as it related to EU law. Hence, there is a different focus in the 2022 chapter, leading to the final argument of Snyder that ultimately the best tool through which to govern a sustainable future is normative hybridity. Legal hybridity was not referred to as such in the 1993 article; the analysis proffered then located Commission communications within a hard law framework, with examples of soft law following case law[61] and being the focus of an annulment action before the CJEU.[62] Hybridity became part of the discussion of soft law later in the 2000s and is embraced by Snyder in the 2022 chapter.[63]

B. Rethinking Soft Law

i. *Soft Law: A Spectrum*

Snyder uses his definition of soft law as a springboard for the re-evaluation of his thinking in the 2022 chapter. He notes how the dichotomy between hard and soft

[60] He also references regulation (are standard setters the 'new global rulers'?) and transnational law (either an unruly pluralism of transnational legal orders or a transnational normative repertoire spatially embedded locally, regionally and nationally).

[61] Communication from the Commission (n 39) 2–3; *Cassis de Dijon* (n 40).

[62] See, eg, Case C-366/88 *Re FEOGA Inspections: France v Commission* [1990] ECR I-357.

[63] DM Trubek, P Cottrell and M Nance, 'Soft Law, "Hard Law" and EU Integration' in G de Búrca and J Scott (eds), *New Governance and Constitutionalism in Europe and the US* (Oxford, Hart Publishing, 2006).

law inherent in the definition obscures the full range of norms that may exist, noting how this range can be captured by concepts such as legalisation and, as discussed above, a spectrum approach.[64] Hard law – binding and creating recognisable legal obligations enforceable through the courts – is enacted by the state (or the supra-national EU). Soft law does not create legal obligations, save perhaps for the author of the measure who may be bound by it.[65] Snyder is careful not to use the term 'enforceability' for soft law, instead revisiting the term 'effectiveness' and is also more equivocal about that, noting that effectiveness usually depends on social practices and institutions other than courts. The use of the word 'usually' also alerts us to the uncertainty in the case law of the CJEU, the extent to which soft law can form the basis for an annulment action, and the status of EU soft law before national courts,[66] which have the nebulous obligation to take it into account.

ii. Soft Law: Authorship

Snyder notes that the authorship of soft law is shared. The state, the EU, international bodies and/or private actors can all issue soft law measures. Private actors are often standard setters, and those standards may be legally binding and capable of having legal effects.[67] The question of authorship can be blurred, with legislation supporting forms of self-regulation by industry actors (co-regulation); and voluntary standards can also be adopted by private actors, such as highly technical standards or environmental standards. Snyder specifically mentions soft law as a key aspect of transnational governance where standards may be given legal effect – for example, the CJEU held that it could provide an interpretation of technical standards adopted by private bodies under the purview of an EU directive, as such standards constituted part of EU law.[68] Looking at the regulatory nature of soft law also supports Snyder's view that the bifurcation between hard law (following legally well-defined processes) and soft law (not doing so and hence more in the political than the legal realm) minimises or hides both the inherently political nature of hard law and the processes whereby it is created and implemented. Snyder goes so far as to suggest that this particular distinction is extremely misleading while differences remain as to outcomes and the extent to which norms can impose obligations that can be enforced by the state.

[64] Terpan (n 14).

[65] See Joined Cases C-189, 202, 205, 208 and 213/02 *Dansk Rørindustri* [2005] ECR I-5425 for a discussion of the principle of legitimate expectation.

[66] *Grimaldi* (n 38).

[67] For an overview, see C Scott, 'Standards-Setting in Regulatory Regimes' in R Baldwin, M Cave and M Lodge (eds), *The Oxford Handbook of Regulation* (Oxford, Oxford University Press, 2010). Snyder mentions standard setting in the context of transnational law, but as Scott reminds us, standards can be set a different level of governance down to and including individual contracts.

[68] Case C-613/14 *James Elliott Construction Ltd v Irish Asphalt Ltd* EU:C:2016:821.

iii. Soft Law Scholarship

Snyder briefly outlines the trajectory of research on soft law in the EU: starting with Senden's now-classic 2004 text, which was the first in-depth treatment,[69] then Mörth's multidisciplinary edited collection[70] and J Scott and Trubek's 2002 article on the EU ill-fated governance tool, the Open Method of Coordination, distinguishing it from the Community method of law making in the EU.[71] Seeing soft law as part of the regulation landscape, he refers to C Scott's edited collection on regulation and his analysis of post-regulatory governance,[72] before mentioning Trubek, Cottrell and Nance's first analysis of hybridity: the combination of hard and soft law in the same policy area.[73] In more recent years, Ştefan undertook the first book-length study of soft law in the CJEU pointing to the emergence of hybridity, judicialisation and constitutionalisation.[74] Finally, Eliantonio, Korkea-Aho and Ştefan have moved the focus to soft law in the EU Member States.[75] Snyder also provides an extensive bibliography (241 references), which he hopes will be of value to students, but in fact is a rich resource for all soft law scholars.

iv. Soft Law: Hard Law

While eschewing the dichotomous relationship between hard and soft law, Snyder devotes a section of the chapter to hard law. Drawing on Marxism, he notes how the state acquired a monopoly on the term 'law', marginalising other non-state normative forms including soft law. Just as the state has a monopoly on law, it also has a Weberian monopoly on legitimate force, which means that only the state can enact binding norms. Snyder reminds us that this analysis ignores the considerable range of sanctions that can exist, such as naming and shaming. For example, the EU Internal Market compliance scoreboard is well established and has been deployed in other spheres in the EU, including the Justice Scoreboard.[76] The success of such soft sanctions is debated,[77] but nonetheless, legal pluralism would

[69] Senden (n 9).

[70] U Mörth (ed), *Soft Law and Governance: An Interdisciplinary Analysis* (Cheltenham, Edward Elgar, 2009).

[71] DM Trubek and J Scott, 'Mind the Gap: Law and New Approaches to Governance in the European Union' (2002) 8(1) *European Law Journal* 1.

[72] C Scott (ed), *Regulation* (Dartmouth, Ashgate, 2003); C Scott, 'Regulation in the Age of Governance: The Rise of the Post-regulatory State' in J Jordana and D Levi-Faur (eds), *The Politics of Regulation* (Cheltenham, Edward Elgar, 2004).

[73] Trubek et al (n 64).

[74] O Ştefan, *Soft Law in Court: Competition Law, State Aid, and the Court of Justice of the European Union* (Alphen aan den Rijn, Kluwer, 2012).

[75] Eliantonio, Korkea-Aho and Ştefan (n 6).

[76] For the Internal Market Scoreboard, see https://single-market-scoreboard.ec.europa.eu/_en. For the most recent justice scoreboard, see European Commission, 'The 2022 EU Justice Scoreboard, Communication to the European Parliament, the Council, the European Central Bank, the European Economic and Social Committee and the Committee of the Regions' COM (2022) 234.

[77] See, eg, K Moumoutzis and S Zartaloudis, 'Europeanization Mechanisms and Process Tracing: A Template for Empirical Research' (2016) 54(2) *Journal of Common Market Studies* 337.

suggest there can be many sites for legal norms. Snyder, however, seems equivocal on this point. He is keen to reject the bifurcation of hard law and soft law, while including a section on hard law in the chapter. He acknowledges a plurality of authors and of legal norms, while also noting that people (by which he seems to mean the general public) see 'law' as state law.

C. The Rule of Law

Whither the rule of law, given this equivocation? Again, starting from a Marxist perspective, Snyder notes how the thick version of the rule of law is associated with hard law and the state, while this is less clear-cut in relation to the more process-orientated thin version,[78] but also notes how the rule of law is a Western construct that served to legitimate colonisation and associated exploitation. Human rights, seen as an inherent part of a thick description of the rule of law, are not absolute, raising the question of who decides how to balance competing rights. Snyder, echoing Grimm,[79] raises concerns about how the CJEU has equated the EU four freedoms with human rights perhaps most famously in the *Laval* case.[80] However, he does not agree with Grimm that sovereignty protects democracy, given the contested nature of the concept of sovereignty.[81] Finally, in this section he returns to transnational law and the capacity of international bodies to perform state functions, thereby leading to a legal pluralism that embraces hard and soft law. Hence, while acknowledging the fluidity and complexity of the concepts of law and state, Snyder ultimately if guardedly sees transnational law and legal pluralism as the concepts that best explain these complexities.

D. Governance by Contract

Turning to executive management – governance by contract – Snyder notes how in the international context, a Memorandum of Understanding (MoU) is only as binding as the parties expressly say it is, and is often not binding at all. From this, he turns to Economic and Monetary Union (EMU) and specifically the responses to the eurozone crisis, where ultimately the European Stability Mechanism was adopted as an international treaty outside the EU legal framework by all the then

[78] For an overview of the rule of law, see B Tamanaha, *On the Rule of Law: History, Politics, Theory* (Cambridge, Cambridge University Press, 2004).

[79] D Grimm, 'Europe's Legitimacy Problem and the Courts' in D Chalmers, M Jachtenfuchs and C Joerges (eds), *The End of the Eurocrats' Dream: Adjusting to European Diversity* (Cambridge, Cambridge University Press, 2016).

[80] Case C-341/05 *Laval un Partneri Ltd* ECLI:EU:C:2007:809. See also Case C-438/05 *International Transport Workers' Federation and Finnish Seamen's Union v Viking Line ABP and OÜ Viking Line Eesti* ECLI:EU:C:2007:772.

[81] D Grimm, *Sovereignty: The Origin and Future of Political and Legal Concept* (New York, Columbia University Press, 2015).

Member States except the UK.[82] Other responses to the crisis constituted the MoU bailouts for each of the indebted eurozone members.[83] These measures marked the contractualisation of the bailout conditions between the individual state and the 'Troika' (the European Commission, the European Central Bank and the International Monetary Fund), largely outside, but deemed to be consistent with, the constitutional constraints of the EU and the those states.[84] These MoUs, operating in the realm of soft law, were followed by EU regulations.[85] Even with this later transformation, in Snyder's view, the process surrounding the crisis marked executive management as a new form of governance in the EU.

When describing EMU as it was originally constructed, Snyder does describe it as an unworkable hybrid. On the one hand, there was complete monetary union in the eurozone fully supported by binding legal norms, including Treaty provisions,[86] while on the other hand, there was no economic union, only economic coordination, rendering EMU itself a misnomer. The Stability and Growth Pact moved from soft law guidance, reporting and recommendations to the binding and punitive excessive deficit procedure, which, it very quickly became apparent, would not be invoked.[87] This experience – where asymmetric formation in law leads to urgent intergovernmental responses when a crisis arises – suggests that where there is a (well-documented and recognised) legal gap, when the system is subjected to pressures, the responses will be outside binding legal frameworks. The COVID-19 crisis did see first temporary, soft law responses (for state aid)[88]

[82] Treaty Establishing the ESM, signed on 2 February 2012, https://www.esm.europa.eu/legal-documents/esm-Treaty.

[83] European Commission, Directorate-General for Economic and Financial Affairs, 'The Economic Adjustment Programme for Cyprus', European Economy Occasional Papers 149/2013; European Commission, Directorate-General for Economic and Financial Affairs, 'The Economic Adjustment Programme for Greece', European Economy Occasional Papers 61/2010 (first of two programmes); European Commission, Director-General for Economic and Financial Affairs, 'The Economic Adjustment programme for Ireland', European Economy Occasional Paper 76/2011); European Commission, Director-General for Economic and Financial Affairs, 'The Economic Adjustment programme for Portugal', European Economy Occasional Paper 79/2011;); European Commission, Director-General for Economic and Financial Affairs, 'The Economic Adjustment Programme for Spain', European Economy Occasional Paper 103/2012.

[84] Case C-370/12 *Pringle v Government of Ireland and Others* ECLI:EU:C:2012:756; *Pringle v Government of Ireland and Others* [2012] IESC 47 (Irish Supreme Court); Case C-62/14 *Peter Gauweiler and Others v Deutscher Bundestag* ECLI:EU:C:2015:400; BVerfG, *Judgment of the Second Senate of 21 June 2016* – 2 BvR 2728/13 (German Federal Constitutional Court).

[85] Regulation (EU) No 472/2013 of the European Parliament and of the Council of 21 May 2013 on the strengthening of economic and budgetary surveillance of Member States in the euro area experiencing or threatened with serious difficulties with respect to their financial stability [2013] OJ L140, 27 May, 1; Regulation (EU) No 473/2013 of the European Parliament and of the Council of 21 May 2013 on common provisions for monitoring and assessing draft budgetary plans and ensuring the correction of excessive deficit of the Member States in the euro area [2013] OJ L 140, 27 May, 11.

[86] Title VII TFEU.

[87] D Hodson and I Maher, 'Soft Law and Sanctions: Economic Policy Coordination and Reform of the Stability and Growth Pact' (2004) 11(5) *Journal of European Public Policy* 806.

[88] European Commission, Communication, 'Coordinated economic response to the COVID-19 Outbreak' COM (2020) 112 final, 13 March; see O Ştefan, 'Entrenching Emergency Soft Law' *European Law Blog* (12 April 2022), https://europeanlawblog.eu/2022/04/12/entrenching-emergency-soft-law.

followed by legislation, which, tellingly, includes the post-COVID-19 support package involving major borrowing by the EU and spending within the Member States.[89]

E. Normative Hybridity

This experience of soft law supplementing and leading to hard law points to the hybrid nature of those measures across a wide range of policy fields, both within the EU and internationally. The challenge is how to manage what Snyder calls this internormativity. A key concern is one of inclusion. The forms of nodal governance[90] that inform the emergence of soft law can be opaque and exclusionary, thereby undermining democratic inputs and legitimation. Snyder warns that we cannot rely on courts to ensure this, and that all non-majoritarian institutions have a responsibility to ensure participation, legitimacy and accountability in decision making.[91] To realise this responsibility will require greater proceduralisation: legitimation is achieved in part through a process appropriate to the locale and exercise of power. He especially highlights how attention needs to be focused on that other key tool of governance, the network,[92] with algorithmic governance posing particular challenges. In concluding, he notes the multifarious challenges that society now faces, including climate change and inequality, which call for the rethinking of economic systems of capitalism. He acknowledges the weight of the challenge for legal scholars, reaching the surprising conclusion that 'it is time to abandon the label "soft law"'. He reminds us that the term is an oxymoron,[93] as the use of the word 'law' is misleading and redundant. The reader then realises that – unusually for a work of legal scholarship – Snyder is perhaps poking fun at us as he suggests the term 'soft law' be replaced by 'bamboo'. Bamboo is characterised by its strength and visibility, and is easily recognisable, fast-growing, resilient and flexible. More seriously, he notes that because of the way in which soft law, hard law, executive management and the roots of big data (the last of these is not discussed in the chapter) are so heavily intertwined that hybridity is now the rule and not the exception.

[89] The NextGenEU programme is a temporary post-recovery package worth more than €800 billion; see Regulation (EU) 2021/241 of the European Parliament and of the Council of 12 February 2021 establishing the Recovery and Resilience Facility [2021] OJ L57, 18 February, 17. See the discussion in O Ştefan, 'Soft Law Making at the European Commission: Not Much of a One-Institution Show' in Eliantonio, Korkea-aho and Mörth (n 1).

[90] On nodal governance generally, see S Burris, M Kempa and C Shearing, 'Changes in Governance: A Cross-Disciplinary Review of Current Scholarship' (2008) 41 *Arkon Law Review* 1.

[91] The forms of accountability can vary depending on the regulatory context; see generally MW Dowdle (ed), *Public Accountability: Designs, Dilemmas and Experiences* (Cambridge, Cambridge University Press, 2006).

[92] I Maher, 'Revisiting Soft Law: Governance, Regulation and Networks' in Eliantonio, Korkea-aho and Ştefan (n 6).

[93] Jääskinen notes that soft law is and is not law depending on which perspective of law one applies; see Jääskinen (n 51) 363.

V. Conclusion

This exegesis of two key works of Professor Snyder shows how soft law has developed both as a form of governance in the EU and as a focus of legal scholarship. The 1993 article, while providing the all-important definition of soft law, in fact sees it as one and not the central tool for achieving effectiveness of EU law. The focus is on the European Commission, with soft law largely being seen through the lens of communication. By 2022, the literature on soft law in the EU had grown exponentially, the CJEU has had to grapple with it increasingly, and national courts are faced with the unenviable task of taking it into account in their deliberations. The responses by the EU to the eurozone crisis were shaped initially largely by soft law and in a way that underlines concerns for democratic accountability and legitimacy. The extent to which soft law has become entrenched as a governance tool in the EU makes it difficult if not impossible to disentangle it or wish it away. Instead, while the challenges that the EU faces are formidable and require long-term responses for law and its effectiveness, for constitutionalisation and for legitimation, soft law remains. Not only does soft law remain, but it also needs to be seen as an inescapable if not essential tool of governance. As such, the challenge becomes one of ensuring a proceduralisation that retains soft law within the boundaries of EU (and institutional) competence, that minimises contractualisation at the intergovernmental level, and that ensures sufficient transparency and inclusion for its legitimation.

3

The Asian Infrastructure Investment Bank as a Site of Governance

MARK FELDMAN*

I. Introduction

The Asian Infrastructure Investment Bank (AIIB), based in Beijing, is now the world's second-largest multilateral development bank (MDB) by membership,[1] with 105 approved members,[2] including 54 approved non-regional members.[3] Financing infrastructure projects 'for the development of Asia, from the Pacific to the Mediterranean',[4] the AIIB is a global institution that retains strong regional characteristics. Given its global membership, the AIIB's potential to influence MDB governance is exceptional. Contributing to the AIIB's potential as a rule maker is the timing of its establishment, which followed years of widely expressed frustration with delayed governance reforms at major MDBs,

* The author thanks Susan Finder for valuable comments on an earlier draft of this chapter and Huang Xinxin and Tian He for excellent research assistance.

[1] KYA Haga, 'The Asian Infrastructure Investment Bank: A Qualified Success for Beijing's Economic Statecraft' (2021) 50 *Journal of Current Chinese Affairs* 391, 403.

[2] MA Weiss, 'Asian Infrastructure Investment Bank' (*Congressional Research Service*, 17 March 2022), https://crsreports.congress.gov/product/pdf/IF/IF10154: 'By the time the AIIB's Articles of Agreement were signed in December 2015, the Bank had 57 founding members, representing every region except North America. As of March 2022 membership has almost doubled, to 105 members.'

[3] See 'Members and Prospective Members of the Bank, Non-regional Members' (*Asian Infrastructure Investment Bank*), https://www.aiib.org/en/about-aiib/governance/members-of-bank/index.html. 'Prospective Members' are members who have been approved by the AIIB Board of Governors, but have not yet completed all required actions for membership. See, eg, 'AIIB Welcomes Two New Prospective Members' (*Asian Infrastructure Investment Bank*, 31 December 2019), https://www.aiib.org/en/news-events/news/2019/AIIB-Welcomes-Two-New-Prospective-Members.html, announcing that the AIIB Board of Governors 'has adopted resolutions approving two applicants to join the Bank, bringing its total approved membership to 102 … The two prospective members will officially join AIIB once they complete the required domestic processes and deposit the first installment of capital with the Bank.'

[4] N Lichtenstein, *A Comparative Guide to the Asian Infrastructure Investment Bank* (Oxford, Oxford University Press, 2018) 1.

including the world's largest MDB, the World Bank[5] and the International Monetary Fund (IMF).[6]

As an MDB with global membership, the AIIB can be viewed – and examined – as a site of governance within the framework developed by Professor Francis Snyder. Globalisation, under this framework, is governed by the 'totality' of a 'multiplicity' of sites of governance 'throughout the world'.[7] Each site of governance 'is a locus of decision-making with the authority to settle disputes'[8] that has structural ('comprising institutions, norms and dispute-settlement processes')[9] and relational ('relations between the site and other sites of governance')[10] dimensions. A site's structures and relations interact and influence one another.[11]

The AIIB's relationships with other MDBs as well as governments have influenced its structures; those structures, in turn, have encouraged the AIIB to further accelerate its relationship-building efforts. The AIIB's relationships have often encouraged adherence to established MDB practices, but at times have encouraged – indeed, arguably required – innovation. An additional AIIB relationship – with China's Belt and Road Initiative (BRI) – has received considerable attention due to a lack of clarity concerning the contours of the relationship and, by extension, the potential impact of the relationship on the AIIB's structures.

Regarding adherence to established MDB practices, one of the two core goals of the AIIB, as set out in its Articles of Agreement, is to 'promote regional cooperation and partnership in addressing development challenges by working in close collaboration with other multilateral and bilateral development institutions'.[12] In practice, such collaboration has included co-financing arrangements with other MDBs,[13]

[5] The World Bank is 'the oldest and the largest of the MDBs'; the World Bank Group includes the International Bank for Reconstruction and Development (IBRD), the International Development Association (IDA), the International Finance Corporation (IFC), the Multilateral Investment Guarantee Agency (MIGA) and the International Centre for Settlement of Investment Disputes (ICSID). See RM Nelson, 'Multilateral Development Banks: Overview and Issues for Congress' (*Congressional Research Service*, 11 February 2020), https://sgp.fas.org/crs/row/R41170.pdf; Weiss (n 2).

[6] The IMF, 'whose mandate is to ensure international financial stability, is not an MDB'. Nelson (n 5).

[7] F Snyder, *The EU, the WTO and China: Legal Pluralism and International Trade Regulation* (Oxford, Hart Publishing, 2010) 32.

[8] ibid 49.

[9] ibid.

[10] ibid.

[11] ibid.

[12] 'Articles of Agreement' (*Asian Infrastructure Investment Bank*, 29 June 2015), art 1(1), https://www.aiib.org/en/about-aiib/basic-documents/_download/articles-of-agreement/basic_document_english-bank_articles_of_agreement.pdf.

[13] See C Humphrey, 'From Drawing Board to Reality: The First Four Years of Operations at the Asian Infrastructure Investment Bank and New Development Bank' (2020) Working Paper of the G-24 and Global Development Policy Center of Boston University, 10, https://www.bu.edu/gdp/files/2020/04/Humphrey_AIIB.NDB_.April2020.FINAL_.pdf: 'AIIB has relied heavily on co-financing with existing MDBs, making use of their project preparation capacity, administrative procedures and environmental and social safeguard frameworks. Just under half (49%) of AIIB's approved projects through 2019 (41.5% of total financing) are co-financed with other MDBs, mainly the World Bank Group, ADB and EBRD, two with the European Investment Bank and one each with the Eurasian Development Bank and the Islamic Development Bank.' See also 'Partnerships' (*Asian Infrastructure Investment Bank*),

cooperation framework agreements with MDBs,[14] and a joint MDB climate action statement delivered at the 2021 United Nations Climate Change Conference (COP26).[15] The AIIB has highlighted how collaboration with other MDBs promotes 'harmonization of policies' and the development of 'common approach[es]' to project management.[16] Adherence to international standards is reinforced by the AIIB's global membership. As observed by the AIIB's President, Jin Liqun: 'Only when you have very high standards could you hope to bring a number of countries, particularly countries in the West, to join and to work with you.'[17]

Regarding innovation, many AIIB members had been frustrated by the slow pace of reforms at major MDBs and the IMF, particularly with respect to the disproportionately weak voice of emerging economies at those institutions. Concerns were also raised about potential conflicts of interest arising from the 'dual' duties of World Bank directors, who must balance a representational duty to a director's government with a fiduciary duty to the World Bank as an institution.[18] The slow pace of reforms in those areas created a need for innovation, which the AIIB has pursued in a number of areas, including the adoption of measures that reflect the 'desirability of a greater voice for regional and smaller members'[19] as well as the development of a non-resident Board, which avoids 'co-managerial' dynamics associated with resident MDB Boards.[20]

The AIIB's path to becoming the world's second-largest MDB by membership has required a careful balance of 'Heritage and Innovation'[21] – a commitment to established MDB standards and practices alongside responsiveness to long-held

https://www.aiib.org/en/about-aiib/who-we-are/partnership/index.html (the AIIB has signed co-financing framework agreements with the World Bank, the Asian Development Bank and the European Bank for Reconstruction and Development).

[14] 'Partnerships' (n 13) (listing many MDBs that have signed memoranda on joint cooperation with the AIIB).

[15] 'Collective Climate Ambition – A Joint Statement at COP26 by the Multilateral Development Banks' (*Asian Development Bank*, 5 November 2021), https://www.adb.org/news/collective-climate-ambition-joint-statement-cop26-multilateral-development-banks. The Joint Statement emphasises the importance of coordination for achieving the goals of the Paris Agreement, with MDBs committing to pursue 'an active coordination and partnership approach with organizations and coalitions' when implementing their climate strategies to achieve the Paris Agreement goals.

[16] 'Environmental and Social Framework' (*Asian Infrastructure Investment Bank*, February 2016), 6, https://www.aiib.org/en/policies-strategies/_download/environment-framework/20160226043633542.pdf.

[17] 'How We Rebuild: A Conversation with President Jin Liqun on the Asian Infrastructure Investment Bank's Fifth Anniversary' (*The Brookings Institution*, 25 January 2021) 8, https://www.brookings.edu/wp-content/uploads/2021/01/20210125_aiib_transcript.pdf.

[18] 'Repowering the World Bank for the 21st Century: Report of the High-Level Commission on Modernization of World Bank Group Governance' (October 2009) 31–32, <https://ycsg.yale.edu/sites/default/files/files/world_bank_governance_report.pdf.

[19] Lichtenstein (n 4) 37.

[20] 'Repowering the World Bank for the 21st Century' (n 18) 40: 'A Board abiding by sound governance principles should not have a co-managerial role.'

[21] Lichtenstein (n 4) 36.

frustrations of governments over delayed MDB reforms. Interactions between the AIIB's structures and relations have played a central role with respect to the AIIB's adherence to international best practices, as well as the AIIB's development of innovative approaches to MDB governance. Those interactions have ultimately led to a Beijing-based MDB that can be viewed, under Snyder's framework, as a unique and consequential site of governance.

II. Sites of Governance

Under Snyder's framework, sites of governance represent, collectively, 'a new form of global legal pluralism'[22] in which globalisation is governed by 'the totality of strategically determined, situationally specific and often episodic conjunctions of a multiplicity of sites throughout the world'.[23] Snyder views global legal pluralism as one conception of how globalisation is governed.[24] Legal pluralism 'has been defined as "the presence in a social field of more than one legal order"'.[25] As developed by Sally Falk Moore, various 'social fields' – 'to which an individual "belongs"' – are 'interposed' between 'the body politic and the individual'; such social fields 'have their own customs and rules and the means of coercing or inducing compliance'.[26]

Each site of governance, under Snyder's framework, has two dimensions: 'a structural dimension, comprising institutions, norms and dispute-settlement processes; and a relational dimension, which refers to relations between the site and other sites of governance'.[27] Those two dimensions interact: 'Structures affect, condition or determine relations. In turn, relations affect, condition or determine structures.'[28] Global legal pluralism, as developed by Snyder, 'concentrates' on those two dimensions of sites of governance and on 'the role of strategic actors in supporting, sustaining and transforming' the two dimensions;

[22] Snyder (n 7) 22.
[23] ibid 32.
[24] ibid 25.
[25] ibid 29, quoting J Griffiths, 'What is Legal Pluralism?' (1986) 24 *Journal of Legal Pluralism* 1.
[26] SF Moore, 'Law and Social Change: The Semi-autonomous Social Field as an Appropriate Subject of Study' (1973) 7 *Law & Society Review* 719. See also P Zumbansen, 'Defining the Space of Transnational Law: Legal Theory, Global Governance, and Legal Pluralism' (2012) 21(2) *Transnational Law & Contemporary Problems* 305, 33: 'Legal sociology and legal pluralism, in particular, have long been developing tools to scrutinize the tension between official and unofficial norm creation, between hard and soft law, and between what at least in the West has often been depicted as a juxtaposition of state law-making on the one hand and private ordering or social norms on the other.' See also PS Berman, 'Global Legal Pluralism' (2007) 80 *Southern California Law Review* 1155, 1170: 'legal pluralists have studied those situations in which two or more state and non-state normative systems occupy the same social field and must negotiate the resulting hybrid legal space'.
[27] Snyder (n 7) 49.
[28] ibid 49.

such strategic actors include corporations, governments and non-governmental organisations.[29]

Considered within Snyder's sites of governance framework, the AIIB possesses a structural dimension and a relational dimension that do indeed interact and influence one another, and at the same time are supported and transformed by a range of strategic actors, both public and private. The structural and relational dimensions of the AIIB are discussed in turn below.

III. The Structural Dimension of the AIIB

The AIIB commenced operations in 2016 with 57 Founding Members,[30] following negotiations from 2013 to 2015 and the entry into force of the AIIB's Articles of Agreement in December 2015.[31] As discussed by Natalie Lichtenstein:

> The specific proposal for AIIB was floated in October 2013 by Chinese President Xi Jinping during a Southeast Asian visit, focused on the infrastructure needs of Asia … by October 2014, 22 Asian countries, organized by China, had concluded a Memorandum of Understanding on Establishing the Asian Infrastructure Investment Bank. These countries, joined in the subsequent Charter negotiations by 37 others from Asia, Europe, Africa and Latin America, agreed on the AIIB Charter, signed in June 2015.[32]

As set out in the AIIB's Articles of Agreement, the purpose of the AIIB is to, first, invest 'in infrastructure and other productive sectors' in order to 'foster sustainable economic development, create wealth and improve infrastructure connectivity in Asia' and, second, to 'promote regional cooperation and partnership in addressing development challenges by working in close collaboration with other multilateral and bilateral development institutions'.[33] Many observers have highlighted the role of the AIIB in responding to an existing infrastructure 'gap'[34] in Asia, where demand for infrastructure greatly exceeds supply, due to

[29] ibid 92.

[30] See 'Introduction, Five Key Accomplishments' (*Asian Infrastructure Investment Bank*), https://www.aiib.org/en/about-aiib/index.html.

[31] See 'AIIB's Charter Enters into Force on 25 December 2015' (*Asian Infrastructure Investment Bank*, 16 January 2016), https://www.aiib.org/en/news-events/news/2016/AIIBs-Charter-Enters-into-Force-On-25-December-2015.html.

[32] N Lichtenstein, 'Governance of the Asian Infrastructure Investment Bank in Comparative Context' in P Quayle and X Gao (eds), *AIIB Yearbook of International Law 2018* (Leiden, Brill, 2018) 88.

[33] 'Articles of Agreement' (n 12), art 1(1).

[34] M Huang, N Chen and Y Chen, 'An Analysis on the Potential Competitiveness of the Asian Infrastructure Investment Bank' (2017) 23(2) *Asia-Pacific Development Journal* 19, 27: 'there is still a wide gap between infrastructure financing need and supply. For example, the Asian Development Bank Institute expects the demand of the 32 developing members of ADB for non-cross-border infrastructure investment will amount to $8.22 trillion during the period of 2010–2020'.

a combination of insufficient capacity,[35] competing MDB policy priorities[36] and inefficiency.[37]

The structural dimension of the AIIB has been shaped, in significant part, by two competing forces, which can be understood as 'Heritage and Innovation'.[38] Regarding heritage, the AIIB starts with a '"bone structure" that fits squarely within the MDB family history', including the AIIB's mandate (which extends beyond infrastructure connectivity to include 'other productive sectors'), capital and financial structure (which 'hew closely to accepted rules for sound financial management'), membership rules (which 'build on the rules and practices of others') and a 'three-tiered governance structure' consisting of a Board of Governors, a Board of Directors and a President (which 'rest on a well-polished foundation').[39]

Regarding innovation, the area of governance in particular 'has seen a considerable number of innovations',[40] including a non-resident Board of Directors (which is innovative but not unique, given that the AIIB Board of Directors is 'among the non-resident MDB Boards'),[41] a President position that is 'limited to two terms',[42] an 'open, transparent and merit-based process' for selecting

[35] See J Ransdell, 'Institutional Innovation by the Asian Infrastructure Investment Bank' (2018) 9(1) *Asian Journal of International Law* 125, 130 ('Even with investment from the AIIB, demand for MDB infrastructure loans in Asia is forecast to outpace supply'); H Yu, 'Motivation Behind China's "One Belt, One Road" Initiatives and Establishment of the Asian Infrastructure Investment Bank' (2017) 26 *Journal of Contemporary China* 353, 359 ('For instance, the Director General of the Cambodia Chamber of Commerce states that Cambodia badly needs more foreign investment to construct deep-water ports and other infrastructure facilities to accommodate large-scale cargo ships … However, the World Bank and the Asian Development Bank (ADB) combined do not have adequate capacity to meet this huge investment demand').

[36] See, H Wang, 'From "Taoguang Yanghui" to "Yousou Zuowei": China's Engagement in Financial Minilateralism' (2014) CIGI Papers No 52, 3: 'Chinese officials point out that the World Bank and the ADB [Asian Development Bank] have focused their attention on poverty reduction and provided very limited investment in infrastructure. They claim that the [AIIB] will help developing countries in the region, especially low-income countries, to meet their infrastructure financing needs.' See also 'How We Rebuild: A Conversation with President Jin Liqun on the Asian Infrastructure Investment Bank's Fifth Anniversary' (*Brookings Institution*, 25 January 2021), https://www.brookings.edu/events/how-we-rebuild-a-conversation-with-president-jin-liqun-on-the-asian-infrastructure-investment-banks-fifth-anniversary ('over the last three or four decades', the World Bank and Asian Development Bank have appeared to focus on poverty reduction 'which is vitally important', but will leave the banks 'with less capital to be invested in infrastructure') (comments of Jin Liqun).

[37] MA Weiss, 'Asian Infrastructure Investment Bank (AIIB)' (*Congressional Research Service*, 3 February 2017) 12, https://digital.library.unt.edu/ark:/67531/metadc958727/m1: 'according to Yukon Huang, a former World Bank director for operations in Asia and Europe, many standards and procedures of existing MDBs are "frustratingly bureaucratic, costly and ill-suited to dealing with the real needs of client borrowers"' (quoting Yukon Huang, 'China Has a Role to Play in Setting the "Right" Standards' *Financial Times* (8 April 2015)).

[38] Lichtenstein (n 4) 36. Bin Gu and Chengjin Xu similarly have observed that AIIB corporate governance 'boasts a dual characteristic of heritage and innovation … vis-à-vis the traditional multilateral development bank (MDB) family'. B Gu and C Xu, 'International Organizations and Corporate Governance: The Case of the AIIB' (2022) 30(2) *Asia Pacific Law Review* 309.

[39] Lichtenstein (n 4) 37.

[40] ibid 36.

[41] ibid.

[42] ibid 37.

the President and Vice Presidents which 'sets a new legal standard',[43] and a set of measures[44] that 'acknowledge' the 'desirability of a greater voice for regional and smaller members'.[45]

With respect to the AIIB's structural dimension, this combination of heritage and innovation has contributed greatly to the Bank's rapid growth in membership by simultaneously assuring governments that the Beijing-based MDB would largely track well-established MDB practices, while, at the same time, addressing long-standing and widely expressed frustrations with delayed governance reforms at major MDBs, which are discussed below.

A. Delayed MDB Governance Reforms

A 2009 report prepared by the High-Level Commission on Modernization of World Bank Group Governance[46] found that aspects of World Bank governance had become outdated in light of changes to the global economy occurring over the six decades following the establishment of the World Bank in the 1940s. As stated in the report, the World Bank Group's:

> [D]ecision-making process is widely seen as too exclusive, offering many member countries too little voice and too few opportunities for participation ... [a]nd certain conventions and practices have contributed to the perception that the institution is accountable and responsive only to a handful of shareholders at best. These weaknesses spring in large measure from the fact that the World Bank's governance – forged in the 1940s – has not kept pace with historical change.[47]

The prior year, Henry M Paulson, who then served as United States Secretary of the Treasury, similarly had called for:

> [C]ontinued reform of the International Financial Institutions like the World Bank and the IMF to allow for greater participation of developing nations. The pressure on these institutions to respond swiftly and effectively has never been greater. But they

[43] ibid.

[44] Those measures include: (i) a special allocation of 600 Founding Member votes to all members who qualified as Founding Members; (ii) priority accorded to Founding Members regarding the rotation for Directors and Alternate Directors on the Board of Directors; and (iii) according each member an equal number of basic votes, which are set as a percentage of total votes rather than as a fixed number of votes, thereby benefiting smaller shareholders 'even as the overall number of share votes grows with capital increases over time' (Lichtenstein (n 4) 29). Founding Members are those members who deposited an instrument of ratification by December 2016; see Ransdell (n 35) 136.

[45] Lichtenstein (n 4) 37.

[46] 'Repowering the World Bank for the 21st Century' (n 18). The Commission 'was created by World Bank Group President Robert B. Zoellick in October 2008 to focus on the modernization of World Bank Group governance so the World Bank Group can operate more dynamically, effectively, efficiently, and legitimately in a transformed political economy'. (Johannes F Linn, 'The Zedillo Commission Report on World Bank Reform: A Stepping Stone for the G-20 Summits in 2010' (*Brookings*, 18 November 2009), https://www.brookings.edu/articles/the-zedillo-commission-report-on-world-bank-reform-a-stepping-stone-for-the-g-20-summits-in-2010, quoting the World Bank website).

[47] 'Repowering the World Bank for the 21st Century' (n 18) ix.

> are constrained by outdated governance structures and policies. Since coming to Washington, I have consistently said that for these institutions to remain relevant, their membership must reflect seismic shifts in the global economy.[48]

More than a decade after such calls for reform, the disproportionately weak voice of emerging economies at the World Bank and IMF persists. In a 2022 essay by Srinivas and Hofman, the authors observe that the BRICS' (Brazil, Russia, India, China and South Africa) share of gross domestic product measured in Purchasing Power Parity (PPP) terms 'rose from about 18% in 2000 to about 31% by 2020', but that 'the role and voice of these countries in the global financial architecture as measured by their voting shares … does not adequately reflect this new economic reality'.[49]

Frustrations with the slow pace of governance reforms at major MDBs and the IMF have been widely expressed.[50] As stated in a Congressional Research Service

[48] 'Remarks by Secretary Henry M. Paulson, Jr. at The Ronald Reagan Presidential Library' (*US Department of the Treasury*, 20 November 2008), https://home.treasury.gov/news/press-releases/hp1285.

[49] PS Srinivas and B Hofman, 'New Development Bank's Role in the International Financial Architecture' *Global Policy* (25 July 2022), https://www.globalpolicyjournal.com/blog/25/07/2022/new-development-banks-role-international-financial-architecture. See also Yu (n 35) ('as of December 2015, China's total holding in the ADB was … only 6.45%, whilst Japan and the US held 15.62% and 15.51% respectively'); Humphrey (n 13) 2–3 (emerging markets and developing economies 'for decades have complained that policy and operational decisions at the legacy MDBs have been controlled by G7 nations and the U.S. in particular. These complaints have become louder in recent years as the economic weight of many EMDCs – especially China – has grown sharply, but their voting power at the legacy MDBs has not kept pace … For example, Japan has almost triple the voting power of China (15% to 5.5%) at ADB, despite an economy about one-fifth the size, while India has similar voting power to Canada at the World Bank (2.9% to 2.5%) even though its economy is about 10 times larger').

[50] See H Wang, 'The New Development Bank and the Asian Infrastructure Investment Bank: China's Ambiguous Approach to Global Financial Governance' (2019) 50(1) *Development and Change* 221, 223 ('Developing countries had long sought to gain greater representation at the World Bank and the [IMF] but the so-called voice reform in those institutions had been slow and limited'); Ransdell (n 35) 125 ('Chinese grievances with incumbent MDBs largely reflected broader dissatisfaction among borrower countries'); A Krishnan, 'The Dragon Raises a Lair: India Backs the China-Led Superbank' *India Today* (20 January 2016), https://www.indiatoday.in/magazine/neighbours/story/20160201-china-led-superbank-asian-infrastructure-investment-bank-828327-2016-01-20 ('"We are now not entirely dependent on Bretton Woods institutions, that is a basic reason [for India's decision to join the AIIB]" India's representative on the AIIB's 12-member board of directors, additional secretary in the ministry of finance Dinesh Sharma, told *India Today*. "We have been banging our head for reforms at the IMF and World Bank, but they are delaying"'). See also Haga (n 1) 394 ('After the 2008 Global Economic Crisis, Beijing found frustrating the slow pace of governance reforms within the US-dominated IFIs [international financial institutions] … China had the economic capability to contribute more, but the US Congress was resistant to authorizing any changes'); RM Nelson and MA Weiss, 'IMF Reforms: Issues for Congress' (*Congressional Research Service*, 9 April 2015) 13, https://crsreports.congress.gov/product/pdf/R/R42844/14 ('In order for key parts of the reform package to take effect, IMF rules dictate that the reform must be formally accepted by three-fifths of IMF members … Under this formula … approval by the United States, the IMF's largest stakeholder, is essential. To date, no action has been taken by [the US] Congress on the necessary legislation').

report, the AIIB and the Shanghai-based New Development Bank (NDB) 'are the first two major MDBs to be created in decades' and, in the view of their proponents:

> [A]ddress the long-held frustrations of many emerging markets and developing countries that the governance of existing institutions, including the World Bank and the IMF, has not been reformed to reflect their growing importance in the global economy. For example, the NDB has stressed that, unlike the World Bank and IMF, each participant country will have equivalent voting rates and none of the countries will have veto power.[51]

Although the NDB's departure from existing MDB governance models is sharper than that of the AIIB,[52] the AIIB nevertheless provides a clear alternative, in terms of governance, to existing major MDBs. From its inception, the AIIB has been distinctive, given that the organisation was 'initiated entirely by non-Western states'.[53] Regarding particular aspects of governance, the AIIB's preference for a non-resident Board of Directors – which provides a bold alternative to the existing practice of many major MDBs – merits close consideration.

B. The AIIB's Departure from the MDB Resident Board Model

Chris Humphrey notes that although 'China proved willing to be flexible' in AIIB discussions with European states concerning many established MDB standards (including environmental and social safeguards), China was less flexible in discussions concerning a non-resident Board; European opposition to a non-resident Board was 'unsuccessful'[54] and China ultimately preferred to depart from the established practice of many MDBs by adopting a non-resident Board.[55]

The AIIB's adoption of a non-resident Board has been strongly criticised by some observers. For example, Robert Orr, who had served as US Ambassador

[51] Nelson (n 5) 17–18. Each of the five NDB members 'subscribes US$10 billion … of the bank's capital and has 20 per cent of the votes' (Wang (n 50) 226).

[52] Regarding voting power in particular, the AIIB maintains a weighted voting system in which voting power is not distributed equally among members. Specifically, an AIIB member's voting power consists of the sum of its share votes (corresponding to the number of shares of stock held by a member), basic votes (an equal number of which are allocated to each member) and (where applicable) Founding Member votes. See Lichtenstein (n 32) 102.

[53] Ransdell (n 35) 126.

[54] Humphrey (n 13) 3.

[55] Natalie Lichtenstein has identified many MDBs that rely on resident Boards (including the African Development Bank, the Asian Development Bank and the European Bank for Reconstruction and Development), but at the same time has identified several 'international financial institutions that have functioned for decades with non-resident Board mechanisms', including the Council of Europe Development Bank and the Caribbean Development Bank: Lichtenstein (n 32) 94. Lichtenstein further observes that 'discussions on the IBRD and IMF Charters at Bretton Woods in 1944 featured a debate on residency, which was not settled in favor of resident boards until the inaugural meeting of the Board of Governors in 1946': Lichtenstein (n 32) 95.

to the ADB and as Dean of the ADB's Board of Directors, argued that 'without a permanent board that has day-to-day oversight' of the AIIB's operations, the Bank's 'ability to ensure' that the interests of taxpayers (who are represented by the Bank's shareholders) are 'guaranteed' is 'greatly diminished'.[56] Orr further argued that the absence of a resident Board inhibited 'transparency and accountability' and reinforced 'a perception by some that the AIIB will be much more centrally controlled by the Chinese government than is the case with the largest shareholder in other MDBs'.[57] In Orr's view, establishing a resident board would have removed 'one of the major concerns of Washington and Tokyo' with respect to the AIIB.[58]

But the AIIB's departure from the past practice of many major MDBs with respect to Board residency received positive reactions from many observers[59] and was consistent with pre-existing criticism of MDB resident Boards, which – like other criticism of MDB governance – had not been adequately addressed by existing MDBs.[60]

Indeed, the Modernization of World Bank Group Governance report raised concerns in connection with a 'dual duty' issue faced by World Bank directors, who, as noted above, must balance two separate duties: a representational duty to

[56] RM Orr, 'Why the Asian Infrastructure Investment Bank Needs Resident Directors' *China Dialogue* (23 August 2016), https://chinadialogue.net/en/business/9206-why-the-asian-infrastructure-investment-bank-needs-resident-directors.

[57] ibid. See also Weiss (n 2) 2 ('China's large voting power combined with the AIIB's nonresident executive board have led some analysts to question the AIIB's independence from China's leaders'); GT Chin, 'Asian Infrastructure Investment Bank: Governance Innovation and Prospects' (2016) 22 *Global Governance* 11, 16 ('Skeptics have derided Beijing as trying to give the [AIIB's] management more unchecked power over the institution. For example, Edward Truman, a former senior US treasury official, remarked that "I understand why the [United States] or other advanced countries prefer the resident board … We do not trust the likely management"') (citing Lingling Wei and Bob Davis, 'China Forgoes Veto at New Bank to Win Key European Nations' Support' *Wall Street Journal* (23 March 2015), https://www.wsj.com/articles/china-forgoes-veto-power-at-new-bank-to-win-key-european-nations-support-1427131055); DCK Chow, 'Why China Established the Asia Infrastructure Investment Bank' (2016) 49(5) *Vanderbilt Journal of Transnational Law* 1255, 1261 ('the establishment of the AIIB brings within the control of the Chinese Communist Party, for the first time, a prestigious multilateral organization consisting of many of the closest allies of the United States, but without the presence of the United States or Japan').

[58] Orr (n 56).

[59] See Gu and Xu (n 38) 6, discussing advantages of non-resident Board model for MDBs, including the reduction of 'large financial and human cost for the Bank', reducing potential conflicts of interest associated with 'dual role' of MDB directors (who represent both a government and the institution) and eliminating the 'co-managerial problem by delegating project approval authority to the President'; M Callaghan and P Hubbard, 'The Asian Infrastructure Investment Bank: Multilateralism on the Silk Road' (2016) 9 *China Economic Journal* 116, 132, observing that the 'AIIB adoption of a non-resident board opens the possibility of a more effective board that provides strategic oversight and direction to the bank, as well as holding management accountable for its performance', which if achieved would be 'a major advance on the arrangement in the World Bank and ADB'; such an achievement, however, would require the 'roles, responsibilities and expectations of the board and management' to be 'clearly articulated'. See also Chin (n 58) 16: 'Forgoing a resident board could save friction and governance costs for the AIIB and allow the money to be redirected for loans, investment, technical assistance, policy advisory, or training purposes.'

[60] See, eg, Gu and Xu (n 38), who stated that the Modernization of World Bank Group Governance report 'effected no change on Board residency in the World Bank'.

a director's government and a fiduciary duty to the World Bank as an institution.[61] These two duties, the report found, 'conflict at least occasionally'.[62] Responding to that conflict, the report recommended that 'the political level of the Executive Board should be elevated and its role reoriented toward strategy definition and oversight',[63] with responsibility for approval of all World Bank Group financing operations being 'transferred to Management', which would 'eliminate the conflict of interest that is currently embedded in the Executive Board's decision-making process'.[64]

The AIIB's non-resident Board model is strikingly consistent with that recommendation. As observed by Bin Gu and Chengjin Xu, the AIIB's founders designed a non-resident Board of Directors during negotiations from 2013 to 2015, which allowed the AIIB:

> [T]o avoid the problems brought forth by an executive Board in traditional MDBs: the dual position of the Directors and the co-managerial dilemma between the Board and management ... A non-resident Board enables the MDB to function as an autonomous international organization, free from daily operating interventions by Board members.[65]

Notably, the European Investment Bank – an 'atypical MDB' that had adopted a non-resident Board – 'contributed substantially to the drafting of the AIIB charter, with its non-resident Board arrangement being an immediate inspiration for the AIIB'.[66]

The non-resident Board 'makes the bank president more directly responsible than the presidents of other MDBs for managing projects successfully'.[67] One related criticism of the AIIB's non-resident Board model is the risk – identified by some observers – that there might be insufficient oversight of the AIIB President.[68]

[61] 'Repowering the World Bank for the 21st Century' (n 18) 31–32.
[62] ibid.
[63] ibid 36.
[64] ibid 40. The 2018 Report of the G20 Eminent Persons Group on Global Financial Governance similarly recommended that MDB Boards should focus on strategic issues. See 'Making the Global Financial System Work for All', Report of the G20 Eminent Persons Group on Global Financial Governance (October 2018), 26, https://www.globalfinancialgovernance.org/report-of-the-g20-epg-on-gfg: 'Boards should focus on strategic issues and directions and move away from a disproportionate tilt towards operational decision making and transactional functions ... consideration should be given to IMF, World Bank and other MDBs amending their Articles of Agreement where necessary, to allow for delegation of appropriate decision-making responsibilities to the Managements of the respective institutions.'
[65] Gu and Xu (n 38). See also Ransdell (n 36) 141: 'In a resident BD [Board of Directors] arrangement, executive officers generally provide managerial services and conduct preliminary investigations before presenting to the directors ... This dynamic often yields potentially disruptive director-management tensions.'
[66] Gu and Xu (n 38).
[67] Haga (n 1) 401.
[68] See R Wihtol, 'The New Development Banks: Paradigm Shift or Poor Imitation?' *The Interpreter* (28 November 2019), https://www.lowyinstitute.org/the-interpreter/new-development-banks-paradigm-shift-or-poor-imitation ('the AIIB has a non-resident board that meets quarterly and has delegated project approval to the Chinese president, Jin Liqun. China justified this arrangement on efficiency grounds, but some prospective members, most notably Australia, raised concerns that this would

Measures adopted by the AIIB in 2018 and 2019 – the Accountability Framework[69] and Oversight Mechanism,[70] respectively – address such criticisms by enhancing institutional oversight of the President.[71]

The Accountability Framework establishes four safeguards: three internal and one independent.[72] The three internal safeguards are composed of the Bank's operational management ('whereby project reviews pass through the Screening Committee, the Executive Committee and the Investment Committee'), compliance and risk management, and internal audit function.[73] The fourth safeguard is provided by the Complaints-resolution, Evaluation and Integrity Unit (CEIU), which consolidates the three separate oversight functions – project-related complaints, project evaluation and anti-fraud/anti-corruption efforts – 'under one roof'.[74]

The Oversight Mechanism establishes a 'Directors' Forum' – sessions at which Directors have the opportunity 'to share information and exchange views' among themselves and the CEIU Managing Director.[75] Directors' Forum sessions are chaired by the 'Dean of the Board', a position created by the Oversight Mechanism.[76] The Dean 'shall be the longest serving Director of a different nationality to that of the President, and who is willing to take on the role'.[77] The AIIB President does not attend Directors' Forum sessions.[78]

Broad 'dissatisfaction among borrower countries'[79] arising from 'slow and limited'[80] reforms at major MDBs and the IMF created a need for innovation at

weaken oversight'); Ransdell (n 35) 139 ('The Super Majority required to elect the AIIB President grants China significant, if not unlimited, control over the President, which is especially significant considering the AIIB's lack of a resident BD [Board of Directors]'); Chow (n 57) 1288–89 ('If the work of the AIIB directors is similar to the work of directors of large business corporations, the directors' quarterly meetings will consist of reports by the management and a casting of votes on issues that have been already prepared for discussion by the management team, all handpicked by the President').

[69] See 'Accountability Framework' (*Asian Infrastructure Investment Bank*), https://www.aiib.org/en/about-aiib/governance/accountability-framework/index.html.

[70] See 'Oversight Mechanism' (*Asian Infrastructure Investment Bank*), https://www.aiib.org/en/about-aiib/governance/oversight-mechanism/index.html.

[71] See Gu and Xu (n 38), who observe that there is 'no formal process for the Board to evaluate presidential performance in the World Bank, which has long been criticized … Therefore, it is sensible for the AIIB to design the Directors' Forum [established by the Oversight Mechanism] for appropriate checks and balances against the President, complementing the CEIU [Complaints-Resolution, Evaluation, and Integrity Unit established by the Accountability Framework] in the context of a non-resident Board in particular'.

[72] ibid.

[73] ibid.

[74] ibid.

[75] 'AIIB Paper on the Oversight Mechanism' (*Asian Infrastructure Investment Bank*, 10 July 2019) para 39, https://www.aiib.org/en/about-aiib/governance/_common/_download/paper-on-the-oversight-mechanism-public.pdf.

[76] ibid.

[77] ibid para 41.

[78] Gu and Xu (n 38).

[79] Ransdell (n 35) 125.

[80] Wang (n 50) 223.

the AIIB. Regarding the development of the AIIB's non-resident Board in particular, the European Investment Bank played a key role as both an 'inspiration' for the model generally and, more specifically, a contributor during the drafting of the AIIB charter.[81] Such interactions illustrate how the AIIB's relationships with governments and MDBs have shaped its structures, including innovative aspects of its governance models.

At the same time, maintaining close relationships with a wide range of governments has required the AIIB to make firm commitments to international best practices. As recently stated by AIIB President Jin Liqun: 'Only when you have very high standards could you hope to bring a number of countries, particularly countries in the West, to join and to work with you.'[82] The Accountability Framework and the Oversight Mechanism reflect recent efforts by the AIIB to maintain such standards by developing 'appropriate checks and balances'[83] in a context where there is no resident Board to provide 'day-to-day oversight'[84] of the AIIB's operations.

As noted above, the AIIB's path to becoming the world's second-largest MDB by membership has required a careful balance of 'Heritage and Innovation'.[85] The AIIB's structures have had to respond to long-held frustrations of governments over delayed MDB reforms, while, at the same time, reassuring governments that the Beijing-based MDB would adhere to international best practices. The AIIB's respect for heritage, as reflected in the Bank's adherence to international standards, is discussed below.

C. The AIIB's Adherence to International Best Practices

Criticism of the AIIB has often focused on whether it would adhere to international standards.[86] But the AIIB's commitment to international standards – captured in significant part by its embrace of 'lean, clean and green' operations – was made clear even before its formal launch of operations. In December 2015, discussing the launch of the AIIB, Jin Liqun stated:

> Our operations will be lean, clean and green. That means keeping a check on bureaucracy and maintaining a relatively flat organizational structure; managing costs and using modern technology effectively; and avoiding duplication and overlap of functions … It also means fostering an institutional culture based on professional integrity and

[81] Gu and Xu (n 38).
[82] 'How We Rebuild' (n 36) 8.
[83] Gu and Xu (n 38).
[84] Orr (n 56).
[85] Lichtenstein (n 4) 36.
[86] See Weiss (n 2) 2 ('Some observers argue that competitive pressure from the AIIB and China's bilateral sources of financing may lead some MDBs to reconsider the World Bank's international best practices in procurement policies and other safeguards'); Nelson (n 5) 12 ('Whether the AIIB embraces strong environmental and social safeguards, and other policy-related conditions, remains a concern for

> exemplary governance, with no tolerance for corruption … Finally, it means concern for sustainability … The management of environmental … and social risks and impacts is central to successful development outcomes.[87]

Responses to the AIIB's commitment to 'lean, clean and green' practices have ranged from positive[88] to sceptical.[89] But the extraordinarily rapid growth in the Bank's global membership – notwithstanding serious governance-related concerns raised by major economies such as the US and Japan[90] – is clear,[91] which reflects, at a minimum, significant levels of confidence in the AIIB's commitment to its stated principles. For an MDB to achieve the 'very high standards'[92] that are required to attract global participation, a significant degree of respect for heritage – in the sense of adherence to core structures found 'within the MDB family history'[93] – is required.

The AIIB's structural dimension has been shaped by the competing forces of heritage and innovation. With respect to each of those forces, the AIIB's experience reflects, under Snyder's sites of governance framework, the interaction of

many analysts, including Members of Congress, who played a major role in establishing robust safeguard policies at the MDBs and have used U.S. leadership at the institutions to advance best practices on these issues').

[87] J Liqun, 'AIIB to Benefit Asia and Beyond' *China Daily* (28 December 2015), https://www.chinadaily.com.cn/bizchina/2015-12/28/content_22838181.htm.

[88] See B Gu, 'Chinese Multilateralism in the AIIB' (2017) 20 *Journal of International Economic Law* 138: 'It is the commitment of the AIIB membership to "lean, clean and green" that makes the arrangement of infrastructure financing an indivisible whole. And such arrangement generates among AIIB membership expectation of "diffuse reciprocity" – that is, the arrangement expects to yield a rough equivalence of benefits among AIIB membership in the aggregate and over time.'

[89] See G Grieger, 'Asian Infrastructure Investment Bank: How Lean, Clean and Green is the AIIB?' (*European Parliamentary Research Service*, 12 February 2021) 12, www.europarl.europa.eu/thinktank/sv/document.html?reference=EPRS_BRI%282021%29679086: 'The AIIB's catchy "lean, clean and green" slogan has raised huge expectations. However, the bank has not become a leader in setting green standards.'

[90] See Chow (n 57) 1259 ('Given China's track record, the United States argued that the AIIB would become a rival to the World Bank and IMF in lending but would not follow the best practices in international lending promoted by these institutions, such as making loans to countries conditional on the recipients' commitment to transparency, non-corruption in government, environmental sustainability … among other conditions'); J Garnaut and P Wen, 'Cabinet Split over "Asian Bank" after UK's Shock Support' *Sydney Morning Herald* (13 March 2015) ('Foreign Minister Julie Bishop and her department have argued that Australia should use its bargaining power by holding out [on joining the AIIB] until China commits to international standards that are consistent with Australia's vision of an open, rules-based regional order'); KV Kesavan, 'US-Japan Dilemma over China-led AIIB' (*ORF*, 1 April 2015), https://www.orfonline.org/research/us-japan-dilemma-over-china-led-aiib ('Foreign Minister Fumio Kishida commented on March 30 that Japan has not received any clear assurances dispelling its concerns on the bank's governance').

[91] See Weiss (n 2) 1: 'By the time the AIIB's Articles of Agreement were signed in December 2015, the Bank had 57 founding members, representing every region except North America. As of March 2022, membership has almost doubled, to 105 members.'

[92] 'How We Rebuild' (n 36) 8.

[93] Lichtenstein (n 4) 37. See also Callaghan and Hubbard (n 59) 134: 'To deflect criticism that the AIIB will not meet the environmental and social standards espoused by the World Bank and ADB, China's President Xi Jinping gave assurances that the new bank would adhere to the "good practices" of existing international lending institutions.'

structures and relationships. Relationships with a global set of governments and MDBs have reinforced the AIIB's commitment to established, international standards. However, at the same time, relationships with a large set of governments frustrated by the slow pace of MDB reforms have encouraged – and, indeed, arguably required – bold innovations in governance. The relational dimension of the AIIB is discussed below.

IV. The Relational Dimension of the AIIB

The relational dimension of a site of governance, under Snyder's framework, concerns relations between the site and other sites of governance. As discussed above, a site's structural dimension and relational dimension interact and influence one another, as well as being influenced by strategic actors, including corporations, governments and non-governmental organisations.

The AIIB's relations with other sites of governance have influenced its structures. One example (discussed above) is its close relationships with other major MDBs, which encourage convergence in standards.[94] Indeed, one of its two core goals is to promote regional cooperation on development through 'close collaboration with other multilateral and bilateral development institutions'.[95] Such collaboration, in turn, can promote rule harmonisation. As stated in the AIIB's Environment and Social Framework:

> The Bank aims to promote harmonization of policies with multilateral development banks and bilateral development organizations with which it co-finances Projects to reduce the burden of multiple requirements on Clients. When co-financing a Project with these other financial institutions, the Bank seeks to cooperate with them with a view to adopting a common approach to appraisal, environmental and social management requirements, monitoring and reporting regarding the Project.[96]

The AIIB's relations with a larger-than-anticipated number of governments – in particular, European governments – has also influenced its structures. As stated by Yun Sun:

> The enthusiasm of European countries to join the AIIB was a welcome surprise for China. Beijing rapidly adapted its position to welcome European countries as well as African and Latin American countries as Prospective Founding Members (PFMs) … [the AIIB's Articles of Agreement] made many pledges to honor international best practices on the environment, society, disclosure, procurement, debt sustainability, and oversight mechanism in line with the principles of transparency, openness,

[94] See the discussion above concerning the AIIB's co-financing arrangements with other MDBs, cooperation framework agreements with MDBs, and joint MDB climate action statement delivered at COP26.

[95] 'Articles of Agreement' (n 12), art 1 (1).

[96] 'Environmental and Social Framework' (n 16) 6.

> independence and accountability … The key reason that China adapted its positions and accepted an AIIB different from its earlier design is the role of the international community. The pivotal event was the decision by leading European economies in late March [2015] to join.[97]

Although the AIIB's global relationships with MDBs and governments have in many ways strengthened global confidence in the Bank's structures, another AIIB relationship – with China's BRI – has to some extent raised questions about those structures.

The AIIB–BRI relationship has received considerable attention due to the significant criticism that has been directed at the BRI[98] as well as a lack of clarity concerning the precise contours of the relationship. Views emphasising the closeness of the AIIB–BRI relationship tend to be quite critical of both initiatives.[99] The 'close timing' of the first announcements of the BRI and the AIIB (in late 2013) 'as well as their common emphasis on infrastructure development and Beijing's willingness the shoulder the huge financial burdens of both plans, might naturally cause observers to view them in tandem and assume their operations would be similar'.[100] In addition, there is substantial overlap between AIIB membership and

[97] Y Sun, 'How the International Community Changed China's Asian Infrastructure Investment Bank' *The Diplomat* (31 July 2015), https://thediplomat.com/2015/07/how-the-international-community-changed-chinas-asian-infrastructure-investment-bank. See also Haga (n 1) 404: 'Even during the process of negotiations, European members in particular urged the bank to introduce environmental and social safeguards and other standards into project oversight and procurement regulations.'

[98] See JJ Lew and G Roughead (Chairs) , J Hillman and D Sacks (Project Directors)), 'China's Belt and Road, Implications for the United States' (*Council on Foreign Relations*, March 2021), 3–4, https://www.cfr.org/report/chinas-belt-and-road-implications-for-the-united-states/findings (China advancing BRI in 'worrying ways' that 'subsidize privileged market entry for state-owned and non-market oriented Chinese companies' and offer 'quick and easy infrastructure packages that forego rigorous environmental- and social-impact assessments'); Venkateswaran Lokanathan, 'China's Belt and Road Initiative: Implications in Africa' (*ORF Issue Brief*, 24 August 2020), https://www.orfonline.org/research/chinas-belt-and-road-initiative-implications-in-africa ('despite China's projects being executed in consultation with the local governments, the bidding processes for these projects are opaque and bribes are often paid to local officials'). Similar criticisms of the BRI have been raised for a number of years; one response by China has been to develop an approach of 'open, green and clean cooperation' for the BRI. See 'Xi Jinping Attends the Opening Ceremony of the Second Belt and Road Forum for International Cooperation (BRF) and Delivers a Keynote Speech', Second Belt and Road Forum for International Cooperation (27 April 2019), http://beltandroadforum.org/english/n100/2019/0429/c22-1391.html; J Tower and J Staats, 'China's Belt and Road: Progress on "Open, Clean and Green"?' *United States Institute of Peace* (29 April 2020) ('The BRI had become synonymous with environmental degradation, corruption, and lack of transparency, and China's top officials pledged new approaches').

[99] See K Horta and W Wang, 'The Beijing-Led Asian Infrastructure Investment Bank: Global Leader in Infrastructure, at What Cost?' (*Heinrich Böll Foundation*, May 2020), who note that the BRI and the AIIB 'were initiated by the same leadership, in the same year, and for the same purpose … in view of growing concerns on the lack of accountability and transparency practices associated with Beijing-led investments and projects around the world, European and like-minded members of the AIIB must redouble their efforts to closely scrutinize the Beijing-led institution's investments'. See also Callaghan and Hubbard (n 59), 124: 'the concern that AIIB funds would be used to pursue China's strategic objectives was at least one of the objections put by Australia's foreign minister in arguing against Australia's early participation in the bank'.

[100] Haga (n 1) 395.

BRI participation;[101] one noteworthy example of such overlap is Oman, where a broadband network project has been co-financed by the AIIB and the Silk Road Fund,[102] a Beijing-based, state-owned fund focused on BRI projects.[103]

But the significance of AIIB–BRI relationship generally, and the AIIB-Silk Road Fund co-financing arrangement in Oman in particular, should not be overstated. Co-financing arrangements with other MDBs (rather than state-owned funds) have been far more common for the AIIB: 'Just under half (49%) of AIIB's number of approved projects through 2019 (41.5% of total financing) are co-financed with other MDBs.'[104] In addition, India – which is not a BRI participant[105] – has received about one-third of all AIIB funding.[106] Simply put, the AIIB 'finances projects both within and outside the places covered by the Belt and Road Initiative'.[107] Regarding future financing trends, the AIIB has set a goal of 50 per cent of approved financing to be private sector financing by 2030.[108] Regarding the AIIB–BRI relationship in particular, AIIB President Jin Liqun has stated: 'We operate by our standards, by our governance. The Belt and Road is a marvelous program … but we have our standards.'[109]

[101] See Grieger (n 89) 11: 'Given BRI's large scope and initially overlapping focus on Asia and infrastructure construction, many AIIB projects are inevitably located in BRI corridors.'

[102] See 'Silk Road Fund Entered into a Participation Agreement with Asian Infrastructure Investment Bank (AIIB) for Oman's National Fiber Optic Broadband Network Project' (*Silk Road Fund*, 7 November 2018), http://www.silkroadfund.com.cn/enwap/27389/27391/37556/index.html.

[103] See 'Silk Road Fund', www.silkroadfund.com.cn. Another example of AIIB–BRI cooperation would be the AIIB's decision to serve as Administrator for, and host the Secretariat of, the Multilateral Cooperation Center for Development Finance (MCDF), 'a multilateral coordination mechanism' established by the Chinese Ministry of Finance and several MDBs (including the AIIB)'; see Haga (n 1) 406. The MCDF had been a deliverable at the 2017 Belt and Road Forum. See State Council, People's Republic of China, 'List of Deliverables of the Belt and Road Forum for International Cooperation' (16 May 2017), https://english.www.gov.cn/news/top_news/2017/05/16/content_281475657209052.htm, s IV ('Enhance Financial Cooperation, Promote Financial Connectivity'), para 4: 'The Ministry of Finance of China signed the memoranda of understanding on collaboration on matters of common interest under the Belt and Road Initiative with the Asian Development Bank, the Asian Infrastructure Investment Bank, the European Bank for Reconstruction and Development, the European Investment Bank, the New Development Bank and the World Bank Group.'

[104] Humphrey (n 13) 10.

[105] See PTI, 'India Refuses to Endorse China's Belt and Road Initiative' *The Hindu* (4 December 2021), https://www.thehindu.com/news/national/india-refuses-to-endorse-chinas-belt-and-road-initiative/article61827373.ece.

[106] See A Krishnan, '"One-Third of Funding by AIIB Has Gone to India"' *The Hindu* (26 September 2020), https://www.thehindu.com/business/Industry/one-third-of-funding-by-aiib-has-gone-to-india/article32699050.ece.

[107] GJ Sanders, 'The Asian Infrastructure Investment Bank and the Belt and Road Initiative: Complementarities and Contrasts' (2017) 16 *Chinese Journal of International Law* 367, 368.

[108] 'How We Rebuild' (n 36) 5.

[109] E Glenn, 'China-Backed AIIB Touts Growth, Sustainability' *Reuters* (17 June 2017), https://www.reuters.com/article/us-aiib-asia-china-idUSKBN199061. See also DF Gordon, H Tong and T Anderson, 'Beyond the Myths – Towards a Realistic Assessment of China's Belt and Road Initiative: The Development-Finance Dimension' (*International Institute for Strategic Studies*, March 2020) 23, https://ispmyanmarchinadesk.com/wp-content/uploads/2020/12/BRI-Report-Two-Beyond-the-Myths-Towards-a-Realistic-Assessment-of-Chinas-Belt-and-Road-Initiative.pdf: 'despite the early assumption by many critics outside China that the AIIB and the BRI would both be dominated by top-down directives dictated by Beijing, the AIIB has developed into a globally accepted, trusted and independent MDB'.

The AIIB's relationships with MDBs, governments and the BRI illustrate how its relational dimension has interacted with its structural dimension. Promoting regional cooperation through 'close collaboration with other multilateral and bilateral development institutions'[110] encourages rule harmonisation and the adoption of 'common approach[es]' to project management.[111] Relationships with a global set of governments have reinforced the importance of adhering to international standards. Relationships with a large set of governments frustrated by the slow pace of governance reforms at major MDBs and the IMF have also underscored the importance of innovation to address long-standing concerns, in particular over the disproportionately weak voice of emerging economies at those institutions. And the AIIB's relationship with the BRI – including the potential impact of that relationship on the AIIB's structures – has attracted considerable attention due to, in significant part, uncertainty surrounding the precise contours of the relationship and, by extension, the potential impact of the relationship on the AIIB's structures.

V. Conclusion

As the second-largest MDB by membership, the AIIB has already had a significant impact on MDB governance. When examined under Professor Snyder's sites of governance framework, the structures and relations of the AIIB have indeed influenced one another and provide an important model for the global governance of MDBs.

Relationships with a global set of governments and MDBs have reinforced the AIIB's commitment to established, international standards. However, at the same time, relationships with a large set of governments frustrated by the slow pace of MDB reforms have encouraged – and, indeed, arguably required – bold innovations in governance. Such innovations include measures that reflect the 'desirability of a greater voice for regional and smaller members'.[112] Innovations also include the adoption of a non-resident Board of Directors, which addresses efficiency concerns as well as concerns over potential conflicts of interest associated with the 'dual' duties of resident MDB directors, who must balance a representational duty to their respective governments with a fiduciary duty to the MDB as an institution.[113]

The AIIB's relationship with the BRI has also received considerable attention, due to, in significant part, uncertainty surrounding the precise contours of the relationship and, by extension, the potential impact of the relationship on the

[110] 'Articles of Agreement' (n 12), art 1(1).
[111] 'Environmental and Social Framework' (n 16) 6.
[112] Lichtenstein (n 4) 37.
[113] 'Repowering the World Bank for the 21st Century' (n 18) 31–32.

AIIB's structures. Although there is substantial overlap between AIIB membership and BRI participation as well as a 'common emphasis on infrastructure development',[114] the AIIB, as was made clear by President Jin Liqun, operates according to its own standards.[115] In addition, increasing reliance on private sector financing by the AIIB should help to address lingering concerns over the potential impact of the AIIB–BRI relationship on AIIB structures.

The AIIB provides a compelling illustration of Snyder's sites of governance model in significant part because the Bank itself has expressly recognised and embraced the connection between structures and relations. A core purpose of the AIIB is to promote regional cooperation on development through 'close collaboration with other multilateral and bilateral development institutions';[116] such collaboration, in turn, promotes 'harmonization of policies' and the adoption of 'common approach[es]'[117] to project management. The interactions of the AIIB's structures and relations have ultimately led to a Beijing-based MDB that can be viewed as a unique and consequential site of governance.

[114] Haga (n 1) 395.
[115] Glenn (n 109).
[116] 'Articles of Agreement' (n 12), art 1(1).
[117] 'Environmental and Social Framework' (n 16) 6.

4

Public Ethics in the EU Institutions: From Self-Regulation to Independent Oversight?

ALBERTO ALEMANNO

I. Introduction

In the autumn of 2000, I had the good fortune of being enrolled on Francis Snyder's mandatory course on EU Institutional law at the College of Europe in Bruges. This class marked not only my first encounter with the Socratic method but also with Francis' law in context approach, two events that proved to be as disruptive as they were opportune for the legal education of a continental law student. This encounter profoundly defined not only my teaching but also the research agenda I have been developing over the last two decades around the democratisation of EU decision making through the design of new participatory and accountability channels. It is against this backdrop that this chapter provides a contextual analysis of one of the most neglected, legally fragmented, undersystematised yet vital areas of EU Institutional law: the public ethics and integrity regime applicable to EU decision makers.[1]

The EU has, over time, put in place ethical standards governing the conduct of its institutions' staff and members to prevent or at least mitigate against the risks of unethical behaviour.[2] It did so on the assumption that what matters today is not

[1] For some notable exceptions, see, eg, M. Cini, 'Ethics Management in the European Commission' in M Egeberg (ed) *Institutional Dynamics and the Transformation of Executive Politics in Europe* (CONNEX Report Series No 03, 2007) 119; M Cini, 'Institutional Change in the European Parliament: Balancing Legislative Ethics and Parliamentary Independence' (2019) 25(2) *Journal of Legislative Studies* 314; A Năstase, 'Managing Ethics in the European Commission Services' (2013) 15(1) *Public Management Review* 63.

[2] These are essentially framed as rights, duties and qualities of EU members and staff, and indicate overall what is considered as appropriate behaviour from them.

only *what* public institutions do (output legitimacy) and *who* does it (input legitimacy), but also *how* it gets done (throughout legitimacy).[3] The resulting EU ethical and integrity framework appears in general more comprehensive and sounder than in most Member States.[4] Yet, a contextual examination of such a regime unveils a richer understanding of its underlying rationale and overall effectiveness.[5] Thus, the multiple cases of unethical behaviour in the EU Institutions that emerged over time have revealed significant systemic shortcomings[6] to the point of ultimately harming EU citizens' trust in democratic institutions and politics.

Acknowledging these far-reaching problems, European Commission President Ursula von der Leyen pledged, when entering office, to create one independent ethics body common to all EU Institutions in an effort to put an end to the current fragmentation of the enforcement mechanisms.[7] The establishment of such a body has also prominently been called for by civil society organisations, notably Transparency International,[8] and appears among the political priorities of the Vice President of the European Commission for Values and Transparency.[9] Likewise, the Council of the EU expressed its support for 'the further improvement of harmonised [ethics] frameworks within and across the EU Institutions based on closer inter-institutional cooperation and the exchange of best practices with a view to strengthening trust in the EU as a whole'.[10]

Against this backdrop, this chapter discusses how to improve the current EU ethics system by focusing on both elected/appointed members, such as MEPs or European Commissioners, respectively, and EU Institutions' career staff. The chapter is organised as follow. Section II unpacks the EU ethics framework by first providing a detailed legal analysis of the existing ethics standards applicable to both EU Institutions' members and their staff. It then examines the oversight mechanisms existing within the European Commission, Parliament as well as within the EU public administration (eg, the European Anti-Fraud Office (OLAF))

[3] See, eg, VA Schmidt, 'Democracy and Legitimacy in the European Union Revisited: Input, Output and 'Throughput'' (2013) 61 *Political Studies* 2, 22.

[4] European Court of Auditors, Special Report No 13/2019: 'The Ethical Frameworks of the Audited EU Institutions: Scope for Improvement', Luxembourg.

[5] For a law in context analysis of the effectiveness of EU law, see F Snyder, 'The Effectiveness of European Community Law: Institutions, Processes, Tools and Techniques' (1993) 56 *MLR* 19.

[6] Transparency International, European Union Integrity System reports, 2021, https://transparency.eu/euis.

[7] U von der Leyen, 'A Union That Strives for More, Political Guidelines for the Next European Commission, 2019–2024': 'I will support the creation of an independent ethics body common to all EU institutions. I will engage and work closely with the other institutions to make this happen.' See https://op.europa.eu/en/publication-detail/-/publication/43a17056-ebf1-11e9-9c4e-01aa75ed71a1.

[8] The EU Integrity System report, Transparency International EU, 2014. The EU Integrity System report is the result of research conducted by the Transparency International EU Office over a nine-month period in 2013–14.

[9] President von der Leyen's mission letter to Věra Jourová, 5: 'I want you to work together with the European Parliament and the Council on an independent ethics body common to all EU institutions.' Available at: https://ec.europa.eu/commission/commissioners/sites/comm-cwt2019/files/commissioner_mission_letters/mission-letter-jourova-2019–2024_en.pdf.

[10] European Court of Auditors (n 4).

tasked to enforce such ethics standards. In so doing, it focuses in particular on these bodies' prerogatives – from the right to initiate an investigation, monitoring to the power of investigation, and sanction. Section III identifies and discusses the major structural limitations of the current EU ethics framework by underscoring its fragmentation across and within EU Institutions, weak enforcement by its multiple, politically driven oversight bodies (most prominently within the European Parliament and the European Commission), as well as its limited awareness and uptake within both the EU Institutional and political contexts. To address and overcome existing limitations, section IV proposes the creation of a permanent, and independent EU ethics body common to all EU Institutions to prevent, or at least mitigate against, the risk of unethical behaviour.

II. The EU Ethical and Integrity System

The EU lacks a harmonised ethics and integrity framework common to all its institutions, be they members or staff (generally referred to as EU public servants).[11] As a result, various, bespoke ethical and integrity regimes coexist under EU law, each with its own ethics standards and obligations (see section II.A below), and different enforcement mechanisms (see section II.B below) that – through the exercise of a variety of monitoring, investigatory and sanctioning powers – ensure their respect.

A. EU Ethical and Integrity Standards

EU ethics and integrity standards of conduct are scattered across multiple legal sources, ranging from the EU Treaties to dedicated Rules of Procedure to Codes of Conduct and, in the case of EU officials, EU Staff Regulations.[12]

[11] The Council of the EU is the only major institution without an ethical framework governing the work of its members, namely representatives of the Member States. When it comes to agencies, no horizontal requirements in relation to ethics are applicable (except for staff; see arts 1a(2) and 110(2)ff of the Staff Regulations). Instead, the precise ethical standards applicable are first to be found in each agency's establishing regulation and in any further relevant secondary legislation. Two texts have been adopted in an effort of harmonisation: a Common Approach on Decentralised Agencies (2012) and Guidelines on the prevention and management of conflicts of interest in EU decentralised agencies (2013). The European Investment Bank (EIB) has an 'Ethics and Compliance Committee' to rule on any potential conflict of interest by providing opinions on any ethical matter concerning members of the Board of Directors or the Management Committee, regulated in their respective Code of Conduct or in related relevant provisions. See the Operating Rules of the Ethics and Compliance Committee (ECC) set out the provisions applying to the Ethics and Compliance Committee of the European Investment Bank, https://www.eib.org/en/publications/operating-rules-of-the-ethics-and-compliance-committee. Similarly, the European Central Bank has established an ethics framework (2015/C 204/04) as well as OLAF. See art 4 of the Rules of Procedure of the OLAF Supervisory Committee [2011] OJ L308/114.

[12] The European Code of Good Administrative Behaviour offers the only harmonised, interinstitutional document.

While the Treaties merely contain references to legal principles such as independence, integrity, confidentiality and discretion, other sources translate them into more concrete and tangible standards of conduct.[13] A common core of ethics principles – applicable throughout and after[14] the end of the term of office – exists,[15] consisting of:

(i) independence;
(ii) integrity and discretion in office;
(iii) obligation of professional secrecy; and
(iv) integrity and discretion post mandate.

As both members and staff are asked to act solely in the public interest and refrain from obtaining or seeking any direct or indirect financial benefit or reward, central to the application of these principles is the concept of conflict of interest. This emerges wherever public officials are, or are perceived to be, confronted with a situation where their private interests diverge from the duties of their position.[16] Such a situation of conflict may arise during or after[17] the term of the mandate or service, but also in relation to situations that occurred before.[18]

There are specific regimes defining, inter alia, a gift policy, outside activities and assignments while in office that help members and staff to preventively know what conducts are compatible with the office.

The determination of the normative content of these ethics and integrity standards is currently left to dedicated bodies. These range from ad hoc committees governing the application of the standards to the members of the European Parliament and Commission to, in the case of EU officials, institution-by-institution Appointed Authorities helped by Disciplinary Boards, as well as, ultimately, the General Court of the EU (following the suppression of the EU Civil Service

[13] For an analysis of the legal status and normative content of ethics and morality under EU law, see M Frischhut "EU': Short for 'Ethical' Union? The Role of Ethics in European Union Law' (2015) 75(3) *Heidelberg Journal of International Law* 531.

[14] The only exception being the European Parliament, whose members are not subject to the respect of any ethical standard after the end of their mandate; in other words, no post-employment restrictions are foreseen.

[15] The only exception being the Council of the EU, whose members are not subject to the respect of any ethical standard, be it during or after their mandate. See n 11 above.

[16] This definition is offered by art 3(1) of the Code of Conduct for MEPs, whereas art 2(6) of the Code of Conduct for Members of the Commission, as reformed in 2018, reads: 'A conflict of interest arises where a personal interest may influence the independent performance of their duties. Personal interests include, but are not limited to, any potential benefit or advantage to Members themselves, their spouses, partners or direct family members. A conflict of interest does not exist where a Member is only concerned as a member of the general public or of a broad class of persons.'

[17] A duty to notify the relevant institution within two years of leaving the service applies to the staff as well as members of the Commission (three years for the President). This is because they continue to be subject to certain obligations, such as integrity and discretion. Despite receiving a transitional allowance, former MEPs have no limitation on their future employment.

[18] While members are required to make a declaration of interests, the staff should merely inform the institution of any potential or actual conflict via 'a specific form'. Based on the latter information, the Appointing Authority should verify whether a candidate has a personal interest impairing their independence or any conflict. See art 11 of the Staff Regulations.

Tribunal) as well as the Court of Justice. As the decision practice of these different bodies varies and is characterised by limited publicity, its visibility remains to the point of making a systematic study of the normative contents of the various ethics standards virtually impossible.[19] While the EU Courts' decisions are public, those adopted by ad hoc committees on members of the EU Institutions are not.

The resulting normative fragmentation among ethics standards prevents the emergence of consistent interpretative and enforcement practices. While cross-institutional harmonisation might not always be warranted, some common approaches might be required. This might entail the adoption of one or more commonly agreed definitions of conflict of interest to start with.

B. EU Ethical and Integrity Oversight Systems

The respect of these ethics standards and integrity obligations is entrusted to a variety of oversight mechanisms of different natures, including ad hoc advisory committees – such as the EU Parliament Advisory Committee on the Conduct of Members (PACCM)[20] and the EU Commission Independent Ethical Committee (CIEC).[21] In the case of EU officials, the Stature foresees institution-by-institution Appointed Authorities helped by Disciplinary Boards, whose decisions are subject to the judicial review of the General Court of the EU (following the suppression of the EU Civil Service Tribunal). Last but not least, the Court of Justice enjoys an exclusive competence in determining the unethical conduct of the Members of the European Commission.[22] In addition, OLAF investigates serious matters

[19] While the opinions of the Commission's ad hoc committee are published upon the decision of the President of the Commission, those adopted by its parliamentary counterpart are generally not subject to the same level of publicity. It is the Parliamentary President's reasoned opinion, which may be based on the committee's advice, that is generally notified to the Member of the European Parliament and announced in plenary.

[20] The Advisory Committee on the Conduct of Members is the body responsible for giving members guidance on the interpretation and implementation of the Code of Conduct. At the request of the President, the Advisory Committee also assesses alleged breaches of the Code of Conduct and advises the President on possible action to be taken. The Advisory Committee is composed of five members, who are appointed by the President on the basis of their experience and of political balance between the Parliament's political groups. Each of the five members serves as chairperson for six months, on a rotating basis. The President also nominates one reserve member for each political group not otherwise represented in the Advisory Committee. See Code of Conduct for Members of the European Parliament with Respect to Financial Interests and Conflicts of Interest, https://www.europarl.europa.eu/pdf/meps/Code%20of%20Conduct_01-2017_EN.pdf.

[21] The members of the Committee serve for terms of three years (renewable once) and are appointed by the President of the European Commission. They advise the Commission on whether the planned activities of Commissioners after leaving office are compatible with the Treaties. The President may also seek the advice of the Independent Ethical Committee on any other ethical question relating to the Code of Conduct for the Members of the European Commission. See Advisory Committee on the Conduct of Members – Rules of Procedure, https://www.europarl.europa.eu/pdf/meps/Rules_of_Procedure_EN.pdf.

[22] Articles 245 and 247 of the Treaty on the Functioning of the European Union (TFEU).

relating to the discharge of professional duties constituting a dereliction of the obligations of EU officials liable to result in disciplinary or, as the case may be, criminal proceedings, or an equivalent failure to discharge obligations on the part of members of institutions and bodies.[23] However, the disciplinary recommendations issued by OLAF exclusively concern the 'serious misconduct' of EU staff or members of the EU Institutions and are directed to the authority having disciplinary powers in the institution concerned. Therefore, the primary responsibility for the enforcement vis-a-vis members belongs to the president of each EU Institution, who may refer to advisory ethical committees, as mentioned above, for advice. In particular, in the case of the EU Commission, the President may ask a Commissioner to step back any time,[24] and when infringements qualify as 'serious misconducts' by a member of the Commission, the College of Commissioners may seise the Court of Justice.[25] When it comes to the members of the European Parliament, it is the President who is tasked, with the assistance of the PACCM and – in case of appeal – the Bureau,[26] to impose penalties. However, when it comes to the suspension or removal from one or more of the offices of an MEP,[27] the Rules of Procedure entrust this power to the President (right of initiative), the Conference of Presidents (decision to proceed) and the Parliament itself (actual sanction). Ultimately, the institutional role played by the Presidents of these two institutions, combined with their respective political colour and the fact that they are both party and judge of the ethics regime, casts doubt on the suitability of their offices to play such an oversight role.[28]

In fact, no EU ethics body – with the limited exception of OLAF (in the case of 'serious misconduct' and the EU Ombudsman (when overseeing how the EU ethics bodies operate)[29] – enjoys the right to initiate investigations whenever it finds it reasonable. Moreover, no mechanism enables third parties to prompt a verification. Only the Presidents of the Parliament[30] and the Commission *may* do so. When it comes to the staff, the initiative belongs to the Appointing Authority, assisted as the case may be, by the Disciplinary Board (one per each institution, agency or body), OLAF or a national court.[31] While OLAF's director-general

[23] Article 5 of the OLAF decision read in light of art 3 of the same decision and art 5 of the OLAF Regulation.

[24] Article 17(6) of the Treaty on European Union (TEU): 'A member of the Commission shall resign if the President so requests.'

[25] Articles 245 and 247 TFEU.

[26] Article 72 of the Decision of the Bureau of 19 May and 9 July 2008 concerning implementing measures for the Statute for Members of the European Parliament [2009] OJ C159, 13 July, 1–24.

[27] Rule 21 of the Rules of Procedure of the EU Parliament.

[28] This is also true for advisory ethics bodies whose composition and appointment procedure raise questions about their independence. Members are appointed by the Commission, on a proposal from the President. In the case of Parliament, the Committee is only composed of MEPs and not independent ethics professionals.

[29] Article 228(1) TFEU.

[30] Article 8 of the Code of Conduct of MEPs.

[31] Where there is evidence that a breach of Staff Regulations may have occurred, the Appointing Authority may decide to open an administrative inquiry.

has the power to open an internal administrative investigation within an EU Institution acting on his or her own initiative,[32] the exercise of such a right in relation to ethical conduct is made conditional on the existence of 'serious facts linked to the performance of professional activities which may constitute a breach of obligations' by staff or members. This leaves uncovered an area of minor ethical misconducts in relation to which no real investigative authority exists and is exercised. It must be noted that insofar as OLAF acts independently from other EU Institutions, including the very same EU Commission that has created it, no current EU oversight system or body is in a position to oversee the exercise of OLAF's right of initiative.

When it comes to monitoring, the EU Staff Regulations imposes a duty on officials when they become aware of facts giving rise to a presumption of the existence of illegal activities as well as conduct which may constitute a serious failure to comply with an official's professional duties, including of an ethical nature, to inform their authorities or OLAF.[33] However, the EU does not provide harmonised staff whistleblower protection. Thus, while OLAF actively encourages citizens to report fraud anonymously on a secure website, the European Commission's guidelines discourage anonymous reporting and the Parliament's rules forbid staff from acting anonymously.[34] In addition, the Parliament fails to protect accredited parliamentary assistants (APAs) who report fraud and wrongdoing by their own MEP.[35] Third parties can also write letters or complaints to the relevant institutions.

The privileged instrument used to prevent the breach of ethics and integrity rules – mainly of the principles of independence and integrity – by members are declarations of interests. Yet, as this analysis of the enforcement mechanisms shows, these declarations appear largely deficient. This is the conclusion reached the European Court of Auditors' 2019 Special Report.[36] While both MEPs and Commissioners are required to regularly submit and update declarations of financial interests, the correctness, completeness and compatibility of these declarations with the respective codes of conduct are not checked according to any written standard procedure.[37] The only check conducted is a check 'for general plausibility, that means to ensure that [declarations] contain no manifestly erroneous, illegible or incomprehensive information, based on available information', as conceded by the Commission in response to the report.[38] As a result, there is considerable uncertainty among Commissioners, MEPs and staff as to the importance of diligence when filing declarations. When it comes to the MEPs, it is quite common to come across suspiciously empty or deliberately false, fictitious, possibly self-ironic

[32] Article 5 of the OLAF decision read in light of art 3 of the same decision.
[33] ibid art 4.
[34] ibid art 22(a)–(c).
[35] ibid.
[36] European Court of Auditors,(n 4) 60.
[37] Recommendation 1(c): ibid 37, as well as paras 46–50. ibid.
[38] ibid, p 2 of the Annex – EU Commission response.

declarations, as symbolised by an MEP declaring in 2012 to have been 'Master of the Universe'[39] before his election.

In fact, the EU ethics framework provides limited or no power of investigation over the EU Institutions themselves regarding breaches of ethics standards. The Commission Independent Ethics Committee (IEC) may ask for additional information to the Commission through its Secretariat General or from the (former) members directly by asking clarifications and more specific information and/or inviting him or her to a hearing. In other words, both the Commission IEC and the PACCM, within the remit of their respective institutions, have only direct access to existing internal sources of information. However, this presupposes that such a relevant information has already been collected by the institution itself, *quod non* on most occasions. Moreover, no EU ethics body enjoys a fact-checking authority that would work with EU and national public bodies, such as tax authorities. Yet both prerogatives are required to ensure the effectiveness of the ethics oversight.

When it comes to sanctions, these may be classified in four main categories: first, measures that primarily affect an official's reputation (eg, a call to order, written warnings, reprimands and publicity); second, measures that affect an official's position within the organisation (eg, relegations in step and downgrading for staff, temporary suspension from participation in all or some of the activities of the Parliament for MEPs, such as rapporteurships, Committee Chairmanships and relocation of files for Commissioners); third, measures that irreversibly alter the relation between the officials and the organisation (eg, removal from post); fourth, some sanctions that may be accompanied by – or consist alone of – financial decisions (eg, temporary forfeiture of entitlement to the daily subsistence allowance for MEPs and the deprivation of right to pension or other benefits in the case of members of the Commission and staff).

III. Structural Limitations of the EU Ethics System

While many elements of an ethics infrastructure are in place in the EU, the absence of a systematic approach has led to a framework with no clear indication of what the ethics infrastructure is and how it works. In particular, three major structural limitations emerge. First, the EU ethics system applicable to members – be they elected or appointed – is highly fragmented, with each EU Institution having its own dedicated framework, limited in its independence and lacking adequate investigatory authority. It comes as no surprise that their sanctioning powers are seldom used. In the case of the European Parliament, the enforcement of ethics rules towards members occurs in the absence of predictable rules of procedure and with limited

[39] 'MEPs not serious about transparency', *EU Observer*, 19 July 2012, https://euobserver.com/institutional/117009; declaration received by the European Parliament in March 2012, https://www.europarl.europa.eu/ep-dif/96710_01-03-2012.pdf.

publicity.[40] Second, this situation is further aggravated by limited awareness and guidance regarding the ethics standards applicable to EU Institutions' members and staff. In turn, this inevitably translates into limited, lax enforcement. Let us briefly unpack each of these structural features of the EU ethics system.

A. Fragmentation and Weak Enforcement with Limited Independence and Investigatory Powers

As illustrated above, the EU ethics system applicable to members – be they elected or appointed – is highly fragmented, with each EU Institution having its own dedicated framework. In addition to the fragmentation of the EU ethics institutional oversight system across EU Institutions, this is further complicated by the existence of a parallel ethics framework – this time common to all EU Institutions – for their career staff. This leads to uncertainty about the interpretation and enforcement of standards.

An *excursus* of the enforcement practice suggests that only few cases have led to the imposition of penalties for the members of the EU Institution.[41] This can be explained by the limited – or even absent[42] – power of investigation of the EU Institutions themselves regarding breaches of ethics standards, and limited coordination with national authorities.

However, where the Appointing Authority or OLAF becomes aware of evidence of failure by the staff, it may launch administrative investigations in order to verify whether such failure has occurred.[43] OLAF can do the same vis-a-vis members too, yet its competence to investigate is limited to 'serious misconducts' and not all ethical standards breaches. This leaves open an entire category of misconducts by members that, by failing to qualify as 'serious', may escape the investigatory powers of OLAF, as well as the initiative by the (Presidents of the) Commission and the Parliament vis-a-vis their own members.

[40] Historically parliamentary ethics systems have lagged beyond other systems of public and professional ethics, mainly due to the parliamentary preference for self-regulation and by virtue of the constitutional principle of parliamentary privilege. See, eg, M Cini, 'The Regulation of Ethics in the European Parliament', *UACES 44th Annual Conference*, Cork, Ireland, 1–3 September 2014.

[41] For the Commission, see, eg, JP Kuijper, 'Misteps by Commissioners: Legal or Political Sanctions?' in F Amtenbrink, *The Internal Market and the Future of European Integration: Essays in Honour of Laurence W. Gormley* (Cambridge, Cambridge University Press, 2019); for the European Parliament, see Advisory Committee of the conduct of Members, Annual Reports from 2015 to 2018 (during the 2014–19 legislative term, the Advisory Committee dealt with a total of 26 MEPs involved in potential breaches of the Code of Conduct, although none of them was sanctioned).

[42] The Parliament has no power of investigation over its own members who are accountable to their voters and enjoy a free mandate. See European Court of Auditors (n 4) Annex – European Parliament response. Yet insofar as citizens do not have access to the information to judge their representatives, be that due to missing checks on the veracity of financial interests or to the incomplete information on lobby meetings, this accountability does not exist.

[43] Article 86 of the Staff Regulations.

When ethical breaches come to light, this is not usually due to systematic checks by the European Parliament or internal reporting, but rather journalistic investigations. In particular, efforts to deter the filing of incomplete or inaccurate declarations by members are further hampered by the very limited sanctioning powers, in particular in relation to MEPs. An additional layer of complexity in the enforcement of ethics standards has to do with often overlapping considerations of political nature that blur the evaluation of the ethical conduct. Ultimately, the fact that the different institutions, which do have sanctions at their disposal, apply only very limited ones – if at all – questions the overall effectiveness of the EU ethics framework.

B. Limited Awareness and Guidance Regarding the Ethics Standards Applicable to EU Institutions' Members and Staff

There is also limited awareness and knowledge about the existing ethics rules, reporting and sanction mechanisms. As a recent European Court of Auditors (ECA) Special Report found,[44] staff across all institutions are largely uninformed about their ethics rights and duties, and lack awareness about existing rules and reporting and sanctioning mechanisms. In a survey conducted for the very same report, only about half of the staff members of the audited EU Institutions considered their own knowledge of the ethical frameworks to be good or very good. More than half had never received any kind of ethics training and more than two-thirds found the guidance provided to them on ethics issues unspecific and lacking real-life examples. The ECA further discovered that knowledge about reporting mechanisms for unethical conduct was insufficient amongst almost 70 per cent of staff members. While there are clear, although non-uniform, rules on how to deal with gifts offered to EU staff, there is no mechanism determining what happens if somebody accepts a gift or entertainment *against* those rules, and it is not evident that staff actually know about their entitlements and duties regarding this issue. This not only means that staff members may be breaking rules while believing that they are acting correctly and meaning to do so, but also that possible forms of wrongdoing are under-reported and their clearance inconsistent.

In these circumstances, although de jure 'institutions have, to [a] large extent, adequate ethical frameworks in place',[45] in practice, the EU ethics framework proves incapable of effectively preventing – and adequately sanctioning – major breaches of EU ethics standards and to make staff (and even more so members) aware of the ethics framework.

With a diverse variety of national ethics systems developed in EU Member States and beyond over years and decades, there are invaluable lessons to be learnt. Indeed, as EU Member States face similar challenges and have over time developed a variety of ethics frameworks, the next section looks at these models in order to

[44] European Court of Auditors (n 4) para 26.
[45] ibid para 26.

identify an ideal model for the EU to follow, while ensuring the respect of its existing ethics standards.

IV. Towards an EU Ethics Body

To address and overcome the limitations previously identified in the current EU ethics framework, this section proposes the creation of a single EU ethics body. This ideal EU ethics body would be common to as many EU Institutions, agencies and bodies as possible and would cover both members and staff.

Unlike any of the existing EU ethics committees, this newly established EU ethics body should be, first of all, (i) independent and, second, competent to (ii) give advice, (iii) monitor, (iv) investigate, and (v) sanction any unethical behaviour committed during and after the term of office or service.

As originally proposed in 2000 (without much success),[46] this dedicated ethics body could be established through the conclusion of an Inter-institutional Agreement (IIA) among the Commission, the Parliament and the Council, and be left open to other EU Institutions and bodies upon their demand.[47] However, its scope and mandate should be considerably broader and draw inspiration from the French Haute Autorité pour la Vie Publique (HATVP).[48] This body would be in charge of monitoring and sanctioning the respect of existing ethics standards, namely the respect of the ethical conduct of members and staff. Indeed, the body could also be given authority over the public register of lobbyists and could monitor and enforce the compliance by lobbyists and lobbied – be they Commissioners, MEPs, their assistants and staff – with lobbying rules. Should additional formal obligations be imposed on EU Institutions' members and staff when it comes to their relations with organised interests, the respect of these rules could also be entrusted to the EU ethics body. Moreover, it might also provide advice, possibly separated by a firewall from monitoring and sanctions.

A. Independence and Composition

Unlike the existing EU highly decentralised model, national experiences suggest that a one-stop-shop authority may offer a more independent, effective and consistent institutional design. However, the EU attempt at setting up a centralised Advisory

[46] Proposal for an Agreement between the European Parliament, the Council, the Commission, the Court of Justice, the Court of Auditors, the Economic and Social Committee and the Committee of the Regions Establishing an Advisory Group on Standards in Public Life, EC (2000) 2077.

[47] On the legal nature of this instrument, see the seminal analysis by F Snyder, 'Interinstitutional Agreements: Forms and Constitutional Limitations' in G Winter (ed), *Sources and Categories of European Union Law: A Comparative and Reform Perspective* (Baden-Baden, Nomos, 1996).

[48] See, eg, A Leduc, *La lutte anticorruption et l'avenir des institutions politiques françaises* (Paris, L'Harmattan, 2021).

Group on Standards in Public Life for its seven main institutions derailed in 2000.[49] France, Ireland and Canada have each centralised this task to a single entity covering both members and staff. Despite also having one entity covering all aspects of ethics in public life, the UK has a myriad of more specific ethics bodies granted with more powers than the Committee on Standards in Public Life (CSPL).[50]

Moreover, the composition of the various EU ethics oversight mechanisms also casts doubt on their respective independence in relation to members.[51] Not only are the Presidents of the Parliament and the Commission both party and judge when ensuring the respect of their respective ethics framework, but they are also in charge of proposing the members of their advisory bodies.

To ensure its independence, its members would no longer be exclusively appointed by the same institution,[52] but would instead be selected by a variety of institutional actors and from different backgrounds. Some members may sit de jure in the committee due to their past functions. Examples include the former Presidents (or vice-presidents) of the European Court of Justice and of the Court of Auditors, as well as the former European Ombudsman.[53]

B. Advisory Role

In the EU ethics system, only the Commission and the parliamentary ethics bodies play an advisory role to their respective institution by essentially providing advice on how to interpret and apply ethical standards to individual cases. While the advice to the Parliament President is confidential, that to the Commission is rendered public upon the adoption of its final decision. Therefore, there is no general advisory function that could offer guidance to both staff and members before engaging in a given conduct.

The proposed ethics body should be entrusted with advisory authority to be able to provide advice both *in abstracto* and *in concreto*. This would enable anyone – be it staff or a member – to ask for advice on the interpretation of an ethical standard in relation to a given conduct. This is common practice in France,

[49] Proposal for an Agreement between the European Parliament, the Council, the Commission, the Court of Justice, the Court of Auditors, the Economic and Social Committee and the Committee of the Regions establishing an Advisory Group on Standards in Public Life, EC (2000) 2077.

[50] See R Dobson Phillips, 'British Standards Landscape: A Mapping Exercise' (2020), report commissioned by the UK's Committee on Standards in Public Life, https://assets.publishing.service.gov.uk/government/uploads/system/uploads/attachment_data/file/867642/Standards_Landscape_Final_Version__1_.pdf.

[51] When it comes to staff, the members of the Appointing Authority, the Staff Committee and the Disciplinary Board are, by definition, public servants. See arts 5–6 of Annex IX of the Staff Regulations.

[52] Article 12(4) of the Code of Conduct for Members of the Commission; art 7(2) of the Code of Conduct for the Members of the European Parliament.

[53] Former EU officials would be eligible to join as members of the EU Ethics Body only insofar as they are retired officials and exercise no other functions. Thus, for instance, some former Secretary-Generals of the EU Commission continue working for the EU administration in different functions. The same is true for former Presidents of the EU institutions who exercise other activities that might potentially conflict with those they would be called upon to exercise when joining the EU Ethics Body.

where individual members or staff can directly address them to receive such personal advice.[54]

C. Monitoring Role

When it comes to monitoring, none of the existing EU ethics frameworks enjoys autonomous monitoring capacity. As a result, they tend to be reactive as opposed to proactive. Thus, when breaches come to light, this is not usually due to systematic checks by the EU Institutions or internal reporting, but rather journalistic work. If the collection of declarations of financial interests responds to a preventive logic, the respective EU ethics bodies fail to ensure a regular, efficient and standardised examination of declarations regarding possible conflicts of interests by limiting their verification to a 'plausibility check'. Moreover, the EU lacks a public registry of all declarable information.

Yet, in order to be able to monitor potential breaches of ethical standards and obligations, the proposed body must be able to build upon both internal/external input as well as an autonomous and centralised collection system, notably one for the declarations of financial interests. For that purpose, the IIA would first pool together the existing monitoring capacity of the various EU ethics systems. In particular, by coordinating the existing reporting systems, the body could offer a one-stop-shop mechanism for both internal (EU officials) and external reports.[55] Moreover, the body would also collect and make publicly available declarations of assets, income and other interests – as currently required both for members and staff – and perform in-depth checks for correctness and for possible conflicts of interest. This could be realised through the creation of an EU public registry of all declarable information, by staff and members, within the limits posed by personal data protection rules in the EU Institutions.[56] It is on the basis of all the available information that the body would be empowered to undertake a standardised examination of declarations regarding possible conflicts of interests, by going beyond today's plausibility check.

D. The Right to Initiate Investigations

As previously noted, no current EU ethics body enjoys a right to initiate investigations whenever they would find it reasonable,[57] the only exceptions being OLAF,

[54] Article 20(1)(5°), Loi n°2013-907 du 11 octobre 2013 relative à la transparence de la vie publique.

[55] However, in the absence of harmonised staff whistleblower protection, their input will be limited.

[56] Regulation (EU) 2018/1725 of the European Parliament and of the Council of 23 October 2018 on the protection of natural persons with regard to the processing of personal data by the Union institutions, bodies, offices and agencies and on the free movement of such data, and repealing Regulation (EC) No 45/2001 and Decision No 1247/2002/EC, PE/31/2018/REV/1 [2018] OJ L295, 21 November.

[57] With the limited exceptions of the EU Ombudsman and the Director-General of OLAF and the Parliament's President's obligation to forward complaints which are not obviously false or in bad faith.

in the case of 'serious facts', and the EU Ombudsman, when overseeing how the EU ethics bodies operate.[58] Moreover, no mechanism enables third parties to prompt a verification: only the Presidents of the Parliament[59] and the Commission *may* do so.

Hence the suggestion to legally foresee for such a right of initiative to be delegated to the body itself. This delegation of authority being inherent to their procedural autonomy may take place with the delegation doctrine as formulated by the Court of Justice in *Meroni*.[60] Importantly, based on the example provided by the HATVP,[61] it could be envisaged that third parties – including previously identified non-governmental organisations (NGOs) fighting corruption – could inform the body of any misbehaviour and prompt an assessment.

E. Investigatory Powers

As discussed above, the EU ethics and integrity framework provides limited or no power of investigation to the EU Institutions themselves for breaches of ethics standards. Moreover, no EU ethics framework, be it of the Commission or of the European Parliament, enjoys fact-checking authority that would work with EU and national public bodies such as tax authorities. OLAF does have investigatory powers, but in relation to 'serious misconducts' only, thus leaving uncovered a wide zone of forms of ethical misconduct by both staff and members.

At the EU level, the Commission IEC may ask for additional information from the Commission through the Secretariat General, or from the (former) members directly by asking for clarifications and more specific information and/or inviting him or her to a hearing. In other words, both the Commission IEC and the PACCM, within the remit of their respective institutions, only have direct access to existing internal sources of information.

Here the IIA could pool together existing investigatory powers, as they are presently enjoyed by the relevant institutions – from the ethics bodies overseeing members to the individual disciplinary boards for staff – and entrust their exercise to the body itself. However, the IIA must regulate these administrative inquiries so as to ensure the protection of the fundamental rights of the persons concerned, as required by Article 52 Charter of Fundamental Rights. OLAF already satisfies that condition, as it does the Appointing Authority vis-a-vis the staff.[62] One

[58] Article 228(1) TFEU.

[59] Article 8 of the Code of Conduct of MEPs.

[60] See Judgment in Case 9/56 *Meroni v High Authority* EU:C:1958:7. The *Meroni* doctrine has been reinterpreted by the Court in *Short Selling* – see Judgment in the Case C-270/12 *UK v Parliament & Council* EU:C:2014:18.

[61] The French HATVP enjoys the right to initiate an investigation about an individual when it deems it necessary. See art 20(2), Loi n°2013-907 du 11 octobre 2013 relative à la transparence de la vie publique. See also, inter alia, arts 7, 18-6 and 18-7 of the same text.

[62] Art 2(1) of Annex IX (Disciplinary proceedings) of the Staff Regulations.

may therefore also argue that the proposed body should exercise its investigatory authority vis-a-vis both staff and members in line with the guarantees currently foreseen in the Staff Regulations, as well as the Parliament's Rules of Procedure[63] and the Commissioners' Code of Conduct. This is needed for the handling of that category of members' misconduct that, by failing to qualify as 'serious', escapes OLAF's investigations. Moreover, the exercise of the body's investigatory authority must be coordinated with OLAF – which in turn is in the process of defining its own relationship with the European Public Prosecutor's Office – and its prerogatives. To this end, the IIA must expressly confer upon the body investigatory competence for every instance of alleged ethical misconduct that has not led OLAF to open an administrative enquiry.

F. Sanctions

When it comes to sanctioning powers, the proposed body could be entrusted with some (but not necessarily full) authority. For staff, the body would take over from the Appointing Authority – through an enabling clause in the Staff Regulations[64] – and adopt any of the penalties foreseen for a breach of an ethical obligation. When it comes to members, the IIA can grant the body sanctioning authority in relation to 'soft' penalties (ie, reputational) and those affecting the position of the member within the institution, but not necessarily those that are of an irreversible nature, such as termination. Thus, for instance, being the compulsory retirement of a Commissioner being foreseen by the Treaty, this penalty can only be requested by the President of the Commission or the Commission itself.[65] When it comes to the early termination or suspension of an office of an MEP,[66] the Rules of Procedure entrust the power of initiative to the President – as well as the Conference of Presidents – and the actual sanctioning power to the Parliament itself. As such, the transfer of such a prerogative to the ethics body seems less automatic than that for soft penalties.

In any event, the decisions of the body should be legally binding for the recipient member, staff and institution. As such, they would be legally reviewable before the Court of Justice. Moreover, the body's activities would be subject to possible complaints to the EU Ombudsman, who can make non-binding decisions in the case of maladministration. The body, like any other body, would not be legally mandated to follow the Ombudsman's recommendations.

[63] Rule 174(2) of the Rules of Procedure of the EU Parliament, as well as r 21 and art 72 of the Decision of the Bureau of 19 May and 9 July 2008 concerning implementing measures for the Statute for Members of the European Parliament.

[64] Be it art 9(1)a or art 2(2) of the Staff Regulations.

[65] Articles 245 and 247 TFEU.

[66] Rule 21 of the Rules of Procedure of the EU Parliament.

G. How to Set Up an EU Ethics Body

To sum up, this chapter proposes concluding an IIA between two or more EU Institutions aimed at pooling together – within the framework of their respective procedural autonomy – the monitoring of the respect for the ethical standards to an Inter-institutional Body (IIB), both for members and staff, as well as entrusting investigatory and partial sanctioning power to it. In particular, when it comes to the staff, the present disciplinary system would be split into two procedures: one for ethical violations that would be outsourced to the ethics body – essentially conflict of interests – and another for the violation of the remaining professional obligations under the current staff disciplinary procedure. As for members, the body could only inflict soft penalties, such as reputational penalties and those entailing a change in the position within the relevant EU Institution, leaving the irreversible ones (essentially those foreseen by the Treaty for Commissioners and the Rules of Procedure of the European Parliament for MEPs) to the present ethics regime as foreseen in the Treaties. The IIA could even foresee the possibility to entrust to the body the verification of the respect of lobbying rules as well as providing interpretative advice.

Last but not least, while the set-up of such a new ethics body presupposes a significant increase in budget and personnel currently allocated to the various EU ethics frameworks and bodies, its benefits are set to outweigh such high costs.

V. Conclusion

This chapter has provided a systematic analysis of the existing EU ethics and integrity framework by focusing on both its standards and enforcement mechanisms. After having identified its major flaws, it has put forward the proposal for the creation of a single, permanent and independent EU ethics body to be established in order to reduce the risk of unethical behaviour to a minimum. One of the advantages of such a construct is that – as the relevant EU Institutions and bodies would act within the framework of their respective procedural autonomy – it would facilitate a more coherent, effective practice throughout the institutions.

It has also demonstrated that the proposed body can legally be established under EU law to set up such a body by pooling together existing monitoring, investigatory, sanctioning and advisory powers.

In order for this to occur, this chapter recommends the conclusion of an IIA between the European Commission and the Parliament (and possibly the Council), and open to more EU Institutions that could voluntarily join, aimed at entrusting – within the framework of their respective procedural autonomy – the respect of the existing ethical standards to an interinstitutional body. The agreement between the institutions involved would set out the basic arrangements for their cooperation and coordination to ensure that the ethical regime applicable to the respective EU Institution, members and staff is upheld.

There are several reasons supporting the establishment of a common EU ethics body.

First, unlike any of the existing EU ethics bodies, the newly established body would be independent and competent to ensure the enforcement of unethical behaviour committed by both appointed/elected members and staff. In particular, by agreeing on a stronger mechanism to control the declaration of interests of the members and staff of the EU Institutions and monitor their respect, this new system of enforcement of ethics requirements would not only be more effective than the current EU Institutions' individual frameworks – through new additional powers – but would also be more independent and permanent.

Second, while an IIA-powered ethics body cannot fully overcome the current fragmentation of EU ethics frameworks, it can – by pooling together their respective enforcement mechanisms – favour common approaches to concretise the application of the existing ethical obligations.

Third, high ethical standards contribute not just to output-oriented (*what*) legitimacy, but also to throughput legitimacy (*how*). In other words, the stronger the EU ethics system, the higher the level of trust in the operation of the EU. This is because any unethical behaviour by staff and members of the EU Institutions and bodies attracts high levels of public scrutiny and reduces trust in the EU as a whole.

Fifth, by preventing and mitigating the risk of ethical misconduct, a strong and credible EU dedicated ethics system could become a model for other public administrations and political bodies within and across the EU.

Ultimately, amid growing public scrutiny over the EU's democratic operation, the time has come for the EU Institutions themselves to take existing EU public ethics standards and their enforcement more seriously.

5

The Transnationalisation of the Foreign Investment Contract

An Unrealised Myth

M SORNARAJAH

I. Introduction

Professor Snyder wrote extensively on law and development in the newly independent countries.[1] The topic of foreign investment contracts has much to do with development. His interest in globalisation and the harmonisation of laws has relevance to the subject of transnational law. Given that he had interests in both development and transnational law, the consideration of the subject of foreign investment contracts in a work in his honour is appropriate.

When transnational law came to be discussed in its formative days by some of its progenitors, one area that was chosen for study, particularly by Judge Philip Jessup, was the existence of foreign investment contracts, which, he suggested, were subject to transnational law. Around the time that Jessup wrote his book on *Transnational Law*,[2] there was an effort to create a law that would ensure that foreign investment contracts, especially in the petroleum area, are kept secure by

[1] F Snyder, 'The Failure of "Law and Development"' (1982) 3 *Wisconsin Law Review* 373; F Snyder, 'Labour Power and Legal Transformation in Senegal' (1981) 21 *Review of African Political Economy* 26; F Snyder, 'Colonialism and Legal Form: The Creation of "Customary Law" in Senegal' (1981) 19 *Journal of Legal Pluralism*, 49; F Snyder, 'Law and Development in the Light of Dependency Theory' (1980) 14(3) *Law and Society Review* 723 (Special Issue on 'Contemporary Issues in Law and Social Science'); F Snyder, 'Legal Innovation and Social Change in a Peasant Community: A Senegalese Village Police' (1978) 48(3) *Africa* 231. My favourite article is F Snyder, 'Law and Development in the Light of the Dependency Theory' (1980) 14 *Contemporary Issues in Law and Social Science* 783. Later, this interest seems to focus on economic globalisation: F Snyder, 'Governing Economic Globalization: Global Legal Pluralism and European Law' (1999) 5 *European Law Journal* 334; F Snyder, 'Economic Globalization and the Law in the 21st Century' in A Sarat (ed), *The Blackwell Companion to Law and Society* (New York, Blackwell, 2003).

[2] P Jessup, *Transnational Law* (New Haven, Yale University Press, 1956). On this work, see P Zumbansen (ed), *The Many Lives of Transnational Law: Critical Engagements with Jessup's Bold Proposal* (Cambridge, Cambridge University Press, 2020).

subjecting them to an immutable supranational system of law. Given the decolonisation that was taking place, the administrations being set up in the newly independent oil-producing countries could not be expected to honour contracts, especially those that were made during colonial times and were not to the advantage of the new states. The newly independent states sought to restructure their economies so as to end the economic dominance of the foreign corporations over their oil and natural resources sectors. Those in the developed world, the world of the former imperialist powers, were intent on ensuring that their supplies of oil and other natural resources, which fuelled their industries and ensured their prosperity, continued without interruption despite decolonisation. The developed states and the oil corporations saw the need to create a system that would ensure this even after the ending of colonialism so that their dominance over oil continued. The way out was the construction either of a new system of law, a supranational system that was beyond change by the newly independent states. Later, the project became more ambitious with the suggestion that this transnational system was no different from international law. Gunboat diplomacy being no longer possible, the law became the weapon through which dominance was to be maintained. The attempt was to ensure that law became an instrumental agency through which there was continued dominance over the natural resources sectors of the newly independent states. There has been an effort to continue with this law to the present times, though that effort has become increasingly dented.

The process of affirming that a foreign investment contract made with a state or its entity was not a domestic contract but was subject to a supranational regime, if not international law, was asserted as the decolonisation period began. Theoretical difficulties arising from the prevailing positivist philosophy prevented international law from applying to such contracts, as the multinational company lacked legal personality in positivist international law. International law was seen as a law between states prior to the Second World War. Only sovereign states were actors within international law.[3] Hence, the idea of transnational law, a supranational system that stood higher than domestic law but lower than international law, was adopted as the solution. This law became the basis for the argument that state contracts in the oil and natural resources sectors could not be changed without incurring heavy damages as the contracts were protected under transnational law. But, progressively, the view that international law was no different from transnational law became the dominant position.

This assiduous attempt to establish an international contract law was characterised as a myth.[4] It was a change in the existing law attempted to ensure that the control over natural resources of the newly independent countries could be

[3] With the rapid rise of the human rights movement in international law, positivism came to be displaced, but it was convenient for the Western international lawyers to continue with the view that multinational corporations did not have personality in international law so as to avoid their accountability.

[4] This was principally in an article written by the present author: M Sornarajah, 'The Myth of International Contract Law' (1979) 13 *Journal of World Trade Law* 108.

continued through mechanisms of international law.[5] The project itself depended on the creation of mechanisms which would give teeth to the myth. These efforts were met by the developing states through their drive towards insisting on the application of their own law to natural resources transactions best encapsulated in the General Assembly Resolutions on the New International Economic Order (NIEO). These efforts were reflected in the domestic legal systems of resource-producing states, in the administrative structures created to control natural resources through state corporations and the contractual structures reflecting continuous administrative control over resource exploitation. With the present emphasis on regulatory controls, despite the efforts of competing mechanisms, the effort to create a transnational or international law on state contracts involving resource exploitation, or any other foreign investment transaction, must still be considered a myth. There were two competing ideas at play. The interests of the oil importing states and the multinational corporations were in securing a law that delocalised the state contract by subjecting it to a supranational system. The interests of the oil-producing states was to ensure that the contract was localised within their domestic legal system. The two ideas clashed. The clash still continues. As long as the notion that the law that applies to the state contract is domestic law, which was the original position taken in international law, the competing notion that international law applies to state contracts in the natural resources sector or in other sectors will remain a myth, despite the strenuous efforts that have been made to concretise that myth.

II. The Construction of the Myth

There was overwhelming acceptance prior to the period of decolonisation after the Second World War that the law applicable to a contract made by a state with a foreign commercial entity was the domestic law of that state.[6] This was a logical view. The contract was formed within the state. It was to operate within the territory of the state. It employed personnel within the states. It concerned the exploitation of the vital resources of the state. Besides, there was nothing in international law that applied to the formation or the operation of such contracts.[7]

[5] R Dolzer, *Petroleum Contracts and International Law* (Oxford, Oxford University Press, 2018); L Cotula, 'Investment Contracts and International Law: Charting a Research Agenda' (2020) 31 *European Journal of International Law* 353.

[6] *The Serbian Loans Case* [1929] PCIJ Series A 1.

[7] There was plenty of authority prior to decolonisation that the law that applied to state contracts was domestic law and not international law. In fact, in the three cases where the idea of transnational law was first articulated – the *Abu Dhabi Arbitration* (1951) 18 ILR 44, the *Qatar Arbitration* (1953) 20 ILR 534 and the *Aramco Arbitration* (1958) 28 ILR 117 – the arbitrators uniformly acknowledged that the law that would ordinarily apply was the law of the host state, but that they had to construct a law on the basis of general principles because the domestic laws of the states involved lacked sophistication. See M Sornarajah, 'The Battle Continues: Rebuilding Empire through the Internationalization of State Contracts' in J van Berstoff and P Dann (eds), *The Battle for International Law: South-North Perspectives in the Decolonization Era* (Oxford, Oxford University Press, 2019) 175.

During the colonial era, there was no need to change this rule, as the law that operated was the law of the imperial system. As imperial rule came to an end, there was a need for a secure system that ensured the continued dominance over the oil and natural resources sectors by the corporations of the former imperial powers. The making of a supranational system of law for the protection of state contracts in resource-related transactions was through the employment of low-order sources of international law. The use of arbitration to settle disputes from such contracts and the writings of publicists in support of the evolution of the system were instrumental in the establishment of a mechanism that could be promoted.[8] While this attempt was being made, the developing countries asserted their right to control their natural resources, which were the mainstay of their economies. They did this largely through the collective assertion of a right of states to control their natural resources in several United Nations General Assembly Resolutions, principally the Resolution on the Permanent Sovereignty over Natural Resources, which came to be embodied in the later Resolutions on the Charter of Economic Rights and Duties of States (CERDS) and the New International Economic Order.[9] What is important to note is that they were merely asserting the pre-existing international law that referred state contracts to the domestic legal system in which the contract was made and in which it operated. They were not asserting a new principle. It is rudimentary that resources occurring within the territorial jurisdiction of a state are subject to the law of that state. Every developed country accepted this proposition. The fact that developing countries had to assert the proposition vigorously is indicative of the efforts that were being made to create new law that tied up the exploitation of their natural resources to serve the interests of the developed world. There was a need for them to resist this development.

III. The Course of the Myth of International Contract Law

As indicated, the clear rule in international law during the first half of the twentieth century was that there was no international law relating to a contract between a state and a foreign private party. This has been stated many times over by authoritative tribunals. The Permanent Court of International Justice approved the rule in

[8] There was intense scholarly activity to promote this change: see, eg, Lord McNair, 'General Principles of Law Recognized by Civilized Nations' (1958) 33 *British Yearbook of International Law* 1; R Jennings, 'State Contracts in International Law' (1961) 18 *International and Comparative Law Quarterly* 987.

[9] The various General Assembly Resolutions beginning in 1961 asserted the permanent sovereignty of the state over natural resources and right of a state to control its economy. They were packaged together in the form of the New International Economic Order (NIEO). The norms articulated in these resolutions remain alive. See M Sornarajah, 'The Return of the NIEO and the Retreat of Neoliberal International Law' in S Bhuiyan et al (eds), *International Law and Developing Countries: Essays in Honour of Kamal Hussain* (Leiden, Martinus Nijhoff, 2014).

the *Serbian Loans Case.*[10] The *Anglo-Iranian Oil Company Case*,[11] which involved in effect the nationalisation of the British oil company that was the forerunner of British Petroleum, was a case brought by the UK against Iran, an interstate dispute submitted to the International Court of Justice. It was accepted at the time that the oil company could not have brought proceedings for violation of international law, for the simple reason that international law applied only as between states according to the prevailing positivist theory.[12] Besides, there were no tribunals that could have entertained such litigation. The British used naked power to deal with the situation. The *Rosemary Case*[13] involved the diversion of a ship carrying Iranian oil to the then British port of Aden, where the ownership of oil was litigated. The Aden court held that the oil belonged to the British company as the oil fields from which it was extracted was wrongfully taken from the British company by the Iranian government.[14] A coup inspired by the US and the UK ousted the democratically elected Marxist Prime Minister of Iran, Mohammad Mossadegh, and replaced him with the Shah of Iran, who resumed a pro-Western policy that served the interests of the oil company.[15] Gunboat diplomacy and covert undermining of legitimate governments ensured economic dominance of weaker states, as the events in Iran demonstrated. In addition, there were other avenues of achieving ostensible legitimacy. Power and pliant courts were willing tools that provided cloaks to cover illegitimacy, as the *Rosemary* situation illustrated. But, with freedom struggles all over Africa and Asia, the writing was on the wall that this era was about to pass.

A new system had to be created to ensure the dominance of the West in the oil industry, an objective that had guided the foreign policy of Europe and the US. Oil was vital to the continued hegemony of the West, as it fuelled the industries, transport and commerce of the Western world. The instrumental use of international law to elevate the contract into the supranational sphere was the technique used to achieve this objective. This would give immutability to the oil contract for

[10] *Serbian Loans Case* (1929) PCIJ Series A No 20.

[11] *Anglo-Iranian Oil Company Case* (1952) ICJ Rep 93.

[12] The view that multinational corporations do not have personality in international law continues to be repeated in Western textbooks on international law. Consequently, an entity that plays a commanding role in international law escapes accountability, though, under the theory of internationalisation of state contracts and under treaty law relating to investment, it is given the right to sue host states. As such, it has the best of both worlds.

[13] *Anglo-Iranian Oil Company v Jaffrate (The Rose Mary)* [1953] 1 WLR 253.

[14] M Sornarajah, *The Pursuit of Nationalized Property* (Leiden, Martinus Nijhoff, 1986).

[15] The Central Intelligence Agency (CIA) admitted its role in the overthrow of the democratically elected Iranian government. 'CIA Admits Role in 1953 Iranian Coup', *The Guardian*, 19 August 2013. Documents released showed the involvement of the British government. The pro-Western Shah of Iran replaced the Mossadegh government. He was deposed in 1979 by an Islamic Revolution. The events turned out not to be in the interests of the US and the UK, and is an indication of the failure of the repeated instances of interventionist politics by big powers. Mossadegh was an anti-colonial figure committed to democracy and human rights. His removal and replacement by a tyrant led to the return of the Ayatollah Khomeini and the institution of an anti-Western government which has ruled Iran for many years. As has often happened, the US and British intervention had unintended consequences, although this has never stopped them from intervening. Later, they intervened in Iraq and Lebanon, with very similar results.

the duration stated in the contract by putting it beyond the authority of the state to change its terms. If the technique of ensuring dominance in the oil industry is achieved, the same techniques could be used in the case of other natural resources so that the Western states, the former imperial powers, could continue with the economic dominance they had initiated through colonialism and keep the natural resources of the former colonies under their control despite decolonisation. It would be as if decolonisation had never taken place in the economic sphere. The control of the economic sphere would in effect also ensure the control of the political sphere.

Both decolonisation that resulted from the recognition of the principle of self-determination and the prohibition of the use of force by the United Nations, which made the use of gunboat diplomacy illegal, ensured that the old methods of pursuing dominance through coercion were no longer possible. There was a need to put in place a new method of exerting control over natural resources, particularly oil. This project was started in earnest by Western international lawyers, focusing initially on the building-up of a transnational law that would apply to contracts, as well as disputes arising from contracts between multinational corporations and other foreign investors and host states, particularly oil-producing countries.

As stated earlier, the work which gave academic impetus to this project was Judge Philip Jessup's *Transnational Law* published in 1956.[16] This work systematised the existence of a regime of law that stood between domestic law and international law and applied to actors such as multinational corporations, which, from a positivist perspective, did not have personality in international law. Parallel to the publication of this work was the emergence of three arbitrations in the oil sector which adverted to the existence of a law other than domestic law that would apply to disputes in the oil industry. All three arbitrations acknowledged that ordinarily the law of the host state – that is, the law of the Middle Eastern state in which the exploitation of the oil took place – would apply. This was the conventional position in international law.

However, the arbitrations stated that the law of the Middle Eastern states, being primitive, was not suitable to be applied to complex contracts such as petroleum contracts. Hence, they suggested that it was more appropriate to apply general principles of law of advanced legal systems, which would provide more acceptable answers. This reasoning is characterised by a sense of racial superiority. If one looks at the contemporary English law of contract in the classic textbooks of the time, one would find that it was developed through a diet of cases on the sale of carbolic smoke balls, Constable paintings and the hiring of deckchairs in Brighton. None of them involved much complexity. Islamic law provided answers to all of the characteristic cases that arose in contemporary English law. Like English law, Islamic law could have been extended through analogical reasoning,

[16] For an assessment of the impact of the work, see Zumbansen (n 2).

which is what judges do when faced with novel problems. The idea that the law was unsuitable for complex contracts was a ruse that was being used to make a leap into the construction of transnational law that gave immutability to the petroleum contracts. Selectivity was also involved in the choice of the legal systems from which general principles were extracted. Aside from the fact that Asian, African and Latin American systems were ignored, the law of the powerful communist states, the Soviet Union and China, were ignored. The general principles were extracted from a few European capitalist states and foisted on the world as transnational law. The selection was subjective as the arbitrators could not have possibly known the position in all the European systems. They chose a principle that was most consistent with their objective. There was no demonstration that the principle they chose, the sanctity of contracts, was in fact a principle that was common to the European legal systems.

The extraction of the sanctity of contracts as the only relevant principle suited the oil multinationals as it made the oil contract, usually a concession for the exploitation of land for a long period stretching to over half a century, unchangeable for its duration.[17] It was protected by a stabilisation clause which made future changes to the domestic law not applicable to the contract. Once the immutability of the contract is established and maintained through the law, the exploitation of oil becomes assured, if a system for sustaining the principle of sanctity of contract can be built. The principle of sanctity of contracts as the sole general principle was itself a fiction, as the European systems were moving away from the sanctity of contract and recognising defences to liability for breaches of contracts based on inequality in bargaining power, such as duress and undue influence. Mercenary motives and lack of objectivity undermine the legitimacy in the selection of sanctity of contract as a general principle.

The procedural system that was devised, as a compliance mechanism, was arbitration. The substantive law was transnational law, which was soon to be changed to public international law. The devising of this system was based on a series of subterfuges that must be identified prior to analysis. These subterfuges make the existence of an international law on contract a myth that exists only in the realm of fantasy, despite the fact that it has been used in some arbitral tribunals. The fact that habitual errors have been made as to rules of international law does not create law, especially if those errors have been continually contested.[18] These rules, which were made on the basis that the domestic laws of the Middle Eastern states – Islamic law – lacked sophistication, smack of racial arrogance that is no longer acceptable to the large majority of the international community.

[17] H. Wehberg, '*Pacta Sunt Servanda*' (1959) 53 *American Journal of International Law* 775. The use of the principle of treaty law was to elevate foreign investment contracts to a position akin to treaties and make them equally subject to international law. The role that international lawyers played in this perfidious reasoning must be noted. It defied theory, but promoted a purely mercenary interest.

[18] Throughout the assertion of the theory of internationalisation, developing states have argued that the host state laws have primacy over other laws.

IV. The Course of Development of the Myth of International Contract Law

This section is brief, as the present author has recounted the development of this area of the law in other publications.[19] Essentially, the foundations of the law were laid in three petroleum-related arbitrations concerning disputes arising in Middle Eastern states. In all three of them, the arbitrators employed similar reasoning.[20] They accepted that there was no rule that applied to contracts between foreign investors and states apart from the law of the host state. It was, on any choice of law theory, the only law that would be relevant to the contract. Yet, the uniform finding of all three arbitral tribunals was that Middle Eastern law, or Islamic law, was not mature enough to contain principles that could apply to sophisticated contracts on oil exploration. The racist arrogance of this conclusion has already been pointed out. But, after stating this, there is a uniform acceptance that general principles of law should be applied.

The use of general principles of law in these arbitrations provided the connecting link with international law. As general principles of law were a source of international law, principles drawn from general principles were regarded as part of public international law. The argument then came to be made that what applied to foreign investment contracts between multinational corporations and states was public international law.[21] This conclusion depended on the making of subterfuges in relation to international law. The subterfuges that were made towards the creation of the internationalisation of contracts must be identified. Seven distinct subterfuges can be identified in the course of the creation of a transnational law that was later upgraded into international law.

V. Seven Subterfuges Underlying the Myth

The first subterfuge is the effort to confer limited personality on the multinational corporation. The old positivist view was that the multinational corporation did not have personality in the law, despite the fact that many of them exercised

[19] M Sornarajah, *The International Law on Foreign Investment*, 5th edn (Cambridge, Cambridge University Press, 2021).

[20] *Abu Dhabi Arbitration* (1951) 18 ILR 144; *Qatar Arbitration* (1953) 20 ILL 544; *Aramco Arbitration* (1963) 23 ILR 117. Another arbitration involving Iran followed these awards: *Sapphire Arbitration* (1963) 36 ILR 136. Outside of petroleum contracts, the theory was used in other sectors like construction agreements: *Holiday Inns v Morocco* (1974) 2 ICSID Rep 16.

[21] The link was provided by the article written shortly after the Middle Eastern arbitrations by Lord McNair (n 8); A Leiter, 'Protecting Concessionary Rights: General Principles of Law and the Making of International Investment Law' (2022) 35 *Leiden Journal of International Law* 55. Leiter discusses the impact of a small group of English international lawyers on the development of the theories in the field. These men were celebrated as great visionaries, but used their academic cloaks to promote mercenary motives of constructing a law to protect oil interests.

sovereignty and played a leading role in international affairs. They waged wars, conquered territories, committed genocide, and engaged in trade and investment. It was convenient to cover their sins through the denial of personality, as this would mean that there would be no accountability for their several routinely committed illegalities. The shareholders of these companies were the political leaders of the colonial powers. They too escaped liability as they were distinct from the corporations which committed the misdeeds in terms of the law. But the inconvenient factor was that such a lack of personality would mean that the multinational company could not institute proceedings against states to recover damages for expropriations or other measures taken against their interests. For this reason, a technique had to be created to give limited personality to the foreign investor to bring arbitrations against host states. This was done progressively, first by contracts and then through bilateral investment treaties creating a unilateral right in the foreign investor to institute arbitration against the host state. So came about the situation in which the multinational corporations had rights, but bore no duties towards the host state and its people.

The second subterfuge was to create a substantive law that would recognise the stability of contract and property. They are the twin pillars of the modern international investment law. However, international law recognised neither the concept of property[22] nor a concept of a contract between private parties. Both concepts operated within the territory of the state and it was logical that the law that applied to both concepts would be the domestic law of the state. This would not do for investment protection, as the domestic law could be changed by the state to restrict or nullify both concepts. In order to prevent such a result, the idea was thought of lifting these concepts into a higher sphere, namely transnational law, so that they could be granted immutability. Hence, it came about that a transnational law on contract and property was created, though neither concept, outside of the territorial law of the state, could have been based on logic.[23]

The third subterfuge was building a substantive law on which this process of lifting out could be located, and the finding of an explanation for this magical feat of ensuring that the contract accomplished a lift-off outside the domestic sphere and attached itself to the supranational sphere. This was accomplished through the argument that the law that applied to such contracts was to be found in the general principles of law common to all states. Since the contract had an external element, it was argued that it was required by fairness that there should be an international element in the law that applied. It was discovered that the only general principle that applied was the sanctity of contracts. This view was demonstrably false, as

[22] Property was a concept of the domestic law of states. States created property rights within their territory. It was not within the domain of international law.

[23] The protection of property and contract were fundamental to the neoliberal theory that economic relations should be built on the basis of the free market. The rise of the theory is coterminous with the rise of the theory of internationalisation of foreign investment contracts, as well as the notion of absolute protection of foreign investment through the construction of a web of bilateral investment treaties and the case law built on them.

most contract systems of the world had begun to move away from the notion of contractual sanctity by recognising that the contract may be nullified or amended by circumstances such as undue influence, duress or unconscionability due to imbalances in the bargaining power of the parties. The choice of contractual sanctity was one of convenience, not one of real fact.

The fourth subterfuge was the use of the stabilisation clause in the petroleum contract that the law prevailing at the time of entry should not be modified by the state in a manner adverse to the interests of the foreign investor. The contract was insulated from any such change made as a result of the existence of the stabilisation clause. This theory of insulation is based on consent. However, it is one that is inconsistent with the constitutional systems of any state. It is inconceivable that any constitutional system can accommodate a rule that enables the removal of a sovereign right of the state to change a purely domestic obligation by an amending legislation. The notion of the immutability of the stabilisation clause is inconsistent with the general principle that the sovereignty of a state cannot be impeded or restricted by a mere contractual provision.

The fifth subterfuge is the asymmetry of the applicability of the law that has been constructed. It was not to apply to petroleum resources in the developing countries, which were always subject to their domestic laws. So, some altruistic reasoning had to be found in order to explain why the law was different for natural resources in developing countries. The subterfuge was that these states needed economic development and that the only way in which the foreign investment necessary for economic development could be attracted was through the provision of the law that gave the process stability. This was a farcical explanation. Petroleum exploration has taken place in the developing world without any economic development ever taking place. The law that was sought to be created merely ripped off the assets of developing countries to the advantage of the major oil corporations. Economic development which never occurred in any petroleum or natural resources-producing country was hardly a justification for tying the economic base of a country in thraldom to a foreign exploiter. The benefits were one-sided, with pollution and other harms resulting from the exploitation of the resources.

The sixth subterfuge was the devising of a secure compliance mechanism for the system. There was arbitration between states, but an investment dispute will not qualify for such arbitration as one party is a private actor. There was international commercial arbitration between private parties, but, technically, this will not capture the situation of investment disputes as there is a sovereign state involved. Though petroleum contracts began referring to arbitration as a method of dispute settlement and such arbitration clauses were invoked, it was not clear what the nature of the arbitration was. There were obvious public law features in the arbitration, as most disputes arose as a result of state interferences with the contract for public interest reasons. This puts the fact situation involved outside the commercial sphere. The use of commercial arbitration meant that arbitrators untrained in public law dealt with issues relating to governmental decisions in the public interest by applying simple breach of contract rules. The decisions were then enforced through a mechanism of a convention, the New York Convention on the Enforcement of Foreign Arbitral Awards 1957, which was designed for the enforcement of purely commercial awards. The genesis of this system had no logical base.

The seventh subterfuge was that the system was supported by the writings of highly qualified publicists and decisions of tribunals, both subsidiary sources of international law. This enabled the transfer of what initially began as a system of an amorphous transnational law into public international law. Yet, the so-called 'highly qualified publicists' were no more than hired guns. Many had been advisors to the petroleum corporations or handled litigation for them. Many of the arbitrators sought repeat appointments by stating viewpoints that were agreeable to the multinational companies. The agglomeration of these viewpoints of publicists (who were motivated by racial arrogance in condemning the legal systems of developing states as not sufficiently mature) and arbitrators (who had mercenary interests in the outcomes of disputes) can hardly constitute a system of law.

The transnational system or what is now referred to as the international law on foreign investment contracts is flawed by its dependence on seven deadly subterfuges. These subterfuges have attended the origin of the internationalisation of foreign investment contracts and continue to taint them, so that it cannot honestly be argued that there is an international or transnational law on foreign investment contracts.

VI. The Backlash to the Internationalisation of State Contracts: The Myth Exposed

The notion of equality of states is one of the two principles on which the Westphalian order is built, the other being that no state should interfere in the domestic affairs of another state. The system of internationalisation of state contracts runs counter to both principles. It is an asymmetric system built against the interests of developing states with the objective of ensuring that their natural resources continue to be tied up to the multinational corporations, to the advantage of developed states. The fact that such a long string of Western international lawyers consistently supported this offensive principle does not say much for their standing as 'highly qualified publicists'. They were mercenary men[24] lending their names to a theoretically irrational and unjust system that ensured the economic thraldom of the former colonies after their independence. They prostituted their learning to keep the majority of people in the world in perpetual poverty.

As the newly independent states became organised, they began to assert their control over natural resources through a series of resolutions of the

[24] In the initial period at least, no women were represented in this group. There came about many women lawyers who supported this iniquitous system.

United Nations General Assembly, culminating in the Resolution of the New International Economic Order. The principle of permanent sovereignty is regarded by many scholars as an *ius cogens* principle of international law. The strange fact is that such a doctrine had to be articulated, for no Western state would have brooked the idea that any system other than its domestic law would have applied to the exploitation of its natural resources. The fact that it had to be stated by the developing states signalled the continued dominance of these natural resources despite independence. When it was formulated, it was immediately challenged by Western international lawyers who sought to whittle down its scope, in another display of duplicity that ignored the fact that their own states recognised only the relevance of the domestic law when it came to the disposal of natural resources. It was derided as *lex ferenda* by the arbitrator in *Texaco*. It was denied the status of law as it was contained in General Assembly Resolutions. Despite frenetic disavowals of the Western international lawyers, it is now generally conceded that the doctrine is a part of international law which is not much of a concession to make.

The doctrine of permanent sovereignty operates at three distinct levels of the law: it is a part of international law; it has moved into the constitutions of the former colonial states of Africa and Asia; and it forms part of the foreign investment codes of states, where such codes exist. Most importantly, natural resources sectors are operated in the developing states by state corporations in which a monopoly of the sector is vested so that they control the exploitation of the resources. Their control is manifested in the contractual terms on the basis of which the foreign investor operates. The production sharing contract which has replaced the concession agreement in the oil industry is a classic example of this. It contemplates the diminishing role of the foreign investor through stages of the contract until they disappear altogether after recovering their initial outlay and reasonable profits. The scope for internationalisation of the contract diminishes virtually to a vanishing point under such circumstances. The stabilisation clause does not feature in such contracts, as the contracts anticipate and provide for changes at every phase.

These are changes brought about by resistance to the idea of the internationalisation of state contracts through their subjection to international law. The developed world has joined in resisting the old norms they had fashioned because they have now become the largest recipients of foreign investments, particularly from China as well as other industrialising states like India, Brazil and South Africa. The assertion of the exercise of regulatory power to reorder the foreign investment relationship is a feature of the arguments that have been made by the developed states. In making these arguments, they have used terminology that asserts notions of sovereignty, as the Third World did in constructing the NIEO. Equally, in the protection of their national interests, the developed states have begun to use the defence of national security extensively. These states are now on the defensive and will not support expansive theories that affect their national interests. The law can be expected to change and what was a myth will be recognised as such when time passes. The problem is that there could be new oppressors taking the mantle of the developed states in sustaining the myth. The chance of this happening has become remote, as no single hegemonic power will emerge in the multipolar world which will not have a powerful grouping of states to maintain its theory with the requisite vigour.

Since the articulation of the theory of internationalisation, international law as an unfragmented discipline has created obligations on states through multilateral treaties as well as custom that whittles away obligations created by contracts into virtual oblivion. The developments in international law on human rights, environmental protection, protection of the rights of Indigenous people, protection of cultural property, protection of labour standards and climate change have created obligations that states owe to the international community. When these obligations clash (as they often do) with contractual obligations, the latter simply have to give way. In the context of these obligations, the role that a theory of internationalisation can play becomes severely limited. States have to act not only in the public interest but also in the interests of the international community. These interests overwhelm the interest in the protection of private foreign investment.

The free market philosophy which sustained the theory of internationalisation has also receded due to successive economic crises indicating the absence of success of the states accepting the theory. This will also lead to the erosion of the internationalisation thesis. Despite the fact that the theory of the internationalisation of state contracts is diminishing in vigour, there are efforts to keep it alive through feeble means of linking it with developments in investment treaty arbitration. The next section looks at these efforts.

VII. Efforts to Keep the Myth Alive

The resuscitation of the myth of internationalisation is attempted by seeking to link trends in investment arbitration with internationalisation on the basis that the contract now comes to be protected by some developments that have taken place within investment arbitration. The initial weaknesses of such efforts are numerous. First, the theory of internationalisation preceded investment treaty arbitrations which became prominent only after 1991 with the award in *AAPL v Sri Lanka*,[25] which announced that investment treaties contained an offer of arbitration which is accepted by a foreign investor when they bring an arbitration against the state for a treaty violation. Technically, the theory is a stand-alone theory and is used as such today in areas where there are no treaties or where the treaties do not cover the situation. The fact is that in many regions, like Africa, treaties are signed but remain unratified. Hence, arguments based on treaties have little impact on the internationalisation theory. Second, though pressed at one stage that treaty principles constitute customary international law, this argument is no longer taken seriously as treaties contain wide divergences and do not cover all types

[25] *AAPL v Sri Lanka* ICSID ARB/87/3 (27 June 1990).

of investments or investors. That being so, it is difficult to see how developments in investment treaty arbitration can have an impact on the internationalisation theory that is passed off as a principle of international law.

Despite these general objections, the specific manner in which the arguments are developed in connection with the link between the internationalisation thesis and investment treaty arbitration needs to be assessed. The objections relate to two specific situations. The first one is the relevance of the umbrella clause in the treaties which protects all commitments made to the foreign investor, which also involves contractual commitments. The second is the case law that has arisen relating to the fair and equitable treatment provision of the investment treaties. It has been interpreted to include legitimate expectations of the foreign investor. The argument is that the contract is protected as the stability of the contract falls within the range of legitimate expectations that the foreign investor has. Both these arguments need to be considered.

A. The Umbrella Clause

As indicated, the umbrella clause is a catch-all provision of investment treaties that simply states that all commitments made to the foreign investor must be honoured.[26] Not all investment treaties have such a clause. Because of the implications of such a general obligation, the newer treaties that are made simply ignore the clause, thereby reducing the significance of any argument made in reliance of the umbrella clause to support the internationalisation theory. One strand of the case law is completely against attaching any significance to the umbrella clause.[27] This strand points out that if the umbrella clause has the significance it is claimed to have, the provisions of the carefully crafted treaty will cease to have any significance, as its breadth captures more than what the rest of the provisions capture. The clause would render the other provisions of the treaty superfluous. All that would be needed is simply to have the umbrella clause. In the context of this group of cases, no claims can be made that the umbrella clause supports the internationalisation theory by protecting contractual commitments. The precise wording of the clause also matters as regards its coverage.[28] Academic opinions on this diverge as much as the case law does: some give the clause full effect and some argue that violations of contractual commitments are commercial acts, not sovereign acts, which are the object of treaties.[29] There is also considerable divergence within the

[26] An example is: 'Each Contracting State shall observe any obligation it may have entered into with regard to the investments of nationals or companies of the other Contracting Party.' British Model Treaty, art 2(2).

[27] *SGS v Pakistan* (2003) ICSID ARB/01/13 (6 August 2003). In two other cases involving Swiss treaties and SGS, the tribunals agreed with arguments based on the umbrella clauses.

[28] *Noble Ventures v Romania* ICSID ARB/01/11 (12 October 2005).

[29] *CMS v Argentina* 12 May 2005 ICSID Case No ARB/01/8; *Burlington v Ecuador* 2 June 2010 ICSID Case No ARB/08/5.

awards as to whether the umbrella clause applies to contracts made by state entities and subsidiaries or whether there must be direct obligations undertaken by the state.[30]

The significance of umbrella clauses in investment treaties is diminishing as states, conscious of their scope and possible interpretations, are simply leaving them out of their new treaties. Besides, the extent of the divergence of opinion is so great that arguments based on the clauses would lack significant credibility. Consequently, their impact on the internationalisation theory would not make that theory anything more than a myth.

B. Legitimate Expectations and the Fair and Equitable Standard

The fair and equitable standard was a dormant standard that had existed since the very first investment treaty made in 1958. A leading article on it in 1999 stated that no particular meaning could be ascribed to the clause. Suddenly it was awakened by a few arbitrators committed to giving the clause an expansive interpretation. The inclusion of the notion of legitimate expectation for which there was no textual authority in the treaty ensured that the standard became the focal point for future arbitrations. The idea was that, when the state through its statements created in the foreign investor a legitimate expectation as to the stability of the investment, then, measures taken by the state which sunder that expectation create liability on the basis of the violation of the fair and equitable standard. Repetition of the formula virtually by a single arbitrator established the doctrine in investment law. The most focused-upon situation that gave rise to the expectation was the existence of a stabilisation clause in the contract. Yet, after early fascination with the interpretation, a significant level of backtracking has occurred.

There has been a focus on whether the foreign investor's expectations were legitimate so that risky ventures were not covered by the clause. The regulatory power of the state to interfere will not be affected. The competing community interests in the environment, human rights and other factors will negate the expectations of the foreign investor, who must factor these into account in his or her expectations. The contextual approach that is taken to the interpretation of the provision in modern treaty law greatly reduces the original significance of the notion of legitimate expectations.

The attitude to stabilisation clauses has undergone a change quite independently. In *Aminoil Award*,[31] the view was taken that changed circumstances nullify the force of a stabilisation clause and that, in any case, the validity of the stabilisation clause must be limited to the specific period when a new investment

[30] Compare *Strabag v Libya* 29 June 2020 ICSID Case No ARB(AF)/15/1 with *Impreglio v Pakistan* 22 April 2005 ICSID Case No ARB/03/3.

[31] *Aminoil v Kuwait* (1982) 21 ILM 976.

finds its feet. In the context of these developments, the extent to which the stabilisation clause affects the internationalisation theory is, at best, minimal if not non-existent.

Some newer treaties specifically put an end to the notion of legitimate expectations being the basis of violation of any treaty standard. Thus, the Indonesia-Singapore BIT (2021) states that the 'mere fact that a Party regulates, including through the modification of its laws, in a manner that affects the investment or interferes with the investor's expectations, including its expectations of profits, does not amount to a breach of its obligations under this Agreement'.[32] Such formulations put an end to any adventurist interpretations that seek to revive the internationalisation of investment contracts through investment treaties.

Besides being theoretically unsound, the developments in investment treaty arbitration in no way enable the rescue of the internationalisation thesis. Whatever optimistic inferences may have existed when the process of investment treaty arbitration commenced, they have been nullified as time has passed and discretion has prevailed over the expansionist tendencies of solitary arbitrators. In any event, the internationalisation thesis was a stand-alone formula that arose at a time when treaties did not exist. Its modern significance is that they are relevant to situations in which treaties do not cover the investment, as in some oil-producing regions which have shown reluctance to sign investment treaties or where investment treaties were signed but remain unratified. As a stand-alone thesis, the internationalisation theory continues to remain a myth.

C. The Falsity of the New Emergence of an International Law on Contract

The argument that developments in investment treaty arbitration have led to an emergence of an international contract law are misconceived. For one thing, investment treaties do not have sufficient coverage in the world to be treated as creating customary international law. Even if they do, these treaties do not have sufficient uniformity permitting the extraction of uniform principles. The treaty of even a single country undergoes change depending on the period in which it was created.[33] The early investment treaties stressing strong norms of investment protection have given way to the so-called balanced treaties, which do away with the umbrella clause, on which much of the argument of the emergence

[32] Article 11(2).

[33] Thus, for example, the early treaties of Singapore like the Singapore–UK treaty (1987) were intent on investment protection based on the idea that investment promotes economic development, whereas the new treaties like the Singapore–Indonesia treaty (2021) are balanced treaties based on sustainable investment, containing exceptions to liability based on notions of regulatory takings in the public interest, protection of the environment and human rights. This significantly erodes investment protection.

of a new international contract law is based. Even during the short period in which the umbrella clause was taken somewhat seriously, the arbitral awards diverged so significantly that the making of a conclusion as to the emergence of a new international contract law was fictional. Likewise, the newer investment treaties either leave out the fair and equitable treatment clause, which provides fodder for the view relating to the new emergence, or curtail its use to situations of customary international law, specifically that relating to denial of justice. Indeed, some treaties specifically exclude any notion of legitimate expectations being drawn on the basis of the fair and equitable standard. Even a cursory look at the case law on legitimate expectations indicates such divergence that the awards cannot launch a move towards the emergence of a new international law on contract. Such exercises in kite-flying go against rudimentary principles of international law.

D. International Law's Revenge

The mercenary effort made by distinguished Western international lawyers to subvert the course of international law through what were described as 'seven subterfuges' has come back to undermine their efforts. If international law created through general principles was indeed relevant, the modern extraction of general principles of contract law would create surprising results, as domestic systems of contract law have clearly moved away from sanctity of contract, which these men had isolated as the single relevant principle applicable to state contracts relating to foreign investment.

Yet, more importantly, the modern trends in international law have led to the undermining of contractual sanctity and extolling the relevance of the regulatory power of the state to act in the public interest. Such a power will affect contracts that require change, a fact that *Aminoil v Kuwait* forestalled. But, moreover, the rule relating to the primacy attached to the exercise of regulatory powers of the state in the public interest is well established in investment treaty law. The exercise of such powers to protect health, welfare, the environment, human rights, indigenous rights, cultural property and other matters. These cases indicate principles that also apply to state contracts.

When Article 42 of the ICSID Convention (1965) referred to international law, it was taken as a triumph of the theory of internationalisation. Today, the opposite is true. One has to take account of the whole body of international law as it has developed since 1965 as applicable to state contracts. This would include a range of principles to be taken from environmental law, human rights law, labour rights law, the law on Indigenous people, the law on cultural property and the law on climate change. The scope for internationalisation becomes so whittled down as to make that theory of little use in the protection of state contracts. Again, we have to take it that the myth is best laid to rest. One act in the perfidy of Western international law lies in shambles, though efforts will be made to resuscitate it.

VIII. Conclusion

What was characterised as a myth in an article by the present author 41 years ago still remains a myth, despite frenetic efforts to keep it alive. Its formulation was, as pointed out above, based on seven subterfuges that go against the rudimentary principles of international law. The creation and maintenance of the theory of internationalisation of state contracts call into question international law as a neutral discipline and confirm that it is the instrument not only of public power of state, but also of the private power of multinational corporations. In this field, the law is created by tribunals applying low order sources of international law. Human agents feature in the creation of the law as highly qualified publicists and as arbitrators. Both could and have mercenary interests as to how the law is formulated. This exposes the instrumental manner in which certain areas of international law are formulated to advance the interests of the very rich over the very poor of humanity. International law suffers as a result of being the handmaiden of the privileged, creating misery for the majority of the people of the world.

PART 2

Law in Context

6

The EU and Law in Context

The Context

CAROL HARLOW*

I. Introduction

It is widely acknowledged that the contextual study of EC law, later EU law, has contributed to a richer understanding of EC/EU law. In this context, much is owed to Francis Snyder and, in particular, to his groundbreaking collection *New Directions in European Community Law* and his enterprise as founding editor of the *European Law Journal*. This chapter considers the institutions, milieus and debates which fostered the analysis and assessment of EC and EU law as 'an intricate web of politics, economics and law', at the same time as it pointed to the need for critical self-consciousness about the underlying assumptions that scholars (including contextual scholars) bring to their study of law.

II. A New Approach

In 1987, 15 years after the UK signed up to the EC – realistically perhaps the Common Market[1] – Francis Snyder published an article asking for 'new directions' in the teaching and study of EC law. His complaint was the dryness of EC law studies. EC law had 'often been regarded (and taught) simply as a highly technical set of rules, a dense doctrinal thicket into which only the ignorant or the foolish would "jump in and scratch out their eyes", still less try to understand in terms of social theories of law'.[2] It had in this respect been to some

* For an earlier version of this chapter, see C Harlow, 'The EU and Law in Context: The Context' (2022) 1 *European Law Open* 209.

[1] For contemporary British attitudes to accession, see D Nicol, *EC Membership and the Judicialization of British Politics* (Oxford, Oxford University Press, 2001) chs 3, 4.

[2] F Snyder, 'New Directions in European Community Law' (1987) 14 *Journal of Law and Society* 167.

extent 'incorporated into the textbook tradition of English law',[3] a development Snyder attributed to the fact that EC law had been taught in the UK by 'a handful of specialists', most of whom had begun their careers as legal secretaries at the Court of Justice (ECJ). The outcome had been a markedly uncritical and pro-European stance and a narrow focus in teaching and legal literature on the Court and its case law.[4]

Legal positivism and a narrow focus on doctrine and the jurisprudence of the superior courts are not confined to the UK, and very similar criticism could have been levelled at EC legal studies more widely. In the formative period of EC law, the infant institutions were left much to their own devices without the guidance of a constitution in fleshing out their roles. EC lawyers were largely receptive of integrationist doctrine and concerned at the same time to shelter the ECJ from accusations of playing politics by embedding integrationism in the case law. Martin Shapiro, an American observer with law and/political science qualifications, famously described EC constitutional law as 'constitutional law without the politics'. Shapiro attacked presentation of the EC as:

> [A] juristic idea; the written constitution as a sacred text; the professional commentary as a legal truth; the case law as the inevitable working out of the correct implications of the constitutional text; and the constitutional court as the disembodied voice of right reason and constitutional teleology.[5]

This contribution tells us much about the source of ideas on the need for change of direction in EC legal studies.

Shapiro also asked questions about the legal community in which these attitudes had developed. An empirical survey made some years later showed just how homogeneous the legal coterie was. The majority of those writing on law in major EC journals had close links with one or more of the EC institutions. Their conception of law and what law can and should do was widely shared. They were mainly integrationist in persuasion, identifying with the project of European integration both intellectually and socially, with a tendency 'to rally as one around the Court in its patient creation of a genuine supreme legal order'.[6] The first full-length and full-blooded demolition job on the Court's federalising tendencies and integrationist ideology did not come until 1986,[7] and its author, Hjalte Rasmussen, received a trouncing from mainstream EC lawyers, outraged by the idea that the law/politics

[3] ibid 167, citing Karl Llewellyn's *The Bramble Bush: The Classic Lectures on the Law and Law School* (Oxford, Oxford University Press, 2008).

[4] Snyder (n 2) 168.

[5] M Shapiro, 'Comparative Law and Comparative Politics' (1981) 53 *Southern California Law Review* 537, 538. Shapiro's principal target was A Barav, 'The Judicial Power of the European Economic Community' (1980) 53 *Southern California Law Review* 461, but was also applicable to a wider range of scholarship.

[6] H Schepel and R Wesseling, 'The Legal Community: Judges, Lawyers, Officials and Clerks in the Writing of Europe' (1997) 3 *European Law Journal* 165, 176, 186.

[7] H Rasmussen, *On Law and Policy in the Court of Justice* (The Hague, Martinus Nijhoff, 1986).

boundary had been crossed.[8] Looking back on its publication from the distance of the millennium, Harm Schepel observed that this was only natural; the law/politics distinction was central not only to the Court's legitimacy but also to 'the whole project of European integration'. By that time, however, Schepel was able to point to a body of interdisciplinary research to prove his point that lawyers were starting to look outside studies of rules and principles for full explanations of the legal integration process, while social scientists were beginning to integrate the Court and its constitutionalising case law into their work. 'Integrationist orthodoxy' was no longer the only accepted discourse in legal academia and criticising the Court had become 'the trend'.[9]

Snyder was not a member of the coterie of EC lawyers who surrounded and revered the Court. His legal predilections ranged well beyond judicial process to embrace international, pluralist and interdisciplinary affairs. Here his credentials were formidable. After graduating from Yale, he had completed postgraduate studies in law at Harvard and at the Institut d'Etudes Politiques in Paris, but he also had substantial publications on African politics to his credit. At the time of writing *New Directions*, he was teaching at Warwick Law School founded in 1967 with a law in context agenda and an evolving record for its contextual approach to legal education.

Snyder's take on EC law was as 'an intricate web of politics, economics and law' that called out to be studied and understood by 'a political economy of law or an interdisciplinary, contextual or critical approach'.[10] Without jettisoning the established tradition of 'highly sophisticated scholarship concerning legal doctrine' in fields such as institutions, procedures and competition law, Snyder demanded innovation in the teaching and study of EC law. In the study of institutions and processes, for example, scholars should branch out to study institutions other than courts and utilise the theoretical insights and findings of other social sciences. They should bear in mind that economic law extends outside competition and look outside the EC to the world economy, evaluating the place and importance of the EC in the global economy.[11]

Snyder's own work was innovative. He had been working for some time on the Common Agricultural Policy,[12] on which much of the argument in *New Directions*

[8] See, eg, JHH Weiler, 'The Court of Justice on Trial – A Review of Hjalte Rasmussen: *On Law and Policy in the European Court of Justice*' (1987) 24 *Common Market Law Review* 526; T Toth, 'Book Review' (1987) 12 European Law Review 3; M Cappeletti, 'Book Review' (1987) Yearbook of European Law 411; M Shapiro, 'On Law and Policy in the European Court of Justice: A Comparative Study in Judicial Policymaking' (1987) 81 *American Journal of International Law* 1007.

[9] H Schepel, 'Reconstructing Constitutionalization: Law and Politics in the European Court of Justice' (2000) 20 *OJLS* 457, 458–59, a review article of H Rasmussen and R Dehousse, *The European Court of Justice: The Politics of Judicial Integration* (London, Palgrave Macmillan, 1998), a mildly critical law in context study of the Court.

[10] Snyder (n 2) 167.

[11] ibid 169–71.

[12] F Snyder, *Law of the Common Agricultural Policy* (London, Sweet & Maxwell, 1985), translated as *Le droit de la politique agricole commune* (Paris, Economica, 1987).

is based. This would later form the basis for a study of EC law making intended for anthropologists and first published in a book about the anthropology of law.[13] In this study, Snyder advanced the thesis that conceptions of 'interests' and 'interest representation' underlie any study of law in society, serving as analytical tools for understanding legal ideas, institutions and processes, and helping to define the salient features of law's social context. Conceptions of interest also 'underpin any analysis of law that is not solely doctrinal and that considers law to be integral to social and economic relations. Thus they are indispensable to any understanding of the causes and consequences of the creation, reproduction, or transformation of law'.[14]

Snyder challenged legal scholars 'to make explicit the underlying assumptions about law, the state and society which as teachers and students we bring to EC law'. Somewhat audaciously he maintained that 'the general principles on which the EC was founded and which are consecrated in its basic legal texts, 'appear … merely to restate in legal language and in treaty form the underlying assumptions of contemporary capitalist economies'.[15] The EC was 'inherently neo-colonial' – 'acting for the rich and north in its manifold relations with the poor and south'.[16] Snyder asked for a new agenda suggesting that EC law was in need both of 'a social theory of law' and studies from the 'perspective of critical theory'.[17]

III. Critical Legal Studies: The US

Snyder was tapping into an approach fast becoming fashionable in anglophone legal studies. Prior to the 1960s, mainstream legal thinking in the anglophone world can be summarised as predominately formalist, though moderated in the US, where critical legal studies originate, by the well-established influence of American realism. The celebrated account by Morton Horwitz of the crisis and transformation of 'legal orthodoxy' in the years between 1870 and 1960 contains only one reference to critical legal studies, which Horwitz regards as a 'revival and extension' of American realism or a 1960s critique of a contemporary revival of 'neutral principles' theory.[18] Horwitz is not an admirer of neutral principles doctrine, which he castigates as 'one more effort to separate law and politics in American culture', serving similar dogmatic and legitimating functions to 'religious authority'. Ensuing

[13] F Snyder, 'Thinking about "Interests": Legislative Process in the European Community' in J Starr and J Collier (eds), *History and Power in the Study of Law* (New York, Cornell University Press, 1989).
[14] ibid 169–70.
[15] ibid.
[16] ibid.
[17] ibid.
[18] MJ Horwitz, *The Transformation of American Law 1870–1960* (Oxford, Oxford University Press, 1992) 270–71. See also R Mensch, 'The History of Mainstream Legal Thought' in D Kairys (ed), *The Politics of Law* (New York, Pantheon Books, 1982). 'Neutral principles' theory approximates to Shapiro's conception (n 5 above) of 'law without politics'.

'abstract jurisprudential controversies' had 'misled' generations of legal thinkers, so that legal theories, 'developed out of the exigencies of particular politics and moral struggles', had come to stand as 'universal truths good for all time'.[19]

By the time Snyder wrote, the two closely linked movements of critical legal studies and social theories of law were strongly represented in American legal literature. In the US, where the critical legal studies movement started, David Trubek opened a study of social theory in 1972 by boldly declaring that the implicit, a priori conclusions about the role of law were no longer valid; accordingly, we must turn to 'systematic efforts to understand the relationships among the legal, social, economic, and political orders'.[20] This Trubek himself undertook at an exalted, theoretical level in a long article on critical social thought in law, significantly published in the infant *Law and Society Review* founded in 1966. Basing his thesis on a detailed Marxist analysis by Isaac Balbus of the operation of the criminal justice system in three American cities during ghetto riots in the 1960s,[21] Trubek praised the book's combination of quantitative analysis with Marxist explanations of the data, acclaiming it as a unique and noteworthy contribution to the sociology of law.[22] Elsewhere, Robert Unger identified two main approaches in critical legal studies. The first (in common with social theory) treated doctrine as the expression of a particular vision of society and emphasised the contradictory and manipulable character of doctrinal argument. The second took as its point of departure the idea that law and legal doctrine 'reflect, confirm, and reshape the social divisions and hierarchies inherent in a type or stage of social organization such as "capitalism"'.[23] This closely resembles the points made by Snyder in relation to EC legal studies.

More accessible to the public at large was a set of essays on the politics of law edited by David Kairys. The presentation of law and judicial decision making as 'autonomous' in the sense of separate from politics and impersonal was, Kairys wrote, a picture of 'government by law, not people' separate from or 'above' politics, economics, culture, and the values or preferences of judges'.[24] Kairys repudiated this 'popular perception' of the judicial process and claimed on behalf of the collection to be presenting or at least aiming for 'a progressive, critical analysis of the operation and social role of the law in contemporary American society'.[25] Kairys himself fired well-aimed shots at 'the language of legal discourse and mystique of legal reasoning', arguing that they serve a primarily ideological purpose, with

[19] Horwitz (n 18).

[20] D Trubek, 'Toward a Social Theory of Law: An Essay on the Study of Law and Development' (1972) 82 *Yale Law Journal* 1.

[21] D Trubek, 'Complexity and Contradiction in the Legal Order: Balbus and the Challenge of Critical Social Thought About Law' (1977) 11 *Law & Society Review* 527, discussing I Balbus, *The Dialectics of Legal Repression* (New York, Russell Sage Foundation, 1973).

[22] Trubek (n 21) 531.

[23] R Unger, 'The Critical Legal Studies Movement' (1983) 96 *Harvard Law Review* 561, at fn 11.

[24] D Kairys, 'Introduction' in D Kairys (ed), *The Politics of Law, A Progressive Critique* (New York, Pantheon Books, 1977) 1.

[25] ibid 8.

outcomes determined by social and political judgment: 'law is simply politics by other means'.[26] Essays on a wide variety of legal subjects were contributed by legal practitioners and academics, but using methods drawn from sociology, economics, political science and law. This is something like the approach that Snyder was hoping for in EC legal studies.

IV. Follow My Leader: The UK

In the UK, where realism had not yet taken root, formalism and legal positivism were more firmly entrenched. The task of the judge was presented at the time as 'wholly analytical – to discover the previously existing law, and to apply it logically to the case before the court'.[27] British judges did not consider policy questions – or, at least, not openly. Terence Daintith, embarking some years later on a legal analysis of economic policy, referred to 'wide acceptance' in both academic and practitioner circles of the idea that:

> [T]he writer on public law matters should deliberately distance himself from the hurly-burly of economic events and political action and conflict, and should draw a picture of constitutional and administrative law which is purified of non-legal, short-run influences ... In the result, the mainstream of British writing by lawyers about the constitution analyses constitutional principles and structures largely to the exclusion of any consideration of the activities in which the organs of government are engaged or the purposes with which they pursue them.[28]

In fact, by the time Daintith was writing, the influence of legal positivism was on the wane. The first number of the *British Journal of Law and Society* appeared in 1974 and Phil Thomas, its pioneering editor, traced the study of law in society back to nineteenth-century European sources – Durkheim, Marx and Weber – and, in England, Maine and, perhaps more surprisingly, Dicey.[29] The new journal aimed 'to follow this tradition of transcending disciplinary boundaries by taking as its focus the subject area of law in society'.[30] Nonetheless, in an important article in a later issue, Tony Prosser still found it appropriate to express dissatisfaction with

[26] D Kairys, 'Legal Reasoning' in Kairys (ed) (n 24) 16–17.

[27] KC Davis, 'The Future of Judge-Made Public Law in England: A Problem of Practical Jurisprudence' (1961) 61 *Columbia Law Review* 201, 202. See also P Atiyah and R Summers, *Form and Substance in Anglo-American Law: A Comparative Study of Legal Reasoning, Legal Theory and Legal Institutions* (Oxford, Clarendon Press, 1987).

[28] T Daintith, 'Legal Analysis of Economic Policy' (1982) 9 *Journal of Legal Studies* 191. See also T Daintith, 'Law as a Policy Instrument: A Comparative Perspective' in T Daintith (ed), *Law as an Instrument of Economic Policy: Comparative and Critical Approaches* (Berlin, De Gruyter, 1988).

[29] Whether Dicey was or believed himself to be a legal positivist is hotly disputed: see, eg, MD Walters, *Dicey and the Common Law Constitutional Tradition: A Legal Turn of Mind* (Cambridge, Cambridge University Press, 2020); P Cane, 'Dicey as a Legal Theorist' (2022) 85 MLR 247.

[30] P Thomas, 'Editorial' (1974) 1 *British Journal of Law and Society* (later the *Journal of Law and Society*) 1–2. There is more than a hint of Marxism in many critical legal theories of law.

the traditional common law style of public law writing, 'composed exhaustively of rules which pass formal tests of legal validity'.[31] This positivist conception of law, Prosser noted, was closely linked to liberal-capitalism – a point made by Snyder in connection with EC law. Like Snyder, Prosser rejected the 'neutral principles' approach as 'no longer an appropriate means of conceptualising Western societies'.[32] He once again argued for a new, critical theory of public law, which 'should not only describe and explain the operation of state institutions but should also provide the means for an effective critique of them and point the way for their future development'.[33]

In other areas of law, this development was well under way. A year later, in a survey of the field, Harris reiterated dissatisfaction amongst younger scholars with the traditional style of legal studies and the consequential rise of interest in the study of law in society and sociology of law. He found much legal scholarship in sociology, social policy and social administration, though far less in economics, political science and other related disciplines.[34] The *Law in Context* series of legal books was started in 1970 as a vehicle for works that treated law and legal phenomena 'critically in their cultural, social, political, technological, environmental and economics contexts' and broadly, using materials and methods from 'any other discipline that helps to explain the operation in practice of the particular legal field or legal phenomena under investigation'.[35] This was precisely the approach that Snyder had practised and advocated, and in 1990 he published *New Directions in European Community Law*, a re-publication of his earlier work on the Common Agricultural Plan, as the first law in context study of EC law.[36] In the same series, Ian Ward published *A Critical Introduction to European Law* in 1996, which was designed as an examination of EU law in its economic, philosophical, historical and political contexts.

[31] T Prosser, 'Towards a Critical Public Law' (1982) 9 *Journal of Law and Society* 1, 3. Prosser's article was directed solely to English public law, its main thesis being the need for a new critical public law based on a theory of power and new organising concepts of participation and accountability.

[32] ibid 3. See also D Trubek, 'Max Weber on Law and the Rise of Capitalism' (1972) *Wisconsin Law Review* 720.

[33] 'Prosser (n 31) 13–15.

[34] DR Harris, 'The Development of Socio-Legal studies in the United Kingdom' (1983) 3 *Legal Studies* 315. By 1987, A Hunt had published 'The Theory of Critical Legal Studies' (1986) 6 *OJLS* 1; and P Fitzpatrick and A Hunt (eds), *Critical Legal Studies in the United Kingdom* (Oxford, Blackwell, 1987). See also M Krygier, 'Critical Legal Studies and Social Theory: A Response to Alan Hunt' (1987) 7 *OJLS* 26.

[35] Published by Weidenfeld & Nicolson and edited by Robert Stevens, William Twining and Christopher McCrudden, the *Law in Context* series has gone through several emanations, ending with Cambridge University Press, with Kenneth Armstrong as editor. The citation comes from a recent publication.

[36] F Snyder, *New Directions in European Community Law* (London, Weidenfeld & Nicolson, 1990). There were four chapters: 'New Directions' (n 2) (1987), 'Thinking about Interests' (1989), 'Ideologies of Competition: Two Perspectives on the Completion of the Internal Market' (first published 1989) and 'The European Community's Food Aid Legislation: Towards a Development Policy?' (1987).

V. The EC: A New Look

Amongst anglophone EC scholars, Snyder's plea for 'new directions' met with an enthusiastic response. The editors of *New Legal Dynamics*, a set of 'new look' essays published in 1996, presented it as 'part of a trend towards broadening the focus of legal scholarship in the field of European integration' and marking 'the first tentative steps towards the articulation of a new voice for European legal studies'. Scholars would add the tools of interdisciplinary scholarship – comparative politics, international relations, public policy analysis, theories of institutional behaviour etc – to the tools of legal scholarship, defined in *New Directions* terms to include socio-legal studies, postmodernist theory, critical legal studies, law in context etc.[37]

New Legal Dynamics epitomised the law in context approach promoted by Snyder. It comprised a mix of theoretical essays with single-sector studies by specialist legal authors of EU policy areas, ranging from the familiar single market and workers' rights to the less well-known topics of EU citizenship, administrative law and public interest litigation and external affairs (the relationship with the General Agreement on Tariffs and Trade (GATT)). It was, however, only marginally interdisciplinary. Problems of interdisciplinary cooperation were highlighted some years later by Kenneth Armstrong, who suggested that even if political science had discovered the ECJ, it had not discovered law. Armstrong set out 'to integrate the legal dimension into the core of the interdisciplinary network which characterizes European studies' with a contribution that was a substantial exploration of different images of law and courts in political science and legal literature.[38] His focus was on the ECJ, but, rather than providing a conventional analysis of the case law, the article is a serious attempt to link law and its institutions with the political science concepts of intergovernmentalism, neofunctionalism and constitutionalism, while also exploring the relationship between law and governance.

Looking back to antecedents, Jo Shaw set out in her 'Introduction' to *New Legal Dynamics* to draw together the main elements of the new approach around the theme of integration. Snyder's contextual work received a mention, while empirical studies by Slaughter/Burley and Mattli stressed the growing influence of American socio-legal work.[39] Special mention was made of the transformational

[37] J Shaw, 'Introduction' in J Shaw and G More (eds), *New Legal Dynamics of European Union* (Oxford, Clarendon Press, 1995) 1-3. Her thesis is expanded in J Shaw, 'European Union Studies in Crisis? Towards a New Dynamic' (1996) 16 *Oxford Journal of Legal Studies* 231, where she says (at 236): 'EC/EU legal studies have also been, at least until very recently, to a large extent insulated from the theoretical, methodological and contextual influences which have been felt in most other fields of legal study, from, for example, critical legal studies and Marxism, postmodernism, socio-legal studies, economics, social and political theory or feminist theory.'

[38] K Armstrong, 'Legal Integration: Theorizing the Legal Dimension of European Integration' (1998) 36 *Journal of Common Market Studiess* 155.

[39] Key to this body of court-centred empirical work was E Stein, 'Lawyers, Judges and the Making of a Transnational Constitution' (1981) 75 *AJIL* 1. See also A-M Burley and W Mattli, 'Europe before the Court: A Political Theory of Legal Integration' (1993) 47 *International Organizations* 41; W Mattli and A-M Slaughter, 'Constructing the European Community legal System from the Ground up: The Role of Individual Litigants and National Courts', *EUI, RSC* No 96/56 (1996).

constitutional writing of Joseph Weiler, who was to remark of the law in context approach that it was 'of course de rigueur' – the new orthodoxy, which he himself did not overtly espouse.

Snyder, on the other hand, was determined to make it so. In his first editorial in the *European Law Journal*, of which he was the founding editor-in-chief, he announced his intention to 'trace a new path'. His infant journal would represent a new approach to European law: 'Its main purposes are to develop the study and understanding of European law in its social, cultural, political and economic contexts.'[40] This message was repeated in volume 3, where he asserted that it had been one of the tasks of the *Journal* 'to fill the perceived gap in legal scholarship' and encourage authors 'to take the context of European Union law seriously, to rethink how and why it is shaped by – and shapes – the contexts in which it operates, and thus to reconceptualise European Union law itself'.[41] The first issues began as the Editorial Board hoped to go on. Two economists, a sociologist and a political scientist wrote for the first two issues, which contained sector-specific studies of social policy, labour law and EU governance. Significantly, there were not and never have been any case notes. Under Snyder's long editorship and that of his successor, there was no deviation from this path.

In some ways, the *European Law Journal* might be seen as Snyder's chief and longest-lasting contribution to European legal scholarship, but he has also made many others. He was the first to urge legal scholars to abandon the safe areas of competition and labour law, and to provide sector-specific studies of less accessible areas. He encouraged cultural pluralism. The International Workshops for Young Scholars (WISH) provided a platform for young scholars to publish on innovative topics such as food security or religious freedom. Participants gathered in schools from all regions of Europe and the meetings are now held in Beijing. In his own work, Snyder provided a model for law in context and interdisciplinary studies.

The legacy has proved to be enduring. Not so long ago, an email appeared in my inbox announcing the arrival of a new textbook, published perhaps ironically in London. The authors claim to provide 'an explanatory and contextual view of EU law and its impact in a simple and easily accessible yet analytical manner'. The book discusses the power struggles behind any given EU law act to allow for a full understanding of how it developed. The objective is to encourage an appreciation of EU law as a force in the increasingly globalised world rather than as a technical and doctrinal subject – in short, a law in context study.[42]

[40] F Snyder, 'Editorial' (1995) 1(1) *European Law Journal* 1.

[41] ibid.

[42] E Herlin-Karnell, G Conway and A Ganesh, *European Union Law in Context* (London, Bloomsbury, 2021).

7

Still Out on the Weekend

Renewing EU Law in Context

AGUSTÍN JOSÉ MENÉNDEZ

'Two points are crucial, however, to the continuous vitality of our common project: first, that we develop a more critical understanding of European Community law, and second, that we move in new directions.'[1]

'The history of the European Community appears to encapsulate the main trends in the development of Western capitalism since the Second World War.'[2]

I. Introduction

When the *Journal of Law and Society* published Francis Snyder's article 'New Directions in European Law' in 1987,[3] EC law was in the process of becoming a consolidated academic field.[4] As is characteristic in such circumstances, different methodological approaches were emerging, putting forward different ways of 'doing' Community law. Fast forward 35 years and you may be tempted to reach the conclusion that the methodological battle has been won by those defending a contextual approach to EU law. Indeed, pieces claiming to consider EU law in its social, economic, political and cultural context have become standard fare in all journals with an interest in EU law – not least the *Common Market Law Review*, generally perceived as the black-letter law journal of reference in the field.[5]

[1] F Snyder, 'New Directions in European Community Law' (1987) 14 *Journal of Law and Society* 167, at 167.

[2] F Snyder, *New Directions in European Community Law* (London: Weidenfeld & Nicolson, 1990) 12.

[3] Snyder (n 1).

[4] See A Vauchez, *Brokering Europe: Euro-lawyers and the Making of a Transnational Polity* (Cambridge, Cambridge University Press, 2015) for a panoramic view of the forging of the academic field and focusing on the period of consolidation of the 1980s (at 203ff).

[5] See Rebekka Byberg's reconstruction of the first three decades of the *Common Market Law Review*: 'The History of the *Common Market Law Review*' (2017) 23 *European Law Journal* 45. The *Common Market Law Review* welcomed (and continues to welcome) pieces by insiders and by scholars who have been, are or will be institutional actors.

In this chapter I argue that the triumph of contextual approaches to EU law is more apparent than real (much like the success of law in context in legal scholarship in general). It is true that the use of conceptual tools of other social disciplines to reconstruct, analyse and assess EU law has become widespread. But it is also the case, as I will show in section II, that the increased respectability of interdisciplinary goes hand in hand with the loss of its critical edge. In particular, the limits of law as a means of integration in Europe are rarely explored, there is a tendency to naturalise and familiarise the basic concepts of EU law, and there is a parallel lack of appetite for questioning the basic categories around which research is structured, and, finally, we are yet to see the emergence of a research agenda which transcends the interests and concerns of EU Institutions. Such are the bases which in my view require us to double down on contextualism. With such a purpose in view, I put forward the outline of a renewed contextualist agenda for EU legal scholarship that is capable of developing a critical understanding of EU law.

II. No Victory is So Bitter as an Illusionary One: Why the Triumph of EU Law in Context is More Apparent than Real

There is no doubt that EU law scholarship has become increasingly open to the social sciences and the humanities. The combination of sociological, politological, philosophical or economic insights with legal-dogmatic arguments is no longer regarded as eccentric. *Épater les juristes européens* now takes much more than mere resort to interdisciplinarity.

Three were the approaches to Community law which were both in competition and in partial overlap: the law of integration, integration through law, and law in context (see section II.A). Mainstream EU law evolved as a hybrid of the law of integration and integration through law. In particular, integration through law succeeded in making EU legal scholarship curious about, and conversant with, other disciplines, but ended up endorsing the status quo. Law in context acquired a modicum of respectability, but only as an *alternative*, rather idiosyncratic when not eccentric way of 'doing' EU law (see section II.B). The result, as anticipated in the introduction, has been that EU legal scholarship, even if open to interdisciplinarity, lacks the capacity to engage into a sustained criticism of EU law (see section II.C).

A. Three Varieties of Community Law Scholarship

Community law became a thriving academic field in the 1980s. The growth of the number of courses taught at universities, journals founded and books published created the conditions under which three different methodological approaches to the analysis, reconstruction and assessment of Community law flourished: the law of integration, integration through law, and Community law in context.

The main practitioners of the *law of integration* shared the view that Community law was the first manifestation of a new type of legal order characterised by the *reconceptualisation* of sovereignty.[6] In other words, Community law was regarded as the avant-garde of supranational law.[7] Consequently, the new legal order was deemed capable of revolutionising not only international relations but also the constitutional structure of federal and non-federal states, now to be re-approached as an 'oeuvre commune'.[8] Even if curious about the insights stemming from other social sciences, the *law of integration* scholars focused on developing new concepts and new categories with which to *reconstruct* the new legal field. Or in other words, they saw as their main task to lay the groundwork of a legal dogmatics of EEC law.[9] In such a way, they expected to gain support for the claim that a new and distinct legal field was in the process of emerging and being consolidated. For that to be so, it was necessary to separate Community law from both public international law and national public law, not least because such disciplines took the sovereignty of nation-states as their very point of departure. Instead, inspiration was to be found, either implicitly or explicitly, in the categories of classical liberal private law, which not only pre-dated the modern sovereign state, but also fitted the values and purpose (*finalité*) at the very core of the process of integration.[10] As Cappelletti, Weiler and Secombe noticed in 1984, this resulted in a certain penchant for a peculiar form of natural law.[11] The law of integration not only saw the law through the eyes of the institutional actors of the process of European integration (most prominently those working in the Court of Justice or in the legal services of the European institutions), but also addressed itself to such an audience.[12] Indeed, many of the key contributors to the law of integration doubled down as judges or legal counsellors and as the first authors of scholarly works on Community law.

[6] P Pescatore, *Le Droit de l'Intégration* (Leiden, AW Sijthoff, 1972) 31 and 48. The word 'use' is given as 'réaménagement' in the French original.

[7] ibid 48.

[8] ibid 41 (a claim which Pescatore stated argued against the characterisation of the powers of the Community as enumerated).

[9] *cf* P Pescatore, *L'Ordre Juridique des Communautés Europeéennes. Etude des sources du droit communitaire* (Liege, Presses Universitaires de Liège, 1975).

[10] See the memorandum circulated by A Trabucchi to the judges of the ECJ: 'Note a MM Les Juges' in *La Formazione del Diritto Europeo, Giornata di Studio per Alberto Trabucchi nel centenario della nascita* (Padua, CEDAM, 2008) 212–23. See also M Rasmussen, 'Revolutionizing European Law: A History of the *Van Gend en Loos* judgment' (2014) 12 *International Journal of Constitutional Law* 136–63.

[11] M Cappelletti, M Seccombe and J Weiler, 'Integration through Law: Europe and the American Federal Experience: A General Introduction' in *Integration through law: Methods, Tools and Institutions. A Political, Legal and Economic Overview* (New York, Walter de Gruyter, 1986).

[12] A good deal of the US scholarship on Community law had reconstructed EEC law from the perspective of American companies aiming at investing in Europe. See, most obviously, but not exclusively, E Stein and TL Nicholson, *American Enterprise in the European Common Market: A Legal Profile* (Ann Arbor, University of Michigan Press, 1960).

If the advocates of the *law of integration* regarded the EEC as a radically new type of supranational organisation, the scholars who developed *integration through law* affirmed that the EEC was but a new instance of a polity based on the federal principle.[13] Consequently, they devoted their energies to the reconstruction of Community law as the law of a federal order.[14] Not by chance, the key scholar behind the massive international research project[15] which gave shape to the new paradigm was Mauro Cappelletti, a comparatist and committed advocate of the normative ideal of the democratic and social state. This goes a long way towards accounting for two distinctive features of the original *integration through law* scholarship: first, the use of the tools and concepts of both comparative law and political science law to identify and describe the federal traits of the EEC legal and political order;[16] and, second, the forging of a research agenda which encompassed not only the reconstruction of European legal norms with the help of the key concepts and categories of US federal constitutional law,[17] but also the analysis of the institutions and procedures which played a key role in the production of these substantive norms and the mechanisms and procedures which guaranteed their actual implementation (or resulted in their not being applied).[18] The law of integration was chiefly a scholarly enterprise, but one with an agenda that reflected very much the perspective of institutional actors.[19]

Finally, advocates of Community law in context aimed at studying EEC law in its wider social, political, cultural and economic context.[20] The influence, both nominal and substantial, of the 'sociologising' British law in context movement played a fundamental role.[21] It was not by chance that the book that served as a reference for contextualists in the 1990s, Snyder's *New Directions in Community law*,[22] was published in one of the flagship collections of the British law in context movement (the *Law in Context* collection then published by Weidenfeld & Nicolson

[13] Cappelleti, Seccombe and Weiler (n 11) 13–14, 25.

[14] ibid 25.

[15] R Byberg, 'The History of the Integration through Law Project: Creating the Academic Expression of a Constitutional Legal Vision for Europe' (2017) 18 *German Law Journal*, 1531. See also D Augenstein (ed), *'Integration through Law Revisited': The Making of the European Polity* (Farnham, Ashgate, 2012); L Azoulai, '"Integration through Law" and Us' (2016) 14 *International Journal of Constitutional Law* 449.

[16] Cappelletti, Secombe and Weiler (n 11) 16.

[17] ibid 5, 11.

[18] This is what was already characterised in 1984 as a 'total' approach to legal scholarship (ibid 63). Weiler would use again this label in the late 2000s and early 2010s.

[19] Byberg (n 15).

[20] Snyder (n 1); F Snyder, '"Out on the Weekend": Reflections on European Union Law in Context', Working Paper, EUI LAW, 1994/11, 21; F Snyder, 'Editorial' (1995) 1 *European Law Journal* 1.

[21] W Twining, *Law in Context: Enlarging a Discipline* (Oxford, Oxford University Press, 1997); W Twining, 'The Law in Context Movement' in P Cane and J Conaghan (eds), *The New Oxford Companion to Law* (Oxford, Oxford University Press, 2009, https://www-oxfordreference-com.ezproxy.uio.no/view/10.1093/acref/9780199290543.001.0001/acref-9780199290543-e-1271; Snyder, '"Out on the Weekend"' (n 20) 38; C Harlow, 'The EU and Law in Context: The Context' (2022) 1 *European Law Open* 209 reminds the reader that at the time that he laid the groundwork for his contextual approach to EEC law, Snyder was teaching at Warwick Law School, which had been established in 1967 with a clear-cut contextual agenda.

[22] Snyder (n 2).

and now by Cambridge University Press).[23] However, Community law in context was not merely British, but its premises and choices resonated with those of other critical legal movements in continental Europe.[24] The basic premise of contextualists was that a formalist description of the law was insufficient. Knowing the law required having resort to the categories and the conceptual tools of other disciplines, particularly, but not exclusively, the humanities and the social sciences.[25] Once this wider set of perspectives was considered, it was possible not only to tackle better the set of questions which usually occupy legal actors (typically problems of interpretation and application) but also to gain a richer, wider picture of law in society.[26] As a result, Community law in context could account for the role and the limits of law in the process of integration, reflect critically on the very way in which knowledge about EU law was produced, and put forward a wider and more interesting research agenda, emancipated from the interests and concerns of European institutions.[27] The audience which contextualists had in mind was much wider than that of both the law of integration and integration through law. Community law in context was interested not only in the Community law as practised by European institutions, but also as widely experienced in European society.[28]

B. How EU Law Became an Odd Mix of Black Letter Law and the External Semblance of Contextualism

The law of integration, integration through law and Community law in context defined differently the object of research, the concepts and categories central to legal analysis, and, last but not least, the audience which they were addressing. Having said that, there important two sets of overlaps.

[23] A further volume on the constitutional law of the EU, also authored by Snyder, was planned, but was never published in the *Law in Context* collection. Snyder published long texts on the matter (including his 'General Course on Constitutional Law of the European Union' (1998) 6 *Collected Courses of the Academy of European Law* 41), but not a textbook as such.

[24] As reflected in the pan-European composition of the editorial and, especially, the advisory boards of the *European Law Journal*. See Snyder, 'Editorial' (n 20) 2. At the same time, as Harlow (n 21) notes, law in context in general was not unrelated to the thriving critical legal studies movement in the 1970s and 1980s, which also had a number of incarnations in different European countries.

[25] Snyder's writings built especially intense bridges between law and political economy. This had been a hallmark of his 'pre-European' writings, and would also be a hallmark of his writings on Europe, from those on the common agricultural policy (*Law of the Common Agricultural Policy* (London, Sweet & Maxwell, 1985) to those on economic and monetary union ('EMU Revisited: Are We Making a Constitution? What Constitution are We Making?', EUI Working Paper Law 98/6) and international trade (*The EU, the WTO and China: Legal Pluralism and International Trade Regulation* (Oxford, Hart Publishing, 2010).

[26] Snyder (n 2) 12ff.

[27] Snyder, 'Out on the Weekend' (n 20) 15–20, reflecting on his own *Law of the Common Agricultural Policy* (Snyder (n 25) 37ff).

[28] Snyder (n 25) 41.

First, the fundamental object of research of *the law of integration* and of *integration through law* was, rather exclusively, the legal norms produced by European institutions. This went without saying in the case of the law of integration, which defined the breadth and scope of Community law by reference to Community institutions themselves. But was also the case of integration through law, even if in the latter case attention extended to the actual practices of European institutions (as reflected in its consideration of the 'dualistic' character of supranationalism).[29] This focus resulted in the playing down of the transnational dimensions of European legal integration. Moreover, both the law of integration and integration through law elaborated Community law from the standpoint of European institutions and indeed in dialogue with such institutions. As has been noted, the law of integration was literally written in many cases by institutional actors who had been, and retained a partial identity as, scholars.[30] Integration through law was developed in close contact with institutions, and with the keen participation, in the founding book series, of institutional actors.[31]

This first overlap was extremely significant and would indeed prove to be determinant of the path followed by mainstream European legal scholarship in the following three decades, as we will see below. But, second, integration through law and Community law in context also overlapped, in at least three respects. For one thing, both integration through law and law in context embraced innterdisciplinarity: in a clear and unqualified fashion, in the case of Community law in context; and in a more circumscribed way, essentially limited to political science, in the case of integration through law. This convergence around interdisciplinarity was reflected in the very composition of the founding editorial board of the *European Law Journal*, in which we would find both 'integrationalists' and 'contextualists'. For two, both approaches rejected the characterisation of EEC law as a radically new phenomenon (as argued by those who favoured the law of integration). Instead of emphasising an alleged transcendence of sovereignty (and power), they saw EEC law as a new federal order (integration through law) or as another instance of a legal order partially decoupled (at least for the time being) from a nation-state (Community law in context). EEC law, from such a perspective, was neither *sui generis* nor the first instance of a new breed of legal order. As a consequence, last, but not least, both approaches could address an audience larger than that made up of actors in European institutions and had an in-built propensity to engage in a critical fashion with their object of research. In relation

[29] J Weiler, 'The Community System: the Dual Character of Supranationalism' (1981) 1 *Yearbook of European Law* 267; J Weiler, *Il sistema comunitario europeo: struttura giuridica e processo politico* (Bologna, Il Mulino, 1985).

[30] Vauchez (n 4); see also M Rasmussen and DS Martinsen, 'EU Constitutionalisation Revisited: Redressing a Central Assumption in European Studies' (2019) 25 *European Law Journal* 251; and A Boerger and M Rasmussen, 'The Making of European Law: Exploring the Life and Work of Michel Gaudet' (2017) 57 *American Journal of Legal History* 51.

[31] Byberg (n 15).

to the law of integration, Cappelletti was so persuaded of the normative value of the integration process that, as we will see, he was not keen to pass any negative judgement on it.[32] The attitude of other 'integrationists' was similar. Nonetheless, the federal democratic principle stood as a *potential* critical yardstick with which to assess Community law, even when integrationists failed to make actual use of it. For example, when it was claimed that European supranationalism was to be positively assessed, such judgement was based on the premise that the peculiar mix of decisional intergovernmentalism and a federal legal order powered by a federal judiciary characteristic of the Communities was an original way of reconciling unity and diversity, as required by the federal principle.[33] To put it differently, the implicit yardstick being affirmed was that integration had to be rendered compatible with the preservation (if not the fostering) of diversity. This, however, left the door open to a reconsideration of such assessment if the actual way in which the European Communities was structured was to change, ie, where the federal balance would be unsettled. Community law in context, in its turn, had a plurality of possible yardsticks with which to engage critically, not only with EEC law, and later EU law, but also with European legal scholarship itself.

These sets of overlaps resulted in two main possible avenues of development of mainstream Community law. The direction that the discipline mainly took could have been marked by the overlaps between the law of integration and integration through law, or, alternatively, by the overlaps between integration through law and Community law in context.

The outcome came closer to a hybridisation of integration through law with the law of integration than the second alterative. The law of integration offered a theoretical reconstruction of the actual work undertaken since the 1950s by the legal actors who had literally made Community law. At the very same time that it radically challenged a key assumption of national legal dogmatics (the centrality of the state in the legal order), it offered a reassuring methodological continuity (any jurist could recognise the breed of legal dogmatics it proposed). Integration through law, in its turn, had a strong institutional basis (the law department of the European University Institute, the legal identity of which was forged by Cappelletti and Weiler, and which would produce scores of doctoral dissertations in the template of the 'Integration through Law' project) and provided key insights on how to adapt the federal conceptual kit to Community law, thus contributing to provide solutions to specific legal problems.

In this process of hybridisation, integration through law failed to come to terms with the radical transformation with which the Communities experimented in the

[32] Byberg (ibid 1535) establishes a connection between the fact that Cappelletti fought in the resistance and his enthusiastic 'europeismo'. See also PS Graglia, *Unità europea e federalismo. Da 'Giustizia e Libertà' ad Altiero Spinelli* (Bologna, Il Mulino, 1996); and F Tortella, *Un antifascisme européiste: Giustizia e Libertà et le Partito d'Azione (1929–1947)* (Bologna, Il Mulino, 2022).

[33] Cappelletti, Seccombe and Weiler, (n 11) 31–32. See also Weiler, 'The Community System' (n 29) and Weiler, *Il sistema comunitario europeo* (n 29).

late 1980s, with what I have elsewhere described as a long process of constitutional mutation.[34] In particular, the European Monetary System and the *Cassis de Dijon* line of jurisprudence unleashed the power of private actors to force the integration of markets, even if there were no parallel advances on political integration. What was hailed (and keeps on being hailed) as a process of 'mutual recognition' implied, as a matter of fact, a radical change in the balance of power between private and public actors, between supranational representative and less or non-representative institutions, and between the EU and the Member States. The Single European Act facilitated a compensatory regulatory intervention of the Community, but only at the price of radically transforming the European decision-making process away from intergovernmentality, and in such a fragmentary way that there would emerge a clear division of labour between 'market making' (the further unleashing of private power through a more expansive definition of economic freedoms) and 'market correction' (redistributive and social policies). Moreover, the former was easier to achieve than the latter. The Treaty of Maastricht and the Stability and Growth Pact crowned the process of constitutional mutation, entrenching a new constitutional settlement in which economic freedoms, 'free competition' and 'sound money' became the meta-principles of EU law.[35] As a result, integration through law failed to transmit its critical potential to mainstream Community legal scholarship. Step by step, the Communities became very different from how they were when the Integration through Law project was originally conceived. The internal market was recharacterised as a single market, no longer a common market, while the project of a common currency was transformed into one of a single currency. The combined result was the unleashing of centralising forces that could not but undermine the balance between the supranational centre and the member states, the very balance on which, as I have already noted, was premised the positive normative judgment of integrationists. To summarise, the federal equilibrium between a 'federal' law and an 'intergovernmental decision making' which integrationists regarded as foundational of the federal character of Community law was being phased out just at the very time that integration through law was gaining traction and support within the academic field.

Integrationists registered the changes, but failed to draw their full implications. As a result, integration through law kept on assessing Community law as if the constitutional settlement prevalent at the time the approach emerged remained in force. In other words, the tension between theory and reality was solved by means of suspending critical judgement or, in other words, by a characterisation of the constitutional transformation as the realisation of the federal principle without paying attention to the extent to which it was pushing European integration

[34] AJ Menéndez, 'A European Union in Constitutional Mutation?' (2014) 20 *European Law Journal* 127.

[35] AJ Menéndez, 'The Terrible Functional Constitution of the European Union: "Sound" Money, Economic Freedom(s) and "Free" Competition' in M Goldoni and MA Wilkinson (eds), *The Cambridge Handbook on the Material Constitution* (Cambridge, Cambridge University Press, 2023).

away from the federal principle. Cappelletti, perhaps much influenced by a very pessimistic interpretation of post-war Italian constitutional history, welcomed the single market and especially the single currency.[36] Weiler, even if entertaining doubts and with reservations,[37] ended up identifying negative constitutionalism[38] with the federal principle, now reconceptualised as the principle of constitutional tolerance.[39] That this was part of the spirit of the time, of a prevailing vision, is reflected in the fact that similar conclusions were drawn by authors sympathetic to the contextual approach, such as Neil D MacCormick.[40]

But there was more. The integrative force of supranational law, which used to be inextricably linked with the legitimising force of intergovernmental decision making, started to pretend to emancipate itself from the latter. Lawyers started to see in law not only the form of political power, but also a means of integration *fully alternative to politics*, including democratic politics.[41] Failing to register this change, integration through law also mutated, and came to refer to the capacity of the law to serve itself as a means of integration, even if its democratic legitimacy was limited.[42]

Integration through law was influential enough as to generalise resort to insights from other disciplines. The turn to interdisciplinarity was especially

[36] M Cappelletti, 'Evolución de Europa' (2005) *Revista de la Facultad de Derecho, Universidad de la República, Uruguay* 31, originally published as a chapter in M Cappelletti, *Dimensioni della giustizia nelle società contemporanee* (Bologna, Il Mulino, 1994).

[37] J Weiler, 'The Transformation of Europe' (1991) 100 *Yale Law Journal*, 2403, 2477: 'A "single European market" is a concept which still has the power to stir. But it is also a "single European market". It is not simply a technocratic programme to remove the remaining obstacles to the free movement of all factors of production. It is at the same time a highly politicised choice of ethos, ideology, and political culture: the culture of the "market". It is also a philosophy, at least one version of which – the predominant version – seeks to remove barriers to the free movement of factors of production, and to remove distortion to competition as a means to maximise utility. The above is premised on the formal equality of individuals.'

[38] J Weiler, 'In Defence of the Status Quo: Europe's Constitutional Sonderweg' in J Weiler and M Wind (eds), *European Constitutionalism beyond the State* (Cambridge, Cambridge University Press, 2003) 15: '[Our constitutions] are about restricting power, not enlarging it; they protect fundamental rights of the individual.'

[39] ibid 18: 'And yet the current constitutional architecture, which of course can be improved in many of its specifics, encapsulates one of Europe's most important constitutional innovations, the Principle of Constitutional Tolerance.'

[40] N MacCormick, *Questioning Sovereignty* (Oxford, Oxford University Press, 1999) 151–52: '[L]et us consider the institutions that would be most apt to realizing individualistic goods of a primarily instrumental kind. It can be credibly argued that here the only legitimate role for collective decision-making is to secure legal and institutional conditions for the flourishing of free and fair markets. Within markets, individuals rationally pursuing their self-interest do in fact contribute to the satisfaction of the self-interests of others and, in the aggregate, individual decisions taken by each for individual ends work to optimize the aggregate outcome in terms of general interest-satisfaction.'

[41] C Joerges, 'The Overburdening of Law by Ordoliberalism and the Integration Project' in J Hien and C Joerges (eds), *Ordoliberalism and the Rule of Economics* (Oxford, Hart Publishing, 2017).

[42] Not by chance, this came at the very same time that academia came to value non-representative institutions as playing a fundamental role in the definition of the general will. In particular, the alleged legitimacy of rule through law would substitute the lacking democratic legitimacy of European laws and policies.

intense in the wake of the manifold crises experienced by the EU in the late 2000s and early 2010s, which led to a (moderate and rather transitory) challenge to the prevailing history of integration, as an almost unstoppable process of realisation of a set of goals already codified in the founding Treaties.[43] However, in the process, the critical potential of integration through law, which should have been brought to bear given the direction in which the EU mutated, was largely enervated, as we will see in the next section.

C. The Loss of the Critical Edge

Mainstream European legal scholarship could thus be said to be the result of the hybridisation of the law of integration with integration through law. In the process, the field has become open to insights from other social disciplines, as pointed out in the previous section, but at the price of integration through law losing its critical edge. There are three main reasons why this is so.

First, there is a marked 'unlimited optimism' regarding the integrative capacity of EU law or, in other words, there is a tendency to neglect the limits of EU law as a means of social integration. There is a propensity to consider that law can replace other means of social integration, assuming at the end of the day the capacity of EU law of legitimising itself (an assumption which has become increasingly clear among the defendants of the unconditional supremacy of EU law over conflicting national laws). The result is the downplaying of the salience and importance of politics, culture and religion, among others. The incapacity to consider the limits of law also results in a failure to distinguish law from other techniques of social integration, such as governance.

Second, mainstream EU legal scholarship takes for granted the basic concepts and categories with the help of which it organises EU legal norms. In other words, there is barely a critical reflection on the social, political, cultural implications of these concepts. That would imply a critical self-reflection on what the law of integration and integration through law were objectively doing when they were coining concepts apt to the task of conceptualising a 'new legal order' or using concepts sharpened in federal systems to analyse and reconstruct EU law. The objective result, whatever the subjective intentions, is the familiarisation and naturalisation of concepts such as European citizenship, supremacy/primacy, *effet utile*, sound budgetary policy or sound money, which are presented to students and to readers as if they were the technical baggage characteristic of EU law, cloaking in plain sight the social, political, cultural and economic genealogy of these concepts.

[43] A context in which Community law had to consider that the process of integration was not irreversible, as proclaimed by European institutions (not least regarding economic and monetary union) and that, indeed, *disintegration* remained a possibility. In the case of the *Common Market Law Review*, this was reflected in the choice of books being reviewed from 2010. Other journals tackled the issue head-on. See for example, Editorial, 'Disintegration through Law?' 1 (2016) *European Papers* 3.

The third reason why we can conclude that the 'contextual turn' in EU legal studies has failed to leave its full mark in mainstream EU legal scholarship is that the research agenda has barely been altered in the last 30 years. Three features are decisive here:

- First, the number of articles, chapters or books which connect the discussion of constitutional aspects of European integration with the analysis, reconstruction and assessment of specific substantive provisions remains limited. What we usually have is a disconnection between the two or, in other words, general pieces or books which focus on structural principles (institutional relationships, the division of competences, conflicts between supranational and national legal law) and narrowly legal-dogmatic pieces or books which tackle highly specialised sets of principles and rules.
- Second, interdisciplinarity is used in largely instrumental terms, that is, as a means of solving legal-dogmatic problems of interpretation and application of EU law; the result is that interdisciplinarity loses its critical edge, and the categories and concepts through which the underlying social categories go unchallenged.
- Third, even in these terms, the questions which are deemed relevant tend to be those which are regarded as such by European institutions. There are very few examples of themes and *thématiques* discussed by mainstream EU legal scholarship independently of the decisions and debates of European institutions themselves. That is extremely problematic because the European Parliament, unlike national parliaments, lacks the capacity to set the legislative, and political agendas of the EU.

III. A Renovated Contextualist Agenda

In the previous section, I argued that the apparent success of law in context is at best partial and at worst illusory. In this section, I put forward a possible agenda of a renewed contextualist approach to EU law, focusing on what I regard as three fundamental contributions of contextualism: the exploration of the limits of law as a means of integration, the denaturalisation and defamiliarisation of the fundamental concepts with which law is analysed and reconstructed, and the discovery of 'blind angles', of topics and themes neglected by mainstream scholarship.

Two caveats perhaps need to be given here. The first is that the more I read back the contextualist literature, the less original the agenda sketched below seems to me. My point is not to break new ground, but rather to remind the reader of what the road not taken could look like if we took it. The second is that the point is not to create a contextualist orthodoxy. EU law in context, much as law in context in general, has always embraced pluralism in methodological approaches. But there is a massive difference between pluralism and losing any methodological identity, especially the capacity to approach *critically* the object of study and research.

A. The Limits of Law

That EU law has played an important role in the making of the European Communities and in the Europeanisation of nation-states is neither surprising nor the subject of dispute.[44] But a renovated contextual approach to EU law requires us to keep in mind the very limits of law and, specifically, of EU law, at least in a double sense. First, EU law is not the only means of European integration. This implies, among other things, that law be differentiated from other means of social integration. It seems to me that such a task is especially urgent and pertinent regarding governance. Second, we should be aware that EU law cannot undertake the integrative tasks assigned to it in an independent way, not least because EU law cannot self-legitimise. The legitimacy of law, including EU law, cannot but be external to EU law or dependent on its normative properties and on the normative qualities of the consequences brought about by EU law.

i. The Plurality of the Means of Social Integration: Distinguishing Law form Governance

EU law in context should stress not only the extent to which law has been key in the process of European integration, but also the degree to which the capacity of the supranational and the national legal orders to perform their fundamental tasks of solving conflicts, providing templates of individual and collective autonomy, and coordinating action in view of the achievement of collective goals critically depends on their keeping a close relationship to other systems of social integration, not least positive morality. As legal pluralism has insisted, there is more law than EU (and national) law, and there are more social norms than those that qualify as legal. This, however, does not entail that EU law in context should license the overstretching of the concept of EU law; rather, the contrary is true, for two related reasons:

- First, contextualism assumes the importance of the distinction precisely because it makes us aware of the different ways in which social integrative tasks are discharged by law in tandem with other social orders.
- Second, and crucially, the capacities and the normative properties of the different systems of social integration are very different. The replacement of positive morality by law, for example, might well have been required by the degree of

[44] For the role of Euro-jurists in the process of integration, which is related to but different from that of EU law, see Vauchez (n 4).

> complexity of social interaction in modern societies. At the same time, it can be argued that the transformation of law into the key means of social integration created the conditions under which it became conceivable that common actions norms were democratically decided through processes of general will formation (contrary to what is the case with positive moral norms, which, independently of whether they are wise or unwise, are not formed through democratic deliberation and decision making). Social integration through law is therefore not only functionally but also normatively required (something which does not rule out, of course, that many laws may be imposed in an autocratic form, or that despotism may not try to make an instrumental use of the legal form).

These are the two reasons why a renewed contextualist research agenda for EU law should aim at clarifying if everything that is usually labelled as 'EU law' can and should be deemed to be law, or if, alternatively, some of the collective action norms that are usually regarded as being part of EU law are more properly identified as being part of another means of social integration.

Consider, for example, governance. From the late 1990s until the fiscal crisis of the eurozone in 2010, both Euro-jurists and Euro-political scientists devoted a considerable amount of their time to study the different manifestations of 'governance' through 'soft law'.[45] Paradigmatic examples were the 'open method of coordination', structured around a series of benchmarks, and 'European economic governance', constructed around a series of numerical rules, a peculiar hybrid of soft and hard law, characterised by the fact that their operative part of the norms is an economic indicator.[46]

Contrary to government through 'hard' law, governance through 'soft law' was supposed to be detached from the 'classical' concept of sovereignty (and thus especially suited to a political and legal process, such as European integration, allegedly premised on the transcendence of sovereignty): if government was hierarchical, governance was horizontal; if government was rigid; governance, was flexible; if government relied on coercion, governance relied on persuasion. Some political philosophers were so enthusiastic that they regarded European governance mechanisms as an evolutionary achievement which would allow us to reimagine democracy itself.[47] In the aftermath of the eurozone fiscal crisis of the early 2010s, and the way it was 'governanced', we may raise serious doubts not only about the intrinsic qualities of 'governance', but actually about the structural distinct traits of governance and its relationship to law.

[45] A term which, quite paradoxically, seems to have originated in international law, ie, in the very legal template which the ECJ denied was applicable to EU law.

[46] AJ Menéndez, 'Numerical Rules or Political Government, That is the (European) Question' (2022) 20 *Comparative European Politics* 631.

[47] See P Nanz, 'Open Method of Coordination: A Deliberative and Democratic Mode of Governance' (2004) 11 *Journal of European Public Policy* 267.

Contextualism should contribute to this problematisation of governance and to an increasing awareness of the extent to which it constitutes a means of social integration different from law. First, we should pose tough questions regarding the very content of the norms enforced through governance. These were largely presented as responding to technical standards, such as employability and sound budgetary policies. By now we should know better that such standards are not technical, but their definition presupposes and invites political discussion. Yet, are governance norms and procedures as open to democratic decision making as the law? There are serious reasons to doubt this. Second, governance norms were deemed superior because they overcame the necessary connection between law and coercion. With the benefit of hindsight, we should perhaps consider that the coerciveness of law not only increases its efficacy (stabilising the expectations of all its addressees in the process), but in turn renders necessary the foreseeability of the actions or omissions required by the norm if the individual is to be left free to comply or to breach the law. Democratic law is heteronomous at the point of its application, but fosters political and private autonomy at the stage of its elaboration. Can the same be said of governance norms? The fuzziness of the obligations imposed by soft law remains unproblematic only insofar as the breach of such standards (which is decided by the authorities rather *ex post* and not *ex ante*) does not trigger any sanction, or only a very minor one. That, however, has only been the case in formal terms. Under certain conditions, such as those prevailing in the eurozone in 2010 or, for that matter, 2015, shaming and blaming were enough to unleash the forces of capital and force, more effectively than any form of legal coercion, to adopt policies which were openly contrary to decisions taken by democratic electorates.[48]

ii. The Limits of EU Law: Supremacy and the Impossibility of EU Law Generating its Own Legitimacy

There is no doubt that EU law plays a key role in the process of integrating the EU. Supranational legal norms solve conflicts, provide a template for the exercise of public and private autonomy, and play a key role in the coordination of the actions of individuals with a view to achieving collective goals. However, EU law cannot by itself create the conditions under which it can discharge such tasks. While the legitimacy of EU legal norms derives partially from their being produced in compliance with other EU legal norms regulating the production of legal norms (of what would be labelled as 'secondary norms' in the Hartian legal theory),[49] the ultimate source of legitimacy is external to the law,[50] dependent on the normative properties of EU laws (especially of the norms that play a functional constitutional

[48] AJ Menéndez, 'The Existential Crisis of the European Union' (2013) 14 *German Law Journal* 453.
[49] HLA Hart, *The Concept of Law* (Oxford, Clarendon Press, 1960).
[50] Carlos Nino, *Derecho, Moral y Política* (Barcelona, Ariel, 1994).

role in EU law) and on the normative properties of the consequences and implications of EU norms (throughput and output legitimacy).

This is a fundamental insight which tends to be somehow neglected by mainstream EU legal scholarship. Evidence of this neglect is constituted by the way in which the structural relationship between supranational law and national constitutional laws is imagined. It is increasingly the case that it is assumed not only that EU law might prevail over national laws, but also that it should do so unconditionally and out of its own force, not because national norms so establish.

That this was so was rendered painfully evident in the wake of the rulings of the German Federal Constitutional Court (GFCC) in the *Gauweiler* and *Weiss* sagas. In both cases, the substantive underlying conflict revolved around the powers of the European Central Bank (ECB) and, in particular, around the national constitutionality and European validity of some of the so-called 'non-conventional' monetary policies announced or implemented by the ECB. In *Gauweiler*, what was at stake was the validity of the programme of outright monetary transactions that the ECB announced in September 2012, at the height of the European fiscal crisis.[51] In *Weiss*, the dispute concerned the set of policies known as 'quantitative easing'. In both instances, the GFCC took a qualified view of the breadth and scope of the powers of the ECB, grounding its rulings in the need of interpreting restrictively the powers of an institution with a non-democratic legitimacy basis. There was no supremacy of EU law, but merely primacy, the ultimate ground of which is to be found in the constitutional norms of the Member States and the legitimacy basis of which is to be sought not in the formal or substantive properties of the law, but on the democratic authority of fundamental norms. The European Court of Justice (ECJ), on the contrary, favoured a teleological interpretation of the powers of the ECB, considering that eventual effects on national fiscal policy of its 'unconventional' monetary policy decisions were not to be regarded as relevant, even if massive, provided they were 'not intended'. Structural and substantive differences did not escalate into a conflict in *Gauweiler*. The GFCC limited itself to issue an order in which it came very close to arguing that the ECB had breached both German constitutional law and European law, while postponing its final judgment until the ECB answered its request for a preliminary reference. Subsequently, the GFCC signalled its disagreement, but regarded the difference as falling within the margin of reasonability, within which it would of its own accord make European law (as interpreted by the ECJ) prevail. The outcome was very different in *Weiss*. While the GFCC started by posing a set of preliminary questions to the ECJ, it persisted in its conclusion that quantitative easing may breach German constitutional law, and explicitly argued that the ruling of the ECJ was defective, as it did not undertake a proper review of the proportionality of the quantitative easing policy.

[51] Measures which were never enacted as a binding legal act or, for that matter, actually implemented – their mere announcement put an end to the speculation on the break-up of the eurozone.

European institutions and many European legal scholars reacted to the decision not so much by challenging it on substantive terms (I will turn briefly to this below), but by questioning the authority and legitimacy of the GFCC to set whatsoever limits to the primacy of EU law (assuming that the problem has to be solved through the lenses of the unconditional primacy of EU law – that is, de facto on the basis of the acknowledgement of the supremacy of EU law). Interestingly, the European Court of Justice produced a press release which, on the one hand, stated that it never commented 'on a judgment of a national court' and, on the other hand, recalled 'in general' (that is, in supposedly abstract and general terms) that 'a judgment in which the Court gives a preliminary ruling is binding on the national court for the purposes of the decision to be given in the main proceedings'.[52] Two days later, the European Commission repeated the same argument, this time affirming explicitly that, whatever could be the underlying substantive arguments, the conflict had to be seen through the key concept of the primacy of European law.[53] These views were supported by many scholars. They amounted in objective terms to the rejection of any possible limit or check on the authority of EU law, objectively even if probably not subjectively divorcing EU law from its democratic legitimacy basis. There are many possible reasons to criticise the ruling of the GFCC,[54] but not its insistence on the impossibility of solving a conflict between the primacy of EU law and the supremacy of democratic constitutional law by means of making the former prevail in an unconditional fashion. This fails to consider the incapacity of law to self-legitimise itself, which is at the heart of the contextualist approach to law.

The reaction to the ruling of the guardian of German constitutionality also shows the extent to which the characterisation of EU law as an all-powerful means of integration fosters the neglect of the substantive content of EU law, including, quite paradoxically, its substantive socio-economic content. Commentaries on the ruling focused on the 'constitutional issues' and rarely considered the political economy of quantitative easing or its capacity to contribute to the solution of the structural weaknesses of an asymmetric economic and monetary union.

B. Denaturalising and Defamiliarising the Fundamental Concepts of European Law

The second item in a new contextualist agenda of EU law should be the denaturalisation and the defamiliarisation of the fundamental concepts with which EU

[52] 'Press release following the judgment of the German Constitutional Court of 5 May 2020' 8 May 2020, https://curia.europa.eu/jcms/upload/docs/application/pdf/2020-05/cp200058en.pdf.

[53] 'Statement by President von der Leyen', 10 May 2020, https://ec.europa.eu/commission/presscorner/detail/en/statement_20_846.

[54] M Dani, E Chiti, J Mendes, AJ Menéndez, H Schepel and MA Wilkinson, '"It's the Political Economy … !! A Moment of Truth for the Eurozone and the EU' (2021) 19 *International Journal of Constitutional Law* 309.

law is analysed, reconstructed and assessed. Concepts are fundamental tools in the toolkit of all jurists. It is perhaps not an exaggeration to say that this is even more so in the case of Euro-jurists. The hallmark of the latter is to view legal problems through the prism provided by a specific set of concepts, concepts which are (at least at first sight) different from those used in national legal systems (or which were, at least initially, different from those used in national legal systems): primacy, direct effect, pre-emption, economic freedoms, sound budgetary policy, sound money, *effet utile* or *acquis communitaire*.

Contrary to what is generally assumed, concepts are neither technical nor neutral terms. Most legal concepts have been borrowed from the humanities and from other social disciplines. In other words, they were not born as juridical concepts, but rather juridified, made part of the legal order and, in the process, given a specific and concrete meaning. But precisely because this is the case, the concepts are not neutral. They carry with them a normative baggage, either from their extra-juridical origin, from the precise meaning given to them when juridified or for the social purpose and point pursued by the jurists who coin legal concepts.

The sheer novelty and the apparent technical and neutral character of the key concepts in EU law create a serious risk of endorsing, without realising it (or at least not fully), the ideological frame which emerges from their use and overlap. The only way to avoid this is to stop taking the concepts for granted. Instead of assuming that concepts are technical and neutral concepts with an objective meaning that is properly established by jurists engaging in largely apolitical discussions, we should consider not only the extent to which such concepts are largely borrowed from other social disciplines and the extent to which the apparent consensus among European legal actors results not from democratic decisions given form by the law, but from a shared positive morality related to social extraction, but also the major social, political, cultural and economic implications of the specific ways in which we construct such concepts.

In other words, we have to strive to render explicit what is implicit in the choice of a specific set of concepts and the discarding of another set of alternative concepts. In brief, we should consider highlighting the point that most concepts are contested concepts or, in other words, that the specific way in which they are interpreted does not depend on technical, politically neutral arguments, but rather on what are, and cannot but be, normatively loaded choices. And that a similar conclusion can be reached regarding the choice of the concepts through which we reconstruct specific social conflicts in legal terms. What is needed is not only immanent critiques, which take as given the very conceptual framework within which we reason about EU law, but also critiques external to EU law.

In the previous sub-section I considered the conceptual choices made when analysing, reconstructing and sorting out conflicts between national constitutional law and European norms. There is nothing neutral or technical in looking at these problems through the prism of one set of concepts or the other. At the end of the day, whether we solve the conflicts through the prism of an unconditional supremacy of EU law and an unconditional supremacy of national law or, rather, through the supremacy of democratically produced constitutional law is not, I insist, a purely legal-dogmatic question and cannot be reduced to one. The choices have to be grounded normatively.

Similar reflections would apply to all the key concepts in EU law, ranging from European citizenship to economic freedoms, from sound budgetary policy and sound money to reverse qualified majority voting.

C. An Independent Research Agenda: The Blind Angles of European Legal Scholarship

I have already argued in this chapter that the research agenda of Euro-scholars remains too closely defined by European institutions and, especially, by legal actors in European institutions – and in a double sense. First, the research agenda of EU legal scholarship tends to follow the legislative activity of the European legislator, the judicial agenda of the ECJ and the policy agenda of the European Commission. The degree to which funding for research has come to depend on European projects has only aggravated this trend, as research calls predetermine the themes and topics which will be dealt with by scholars. Second, research questions are considered mostly from the standpoint of European institutions and of repeated players before European institutions, and rarely from the standpoint of the European civil society. As a result, the rhythm and the tempo[55] of European legal scholarship are largely predetermined, when not set, by institutions.

Recontextualising the research agenda of European legal scholarship would require rendering research more pluralistic in terms of themes and perspectives.[56] Two possible steps towards such an objective are the following: first, we need a genuine historical approach to EU law, which takes seriously the breaks and discontinuities in the history of European integration; and, second, we have to make part of the research agenda themes which have been long neglected despite their social, economic, political and cultural salience (what I suggest we could label as the blind angles of EU law).

[55] The academic fashionability of specific subjects (European citizenship, the European Constitution, the open method of coordination etc) has followed political or administrative initiatives of European and national institutions.

[56] To make explicit what has remained so far implicit. My point is not to establish a 'contextual police' and reserve the term 'law in context' only to 'true' law in context pieces, whatever that may mean – or, for that matter, to deny the pertinence of pieces of legal dogmatic EU scholarship. It seems to me that, at this point in time, we are lacking not only good contextual pieces, but also sober descriptive pieces providing us with an accurate description of the actual content of the law as practised in the EU. Such pieces can indeed be more inspiring of actual transformation than many 'contextual' pieces.

i. Towards a Non-Whig History of EU Law

Mainstream EU legal scholarship is characterised by its 'Whiggism' or, in other words, by the combination of the following three features. First, the history of EU integration is regarded as a normative triumph, as a history of progress. Through integration, Europe would have overcome its terrible past and become capable of enjoying a happier present and be destined to a bright future. Second, the project of integration would have been largely defined – at least in broad terms– in the founding Treaties of the European Communities. Successive Treaty amendments and big decisions would have 'completed' the original design. From that perspective, the different crises which the EU has experienced have not only revealed the capacity of European integration to endure, but would also have proven to be occasions to overcome the different obstacles to integration.[57] Third, law would be the means of European integration par excellence. From such a perspective, European law would be a progressive force in history, which would have naturally contributed to the realisation of fundamental normative goals, not least peace and prosperity.

Under such a light, the founding Treaties are reduced to programmes which would have been progressively realised through history, instead of complex compromises between liberalisation and protectionism, as the best historical scholarship has shown. Breaks and discontinuities, such as the European Monetary System or the Single European Act, which have transformed not only EU law but also the EU and the Member States as political communities, are proposed again as stages in an unfolding process of 'ever closer union'. This largely pre-empts the critique of the fundamental decisions through which transformations were introduced, be they political acts, legal norms or judicial decisions, to the extent that the latter are presented as the mere implementation of what was already contained in embryo in the founding Treaties. The result is paradoxical: the real existing European Union is not so much the outcome of a struggle, in which objectives are unavoidably reconsidered as circumstances change, but the result of implementing a pre-established programme. What would have changed is not 'integration', but the 'external circumstances' (critically including the states themselves) in which the process would have unfolded. This also fails to consider the extent to which there have been decisive moments in which it has become evident that applying existing EU law would have catastrophic consequences, and therefore there were extremely pressing reasons to breach the norms in force and proceed according to very different norms that were basically established through a de facto emergency executive power. These new norms were later endorsed by the courts, not least by the CJEU.

A non-Whig EU legal scholarship should normalise the history of European law and regard it as being shaped by the same social, political, economic and

[57] It is frequently argued that European crises would not result so much in ruptures, discontinuities and breaks as in the reinforcement of the integration process itself. In other words, integration would accelerate through crisis government.

cultural forces as national legal history. Once we do so, we will realise that EU law is bound to be ambivalent from a normative perspective. In particular, when considered from the standpoint of the democratic and social state, EU law has played both the role of a facilitator of the development of the democratic and social state, and a constraint limiting when not undoing the democratic and social state. The consolidation of the democratic and social state was facilitated by European integration as unfolded in the 1950s and 1960s, and part of the 1970s, because it allowed the simultaneous growth of external trade and the build-up of the power of states to shape their socio-economic structure in line with their politically selected social, economic and cultural goals, all at the very same time that Community law made it possible to realise the objectives of the social state in the transnational and supranational dimensions. However, the Communities already became a deeply ambivalent force in their relationship to the democratic and social state in the late 1970s. By means of unleashing the power of capital holders from the late 1970s, EEC law created the conditions under which the latter were empowered to make use of their rights to private property and entrepreneurial freedom to escape from the constraints imposed to render the social state possible and functional. This shows that European integration per se is not an unqualified blessing or an unqualified curse. Consequently, the key question is not whether there is more or less of Europe, but what is the point and purpose of Europe (*which Europe we want, what we want Europe to do*). This invites the problematisation of present EU law, in line with the objective described in the previous section, namely the denaturalisation and defamiliarisation of the key concepts of EU law. By the same token, we should stress the breaks and discontinuities in the evolution of EU law, and render visible the extent to which such breaks and discontinuities have not always been mended through democratic decision making, but rather frequently through executive intervention or 'judicial statesmanship'.

A key part of the process of normalisation of the history of European integration would be to set the legal history of the EU in its wider, global context. Two main challenges have already emerged in the historiographical literature. The first is far from new and concerns the decisive external constraints that shaped the process of European integration. In the aftermath of the Second World War, Western Europe operated under extremely strong military and geopolitical constraints. To this day, in order to make sense of European defence and foreign policy, one has to take seriously the limits stemming from the far from symmetric relationship between the US and the EU, for example. By the same token, and as Europeans have realised in shock in the last few months, from the 1970s the supply of European energy came to depend on Russian gas, while in the last 30 years the degree of trade dependence on China has grown massively. Without these external entanglements, we cannot make sense of the development of European law. The second challenge remained subdued until recently.[58] It is clear that we cannot make sense of the

[58] But see W Rodney, *How Europe Underdeveloped Africa* (Dar es Salaam, Tanzania Publishing House, 1972); J Galtung, 'The Lomé Convention and Neo-capitalism' (1976) 6 *African Review* 33.

history of Europe without paying due attention to the phenomenon of colonialism, imperialism and neo-imperalism. Hansen and Jonsson's *Eurafrica* and Brown's *The Seventh Member State*[59] have made it impossible to miss the extent to which the same can be said of the EU. Imperialism and neo-imperalism are not part of the past of European integration, but, unfortunately, are part of our present. It suffices to consider the complex arrangements sustaining the CFA franc, which, at the very least, can be said to create a series of bonds which are not obviously in favour of the weaker party.[60]

ii. Blind Spots

I have already pointed to the fact that EU scholarship follows the institutional agenda in a double sense: not only does it tend to focus on the questions which are part of the legislative, judiciary or policy agenda of European institutions, but it also tends to look at those problems from the perspective of the legal actors serving European institutions. The result is not only the neglect of topics, despite the fact that they are socially regarded as highly relevant, but also that even when questions are tackled, the perspective from which they are dealt with may result not so much from the nature and consistency of the underlying socio-economic problems, but from the very way in which institutions perceive the problems. A renewed contextualist programme of research has to tackle these 'blind angles' of EU law scholarship, and both explore new issues and consider old issues from new perspectives.

Perhaps the most obvious example of a major social issue which has been neglected by European law scholarship is caring labour or care work. Community law was built on the basis of a very traditional understanding of work in standard Fordist terms. The case law on the freedom of movement of workers and the rights of workers seemed in the 1970s to be evolving towards a wider and richer understanding of work, which resulted in an expansion of the very concept of 'worker'. Such transformation, however, was arrested by the combined effect of apparently decoupling European rights from work (through citizenship), only to introduce a new discriminating factor in the form of the concept of 'economically active'. First, in the early 1900s, the enshrinement of European citizenship in the European treaties seemed to render somehow obsolete the discussion about who was and who was not a worker, and what would count as work. This was because access to the rights stemming from EU law seemed to be in the process of being extended to all citizens, independently of whether or not they qualified as workers. However, second, in the '10s the ECJ reintroduced conditions for access to European rights

[59] P Hansen and S Jonsson, *Eurafrica: The Untold Story of European Integration and Colonialism* (London, Bloomsbury, 2014); M Brown, *The Seventh Member State: Algeria, France, and the European Community* (Cambridge, MA, Harvard University Press, 2022).

[60] F Pigeaud and NS Sylla, *Africa's Last Colonial Currency: The CFA Franc Story* (London, Pluto Press, 2021).

through the concept of 'economically active'. The latter seems to be even more anchored to a conception of classical waged work than the very concept of 'worker'. It is high time that EU law scholarship challenges the systematic discrimination against caring labour and work, and considers the ways in which we can transform our understanding of what is a good society through a different understanding of how we are useful through different forms of labour to others.

In terms of the need to adopt different perspectives on well-established subjects of research, perhaps that is especially urgent on what concerns the area of freedom, justice and home affairs, especially but not exclusively on what concerns migration and asylum policy. The latter policies have systematically been approached through the prism of national and/or internal security. A clear example of this is the permanent association, often implicit but frequently explicit, between immigration, insecurity and criminality, which has permeated the EU's programmes on the matter since the early days of the Tampere meeting in 1999. This accounts, for example, for the fragmentation of the status of third-country nationals. Instead of a single status, we have such disparate ones as, on the one hand, the holders of blue cards and, on the other hand, seasonal workers. If we want to honour our normative commitments, as reflected in the Charter of Fundamental Rights of the European Union, we have to start by looking at those issues also from the perspective of the forced migrants entering European territory. This is by no means a mere pious intention based on a millenarian hope for universal justice, nor is it a denial of the real importance of migratory flows for a considerable number of public policies, not least the redistributive ones.

IV. Conclusions

In this chapter, I have argued that the popularity of interdisciplinary and contextual studies of EU law is not only a signal of the relevance and salience of EU law in context, but also proof of the capacity of 'black letter' approaches to metabolise methodologies with a sharper critical edge. There is no doubt that EU law in context has made its mark on EU legal scholarship. Proof of this is the fact that it is no longer deemed eccentric to set EU law in its wider political, cultural, economic and social context; rather, presenting a manuscript as a combination of description and contextualisation may increase the chances of seeing it published in the leading EU law journals. Still, EU law scholarship tends to fail to make use of the insights and knowledge stemming from other disciplines to reflect critically on the conceptual tools it uses to reconstruct and describe EU law. By the same token, EU legal scholars rarely reflect on the limits of EU law, ie, on what we can expect EU law can actually achieve as a means of social integration. Perhaps even more worryingly, EU law scholarship has yet to develop a research agenda which takes the necessary distance from the interests and concerns of EU institutions and actors.

All these are among the reasons why we need EU law in context more than ever, as I have argued in this chapter. From even the narrowest possible legal perspective, it must be concluded that the interpretation and application of the norms structuring and organising the European socio-economic structure cannot be regarded as a purely legal-dogmatic task. The law of a process of integration of democratic and social states is bound to be complex and to require, for its reconstruction, interpretation and application, resort to concepts and tools other than technical legal ones – a conclusion that is only rendered firmer by the peculiar path followed by the EC and the EU over the last 30 years.

8

A Genealogy of Constitutional Europe

LEONE NIGLIA*

I. Introduction

We may have shifted away from an understanding of law as monopolised by the state towards seeing it instead as pluralistic. Yet, paradoxically, most scholars of Europeanisation still think of the EU legal order as a legalistic-monistic constitutional order. In other words, the more law (including constitutional law) is, generally speaking, seen as pluralistic, and the more EU law remains predominantly seen, legalistically, as monistic. This chapter overcomes this dogmatic, restrictive view of EU law and its order, and aims at offering a more complex rendering of constitutional Europe: it shows that the EU legal order in itself, as developed in the period up to the start of the twenty-first century, has been an internally pluralistic constitutional construction.[1]

* Financial support is acknowledged from Erasmus+ Jean Monnet, EU (research awards 2021 and 2022) and from Sapienza University (research awards 2020–22). This chapter is also part of a broader research project undertaken under the auspices of the European Union/Universidad Carlos III de Madrid, 'Connecting Excellence' Programme, as 'Connecting Excellence' Research Professor/Investigador Distinguido, Universidad Carlos III de Madrid, Instituto Bartolomé de las Casas, Madrid, Spain (EU/FP7 Grant Agreement No 600371; COFUND 2014–51509). I am also grateful to the British Academy (UK); the Leverhulme Trust (UK); MIUR (Italy); and the University of Michigan (US) for financial support. Thanks to the participants at, and the organisers of, lectures, talks, workshops and conferences at the London School of Economics and Political Science; the University of Cambridge; Harvard University; the University of Heidelberg; the European University Institute; Queen Mary, the University of London; Universidad Carlos III de Madrid; the University of Michigan, Ann Arbor; and Sapienza University, where I have presented ideas on which this chapter is based.

This chapter is an instalment of a series of essays on the state of constitutional Europe. The previous instalments are: L Niglia, 'The New Transformation of Europe: *Arcana Imperii*' (2020) 68 *American Journal of Comparative Law* 151; L Niglia, 'Eclipse of the Constitution: Europe Nouveau Siècle' (2016) 22 *European Law Journal* 132; L Niglia, 'Taking Private Law Rights Seriously: Of Balancing and the Jurisprudence of the Court of Justice of the European Union' in L Niglia (ed), 'Symposium: Balancing in European Law: Anatomy of Judicial Practices' (2013–14) *Cambridge Yearbook of European Legal Studies* 394; L Niglia, 'Form and Substance in European Constitutional Law: The Social Character of Indirect Effect' (2010) 16 *European Law Journal* 439; L Niglia, 'Beyond Enchantment: The Possibility of a New European Private Law' (2009) 28 *Yearbook of European Law* 60.

[1] On European law and pluralism, see L Niglia, *Pluralism and European Private Law* (Oxford, Hart Publishing, 2013); and see the seminal work of Francis Snyder on European law methodologically seen in terms of 'first, the tension between concentration and dispersion; and, second, the tension between

The chapter is divided into three main sections. After considering, in section II, the state of the art of constitutional thinking about the EU against which the chapter is written, the chapter undertakes a two-step analysis.

Judicial actors, I will argue in section III, have weaved the constitutional design with an eye on certain substantive agendas. The constitutional design itself appears more complex than conventionalism would have us believe: there has been a striking parallelism between, on the one hand, contingent political visions (related to a heterogeneity of discrete regulatory concerns) and, on the other hand, judicial decisions. I therefore retrace the making of a constitutional order made out of a heterogeneity of discrete regulatory arenas (that is, agriculture, free movement, competition and social policy) or, in other words, an internally pluralistic constitutional construction.[2]

In section IV, I note that that parallelism challenges us to rethink the established understanding of 'constitutionalisation', in at least two key senses that profoundly rewrite conventionalism. I consider what constitutionalisation has *not* been and what it has been.

First, 'constitutionalisation' has *not* been a legalistic development insulated from the political as per the accounts of a legalistic dynamic of law's hardening[3] as the inevitable outcome of a reading of the texts. Judges have handled legal material with an eye on the surrounding political visions held by governmental actors, through a principled hermeneutical work that mirrors that of constitutional courts in national jurisdictions.

Second, and relatedly, constitutional disciplining in the courtrooms has *not* been comprehensive (that is, the 'hardening' of the law everywhere within the remit of Community law, according to the monistic view) but pluralistic in the sense of being selective. It has been about hardening law in some regulatory areas whilst not in others insofar as they have remained under domestic sovereignty, in tune with the requirements emerging from the underlying political settlement. A plural dimension has operated alongside those very hierarchical *qua* disciplinary constitutional structures that scholarly narratives typically draw upon.

The chapter then concludes that there has never been a blanket (universal) constitutionalisation of individual rights, but a piecemeal (pluralistic) judicial work that has upheld (or not) Community (Union)-based rights depending on the constitutional handling (institutional reflexivity) of the plural requirements of the broader, multilevel politico-constitutional settlement.

power and relativity' (F Snyder, '"Out on the Weekend": Reflections on European Union Law in Context' *EUI Working Paper LAW* No 94/11, 1994, 4–5). See also L Niglia, *The Structural Transformation of European Private Law: A Critique of Juridical Hermeneutics* (Oxford, Hart Publishing, 2023, forthcoming); and L Niglia, 'The New Transformation of Europe: *Arcana Imperii*' (2020) 68 *American Journal of Comparative Law* 151.

[2] On JHH Weiler's distinct thesis (focused on the system of voting in the Council) on this parallelism, see below at section V.

[3] In this chapter 'law's hardening' is meant to indicate not the transformation of soft law into hard law or the enhancing of the effectiveness of law, but rather the lifting of the EU's law status to a 'constitutional' status in the idiosyncratic ways explained in this chapter.

II. An Old Story, a New Reading: Part I

The body of knowledge on the judicial discourse on individuals, rights and enforcement,[4] and on the resulting constitutionalisation of Europe,[5] is contingent on the type of scholarship that has produced it.[6] A body of knowledge that comes from a variety of sources (constitutional and political science scholarship)[7] and that has a complex intellectual history (from doctrine to social science to normative politics)[8] revolves around the belief in the constitutional story as a *legal(istic)* phenomenon.[9]

According to this account, the key figures in this story are the judges of the Court of Justice of the European Union and of the national courts. Its defining conceptual apparatus is the language of constitutional principles and the talk of rights' entitlements. Its driving force is the twin allure of judicial empowerment and judicial legislation. Its ethos is the entrenchment of individual rights vis-a-vis the state.[10] Basically, this story is understood to be an experiment dictated by legal necessity. Even in its most sophisticated rendition, the hardening of the law (*qua*

[4] Notably, a discourse developed ever since Case 26/62 *Van Gend en Loos* [1963] ECR 1.

[5] 'Constitutionalisation' in Europe is customarily defined as 'the process by which the EC Treaties evolved from a set of legal arrangements binding upon sovereign states, into a vertically integrated legal regime conferring judicially enforceable rights and obligations on all legal persons and entities, public and private, within [the sphere of application of EC law]': A Stone, 'Constitutional Dialogues in the European Community' *EUI Working Paper* RSC No 95/38, 1, as quoted, for example, in JHH Weiler, *The Constitution of Europe* (Cambridge, Cambridge University Press, 1999), 221; and B Rittberger and F Schimmelfennig (eds), *The Constitutionalisation of the EU* (Abingdon, Routledge, 2007) 1. This chapter contributes to a growing body of literature on the meaning of constitutionalisation in Europe in its historical evolution, for the more the crisis of Europe has unfolded, the more scholars (including legal historians) have retrospectively revisited the constitutionalisation process: see, eg, articles in the *European Constitutional Law Review* (2014) and in the *European Law Journal* (2015). See also C Joerges, 'Private Law in Europe's Political Economy after the Financial Crisis' in M Ruffert (ed), *European Economy and People's Mobility* (Tübingen, Mohr Siebeck, 2016).

[6] On the interface between legal developments 'out there' and scholarly reconstructions of them in EU law, see Weiler (n 5) 224; PL Lindseth, 'The Perils of a "as if" Constitutionalism' (2017) 22 *European Law Journal* 696.

[7] See respectively Weiler (n 5); and A Stone Sweet, *The Judicial Construction of Europe* (Oxford, Oxford University Press, 2004).

[8] See, critically, Weiler (n 5) 224 et seq.

[9] See K Alter, *Establishing the Supremacy of European Law* (Oxford, Oxford University Press, 2001) 39 (holding that 'legalism remains the dominant paradigm for analyzing legal integration in Europe' also for political scientists). Examples of groundbreaking works that have taken a contextual approach are F Snyder, *New Directions in European Community Law* (Cambridge, Cambridge University Press, 1990); and Weiler (n 5). But the core integration scholarship has chosen another path: '"Law in society" approaches … look at the epistemology of the law, its vision of society: what image does it draw of human relations; what ideologies, justified true-beliefs does it draw on; how do the internal structures of the law reconstruct these; how do legal visions of society compete with other collective visions … with some notable exceptions … this debate is absent from EU studies' (*cf* D Chalmers, 'EU Law and the Failure of the European Social Scientific Imagination' (2004) 4 *EUSA Review* 4). See, critically, Lindseth (n 6) 696.

[10] See F Mancini and DT Keeling, 'Democracy and the European Court of Justice' (1994) 57(2) *MLR* 175, 181 (on the relevance of 'rights' in the process of 'democratisation' of the Community, and on the ECJ being seen as embarking on the job of 'ensuring an adequate level of judicial protection for the individual in spite of the sometimes deficient terms of the Treaty').

constitutionalisation) for the protection of EU-based individuals' rights is seen as traceable less due to policy choices and more to the inevitable result of a 'correct' reading of the text. For, in the words of Judge Mancini, the judges of the Court of Justice managed 'to convince' their domestic interlocutors on the bench that their own interpretation was the best way to decode the available legal material – a story of law-driven, rather than politically driven, integration in which the heroic judges of the Court managed to 'work out the details agreed to in the Treaty of Rome'.[11] In Mancini's vocabulary, lacking any coercive powers to enforce its judgments and aware that they had 'almost no powers that were not traceable to … the persuasiveness of its judgments', the Luxembourg judges 'made the most of these assets'. They employed a 'courteously didactic method' of reasoning that only offered national judges 'clever' renditions of the available legal material. The national judge, thus 'led hand in hand as far as the door', was left with the job of 'crossing the threshold', a job entirely of their own choice, 'but now a job no harder than child's play'. Ultimately, 'the Luxembourg judges won the confidence of their colleagues from Palermo to Edinburgh and from Bordeaux to Berlin'.[12] Individuals' Community (now Union) law-based rights managed to be hardened *qua* 'constitutionalised' against states' recalcitrance to enforce them, only thanks to this ingenuous mechanism through which best interpretations 'inevitably' prevailed, because of the 'cleverly crafting' of legal material by the Luxembourg and national judges.

To be sure, scholarship that has articulated this purely legalistic rendition has been criticised for presenting:

> [T]he Community as a juristic idea; the written constitution as a sacred text; the professional commentary as the inevitable working out of the correct implications of the constitutional text; and the constitutional court as the disembodied voice of right reason and constitutional theology.[13]

Moreover, the established legalistic reading has been subject to criticism in legal scholarship that has explored law's hardening in relation to contextual aspects ('sophisticated legalism') *and* in international relations and comparative politics literature that has explored non-legal factors as the *only* ones that have produced the law's hardening.[14]

[11] K Alter, *The European Court's Political Power* (Oxford, Oxford University Press, 2010) 35.

[12] See GF Mancini, 'The Making of a Constitution for Europe' (1989) 26 *CML Rev* 595, 605–06. Note that, in my view, the legalistic rendition has been masterly summarised by Mancini in the account that I relate in the narrative, but, no doubt, his overall essay must otherwise fall into the camp of a more sophisticated literature (in the narrative this literature is referred to as 'sophisticated legalism') that has taken wider contextual factors into account. For a critical, sophisticated approach, see Weiler (n 5) 192, which also talks of hegemony of the ECJ by way of 'persuasion', but in the context of a wider study that takes political material seriously: 'despite the integrative radicalness of its doctrinal construct … the Court managed to hegemonize the EC interpretive community, and to persuade, co-opt, and cajole most, if not all, of the other principal actors to accept the fundamentals of its doctrine and of its positions in making the constitutional determinations for the Community'.

[13] See already M Shapiro, 'Comparative Law and Comparative Politics' (1980) 53 *Southern California Law Review*, 537, 538 (also quoted in Weiler (n 5) 14–15, who believes that such critical comments 'could be levelled against much of the legal literature on the Community').

[14] For a summary of the legalistic, international relations and comparative politics literature on constitutional Europe, see Alter (n 11) 34 et seq.

Yet, the critics agree with orthodox legalism in assuming that the law's hardening is a 'given' that one cannot but acknowledge.[15] In the words of Alec Stone, constitutionalisation consists of:

> [T]he process by which the EC Treaties evolved from a set of legal arrangements binding upon sovereign states, into a vertically integrated legal regime conferring judicially enforceable rights and obligations on all legal persons and entities, public and private, within [the sphere of application of EC law].[16]

Today, this belief in European law as a constitutional body of rules that compellingly (by the 'inner force of law') entrench rights against the state is here with us to stay. Any pattern of 'deviation' from that belief is read through the legalistic prism, as in the following recent statement by Jürgen Basedow. Basedow proposes a binary opposition between, on the one hand, 'the effectiveness and unity of EU *law*' and, on the other hand, the 'promotion' of '*political agendas*', through 'exploiting' 'their discretion', by the constitutional courts. No doubt this statement reflects the deeply held belief in viewing the work of the European Court of Justice (ECJ) as, to put it in the above-quoted Shapiro's words, 'the disembodied voice of right reason':

> [I]t is problematic that, in practice, *constitutional courts could exploit their discretion to promote political agendas*, which would ultimately undermine the effectiveness and unity of EU law.[17]

A critical scholar, Ulrich Haltern, denounces the persistence of this consciousness in that:

> [T]he CJEU has refused to make any structural revisions *but continues to revere its own history and ironclad logic of EU law coherence.* (Emphasis added)[18]

This shows a 'reverence' of 'its own history and ironclad logic of EU law coherence' that, one must add, is reflected and reinforced in conventional scholarship.

[15] Note, eg, the study of M Pollack, *The Engines of Integration: Delegation, Agency, and Agency Setting in the European Union* (Oxford, Oxford University Press, 2003) 200 et seq (arguing, in response to international politics literature attempting to explain the ECJ case law entirely in relation to states' political interests, that explanations based on the assumption that the ECJ decides the case 'purely on the basis of law' cannot be ruled out – I draw on the synthesis of Pollack's work given by Alter (n 11) 38).

[16] See Stone (n 5).

[17] J Basedow, 'European Integration: *Quo Vadis*? A Critical Commentary on the PSPP Judgment of the German Federal Constitutional Court of May 5, 2020' (2021) 19 *Journal of International and Constitutional Law* 1, 75 (fn 26).

[18] U Haltern, 'Revolutions, Real Contradictions, and the Method of Resolving Them: The Relationship between the Court of Justice of the European Union and the German Federal Constitutional Court' (2021) 19(1) *International Journal of Constitutional Law* 208 (this being the most recent critical account of the state of EU scholarship and jurisprudence as legalistic). Note the widespread view that nothing much has changed in the constitutional material landscape (see JHH Weiler, 'The Transformation of Europe' (1991) 100 *Yale Law Journal* 2405, now in Weiler (n 5), on 'constitutionalisation' as a process that was largely completed in the 1960s and early 1970s, and that remained unaltered in its structure for the subsequent two decades).

In this chapter, I would like to contribute to an understanding of what judges have actually done, given that, in my view, they have acted less as 'the disembodied voice of right reason' and more as engaged voices among the many in the wider community of political and legal actors. Judges will not come out of this account any less heroic: their constitutional role as policy-making institutions capable of influencing major policies and framing rights' protection whilst maintaining independence and trust is no different from the accounts of the constitutional role and function of national courts acting independently of European law, but it is striking how conventionalism keeps thinking of the European constitutional story as a legalistic 'special case' (*Sonderweg*).

The chapter aims at overcoming the law/political division that lies at the core of the accounts of both those who elevate law (as legalism) above everything else and of those who critically discuss the relevance of non-legal factors (political scientists). It proposes to re-read the story of European law and its constitutionalisation as hermeneutic material uttered by the judges acting as engaged interpreters of sets of policies widely shared everywhere else, from the national to the supranational organisational-governance level. From this vantage point, I agree with Karen Alter's conclusive remarks in her book[19] that understanding the 'synergies' between the national and the supranational would self-evidently answer questions such as 'how could it be that the law hardened' or 'how could it be that the states allowed this to happen' better than thousands of (legalistic *or* international relations or comparative politics)[20] theories. This is because, I argue in the remainder of this chapter, the answer lies in acknowledging an exceptional moment of convergence of state policies in European history. Here, as everywhere, a *comparative* study of both political and legal developments in parallel can reveal exactly what theories that focus either on law *or* on politics can only hide – the pedigree of constitutional Europe at the intersection of the national and the supranational. Thus, below I explain that there is a complex interface between the official constitutional story and the surrounding, multilevel political context (both national and supranational). 'Knowledge' must be broadened to include substantive aspects in order for us to unearth the complex genealogy of constitutional Europe.

III. An Old Story, a New Reading: Part II

The role that 'the law' has played in the constitutional story has been overstated at the expense of a more balanced account that would take into consideration the

[19] Alter (n 11) argues that there is a need for scholarly investigations on the 'synergies' between state and European-level actions that managed to 'work' while other synergies (international-domestic) have not. For another recent reminder of the need for both national and supranational stories to be taken seriously in theorising about integration, with particular regard to the 'social' national dimension, *see* C Joerges, 'Unity in Diversity as Europe's Vocation and Conflicts of Law as Europe's Constitutional Form' *LSEQ Papers* 28/2010.

[20] For a summary, see Alter (n 11) 32 et seq.

political. Typically, constitutional scholars tell the story of the aptitude and propensity of judges to weave constitutional material on the basis of which litigants then confidently advance their Community (now Union) law-grounded claims. Political scientists have joined the choir at a later point in time and, although taking an entirely different perspective that focuses on the various contexts,[21] have agreed with the legalist account.[22] That the constitutional story revolves around the ways in which the courts have skilfully handled legal material has therefore become an established belief in both fields.[23]

A major component of this belief is the fiction that developed out of a presumption that, in 'inventing' the supranational constitutional discourse, the judges of the ECJ have acted – to use the vocabulary introduced by Eric Stein – *as if* there had been a true 'constitutional moment'.[24] Notably, the active engagement of national courts in using Article 234 of the EC Treaty (now Article 267 of the Treaty on the Functioning of the European Union (TFEU)) for the pursuit of Community (now Union) policies, through the vigilant behaviour of citizens *qua* litigants[25] was the decisive factor that transformed a set of doctrines normally found in the international law discourse into a constitutional-like script,[26] as judges, lawyers and litigants engaged in a constitutional conversation over rights conceived of in the context of rule-of-law narratives.[27] Thus, doctrinal elements such as direct effect, supremacy, human rights and implied powers have been transformed into instruments for domestic courts to sanction their own states' negligence in complying with the 'international' obligations undertaken in the treaties – with (constitutional) 'solidarity' replacing (international law) 'reciprocity'.[28]

[21] See Alter (n 9) 39 et seq; see also a re-reading of her own work in Alter (n 11), as summarised above.

[22] ibid.

[23] ibid 43 et seq and as discussed in the introduction to this chapter. See also M Pollack, *The Engines of Integration: Delegation, Agency, and Agency Setting in the European Union* (Oxford, Oxford University Press, 2003) 200 et seq, as discussed in n 15 above.

[24] See E Stein, 'Lawyers, Judges and the Making of a Transnational Constitution' (1981) 75(1) *AJIL* 1 (holding that 'the Court … has fashioned a constitutional framework for a federal-type structure in Europe … has construed the … Treaties in a constitutional mode rather than employing the traditional international law methodology').

[25] See Weiler (n 5) (developing further Eric Stein's conceptual framework of analysis based on the 'symbiotic relationship between national courts and the Court of Justice', and explaining how that relationship has been key to the success of the ECJ constitutional move).

[26] See B de Witte, 'The Nature of the Legal Order' in P Craig and G de Burca (eds), *The Evolution of EU Law* (Oxford, Oxford University Press, 1999) 193: 'It is not enough for the Court of Justice to proclaim that Community law rules should have direct effect and should prevail over national law … There is … a second dimension to the matter, which is decisive for determining whether the Court's doctrines have an impact on legal reality: the attitude of national courts' and arguing that this impact has been largely successful.'

[27] See Weiler (n 5) 2419.

[28] ibid 192 et seq. See also further literature drawing on Weiler's work, including L Hancher, 'Constitutionalism, The Community Court and International Law' (1994) 25 *Netherlands Yearbook of International Law* 259, 265–66; and M Maduro, *We the Court* (Oxford, Hart Publishing, 1998) 8. On 'solidarity' replacing 'reciprocity', *see* G Bebr, 'Agreements Concluded by the Community and Their Possible Direct Effect: From International Fruit Company to Kupferberg' (1983) 20 *CML Rev* 35, 71.

Ever since, so the story goes, a true federal-type constitutional discipline, based on a 'habit of obedience' traditionally associated with national (federative nation-state) rather than international obligations,[29] has developed composed of *formal* and *structural* aspects.

The *formal* aspects of such constitutional discipline are the discourse on rights and individuals, and its *structural* aspects, the active cooperation between national courts and the ECJ for the actual protection of individual rights.[30] Structure (judicial cooperation) has transformed form (the discourse of individuals and rights) into a constitutional disciplinary script (the judicial enforcement of Community rights, the flipside of which results in the sanctioning of states' non-compliance vis-a-vis Community obligations). The script is called 'constitutional' because of the 'vertically integrated' legal regime thus produced, conferring as it does rights and obligations on legal persons and entities,[31] which, the argument goes, has transformed the EC Treaties in a system analogous to a constitutional federation.

One can gain a more complex picture of the above set of processes by looking at their underlying substantive policies, in the sense that more is at stake if one looks, beyond the conventional focus on formal and structural aspects, at those substantive choices made in the shadow of legal constitutionalisation – although rarely perceived as such.[32] The phenomenal development of a constitutional framework around the discourse on individuals, rights and enforcement must be seen in the broader context of the political choices made by the key social actors other than the courts, and crystallised around governmental structures, that the courts then respected and elaborated upon in their judgments. Adopting this perspective, below I consider the making of a federal-type 'constitutional discipline' characterised by, and modulated and adapted in relation to, certain specific dominant substantive policies: those contingent choices that crystallised over the years in a

[29] I derive the term 'constitutional discipline' from Weiler (n 5) 191–92: the federal-type constitutional framework introduced by the ECJ involved an 'aggressive and radical doctrinal jurisprudence' whose content can be understood as a 'Community discipline' defined as 'a set of norms governing many of the relations between Community and Member States legal (and political) orders'. See de Witte (n 26) 193, holding, in relation to the doctrines of supremacy and direct effect, that 'the reception of those doctrines at the national level has been rather successful' and detailing the many nuances that have characterised this story – in particular how, in relation to supremacy vis-a-vis constitutional law, 'the essential question is where to draw the line between minor adaptations and essential changes, and, consequently, where to set the limits to the penetration of EC law into the domestic constitutional order', rather than one of whether or not integral reception takes place. By 'discipline', obviously, at this point I am referring more to the outcome ('successful reception') and less to the many nuances that have characterised the processes that have led to the disciplinary outcome, nuances that I will detail in the remainder of this chapter.

[30] For the classical explanation of both aspects, and the adoption of the vocabulary of federal constitutionalism based on the argument-by-analogy that Europe works similarly to the way national federal constitutional systems do, see Weiler (n 5) 24 et seq.

[31] See Stone (n 5).

[32] As noted by Weiler (n 5) 88, fn 198 (referring to 'an interesting feature of the pre-1992 Community: the relative absence of ideological discourse and debate on the right-left spectrum', and adding that '[o]f course I do not suggest that choices with ideological implications were not made. But they were rarely perceived as such').

federal-type system whose substantive foundations remained for a long period the way that Eric Stein captured and described them in the early 1970s – that is, 'in the nature of a market economy tempered by social welfare considerations'.[33]

Below I propose to analyse, in synthetic form, the ways in which 'constitutional Europe' has been organised in four key regulatory arenas: agriculture, free movement, competition and social policy.

After sketching the key aspects of the public policy agendas in the light of which governmental actors have orientated their behaviour in the Community setting through their *legislative and executive-administrative* activities (section III.A), I then consider the position of the CJEU (*judicial* activities) in weaving the constitutional script in relation to such developments in the political process (section III.B). I argue that political material (governmental activities) and legal hermeneutics (the European courts' decisions) have gone hand in hand, trespassing on each other in ways in which the particulars are only now starting to be unveiled in socio-legal, legal comparative, constitutional and theoretical terms.[34]

For the purposes of this chapter, I will confine my analysis to the striking parallelism and correspondence between, on the one hand, *policy visions and plans* in the political realm regarding a contingent distribution of powers between the EU and the Member States in four discrete regulatory domains (free movement, agriculture, competition and social policy) and, on the other hand, judicial *decisions* in the legal realm, before casting an eye (in section IV) on 'constitutionalisation' as a meta-narrative that can be made really intelligible in relation to such hermeneutical interface. I argue that 'European law' is not just about subjecting states to a supranational constitutional law, as in the conventional rendition of the work of the European courts, in that it is about implementing a specific kind of substantively orientated constitutional order. In other words, what developed as the 'new legal order' over the period from 1960 to 2000 consisted less of a monistic constitutional structure (that is, 'a vertically integrated legal regime conferring judicially enforceable rights and obligations on all legal persons and entities, public and

[33] E Stein, *Harmonisation of European Company Laws* (Indianapolis, Bobbs-Merrill Company, 1971) 6.

[34] See A Vauchez, 'The Transnational Politics of Judicialization: *Van Gend en Loos* and the Making of the EU Polity' (2010) 16 *European Law Journal* 1, 7 (holding that 'gentlemen-politicians' – that is, actors being both politicians and lawyers – have played a key role in shaping legal Europe, a socio-legal account that is simultaneously biographical and structural); L Niglia, 'Form and Substance in European Constitutional Law: The Social Character of Indirect Effect' (2010) 16 *European Law Journal* 439 (on the interface between indirect effect in legal discourse and social policy in the political sphere). Note the plea in MA Wilkinson, 'The Reconstitution of Postwar Europe: Lineages of Authoritarian Liberalism' *LSE Working Papers* 05/2006: 'A fuller account of the duality between supranational normative structure and national political power ('dual supranationalism') must therefore reject any formalistic picture of a balanced bifurcation of legal and political pillars and capture their dysfunctional inter-relation' (a plea that refers to the more recent history of integration, and that is intelligible in the light of the analysis proposed in this chapter, focused on the previous period of integration, in terms of a constitutionally grounded inter-relation, as I will discuss it in the remainder of this chapter). For the theoretical argument that there is a great need for descriptive socio-legal studies on the structures of constitutionalism, both in Europe and beyond, see DJ Calligan, 'The Paradox of Constitutionalism or the Potential of Constitutional Theory?' (2008) 28 *OJLS* 343 et seq.

private, within [the sphere of application of EC law]') and more of a plural constitutional constellation of the EU and the Member States' powers distributed across certain domains: free movement, agriculture, competition, social policy. I start with recounting political material (section III.A) before considering the legal material (section III.B).

***

I would like to preface the remainder with a *caveat lector*. Mine is an exercise in re-description. It appears that judges have been acting out of a *Vorverständniss*, to put it in the vocabulary of Joseph Esser[35] – that is, a 'pre-understanding' structured along legal principles *and* substantively motivated out of contingent belief sets that in turn have enjoyed wide consensus in the (European, multilayered) political community. For the purpose of analysis, the chapter re-deploys a hermeneutical material that underlies the political and the legal realms, and that revolves around such defining *Vorverständniss*.

In a Europe that, due to its late modern history, places in the hands of the judges much of the most defining public choices, I argue that the judges engaged in constructing and enforcing European law have been acting, not unlike the work of the national constitutional courts, as 'reflexive institutions' vis-a-vis social and political conflicts, to put it in the words of Pierre Rosanvallon, in the sense that the judges have been putting forward a constitutional *Vorverständniss* that sees constitutional law shaped by a certain contingent kind of common welfare agenda – that is, what has become known in the social sciences as 'embedded liberalist consensus' and as opposed to anarchic and individualistic 'classical international law' interactions among states (in the words of the international law scholar Antonio Cassese).

A. The Political Process as Background to Constitutionalisation

The political actors who gave birth to the integration project in post-Second World War times were wholeheartedly committed to a reconstruction project of a 'welfarist' type at both the nation-state and the Community levels (hereinafter referred to as 'welfarist consensus' or 'settlement').[36]

[35] J Esser, *Vorverständniss und Methodenwhal in der Rechtsfindung* (Frankfurt, Athenäum Fischer Taschenbuch Verl, 1972). For a re-reading of Esser's work, specifically stressing his argument for the possibility and necessity to win consensus on concepts of justice in the relevant political community based on substantive values ('*Sachgerechtigkeit*'), see the seminal article by N Reich, 'Balancing in Private Law' in L Niglia et al (eds) *The Foundations of European Private Law* (Oxford, Hart Publishing, 2011) (adapting Esser's work to make key contemporary European private consumer law cases intelligible).

[36] For details, see A Moravicsik, *The Choice for Europe* (London, Routledge, 1998) 40 et seq; and A Milward, *The European Rescue of the Nation State* (Berkeley, University of California Press, 1992) 27 et seq.

Situated at the interface between the nation-state and the Community, the aim of this reconstruction project was to combine the enjoyment of the wealth-maximising effects of free commerce with the protection of social groups such as farmers and workers. This combination of public policy goals was based on a widely held and agreed-upon rationale: free commerce was seen as the key vehicle for increasing wealth and productivity, which in turn would allow the welfare state to finance its distributive and redistributive programme.[37]

Seen from the vantage point of the states, Europeanisation (the integration project) was 'a creation of the states' (in Milward's words) in the concrete sense of delivering this welfarist consensus-based reconstruction agenda 'for their own purposes'. State governmental actors chose to 'Europeanise' – that is, they actively set in motion the Europeanisation process as part of their chosen dual (combined) goal: the goal of promoting interstate commerce, as part of the idea that export-led growth would bring about high levels of productivity[38] and, at the same time, the goal of ensuring the protection of labour and farmers.[39]

This was a true multilevel project meant to operate simultaneously at the national and supranational levels, given that '[i]ntegration … was the creation of the European nation-states themselves *for their own purposes, an act of national will*' (emphasis added),[40] that is, implementing the post-war consensus among political actors, aimed at creating the conditions for high growth and productivity through export-led trade unconstrained by protectionism, whilst sheltering (in Milward's own words) 'three large, overlapping categories of voters … labour, agricultural producers and a diffuse alliance of lower and middle income beneficiaries of the welfare state', with a view to forging strong bonds of loyalty around the nation-state, in turn 'rescuing the state' from its long-term weaknesses due to their failing to keep the body politic in one piece.[41]

[37] See S Giubboni, *Social Rights and Market Freedom in the European Constitution: A Labour Law Perspective* (Cambridge, Cambridge University Press, 2006), 15 et seq (discussing the 'fiscal dividend deriving from the creation of the common market' for domestic systems of social governance); M Everson 'Law and Non-law in the Constitutionalisation of Europe' in C Joerges et al (eds), *Transnational Governance and Constitutionalism* (Oxford, Hart Publishing, 2004) 149 (referring to the works of Milward (n 36); and G Majone, *Regulating Europe* (London, Routledge, 1996) and elaborating on the related point that 'the driving force behind EEC construction in the 1950s, and even more so, its economic consolidation in the 1980s, was the vital need to overcome national economic stagnation in order to fulfil solidarity-security national social agendas'). For US perspectives, see D Rodrik, 'Globalisation and Labour, or: if Globalisation is a Bowl of Cherries, Why are There So Many Glum Faces at the Table?' in R Baldwin et al, *Market Integration, Regionalism and the Global Economy* (Cambridge, Cambridge University Press, 1999) 117, 141–43; and R Howse, 'From Politics to Technocracy – and Back Again: The Fate of the Multilateral Trading Regime' (2002) 96 *American Journal of International Law* 94. 98 (stressing this positive correlation and citing Rodrik's work).

[38] Milward (n 36) 119 et seq (discussing the Europeanisation of export-led growth and productivity).

[39] ibid 224 (discussing the Europeanisation of agricultural protectionist measures).

[40] ibid 18.

[41] I am drawing on A Milward's widely acknowledged work. The relevance of the national dimension in the design of trade integration has also been emphasised in the literature on trade policy and law: *see* Howse, (n 32) 97: 'This was the miracle of "embedded liberalism" – trade liberalization was embedded within a political commitment, broadly shared among the major players in the trading system of that

As a matter of fact, as I argue below, discrete regulatory arenas were developed and structured through the Community legislative and administrative activities pursuant to the belief that both the free market (export-led growth through fighting against protectionism) and the interventionist elements (protecting 'labour, agricultural producers and a diffuse alliance of lower and middle income beneficiaries of the welfare state') should be implemented in parallel so as to achieve the then dominant public policy goals.

The Community's regimes of economic freedoms, competition, agriculture and social policy were all seen as steps for implementing such a nation-state-based strategy. The driving idea was giving up trade protectionism, with their embracing the strategy of integrating markets through the four freedoms and competition, whilst constructing a pan-European interventionist regime in the area of agriculture (protection of farmers) and, at the same time, allowing states to retain as many of the rest of their social regulatory powers (protection of workers) as possible.

Such a widely shared public policy governmental vision was incorporated into the (multilevel) institutional setting of the Community through the arrangement of a set of concrete regulatory areas, consisting of a mix of *market-based* and *interventionist* (legislative and administrative-executive) tools and techniques.[42]

First, as to *market-based* governance objectives, governments saw in the structuring of a transnational market economy, through the four market freedoms and competition, a powerful way to increase their own finances for the purpose of funding wealth redistribution. The fight against protectionism in trade was seen as material to this strategy. For this reason, the free market elements of this project, as developed in the courtrooms around the promotion of the four freedoms and the fight against distorted competition (as I recount them below), were met favourably in the political process – a political process out of which, in parallel, harmonised rules (secondary legislation, from Directives to Regulations to Decisions) emerged that were strictly functional to the concretisation of the free movement of the factors of production and of market integration through competition.

Second, the *interventionist* elements of this European governance architecture were especially developed in two key areas: agriculture (the Common Agricultural Policy (CAP)) and social policy. In agriculture, a pan-European interventionist regime of controlled prices was constructed. In social policy, the political commitment of states to increase social protection nationally was enabled.[43]

era, to the progressive, interventionist welfare state; in other words, to a particular political and social vision – with greater use of microeconomic intervention, such as indicative planning and public enterprise in European and Japan, whilst tax-and-transfer approaches were more typical of North America … it was the trust that emerged from this basically shared vision that produces acceptance of the differences in approach to the mixed economy and welfare state as between the United State, Europe and Japan.'

[42] See, on institutions, processes, tools and techniques in European law, the seminal contribution of F Snyder, 'The Effectiveness of European Community Law: Institutions, Processes, Tools and Techniques' (1993) 56 *MLR* 19.

[43] See, eg, Giubboni (n 37).

In particular, the CAP was based on a system of controlled prices aimed at protecting and raising the income of farmers, a system that has held sway for decades.[44] The costs entailed in this regime were put on the Community budget. Considering that at least until the early 1990s agricultural and food policy accounted for over 80 per cent of EC legislation and judicial decisions,[45] for some decades supranational Europe has effectively consisted of a massive enterprise aimed at designing a supranational legislative and administrative interventionist regime in the agricultural sector, coupled with a parallel interventionist (protectionist) agricultural regime via common custom duties vis-a-vis non-European countries in the industrial sector.[46]

Another area in which interventionism triumphed was social policy. At the beginning, social policy was conjured up with a view to setting up a European-wide regime.[47] This project proved difficult to realise.[48] It was soon replaced by another kind of interventionist project that kept faith in the goal of protecting workers, but changed the way to achieve that very objective. The words of Scharpf well capture this historic shift:

> [W]here would we now be if, in the 1956 negotiations leading to the Treaties of Rome and the creation of the European Economic Community, French (Socialist) Prime Minister Guy Mollet had had his way? Mollet, supported by French industry, had tried to make the harmonization of social regulations and fiscal burdens a precondition for the integration of the industrial markets. But since he had even more pressing concerns to fend for – opening European markets for French agriculture, support for French colonies – *what he got in the final package was merely the political commitment of other governments to increase social protection nationally*. (Emphasis added)[49]

Thus, the key political actors with access to the Community opted for sheltering domestic social policies from the encroachment of market integration: the apparently 'lost opportunity' of the original harmonisation of social regulations turned out to be a blessing, in that social policy standards were preserved and improved through diversity. It was believed that all the gains coming from free commerce would put government in the position of improving the conditions of workers,[50] and that 'upward harmonisation' around a *spontaneous* convergence of social

[44] F Scharpf, 'The Joint-Decision Trap: Lessons from German Federalism and European Integration' (1988) 66 *Public Administration* 239, 251; Snyder (n 6); F Snyder, 'Ideologies of Competition in European Community Law' (1989) 52 *MLR* 149.

[45] Snyder (n 9) 19; Chalmers (n 9).

[46] Scharpf (n 44) 241. For details on the relevant legislative and administrative measures, see Snyder (n 9).

[47] See Giubboni (n 37) 15 et seq.

[48] ibid.

[49] FW Scharpf, 'The European Social Model: Coping with the Challenges of Diversity' (2002) 40 *Journal of Common Market Studies* 645, 645–46. For an example of the way in which harmonisation was originally conceived, see Stein (n 33) 6 (explaining that Europe's economic system was meant to be about harmonising *social policies*).

[50] Scharpf (n 44) ('national systems of social protection could and did expand rapidly').

policies towards increasingly higher levels of workers' protection would develop.[51] Only harmonised legislative rules strictly functional to the concretisation of free commerce and, in any case, never meant to alter domestic social policies arrangements were politically possible. It was in the light of this consensus that, over the years, a practice developed based on the resistance of governments in the Council of Ministers to change established rules and principles built under the type of social welfare provisions that they had elected as appropriate for themselves.[52] Some see the Community legislative setting as having been 'trapped' (to put it in Scharpf's terms) at any time that attempts have been made at conjuring up common social policy rules fundamentally at odds with domestic laws, or at overcoming domestic laws in the name of an excessive interpretation of market liberalisation values.[53]

En bref, governments have organised the Community process so as to retain the variety of domestic social welfare systems, which in turn have allowed them to implement the welfarist consensus *not* by harmonising social policy throughout Europe, the dream of French politicians in the 1950s that could simply not be possible to realise, *but* by leaving untouched the domestic choices in the field.

Overall, developing discrete regulatory mechanisms consisting of market-based (free movement and competition) and of interventionist (agriculture/CAP) elements, whilst retaining state interventionism in matters of social policy seen as a constituted dimension of the overall embedded liberalist settlement, have allowed governments to achieve a twin objective implicit in welfarist politics ever since post-war times – to promote wealth creation via free commerce whilst shielding from market processes certain social groups key for electoral concerns and, as such, singled out as deserving protection: workers and farmers.

Judicial work has been key in designing this multilevel regulatory framework, as I will discuss below.

B. The Judicial Process

Over the years, the ECJ judges, through the support and collaboration of national courts, have weaved the European constitutional discourse in concert with the choices made in the political process.

The Court of Justice has always been highly sensitive to the consensus that its decisions are bound to attract. For example, it has been noticed that the Court has typically resisted the creation of directly effective rights that might then find opposition among non-judicial actors.[54] I see more structure in the arguments

[51] Giubboni (n 37) 16.

[52] Scharpf (n 44).

[53] ibid.

[54] T Hartley, *The Foundations of European Community Law* (Oxford, Oxford University Press, 1988) 7-879. With regard to the Commission vis-a-vis the Member States, see Stein (n 24) 6 ('the Commission obviously hesitated to aggravate its fragile relationship with member governments by bringing them into the Court … In contrast, most of the "constitutional cases" as well as the cases in which the Court fashioned such concepts as illegal "charges equivalent to custom duties" or "measures equivalent to

regarding consensus as they pertain to the work of the CJEU. Below I note a contamination and a sharing of hermeneutical material across power sites on the one hand, legislative and executive-administrative, as noted above; and, on the other hand, judicial, as I will cover in the remainder of this section.[55]

Over the period considered in this chapter, the ECJ acted in tune with the welfare-orientated choices made within the political process regarding integration through governing the four key regulatory domains. This can be seen in the juxtaposition of a range of key, representative ECJ cases to the political choices structuring the aforementioned welfarist settlement. Each set of cases shows that the Court has acted out of– to put it in comparative constitutional vocabulary – a constitutional 'minimalist agenda' (in the words of Mark Tushnet) grounded on widely shared beliefs among the key social actors and ultimately aimed at intersecting and supporting that very settlement.[56]

A first correlation between the welfarist settlement (under the aspect of the objective of preventing protectionism) and the jurisprudence of the CJEU can be found in the case law on *free movement*. Here the Court judgments had the effect of supporting, and indeed co-determining, the member governments' political interest in preventing protectionism as a way of ensuring export-led growth.

Taking the pursuit of intra-Community trade liberalisation in terms of preventing state protectionism, and that of the unhindered pursuit of commerce in individual Member States in terms of reviewing national measures (assessing the Member States' intervention in the market) as the conflicting economic constitutional conceptions in this area,[57] one can say that free movement constitutional

quantitative restrictions" into tools for striking down national protectionist legislation, were referred to the Court under Article 177 as a result of litigation instituted by individuals or companies against their governments as, for example, in *Van Gend*.'

[55] On contamination and the sharing of hermeneutical material, see the works of, respectively, G Monateri, 'The Weak Law: Contaminations and Legal Cultures' (2001) 3 *Global Jurist Advances* 1; Niglia (n 1); and L Niglia, *The Struggle for European Private Law: A Critique of Codification* (Oxford, Hart Publishing, 2015) (on the sharing of hermeneutical material).

[56] I borrow the term 'minimalism' from the studies of M Tushnet, *The New Constitutional Order* (Princeton, Princeton University Press, 2003); and C Sunstein, *One Case at a Time. Judicial Minimalism on the Supreme Court* (Cambridge, MA, Harvard University Press, 1999) in relation to adjudication in the US, in the sense that the Supreme Court may act out of maximalism or minimalism. In the words of Tushnet, opinions may appeal 'to a collection of principles each of which is shared by some segments of society and that taken together are rather widely shared' (at 131 – and this is what minimalism is about), as opposed to opinions that 'appeal only to those who share the entire set of implications of the deep principles it invokes' (at 138 – and this is what maximalism is about).

[57] For this dichotomy, *see* Opinion of Advocate General Tesauro in Case C-292/92 *Huenemund* [1993] ECR I-6787 ('Is Article 30 of the Treaty a provision intended to liberalize intra-Community trade or it is intended more generally to encourage the unhindered pursuit of commerce in individual Member States?'), as critically discussed in Maduro (n 28) 60: 'The first concept can be summed up with the idea that the aim of Article 30 is to prevent State protectionism. Such protectionism assumes subtle forms which require constant refinement of the criteria used to review national measures. The second concept leads to the transformation of Article 30 into a kind of "economic due process" clause. It is based on a conception of the Economic Constitution of the Community built on the free market, open competition, and a particular view of the kinds of regulation that are acceptable. According to this concept, judicial review of national rules under Article 30 should assess State intervention in the market.'

rights were engineered, in the period under consideration in this chapter, more around an anti-protectionist ethos than around an actual interference through the judicial review of national policy choice *qua* the unhindered pursuit of commerce.[58]

This allowed the ECJ to stay within the welfarist consensus, for its case law revolved around the objective of preventing protectionism, although without interfering with the state social regulations through reviewing them. The Court could in this way ensure that the other side of the equation of the welfarist settlement – the protection of social rights through state law – could not be affected adversely by the force of market integration. In other words, the Court constitutionalised the then dominant public policy goals of the welfarist settlement. It liberated free commerce from interstate protectionism whilst avoiding embracing a free-market ideology that would have meant entertaining an assessment of the quality and degree of interference of the Member States' interventionist choices.

Monographic studies on the four freedoms have shown this discrete approach of the Court, as exemplified by one key dimension of the Court's case law of the relevant period in the area of free movement of goods, insofar as it revolved around the issue of 'whether measures are necessary in order to satisfy mandatory requirements' rather than the balancing of costs and benefits implicated in the measures (the latter being understood as the specific assessment of, and review of, the state's degree of public intervention in the market under Article 30 (now Article 34 TFEU)). This indicates that prevention of protectionism rather than control of the degree of public intervention in the market is what ultimately mattered to the ECJ.[59] The policy objective underlying judicial action revolved around preventing protectionism through the play of the four freedoms, whilst not intruding into and reshaping national economic constitutional arrangements and their social embeddedness.

A second correlation between the welfarist settlement (the objective of preventing protectionism) and the jurisprudence of the CJEU can be found in the case law in the area of *competition*.

Here the case law has been more about integrating markets through abolishing territorial protectionism than entertaining more in-depth forms of control of

[58] See Maduro (n 28) 67–68 (one 'cannot deduce' from the free movement case law of the Court that 'it has a certain "free market" conception of the economic constitution of the EU which is to be protected as a constitutional right and which the Court considers legitimate to impose on public authorities'; that 'the market conception advanced by the Court in the free movement of goods cases is not a neo-liberal one', 'nor is it presented as a fundamental economic right to be upheld by the Court against *public* intervention'; and that 'limits are imposed on State intervention and such case law is more understandable as the product of a "legislateur de substitution" which does not intend to impose a constitutional conception of the market and of economic organisation, but which aims to transfer economic decisions affecting the internal market from State level to Community level, in the pursuit of the judicial harmonisation of State rules the diversity of which is capable of restricting free trade and the optional gains offered by the common market'.

[59] ibid.

national policies through advanced forms of efficiency-based control in at least three senses.[60]

First, as part of the ECJ's strategy of integrating markets by employing the Treaty-based competition law rules, *Consten and Grundig* is an early yet representative case of a Court that has ever since been fully committed to integrate markets through prohibiting any absolute *territorial protectionist partitioning* (ex Article 85 EC Treaty);[61] later on, following a similar integrationist approach aimed at abolishing protectionist partitioning, in *Continental Can* the Court 'continued to expand the scope and enhance the intensity of competition law, relying on the integration imperative for both interpretive guidance and political support' by holding that Article 86 could be applied to the realm of acquisitions.[62] In the words of former judge Ulrich Everling:

> In evaluating the case law of the Court it is necessary to recognise that the competition rules of the Community are placed *in the service of the central objective of the Community*, namely the *opening of the markets* of the Member States. (Emphasis added)[63]

[60] For this argument, see G Monti, *EC Competition Law* (Cambridge, Cambridge University Press, 2007) 51, who summarises the first decades of integration in this way: 'For a long time in the history of Community competition law, the core values of market integration and economic freedom had a higher status than economic efficiency – decisions like *Consten and Grundig* show market integration taking priority over economic efficiency, and exemptions as recent as those in *TPS* and *T-Mobile/O2* show economic freedom to be dominant over economic efficiency.' In *Consten and Grundig*, 'absolute territorial protection was … condemned' (at 51), in line with the fact that '[s]ince the birth of the Community, competition law has been used as a mechanism for integrating the EC market, although the prime drivers for integration were other Treaty provisions, specifically those abolishing protectionist measures and allowing for the free movement of workers, goods, services and capital' (at 39). See also Snyder (n 44).

[61] See Case 56/64 *Consten and Grundig* [1966] ECR 299: According to D Gerber, *Law and Competition in Twentieth Century Europe: Protecting Prometheus* (Oxford, Clarendon Press, 1998) 355, in this case 'the Court signalled the centrality of market integration values and condemned … for market separation' … 'a variety of agreements that manufacturers and distributors were using to separate and protect national markets noting how less attention was given to horizontal agreements from the Commission (and therefore from the Court) because horizontal agreements were 'less obviously and directly related to the paramount goal of integration'. Note in general the following statements by Gerber (at 352–53 et seq): 'The Court … developed competition law as a central tool … to promote integration, structuring the competition law system to achieve that goal' and '[r]eflecting the centrality of the goal of integration, the Court made teleology the cornerstone of its interpretive strategy. As in its constitutional case law, the Court interpreted the treaty's competition law provisions according to its own conception of what was necessary to achieve the integrationist goals of the treaty. It conveyed a clear message that this goal-energized methodology was not merely to be one of a number of principles to be used in interpreting the treaty. It was to be the dominant interpretive method. The Court's teleological discourse carried centralist values. The Court saw a strong Commission as necessary for achieving integration, and it moulded competition law doctrine so as to increase the power of the Commission in relation to national authorities', and referring to the Court's case law on the expansive conception of 'effect on trade' ex Article 85(1) as a way to enhance the integrationist goals. See also Monti (n 60).

[62] Case 6/72 *Europmballage Corporation v Commission* [1973] ECR 215 (*Continental Can*): *see* Gerber (n 61) 360–61.

[63] U Everling, 'Zur Wettbewerbskonzeption in der neuren Rechtsprechung des Gerichtshofs der Europaischen Gemeinschaften' (1990) *Wirtschaft und Wettbewerb* 995, 1000.

Second, mirroring the case law on free movement – avoiding intruding into, and reshaping, national economic constitutional arrangements through 'balancing the costs and benefits of the measures' impeding free movement – the Court has equally shown respect for domestic sovereignty (concerning social welfare policy) in its competition case law, considering its cautious approach in applying the then Articles 85 and 86 EC Treaty for censuring state measures (state aid), with a view to avoiding encroachment on key domestic policy arenas vital to the functioning of welfare state systems.[64]

Third, it has been acknowledged that competition law played a secondary role in the relevant period, in that 'competition law has been used as a mechanism for integrating the EC market, although the prime drivers for integration were other Treaty provisions, specifically those abolishing protectionist measures and allowing for the free movement of workers, goods, services and capital';[65] in other words, the anti-protectionist approach of the Court in the area of the four freedoms remained the overarching benchmark for the overall case law on market integration. This in turn translated into a remarkable judicial input towards propagating the movement of the factors of production (workers, goods, services and capital) and undistorted competition in as-integrated-as-possible markets throughout Europe, in correlation with the public policy objectives of accommodating export-led growth and productivity.

The welfarist consensus-based organisation of the CAP was equally met with a supportive case law of the Court; this was a third correlation between the welfarist settlement (under the aspect of the public policy objective of protecting farmers) and the jurisprudence of the CJEU.

The Court adopted a permissive stance vis-a-vis the Community-controlled prices as discretionarily arranged by the Community legislature and aimed at protecting farmers.[66] Therefore, in the midst of a large jurisprudence aimed at preventing protectionism in both trade and competition, as above noted, was another strand of jurisprudence that validated the European wide CAP system of protected prices of agricultural products. Thus, in *Germany v Council*,[67] the Court famously held that 'in matters concerning the common agricultural policy the Community legislature has a broad discretion'.

As a matter of fact, only exceptionally, in cases of patent discrimination, did the Court intervene to alter the distributive features of the CAP regulatory regime – and, specifically, the levels of prices of milk and milk-related products as chosen by the Community legislature – a representative case being *Bela-Mühle*.[68] In another representative case decided in the context of the litigation on the (then) Community's regime for imported bananas,[69] the Court summarised its previous

[64] See Maduro (n 28) 75 (the ECJ having constantly held that arts 85 and 86 EC Treaty cannot be applied to Member States' measures); Giubboni (n 37) 202.

[65] See Monti (n 60).

[66] See Snyder (n 44) (on the CAP as market structural policy).

[67] Case C-280/93 *Germany v Council* [1994] ECR I-4973, para 89.

[68] Case 114-76 *Bela-Mühle* [1977] ECR 1222 at 1227 and at para 6. See Snyder (n 9) 22.

[69] *Bela-Mühle* (n 68).

established case law by holding that 'in matters concerning the common agricultural policy the Community legislature has a broad discretion … the lawfulness of a measure adopted in that sphere can be affected only if the measure is manifestly inappropriate having regard to the objective [pursued]' and, ultimately, 'submitting the principle of proportionality to the discretion of the institutions' – which, as it has been powerfully argued, means that 'the Court, like the Advocate General, grants them a carte blanche and reduces judicial control to a minimum'.[70]

Here the Court notably managed to reinterpret key components of the disciplinary constitutional vocabulary, such as the principle of proportionality (that is, limiting the latter to cases of 'manifest inappropriateness'), with a view to defending the 'rationality' of the CAP. A truly carte blanche stance was taken, leaving it to the Community institutions full discretion in arranging the CAP on the basis of purely political calculations (that is, the typical discretionary, dirigiste welfarist policy), and even when the perceived disregard of certain fundamental rights, such as the right to property, has been at stake.[71] The Court equally held in the 1980 *Maizena* judgment that Community law was characterised by 'the precedence of the agricultural policy over the Treaty's aims regarding competition'.[72] In 1985, in *Association de defense des brûleurs des huiles usagées*, the Court declared that a range of provisions that, in the view of the claimants, illegitimately obstructed the pursuit of free movement of goods and of free and fair competition rights – that is, 'exclusive zones being assigned to waste-oil collectors, the prior approval of undertakings responsible for disposal, and the possibility of indemnities being granted to undertakings which collect and dispose of waste oils'[73] – were justified under EC law. This illustrates the Court's neat choice to prioritise the market structural policies shaping agriculture (the CAP) over claims for introducing greater levels of competition and of free movement rights in the area of agriculture.

In the area of *social policy (labour)* lies a fourth correlation between the welfarist settlement (under the aspect of the protection of workers) and the jurisprudence of the CJEU.

The Court conjured up only an interpretative obligation of the whole of national law in the light of the relevant EU Directive – requesting national courts to interpret national law, whenever reputed to be 'possible, in the light of the relevant unimplemented (or incorrectly implemented) labour policy directive' ('indirect effect') – rather than outright direct effect,[74] which has effectively been

[70] U Everling, 'Will Europe Slip on Bananas?' (1996) 33 *CML Rev* 401, 418–19.

[71] ibid 419 (noting that this is 'particularly dangerous' if the Court is to take rights seriously; reference to fundamental rights here being to the right to property and the right to protection from bankruptcy as relevant in the context of the banana litigation saga).

[72] See Snyder (n 44) 174; the relevant decision is Case 139/79 *Maizena GmbH v Council of the European Communities* [1980] ECR 3393.

[73] See Snyder (n 44) 174–75: the relevant decision is Case 240/83 *Procureur de la Republique v Association de defense des brûleurs des huiles usagées* [1985] ECR 531.

[74] See Case 14/83 *Von Colson v Land Nordrhein-Westfalen* [1984] ECR 1891 (at paras 26 and 28), reiterated in Case 80/86 *Kolpinghuis Nijmegen BV* [1987] ECR 3969 and in subsequent cases. For details of this argument, see Niglia (n 29).

of service to the political will of the vast majority of states aimed at defending the autonomy of the variety of the states' social policy regimes. The representative case here is *Von Colson*.[75]

In disputes on Community social policy legislation and yet not involving directives and therefore the application of the doctrine of 'indirect effect', in a representative case of the jurisprudence of the time (*Palacios de la Villa*), the Court could held that 'it is … for the competent authorities of the Member States to find the right balance between the different interests involved' on the basis of 'political, economic, social … and/or budgetary considerations and having regard to the actual situation in the labour market in a particular Member State' – for example, in relation to choices regarding the prolonging of people's working life or, conversely, the provision of early retirement.[76]

IV. The New Story, the New Reading: Constitutionalisation Reconceived

On the basis of the above account, the received body of ideas about the constitutional story lends itself to be reformulated; I surmise that one should review the conventional understanding of the 'constitutionalisation' process in the relevant period upon which this chapter focuses.

The constitutional story has certainly been about *formal* (the discourse about individuals and rights) and *structural* (the ritual of judicial cooperation) material. Yet, it has also been about *substantive* choices, in that the judges have been acting in concert with the welfarist settlement. The substantive elements must be taken into account rather than disregarded, as conventionalism does. And the three elements, albeit distinguishable for analytical reasons, must be treated as interrelated aspects of the same story, in the sense that one should leave behind the conventional understanding of 'constitutionalisation' understood as both *legalistic* and *comprehensive*, namely:

> [T]he process by which the EC Treaties evolved from a set of legal arrangements binding upon sovereign states, into a vertically integrated legal regime conferring judicially enforceable rights and obligations on all legal persons and entities, public and private, within [the sphere of application of EC law].[77]

[75] See Giubboni (n 37). Notably, the ECJ has applied indirect effect to cover the enforcement of Community directives in the area of 'private consumer law': *cf* Case C-91/92 *Faccini Dori* [1994] ECR I-3325; Case C-106/89 *Marleasing* [1990] ECR I-4135.

[76] See Case C-411/05 *F Palacios de la Villa* [2007] ECR I-08531, paras 69–71. The Court has confirmed that the Member States enjoy 'broad discretion in matters of social policy' in the remarkable Case C-388/07 *The Incorporated Trustees of the National Council on Ageing v Secretary of State* [2009] ECR I-01569, para 65 (the decision as to whether retirement at 65 breaches age discrimination legislation being left to the Member States).

[77] See Stone (n 5).

As a matter of fact, constitutionalisation has not been a procedural development dictated by the requirements of legal necessity, that is, about 'conferring judicially enforceable rights and obligations on *all* legal persons and entities, public and private' (legalism). And neither has it been about establishing a comprehensive regime of EU law-based rights applicable 'within the sphere of application of EC law', that is, to *all* of the regulatory arenas falling within the remit of Union law (comprehensive legalism). Instead, 'conferring rights' has been an operation driven by substantively orientated concerns.

In turn, within the 'sphere of application of EC law', the law has been constructed selectively: 'conferring' (or not) Community-based 'rights' relative to the requirements of the relevant regulatory arena.

As constitutionalisation has been defined by choices regarding the preferred substantive policies designed in the context of the welfarist consensus of the time, constitutional discipline has accordingly been far from a monolith, in that it has been modulated and adapted depending on the underlying policy choices in the lines of decisions above noted.[78] Thus, asserting (or not) the pre-eminence of EC (EU) law – that is, striking down national legislation through decisions such as *Consten and Grundig*, or, alternatively, validating national legislation such as in *Palacios de la Villa* – was correlated with overarching calculations of political convenience made elsewhere and yet internalised in the courtrooms through a careful principled handling of legal material.[79] Equally, such correlation took place through, respectively (to recall the case law above considered), a range of constitutional 'incoherences' that fly in the face, and show the weakness, of the 'ironclad logic of EU law coherence'.[80] This is illustrated, first, by the 'light touch' interpretation of proportionality so as to validate the wide discretion on the part of the Community legislator in matters of the CAP, as opposed to the more rigorous interpretation of proportionality in other arenas such as free movement. A second illustration is the protection of fundamental rights under the general case law of the CJEU, yet de-activated in the context of the CAP-related litigation (in relation to the right to property). Third, workers' rights based on unimplemented directives were recognised, if claimed vertically, but denied EU based rights' protection, if claimed horizontally, through the indirect effect line of cases. This is a line of jurisprudence that is typically denounced as an unacceptable 'incoherence' of the case law of the CJEU, but one that must be read as effectively allowing the paramount substantive concern of sheltering social policy from market integration.[81]

[78] See above n 29 (on constitutional discipline as consisting of adaptations and changes); see also Niglia (n 1) above, and Niglia (n 55) (on constitutional structural transformations through integration over the course of the past few decades).

[79] Esser (n 5).

[80] See Haltern (n 18).

[81] From this vantage point, one should note that, cases such as Case 14/83, *Von Colson v Land Nordrhein-Westfalen* [1984] ECR 1891 and Case C-91/92, *Faccini Dori* [1994] ECR I-3325 have been criticised in the scholarship for not being consistent or credible in relation to not having advanced the cause of protecting Community-based individual rights in the same way as direct effect cases do (see, eg, G de Burca, 'Giving Effect to European Community Directives' (1992) 55(2) *MLR* 215: interpreting

There was no automatism, considering that judges exercised margins of discretion obviously involved in their principled work, but their decisions were ultimately calibrated towards accommodating rather than ignoring or disrupting the social-welfarist consensus.

Overall, it has been the case less of an abstract and comprehensive constitutionalisation of rights in terms of its classical scholarly rendition,[82] and more of a concrete, pragmatic (and selective) constitutionalising of winners and losers depending on the actual stakes at play, in the sense that constitutionalised sets of rights were set in stone over the years less by technical judicial deliberation aimed at 'best' possible sets of 'persuasive readings' of texts (as per the conventional legal necessity account), and more by engagements in the courtrooms based on constitutional 'readings', which in turn incorporated wider value and policy considerations. The judges, as engaged voices among the many in the wider community of political and legal actors, contributed to the engineering of a contingent, multilevel and differentiated distribution of powers between the EU and the Member States across the aforementioned discrete regulatory domains – far from having constituted an allegedly unified and comprehensive constitutional system described, reductively, as one in which '[t]here simply is no nucleus of sovereignty that the Member States can invoke, as such, against the Community'.[83]

V. Conclusion: 'What is Constitutionalisation?' and Europe

On the basis of the above analysis, I am suggesting a shift to a radically new understanding of Europe's 'constitutionalisation', borrowing a definition of it as adopted elsewhere in constitutional systems, and specifically the argument of Loughlin whereby by 'constitutionalisation', one means:

> [T]he attempt to subject all governmental action within a designated field to the structures, processes, principles and values of a (written) constitution.[84]

the Marshall reasoning as a 'major limitation to the direct effectiveness of directives as they cannot be invoked against individuals'); yet, *Von Colson* and *Faccini Dori* should be regarded no less valuable decisions than *Van Gend* and *Costa v ENEL* in their contributing to the design of Europe's constitutional order, for they have been key to the handling of the social policy stakes in the EU constitutional context in much the same way as *Van Gend* and *Costa v ENEL* have been key to the handling of the free movement stakes (according to the distinct areas considered in this chapter): for further discussion, see Niglia (n 34).

[82] Section II above (references on 'the constitutional story as a *legal(istic)* phenomenon').

[83] K Lenaerts, 'Constitutionalism and the Many Faces of Federalism' (1990) 220 *American Journal of Comparative Law* 205, as cited in JHH Weiler, 'The Transformation of Europe' (1991) 100 *Yale Law Journal* 2405, 2407 (in relation to 'absorption' consisting of the erosion in the 1970s of the 'limited fields' as proclaimed in the jurisprudence of the CJEU in the 1960s).

[84] M Loughlin 'What is Constitutionalisation?' in P Dobner and M Loughlin (eds), *The Twilight of Constitutionalism?* (Oxford, Oxford University Press, 2010) 47, as discussed in D Dyzenhaus Constitutionalism in an Old Key: Legality and Constituent Power' (2012) 1 *Global Constitutionalism* 229.

Europe's constitutionalisation has been no different. Deep down, it has been about 'subjecting' 'governmental action' not just to 'structures and processes' but also (as related) to 'the principles and values of a … constitution' – that is, the web of norms and principles that constituted a constitutional order made out of a heterogeneity of discrete regulatory arenas. Only by abandoning the safe harbours of legalism can one go towards providing new answers, such as those that derive from this chapter, to the fundamental questions concerning 'why governments will not have acted vigorously to change and even neutralise an uncomfortable and dangerous actor – by reducing the powers of the ECJ, trimming its jurisdiction and, if necessary, controlling its personnel'[85] and 'how could it be that the law hardened'.[86] Here as elsewhere, I believe that constitutional adjudication is part of history and not beyond it, interrogating us politically, morally and ethically, and demanding our own critical positioning, from *that* very predicament.

[85] See JHH Weiler, 'A Quiet Revolution: The European Court of Justice and its Interlocutors' (1994) 26(4) *Comparative Political Studies* 510, 525; and Alter (n 11) 32 et seq (addressing the question regarding 'how could it be that the states allowed this to happen'). The best exposition of this riddle remains Weiler, 'A Quiet Revolution', 525, for whom 'the belief in the apolitical and neutral nature of the judicial process is … the reality that counts'. However, I argue that the political branches of Member States' governments did not stop the CJEU because, underneath that 'belief' (which no doubt played a role in keeping the Court 'out of political contestation', as rightly argued by Weiler, albeit, in my view, not an exclusive role: see n 35 on *Vorverständniss*) the Court was no 'enemy' to the Member States, but an 'ally'.

[86] For these 'open questions' see Alter (n 8) 32 et seq.

9

The EU–China Comprehensive Agreement on Investment

A New Beginning?

HENRY GAO

I. Introduction

As one of the pioneers in the study of European trade and investment law and the bilateral economic relationship between the EU and China, Professor Francis Snyder has long recognised the potential for deeper economic integration between the two.[1] His vision for the bilateral economic cooperation bore fruit in the EU–China Comprehensive Agreement on Investment (CAI), which was concluded in principle by the EU and China on 30 December 2020.[2] It was hailed as 'the most ambitious agreement that China has ever concluded with a third country' by the EU[3] and a 'high-level' agreement that matches 'international high-level economic and trade rules' by China.[4] Upon closer examination, however, such rhetoric does

[1] See, eg, F Snyder, *The EU, the WTO and China: Legal Pluralism and International Trade Regulation* (Oxford, Hart Publishing, 2010); F Snyder, *The European Union and China, 1949–2008: Basic Documents and Commentary* (Oxford, Hart Publishing, 2009).

[2] For the EU's announcement, see European Commission, 'EU and China Reach Agreement in Principle on Investment' (30 December 2020), https://ec.europa.eu/commission/presscorner/detail/en/ip_20_2541; for China's announcement, see '中欧领导人共同宣布如期完成中欧投资协定谈判-新华网' (30 December 2020), www.xinhuanet.com/world/2020-12/30/c_1126929012.htm. There has been a rich literature on the CAI since its conclusion. See, eg, PC Mavroidis and A Sapir, 'What is So Special about CAI?' (2022) 30(2) *Asia Pacific Law Review* 348, DOI: 10.1080/10192557.2022.2085414; Q Xu, 'Scoping the Impact of the Comprehensive Agreement on Investment: Liberalization, Protection, and Dispute Resolution in the Next Era of EU–China Relations' (2022) 30(1) *Asia Pacific Law Review* 93, DOI: 10.1080/10192557.2022.2045708; D Pathirana and P Kerneis, 'Market Access for Investment and Services under the EU–China Comprehensive Agreement on Investment: An Appraisal' (2023) 31(1) *Asia Pacific Law Review* 123, DOI: 10.1080/10192557.2022.2117487; and J Chaisse and M Burnay, 'Introduction – CAI's Contribution to International Investment Law: European, Chinese, and Global Perspectives' (2022) 23 *Journal of World Investment & Trade* 497.

[3] European Commission, 'Key Elements of the EU–China Comprehensive Agreement' (30 December 2020), https://ec.europa.eu/commission/presscorner/detail/en/ip_20_2542.

[4] '商务部条法司负责人就如期完成中欧投资协定谈判答记者问', www.mofcom.gov.cn/article/news/202012/20201203027541.shtml.

not appear to be warranted, as the Agreement failed to add much in terms of substance. What, then, explains the rationale for the Agreement? This chapter argues that the key to understanding the Agreement lies not in the narrow commercial interests, but more in the broad strategic and geopolitical considerations of both the EU and China. It concludes with a review of the development of the twin concepts of 'strategic opportunity' in China and 'strategic autonomy' in the EU, as well as what the confluence of these considerations would mean for the future of the CAI.

II. A Critical Summary of the CAI

The CAI includes a total of six sections, which can be further divided into two groups.

The first are the substantive provisions, which includes Section I on objectives and general definitions, Section II on investment liberalisation, Section III on regulatory framework, and Section IV on investment and sustainable development.

The second are the procedural and institutional provisions, which include Section V on dispute settlement and Section VI on institutional and final provisions. These sections are analysed in detail below.

A. Objectives and General Definitions

According to Article 1, the main objective of the Agreement is to 'lay down the necessary arrangements for the liberalisation of investment'. This means that the Agreement is different from the normal Bilateral Investment Treaties (BITs), which have traditionally focused on investment protection, with investment liberalisation included only as a more recent development after free trade agreements such as the North American Free Trade Agreement (NAFTA) started to incorporate investment in its scope. Having investment liberalisation as the main objective also explains the CAI's lack of common BIT provisions on substantive rights for investors, such as expropriation and compensation, fair and equitable treatment, and a minimum standard of treatment. Instead of trying to restrict the regulatory power of the government to protect the rights of investors, the second paragraph of Article 1 explicitly reaffirms that the parties have 'right to regulate within their territories to achieve legitimate policy objectives, such as the protection of public health, social services, public education, safety, the environment, including the fight against climate change, public morals, social security or consumer protection, privacy and data protection or the promotion and protection of cultural diversity'.

For the EU, such explicit affirmation of the regulatory power reflects, on the one hand, the ever-expansive regulatory regime in the EU and, on the other hand, the need to assuage the fears by the EU Member States on the possible encroachment of their domestic regulatory framework by the CAI. From the perspective of China, such carefully crafted clause is also necessary, especially in view of the hard lessons China has learned in the twin World Trade Organization (WTO) cases of *China – Raw Materials* and *China – Rare Earth*, where due to of the lack of explicit reference to the general exception clause of the General Agreement on Tariffs and Trade (GATT), China was denied the right to justify its export restrictions under Article XX. Thus, it is better to spell out these exceptions upfront, even though the preamble does reaffirm the Parties' 'respective rights and obligations under the WTO Agreement'. As I mentioned in another article, such an approach is also reflected in China's negotiating proposal in other forums, such as the e-commerce Joint State Initiative negotiation in the WTO.[5]

The focus on investment liberalisation also means that the agreement will not qualify as a free trade agreement in goods or services. Under the existing WTO framework, these two types of free trade agreement can potentially be justified under the GATT and the General Agreement on Trade in Services (GATS), respectively, so long as they satisfy the necessary requirements therein, ie, Article XXIV GATT or Article V GATS. While the WTO also has another Agreement on Trade-Related Investment Measures (TRIMS), TRIMS does not provide exceptions for an agreement that focuses solely on investment liberalisation. This might raise some interesting legal issues, as I will discuss below in section IV.

The other part of Section I CAI focuses on 'general definitions', or definitions of general terms which are used frequently in the agreement. Such terms include, for example, 'enterprise', 'measure', 'operations', 'investor of a Party', 'non-Party' and 'natural person'. Many of these definitions closely follow those of the WTO Agreements or other free trade agreements and BITs. For example, the definitions on 'measures by Members' and 'services' follow the definitions under Article I.3 GATS verbatim, while the only difference between the CAI definition on 'activities performed in the exercise of governmental authority' and the GATS definition on 'a service supplied in the exercise of governmental authority' is the replacement of 'service' with 'activities'.

At the same time, there are also some definitions which are not really general, but specific to a sector or type of activity. The former includes definitions on 'aircraft repair and maintenance services', 'selling and marketing of air transport services', 'computer reservation system (CRS) services' and 'ground handling services', which are specific to the sector of air transport services and auxiliary air services. The latter is the definition on 'commercial considerations', which only applies to 'covered entities' (which is how the CAI defines state-owned enterprises (SOEs), as explained below) under Article 3bis of Section II CAI.

[5] H Gao, 'Across the Great Wall: E-commerce Joint Statement Initiative Negotiation and China' in S-Y Peng, C-F Lin and T Streinz (eds), *Artificial Intelligence and International Economic Law* (Cambridge, Cambridge University Press, 2021).

B. Investment Liberalisation

Section II CAI is the heart of the Agreement and sets out in detail the investment liberalisation commitments. It starts by noting that it applies to 'measures or treatment adopted or maintained by a Party affecting the establishment of an enterprise or the operation of a covered enterprise by an investor of the other Party in its territory', which essentially means measures affecting investment. Following the tradition of the GATS, it also excludes governmental activities, government procurement, and air transport services and auxiliary air services other than aircraft repair and maintenance services, the selling and marketing of air transport services, CRS services and ground handling services. Audio-visual services are also excluded, probably due to the reservations of certain EU Member States such as France.

Most of the other provisions in Section II can be divided into two broad categories.

First are the market access commitments, which are scheduled pursuant to Article 2. The list of types of market access restrictions under Article 2 closely follows that of Article XVI GATS, except that it does not include the last type of restriction, ie, 'limitations on the participation of foreign capital in terms of maximum percentage limit on foreign shareholding or the total value of individual or aggregate foreign investment'. Instead, such limitations are scheduled under the national treatment restrictions as mentioned below, as they also constitute national treatment discrimination by their very nature. The specific limitations are scheduled in Annex III of the Agreement, ie, the schedule of specific commitments and limitations on market access. It also follows the example of services schedule under the GATS in two ways: first, in the adoption of a positive listing approach, which means that only services sectors explicitly listed in the schedule are subject to liberalisation commitments; and, second, in the adoption of the GATS scheduling format, which includes a horizontal section of limitations or commitments which apply to all sectors, as well as sector-specific commitments which are organised according to sectors and sub-sectors with detailed commitments or restrictions. The only difference is that, unlike the GATS schedules, which include three columns of commitments on market access, national treatment and additional commitments, respectively, the CAI schedules only include the column on market access after the column of sectors and sub-sectors.

Second are the commitments on domestic regulation. More specifically, these include commitments relating to Article 4 (National Treatment), Article 5 (Most Favoured Nation Treatment), Article 3 (Performance Requirements) and Article 6 (Senior Management and Boards of Directors). With respect to these obligations, the Agreement adopts the negative listing approach instead of the positive listening approach on market access commitments. This means that unless a restriction has been scheduled, these obligations are presumed to apply. More specifically, two types of restrictions can be scheduled according to Article 7: existing non-conforming measures scheduled in Annex I, which the parties can continue to maintain but may not make it more restrictive; and reservations scheduled in Annex II, which allow the parties to retain the flexibility to adopt new restrictions in the future.

It is not surprising to see these provisions and commitments on market access and domestic regulations in the Agreement, as they have been quite common in the investment chapters of free trade agreements. But in addition to these, the Agreement has also broken new ground by including two new articles on SOEs and regulatory principles.[6]

Until very recently, provisions on SOEs have been very rare in trade[7] and investment agreements.[8] This only changed in the last decade with the US Model BIT in 2012 and the negotiations on the Trans-Pacific Partnership (TPP), the Transatlantic Trade and Investment Partnership (TTIP), the United States-Mexico-Canada Agreement (USMCA) and the China–US BIT. In addition to this global trend, the inclusion of SOE regulation in the CAI also reflects the EU's long-standing concerns over the market-distorting effects of the anti-competitive behaviours of SOEs at all levels. At the EU level, the Commission issued a Staff Working Document 'On significant distortions in the economy of the People's Republic of China for the purposes of trade defence investigations' in December 2017,[9] which devoted 25 pages to the problem of Chinese SOEs. At the international level, the EU also issued a trilateral statement with the US and Japan on the sidelines of the 11th WTO Ministerial Conference held in Buenos Aries in the same month to address the 'critical concern' of 'unfair competitive conditions caused by … state owned enterprises'.[10] SOE also featured prominently in the EU's new trade strategy document unveiled in February 2021, which calls for new rules on 'competitive neutrality' in view of market distortions created by SOEs[11] and is likely to lead to a proposal for new plurilateral negotiations on the issue in the WTO.[12]

[6] See, eg, X Su, 'Liberalising the Chinese Market: State-Owned Enterprise Disciplines in CAI' (2022) 23 *Journal of World Investment & Trade* 545.

[7] Q Kong, 'Emerging Rules in International Investment Instruments and China's Reform of State-Owned Enterprises' (2017) 3(1) *Chinese Journal of Global Governance* 57.

[8] L Wang and N Gallagher, 'Introduction to the Special Focus Issue on State-Owned Enterprises' (2016) 31(1) *ICSID Review* 1.

[9] 'On Significant Distortions in the Economy of the People's Republic of China for the Purposes of Trade Defence Investigations' (2017) European Commission Staff Working Document SWD(2017) 483 final/2, https://trade.ec.europa.eu/doclib/docs/2017/december/tradoc_156474.pdf.

[10] United States Trade Representative, 'Joint Statement by the United States, European Union and Japan at MC11', http://ustr.gov/about-us/policy-offices/press-office/press-releases/2017/december/joint-statement-united-states.

[11] European Commission, 'Reforming the WTO: Towards a Sustainable and Effective Multilateral Trading System' (April 2021), https://trade.ec.europa.eu/doclib/docs/2021/april/tradoc_159544.1329_EN_02.pdf.

[12] See 'Weyand Proposes WTO Plurilateral on "Competitive Neutrality" Led by EU, U.S.' (*World Trade Online*, 10 March 2021), https://insidetrade.com/daily-news/weyand-proposes-wto-plurilateral-%E2%80%98competitive-neutrality%E2%80%99-led-eu-us.

Interestingly, the term 'state-owned enterprises' or 'SOEs' never formally appears in the CAI. Instead, it is referred to in the Agreement as 'covered entity' under Article 3bis, a seemingly innocuous expression probably carefully chosen to avoid the controversies surrounding SOEs. Moreover, by using 'covered entity', the CAI is also able to expand the coverage from just those owned by the government (either through majority share or majority voting rights), to those where the government has the power to control either the board or the decisions of the enterprises or 'the power to legally direct the actions or otherwise exercise an equivalent level of control in accordance with its laws and regulations'. This is consistent with the WTO jurisprudence on 'public body' in the context of subsidy regulation, where the Appellate Body emphasised the need to 'demonstrate that the government exercises meaningful control over the conduct of [an] entity' and promoted a functional approach on whether the enterprise 'possesses, exercises or is vested with governmental authority'.[13] The last two parts of the definition on 'covered entities' also cover cases of monopoly and duopoly, where ownership by the state is not required. With such a broad definition, the CAI covers most situations where the competitive environment is undermined due to government ownership or control, or monopolistic power of the enterprise.

Article 3bis then listed two obligations for covered entities. The first is the obligation to act in accordance with commercial considerations and provide non-discriminatory treatment in their purchases or sales of goods or services. The EU regards this as a significant achievement and calls the CAI 'the first agreement to deliver on obligations for the behaviour of state-owned enterprises'. But, as discussed below, this is nothing new and simply repeats what was already in China's WTO accession package. The other is the transparency obligation, which grants the right to a party to request the other party to 'supply information about the operations of [a covered] entity related to the carrying out of the provisions of [the Article on SOEs]'. This includes information on ownership and the voting structure, special shares and voting rights, organisational and management structures, annual revenue or total assets, exemptions, immunities and equivalent measures, and government authorities responsible for exercising the ownership function and regulatory power. The list of information seems quite comprehensive and could provide a useful means to nudge China to police the behaviours of SOEs according to CAI requirements. Making the information request a government-to-government exercise also removes the fear of retaliation which might prevent EU firms from venting their complaints to China. It would be interesting to observe whether this provision would work in practice.

The article on regulatory principles requires regulatory authorities to be impartial, non-discriminatory and independent in exercising the regulatory function. Again, here the concern seems to be the uneven administration of regulatory

[13] Appellate Body Report, *United States–Definitive Anti-dumping and Countervailing Duties on Certain Products from China* (11 March 2011) WT/DS379/AB/R 317–18.

measures, given that many SOEs in China enjoy cosy relationships with their regulators built on both historical ties and sharing a common pool of personnel, especially at the most senior level. This is most obvious in the telecommunications sector, where Shang Bing, the former CEO of China Unicom, was promoted to be Vice Minister of the Ministry of Industry and Information Technology, before being appointed as the Board Chairman of China Mobile.[14] Indeed, this also explains the similarity between this article and Section 5 of the WTO Reference Paper on Telecommunications, which lays down the regulatory principles for the telecommunications sector.

C. The Regulatory Framework

The CAI section on the regulatory framework spells out detailed obligations on the regulatory principles, which are further divided into three sub-sections covering domestic regulation, transparency and the financial services sector, respectively. They largely build on corresponding provisions in the GATS, with the sub-section on domestic regulation focusing mainly on licencing and qualification requirements and procedures, as in Article VI GATS; the sub-section on transparency combining the obligations on publication, contact point and provision of information under Article III GATS, and those on administrative proceedings, review and appeal under Article VI GATS; and the sub-section on financial services copying the Annex on Financial Services.

Of course, there are also some innovations in drafting, with the Article on transparency of subsidies being the most interesting. Building on the rules in the WTO Agreement on Subsidies and Countervailing Measures, this Article breaks new ground by expanding the scope of coverage from trade in goods to services, a feat yet to be achieved in the WTO despite the built-in mandate to negotiate rules on services subsidies in Article XV GATS. In addition, the Article also includes a provision on transparency of subsidies, which applies to the following sectors: business services, communication services, construction and related engineering services, distribution services, environmental services, financial services, health-related services (privately funded), tourism and travel-related services, and transport services. According to the Article, information on services in these sectors shall be published no later than two years after the CAI enters into force. The Article further provides opportunities for government-to-government consultations on subsidies with negative effects on its investment interests, but falls short of subjecting such disputes to the full-blown state-to-state dispute settlement system under the CAI.

[14] '工信部副部长尚冰任中国移动董事长奚国华不再担任(图|简历)_中国 …', http://district.ce.cn/newarea/sddy/201508/24/t20150824_6303817.shtml.

D. Investment and Sustainable Development

Provisions on sustainable development has been a key feature in the EU's recent trade agreements, which often cover issues on environment protection, human rights, labour rights and corporate social responsibility.[15] However, such clauses have been missing from the latest investment protection agreements concluded by the EU, probably because the EU also signed free trade agreements with these countries and thus there was no need to put these issues in the investment protection agreements.[16] The CAI, however, is different, as it would be very difficult, at least in the short to medium term, for the EU to conclude a free trade agreement with China due to political reasons. Thus, the CAI breaks with the tradition of the investment protection agreements and includes a section on sustainable development[17] that is divided into three sub-sections.

The first sub-section sets out the context and objectives of the section, with provisions on the overarching principles of on sustainable development as found in the relevant international documents, corporate social responsibility, public participation and sustainability impact review.

The next two sub-sections cover environment and labour rights, respectively, and follow a similar pattern. They both start by recognising the parties' right to regulate, before listing more detailed obligations on the levels of protection: not too lax to attract investment, but at the same time not too harsh so as to 'constitute a disguised restriction of investment or an unjustified discrimination between investors and investments of the Parties'. In particular, the Agreement specifies that the parties shall not, 'through a sustained or recurring course of action or inaction, fail to effectively enforce its [environmental/labour] laws, as an encouragement for investment'. The two sub-sections also call for dialogue and cooperation on investment-related environmental and labour issues between the parties, and require each party to effectively implement the multilateral environmental and labour agreements it has ratified. In addition to the passive obligations noted above, the parties also agree to promote investments favouring green growth and decent work.

In addition to environmental protection and labour rights in general, the Agreement also singled out one key issue in each area. The key issue for environment is climate change, to which both the EU and China have been politically committed. The key issue for labour is forced labour, which includes the obligations in International Labour Organization (ILO) Conventions No 29 and 105,

[15] European Commission, 'Sustainable Development – Trade – European Commission', https://ec.europa.eu/trade/policy/policy-making/sustainable-development.

[16] See the EU's recent investment protection agreements with Singapore and Vietnam.

[17] See, eg, DN Dagbanja, 'The CAI and Sustainable Development' (2022) 23(4) *Journal of World Investment & Trade* 572, DOI: https://doi.org/10.1163/22119000-12340261; X Qian, 'Investment for Green Growth: An Analysis of the CAI Environmental Provisions' (2022) 23(4) *Journal of World Investment & Trade* 628, DOI: https://doi.org/10.1163/22119000-12340263.

two instruments China explicitly committed to make 'continued and sustained efforts on its own initiative to pursue ratification'. This is significant, especially in view of the recent controversy on China's alleged forced labour practices in Xinjiang.

Probably due to the sensitivity of the issue to China, the section on sustainable development is not subject to the normal dispute settlement system of the CAI; instead, it has its own dispute settlement system. The process starts with bilateral consultations between the parties and may proceed to a Panel of Experts if the dispute is not satisfactory resolved within four months. The Panel process largely models after that of the WTO, except without the official adoption and implementation processes. Instead, the Panel report is only supposed to provide a basis for the parties to work out ways to address the dispute. One striking feature of the dispute settlement process in Section IV is the provisions on the transparency of proceedings. For example, the Agreement requires the parties to make the Panel hearing open to the public, and make publicly available the request for consultation and Panel establishment, the submissions and statements of the parties, the Panel report, and the final agreed solution between the parties. In addition, an Article specifically provides for the right for natural and legal persons from a party to participate as amicus curiae in panel proceedings. Once implemented, this would provide unprecedented access for non-governmental organisations (NGOs) on environmental and labour issues from the EU to participate in dispute settlement proceedings involving China. Coupled with the wide range of public-participation rights, the transparency of such proceedings are likely to create strong pressure on China, which can sometimes be even more powerful than binding dispute settlement procedures.

E. Dispute Settlement

The section on dispute settlement[18] adds 'teeth' to the obligations contained in the CAI by providing 'an effective and efficient mechanism' for resolving disputes, albeit with two caveats: first, as the Agreement has yet to include provisions on investor protection, the scope of the dispute settlement mechanism is limited to those within the current Agreement, ie, on investment liberalisation commitments and regulatory principles; and, second, the dispute settlement mechanism in the Agreement is only state to state, and does not include an investor state dispute settlement mechanism, which is typically found in BITs. Of course, this does not mean that the parties do not wish to include these issues; instead, according to

[18] See, eg, H Ascensio, 'The International Settlement of Disputes under the (Draft) CAI' (2022) 23(4) *Journal of World Investment & Trade* 651, DOI: https://doi.org/10.1163/22119000-12340264; J Chaisse and X Ji, 'Stress Test for EU's Investment Court System: How Will Investments Be Protected in the Comprehensive Agreement on Investment?' (2022) 49(1) *Legal Issues of Economic Integration* 101.

Article 3 of Section VI, the parties agree to continue their negotiations to include 'state of the art provisions' on both issues, which they strive to conclude within two years of the signing of the CAI.

The dispute settlement mechanism closely follows that of the WTO and includes confidential bilateral consultation, arbitration by a three-person panel, an interim report and a final report, the determination of a reasonable period of time for implementation, a compliance review, and retaliation in the form of suspension of concessions and other obligations. It also provides for the possibility of resolving the dispute through mediation and a mutually agreed solution, as well as suspension, resumption and termination of panel proceedings. There are also a few innovations compared to WTO rules. For example, the Article on applicable law and rules of interpretation explicitly states that customary rules on interpretation of public international law include those codified in the Vienna Convention of the Law of Treaties. Another example is the Article on transparency, which explicitly makes panel hearings open to the public and grants right to natural and legal persons to submit amicus briefs to the panel. Given the controversy that these issues have raised in the WTO dispute settlement system, such clarifications are quite welcome. The section also contains two Annexes; the Annex on rules of procedure for state-to-state dispute settlement is fully developed, while the Annex on the code of conduct for panellists and mediators is still under discussion at the time of writing.

F. Institutional and Final Provisions

This section is composed of two sub-sections. The first sub-section sets out the institutional framework, which includes an investment committee at the level of Vice President of the European Commission and the Vice Premier of China; a Working Group on Investment at the level of EU Director-General on Trade and Vice Minister of China's Ministry of Commerce (MOFCOM); and a Working Group on Sustainable Development at the senior official level. The second sub-section includes final provisions which address various miscellaneous issues, such as the amendment and termination of the Agreement, general exceptions and security exceptions, provisions on payments and transfers on current accounts and capital movements, and safeguarding and balancing of payment measures. One Article requires the parties to 'have a regular dialogue with non-state stakeholders in a balanced representation of economic, environmental and social interests',[19] which is designed to provide access to government by business firms, NGOs and civil society groups.

[19] Sub-section 2 of Article 1 of the EU–China Comprehensive Agreement on Investment (China–EU) (22 January 2021) (CAI).

Before the conclusion of the CAI, many EU Member States had already concluded many BITs with China, which often include clauses on investor protection and investment state dispute systems absent in the CAI. Thus, the CAI explicitly states that these agreements will remain in place and will 'not be superseded or terminated by this Agreement'.[20] Moreover, the same Article also states that the CAI shall 'be an integral part of the overall bilateral relations as governed by the Trade and Economic Cooperation Agreement or a future Framework Agreement', which implies that the EU and China are expecting the negotiation of a broader trade agreement in the future.[21] The last part of the Article states that 'nothing in this Agreement requires them to act in a manner inconsistent with their obligations under the WTO Agreement', which means that the parties need to comply with the WTO rules at the same time.[22] Of particular relevance here would be the Most Favoured Nation (MFN) principle. While free trade agreements can normally be justified pursuant to Article XXIV GATT or Article V GATS, the exception is not available here as the CAI agreement, with its limited scope, would not be able to satisfy the substantial trade coverage requirements under the two clauses. More specifically, it mainly covers trade in services, and chiefly in one mode of supply: Mode 3 on commercial presence, with some commitments on Mode 4 (movement of natural persons). This would make it hard to justify under the GATS, as Article V explicitly states that such agreements 'should not provide for the a priori exclusion of any mode of supply'.[23] In practice, this means that most if not all of the market access commitments under the Agreement must be granted to other WTO members.

III. An Assessment of the Market Access and Rules Commitments

To prove its point that the CAI is 'the most ambitious agreement that China has ever concluded with a third country', the EU kept emphasising in its summary on the key elements of the CAI that 'China has not made such far-reaching market access commitments with any other partner' (in the manufacturing sector) and 'China has not previously committed openness to foreign investment' (in research and development in biological resources). Yet, a closer examination reveals that such assertions are at best dubious, as many of the concessions are neither 'unprecedented'[24] nor 'not previously committed'. Instead, as the examples below will illustrate, many of these commitments are either already available as part of China's own autonomous liberalisation or have already been agreed by China in other agreements.

[20] ibid sub-section 2, Article 15.
[21] ibid.
[22] ibid.
[23] GATS, fn 1 to Article V.
[24] European Commission (n 2).

A. China's Autonomous Liberalisation

Under China's commitments in Annex I: Entry 6 – Manufacture of Transportation Equipment to the CAI, China agrees to lift two existing restrictions on foreign investments in the automobile manufacturing sector contained in the *Special Administrative Measures for Market Access of Foreign Investment (Negative List)* (2019 edition): limiting foreign investment to no more than 50 per cent shares; and restricting each foreign investor to no more than two joint ventures in passenger cars within the territory of China. According to the entry, both restrictions would be removed 'after 2022'.

However, both restrictions have already been scheduled for removal in the *Special Administrative Measures for Market Access of Foreign Investment (Negative List)* (2020 edition),[25] which was issued in June 2020, or six months before the CAI was concluded. Moreover, according to *(Negative List)* (2020 edition), both restrictions were supposed to be removed 'in 2022', which could take effect long before the CAI obligations kick in. As a matter of fact, such commitments were already noted two years earlier in the 2018 edition of the *Negative List*.[26]

The same entry in China's commitments in Annex I also notes that 'the measures listed in this entry does [*sic*] not apply to investments by foreign investors in the manufacture of new energy automobiles and special purpose automobiles'. Again, however, this is nothing new, as both sectors have already been liberalised in the 2018 edition of the *Negative List*.

Similarly, China's commitments in Annex I: Entry 12 – Telecommunication Services to the CAI allows EU investors to invest in internet data centre service (including content delivery network service), subject to an equity cap of 50 per cent. Again, however, the same commitment was already made by China in the *Hainan Free Trade Port Special Administrative Measures for Market Access of Foreign Investment for (Negative List)* (2020 edition), which was issued a day after the conclusion of the CAI negotiation.[27] While the CAI commitments are arguably broader than the commitments under the *Hainan Negative List*, as the latter does not allow such services to be provided to Chinese territories other than the Hainan free trade port, it would not be hard for firms wishing to avail themselves of such services to move their data centres to Hainan. Moreover, despite restrictions on paper, entrepreneurial firms like Amazon have been reportedly providing cloud services in China through creative legal arrangements since 2013.[28]

[25] 中华人民共和国国家发展和改革委员会，中华人民共和国商务部，'外商投资准入特别管理措施（负面清单）（2020年版）', www.gov.cn/gongbao/content/2020/content_5532623.htm.

[26] 中华人民共和国国家发展和改革委员会,中华人民共和国商务部,'发展改革委商务部令2018年第18号外商投资准入特别管理措施（负面清单）（2020年版）',www.mofcom.gov.cn/article/b/f/201806/20180602760432.shtml.

[27] '海南自由贸易港外商投资准入特别管理措施（负面清单）（2020年版…',www.gov.cn/zhengce/zhengceku/2021-01/01/content_5576049.htm.

[28] G Bensinger, 'Amazon Teams with Companies in China for Cloud Service' (*Wall Street Journal*, 18 December 2013), https://online.wsj.com/article/SB10001424052702304866904579266272134981780.html?st=fcjg25g1xedbxjv&reflink=desktopwebshare_permalink.

B. Pre-existing Commitments in Other Agreements

At the same time, many other commitments in the CAI were already committed in other agreements. For example, under Annex III: Schedule of specific commitments and limitations on market access, China commits to remove all restrictions on insurance and insurance-related services, including life insurance, non-life insurance, reinsurance and services auxiliary to insurance. However, such a commitment has already been made by China in its Phase One Agreement with the US, which states that China shall remove 'the foreign equity cap in the life, pension, and health insurance sectors and allow wholly US-owned insurance companies to participate in these sectors' as well as 'any business scope limitations, discriminatory regulatory processes and requirements, and overly burdensome licensing and operating requirements for all insurance sectors (including insurance intermediation)' by 1 April 2020, or nine months before the conclusion of the CAI.[29]

Moreover, in some parts, EU insurance companies actually got a worse deal compared to US firms. Under the CAI's Annex I: Entry 31 – Insurance, the EU agrees that China will be able to maintain the requirement that the aggregate shareholding percentage of domestic insurance companies in an insurance asset management company shall be no less than 75 per cent, and such restrictions will only be lifted by China 'within three years from the date of entry into force of this Agreement'. In contrast, under the Phase One Agreement, China explicitly affirmed that 'there are no restrictions on the ability of US-owned insurance companies established in China to wholly own insurance asset management companies in China'. As the Phase One Agreement was signed in January 2020 and the CAI is unlikely to come into effect before 2023 (see the discussion on the ratification process below), this means that EU firms lag behind their American counterparts by at least six years before they may establish wholly owned insurance asset management companies in China.

Another widely publicised concession is disciplines on the behaviour of Chinese SOEs, where the CAI requires SOEs to 'act in accordance with commercial considerations in their purchases or sales of goods or services' and accord to EU investors 'treatment no less favourable' than they accord to Chinese investors.[30] Again, this does not add much to China's commitment in its 20-year-old WTO Accession Working Party Report, which already requires it to 'ensure that all state-owned and state-invested enterprises would make purchases and sales based solely on commercial considerations, e.g., price, quality, marketability and availability, and that the enterprises of other WTO Members would have an adequate opportunity to compete for sales to and purchases from these enterprises on

[29] Office of the United States Trade Representative, 'Economic and Trade Agreement between the Government of the United States of America and the Government of the People's Republic of China' (2021) Article 4.6: Insurance Services, https://ustr.gov/countries-regions/china-mongolia-taiwan/peoples-republic-china/phase-one-trade-agreement/text.

[30] CAI, Article 3bis, Covered Entities.

non-discriminatory terms and conditions'.[31] Moreover, the scope of the covered activities is further reduced by a footnote in the CAI section, which explicitly notes that the obligations on non-discriminatory treatment and commercial considerations 'does not apply to situations of trade in goods and to supply of services other than through establishment of an enterprise and operation of a covered investment'.[32] In other words, these two obligations only apply to sale or purchase transactions between Chinese SOEs and EU firms investing in China, but not to EU firms with no commercial presence in China.

As to disciplines on SOEs, the only new thing seems to be an expansive definition adopted by the CAI, which also includes, in addition to firms where the government controls more than 50 per cent ownership or voting rights, those where the government has the power to appoint a majority of the board, control the decisions of the enterprise, legally direct the actions or otherwise exercise an equivalent level of control. However, even on this issue, one may well argue that, with the recent development of the jurisprudence on 'public body' by the Appellate Body in *US – Countervailing Measures (China) (Article 21.5 – China)*,[33] such an expansive definition might no longer be necessary.

IV. The Strategic Dimension

As we can see from the discussions in the preceding section, China's commitments on market access and regulatory issues are not as ambitious as the EU has claimed. Moreover, as most of China's concessions in the CAI schedules are made in the services sector, they would have to be made available to all other WTO members on an MFN basis, even if any concession is entirely new. This is because the Agreement, by covering mainly Mode 3 – commercial presence, cannot be justified as a services FTA under Article V GATS.

On the other hand, the EU's commitments are even more limited compared to China. This is confirmed by the news release by the Commission following the publication of the market access commitments under the CAI, which noted that: 'Any restrictions the EU or its Member States may have in place remain unaffected, as well as the policy space needed, for example, to enable the autonomous measures.'[34]

[31] China's WTO Accession Working Party Report, para 46.

[32] Footnote 8 to Article 3bis of Section II of the CAI.

[33] Appellate Body Report, *United States – Countervailing Duty Measures on Certain Products from China – Recourse to Article 21.5 of the DSU by China* (18 December 2014) WT/DS437/AB/RW.

[34] 'Commission Publishes Market Access Offers of the EU–China Investment Agreement' (*European Union External Action*, 12 March 2021), https://www.eeas.europa.eu/delegations/china/commission-publishes-market-access-offers-eu-china-investment-agreement_en?s=166.

So why then did the EU and China still choose to forge ahead with the CAI, despite the lack of major substantive benefits? In my view, the deal on the CAI must be understood in the broader context of geopolitical strategy, which permeates the whole life cycle of the CAI from its inception and negotiation to its conclusion and ratification.

A. Inception

When people look back at international economic relations in the early twenty-first century, 2013 has to be a watershed year. The year before, China overtook the US as the world's biggest trading nation in goods.[35] In response, the US stepped up its efforts at 'organizing trade relations with countries other than China so that China starts feeling more pressure about meeting basic international standards'[36] on two fronts. First, in the Asia Pacific region, the US continued to push to expand the membership of the TPP. In April 2013, the US finally brought Japan into the TPP, which was the world's third-largest economy and the second-largest economy among TPP members at that time.[37] Second, the US also reached out to the EU across the Atlantic, which led to the launch of the Transatlantic Trade and Investment Partnership (TTIP) negotiations in June 2013.[38]

China responded with its own initiatives. In July 2013, it agreed to drop its blanket restrictions on investment to relaunch the negotiations on the BIT with the US, which has not been making much progress despite being launched in 2008.[39] In September and October 2013, President Xi also announced the land-based Silk Road Economic Belt, which links China with Europe through Central and Western Asia, and the sea-based twenty-first century Maritime Silk Road, which connects China with Southeast Asian countries, Africa and Europe. Later combined as the Belt and Road Initiative (BRI), these would become a key pillar of China's foreign economic policy. In November 2013, China and the EU also announced at the EU–China Summit to launch negotiations for 'an ambitious investment agreement',

[35] 'China Overtakes US to Become Biggest Trading Nation' (*South China Morning Post*, 12 February 2013), https://www.scmp.com/news/article/1148330/china-overtakes-us-become-biggest-trading-nation.

[36] 'Southeast Asian Nations Announce Trade Bloc to Rival U.S. Effort' (*New York Times*, 21 November 2012), https://www.nytimes.com/2012/11/21/world/asia/southeast-asian-nations-announce-trade-bloc-to-rival-us-effort.html.

[37] Office of the United States Trade Representative, 'Transcript of on-the-Record Conference Call by Deputy National Security Advisor for International Economic Affairs Michael Froman and Acting United States Trade Representative Demetrios Marantis' (12 April 2013), https://ustr.gov/about-us/policy-offices/press-office/speeches/transcripts/2013/april/dep-nsa-froman-amb-marantis-cc-tpp.

[38] 'Remarks by President Obama, U.K. Prime Minister Cameron, European Commission President Barroso, and European Council President Van Rompuy on the Transatlantic Trade and Investment Partnership' (*The White House*, 17 June 2013), https://obamawhitehouse.archives.gov/the-press-office/2013/06/17/remarks-president-obama-uk-prime-minister-cameron-european-commission-pr.

[39] P Eckert and A Yukhananov, 'US, China Agree to Restart Investment Treaty Talks' (*Reuters*, 12 July 2013), https://www.reuters.com/article/us-usa-china-dialogue-trade-idUSBRE96A0ZD20130712.

which later morphed into the CAI.[40] Together with the Regional Comprehensive Economic Partnership (RCEP), which was launched in November 2012, the BRI and the CAI became key components in China's strategic toolbox against the US.

B. Negotiation

In January 2014, the first round of EU–China investment agreement took place. The initial progress was rather slow, and two years passed before the two sides reached agreement on the scope of the negotiations.[41] For the next two years, the negotiations made some progress, but the pace was still rather slow. The negotiation could have languished like the ill-fated US–China BIT negotiation, but President Donald Trump's trade war brought a sense of urgency to both the EU and China.

On 22 March 2018, President Trump signed a Presidential Memorandum[42] directing the United States Trade Representative (USTR) to raise tariffs against Chinese products pursuant to the USTR's Section 301 Report into China's Acts, Policies, and Practices Related to Technology Transfer, Intellectual Property, and Innovation, which was issued on the same day.[43] The EU was not spared either, as the US announced additional duties on steel and aluminium imports from the EU in the same month, which finally took effect in June 2018,[44] one month before the imposition of 25 per cent tariffs on Chinese products.

United against a common enemy, the EU and China accelerated negotiations on their investment agreement, which resulted in the exchange of market access offers during the 20th EU–China Summit held in July 2018.[45] As the trade war raged on, the negotiations on the investment agreement also intensified. The 21st EU–China Summit in April 2019 set 2020 as the deadline for 'the conclusion of

[40] European Commission, 'Statement by President Barroso at the Press Conference of the EU–China Summit' (21 November 2013), https://ec.europa.eu/commission/presscorner/detail/en/speech_13_959.

[41] 'EU and China Agree on Scope of the Future Investment Deal', https://policy.trade.ec.europa.eu/news/eu-and-china-agree-scope-future-investment-deal-2016-01-15_en.

[42] 'Presidential Memorandum on the Actions by the United States Related to the Section 301 Investigation' (22 March 2018), https://www.whitehouse.gov/presidential-actions/presidential-memorandum-actions-united-states-related-section-301-investigation.

[43] Office of the United States Trade Representative, 'Findings of the Investigation into China's Acts, Policies, and Practices Related to Technology Transfer, Intellectual Property, and Innovation under Section 301 of the Trade Act of 1974' (22 March 2018), https://ustr.gov/sites/default/files/Section%20301%20FINAL.PDF. For a detailed history of the trade war, see Henry Gao, 'WTO Reform and China: Defining or Defiling the Multilateral Trading System?' 2021 Harvard International Law Journal (forthcoming).

[44] European Commission, 'European Commission Reacts to the US Restrictions on Steel and Aluminium Affecting the EU' (31 May 2018), http://europa.eu/rapid/press-release_IP-18-4006_en.htm.

[45] 'EU–China Leaders' Meeting: EU Must Do More to Tackle Legal Breaches by Chinese Companies in Europe, Say Civil Society Organisations' (*Bankwatch Network*, 14 September 2020), https://bankwatch.org/press_release/EU-China-leaders-meeting-eu-must-do-more-to-tackle-legal-breaches-by-chinese-companies-in-europe-say-civil-society-organisations.

an ambitious EU-China Comprehensive Investment Agreement',[46] which sent the talks into a state of frenzy. Starting from June 2020, 15 rounds of negotiations were held in a short span of one and half years. This was more than double the pace of negotiations in the preceding years, which only averaged four rounds a year.

C. Conclusion

As the agreement was nearing completion, geopolitical forces started to emerge again. After winning the US presidential election, Joe Biden announced on 25 November 2020 that 'America is back – we're at the head of the table again'.[47] This comment sparked anxiety in the EU as many Europeans interpreted this to imply a return to 'the status quo ante of Brussels expected to play second-fiddle to Washington'.[48] As if to make the message even more explicit, on 23 December 2020, Biden's pick for national security adviser Jake Sullivan retweeted[49] a Reuters story[50] dated 18 December on the imminent conclusion of the EU–China investment deal, with the comment that the new administration would 'welcome early consultations with our European partners on our common concerns about China's economic practices'.[51]

The EU, however, had different calculations. First, the EU was not the first to enter a bilateral deal with China; it was simply following the footsteps of the US, which signed the bilateral Phase One deal with China at the beginning of 2020. The EU was concerned that the purchase commitments under the Phase One deal would be fulfilled at the expense of EU exporters.[52] This is why EU trade commissioner Valdis Dombrovskis regarded the CAI as simply 'levelling up' with the US, which secured market access and level playing field commitments from China in the Phase One deal.[53] Second, the Phase One deal also taught the EU important lessons about China's negotiating style. With more than 100 sentences containing

[46] 'Joint Statement of the 21st EU–China Summit' (*European Union External Action*, 10 April 2019), https://eeas.europa.eu/delegations/china_en/60836/Joint%20statement%20of%20the%2021st%20EU-China%20summit.

[47] 'Why Biden is Good News for Germany' (*CNBC*, 25 November 2020), https://www.cnbc.com/2020/11/25/why-biden-is-good-news-for-germany.html.

[48] 'EU–China Deal May Give Biden's Team More Options' (*Asia Times*, December 2020), https://asiatimes.com/2020/12/EU-China-deal-may-give-bidens-team-more-options/.

[49] J Sullivan, (*Twitter*, 22 December 2020), https://twitter.com/jakejsullivan/status/1341180109118726144?s=20.

[50] R Emmott and G Crossley, 'China, EU Aim for Investment Pact by Year-End, Germany Says' (*Reuters* (Beijing), 18 December 2020), https://www.reuters.com/article/EU-China-trade-idUSKBN28S13X.

[51] 'Biden Team Voices Concern over EU–China Investment Deal' (*Financial Times*, 22 December 2020), https://www.ft.com/content/2f0212ab-7e69-4de0-8870-89dd0d414306.

[52] S Lau, 'EU Trade Commissioner Phil Hogan Criticises US–China Phase One Trade Deal, Claims it is Unlikely to Boost Competitiveness or Jobs' (*South China Morning Post*, 17 January 2020), https://www.scmp.com/news/world/europe/article/3046460/eu-review-us-china-deal-any-wto-challenge-says-trade-commissioner.

[53] 'EU and China Agree New Investment Treaty' (*Financial Times*, 30 December 2020), https://www.ft.com/content/6a429460-4bfb-42d4-9191-73ba97dde130.

'China shall' and only five sentences containing 'the United States shall' (including two sentences with 'China and the United States shall'), the Phase One deal proves that China's resistance to one-sided deals may be overcome under certain circumstances. This is also demonstrated in the CAI, not only by the uneven concessions between the two sides, but also by reports that China's request to access the EU's nuclear energy market[54] and the insertion of a Huawei clause[55] were both rejected by the EU, while the EU's demands on commitments on forced labour was accepted by China at the last minute.[56] Third, the EU was worried that, had it waited until the new Biden administration assumed office, it might not have been able to conclude the deal with China. Instead, concluding the deal with China independently is regarded as a major step in achieving the EU's 'strategic autonomy'.[57] Moreover, the EU insisted that such autonomous action should not hinder the cross-Atlantic cooperation, just as the Phase One deal would not do so.[58]

On the other hand, for China, signing a deal before the new Biden administration came into office also had at least three advantages. First, it prevented the new administration from being able to sabotage the deal, as they did not have official channels of communication with the EU before assuming office. Second, it also signalled to the new Biden administration that China always has the option of turning to the EU should the relationship with the US deteriorate further. Indeed, at least by judging from Biden's harsh comments against China on the campaign trail, it would be naïve for China to assume that the new administration would play nice with China. This is especially true when the reckoning under the Phase One deal is taken into account, as China was quite far behind in meeting the purchase targets under the agreement, meeting only less than 60 per cent of the specified targets as of July 2022.[59] Third, a deal with the EU also helps to bolster China's international reputation, which suffered major setbacks in 2020 due to the COVID-19 pandemic and China's aggressive style of diplomacy.[60]

[54] 'Chinese Demands on Nuclear Power Investment Complicate EU Talks' (*Reuters* (Berlin), 23 December 2020), https://www.reuters.com/article/us-EU-China-trade-idUSKBN28X1W8.

[55] F Bermingham, 'China Tried to Punish European States for Huawei Bans by Adding Eleventh-Hour Rule to EU Investment Deal' (*South China Morning Post*, 8 January 2021), https://www.scmp.com/economy/china-economy/article/3116896/china-tried-punish-european-states-huawei-bans-adding.

[56] L Wen, X Heqian and L Zhenhua, 'China's Last-Minute Pledge on Forced Labor Saved Investment Accord, EU Envoy Says' (*CaxingGlobal*, 20 January 2021), https://www.caixinglobal.com/2021-01-20/chinas-last-minute-pledge-on-forced-labor-saved-investment-accord-eu-envoy-says-101652916.html.

[57] P Tamma, 'Europe Wants "Strategic Autonomy": It Just Has to Decide What That Means' (*Politico*, 15 October 2020), https://www.politico.eu/article/europe-trade-wants-strategic-autonomy-decide-what-means.

[58] 'EU and China Agree New Investment Treaty' (n 53).

[59] CP Brown, 'US-China Phase One Tracker: China's Purchases of US Goods and Services in 2020 and 2021' (*PIIE*, 19 July 2022), https://www.piie.com/research/piie-charts/us-china-phase-one-tracker-chinas-purchases-us-goods.

[60] L Silver, K Devlin and C Huang, 'Unfavorable Views of China Reach Historic Highs in Many Countries' (*Pew Research Center*, 6 October 2020), https://www.pewresearch.org/global/2020/10/06/unfavorable-views-of-china-reach-historic-highs-in-many-countries.

Thus, on 30 December 2020, the EU and China concluded in principle the negotiations for the CAI, despite the complaints from the US.[61]

D. Ratification

So far, all the stars seem to have aligned perfectly to guide the CAI from inception to conclusion. However, the successful conclusion of the CAI might well mark the end of good fortune for the CAI. As per EU internal procedure, the text of the agreement shall first go through the necessary legal and technical review, before it is approved by the European Council and translated into all the official EU languages.[62] It will then be referred to the European Parliament, which will decide with a majority vote within a year.[63] Unfortunately, the European Parliament is not really known for being friendly towards China; instead, it has been criticising China for years over allegations ranging from human rights violations to economic aggression.[64] This is not really surprising because, as representatives of the people, the Members of the European Parliament (MEPs) regard their main task as voicing the concerns of their constituencies rather than clinching major trade and investment deals, as the Commission does. Such an approach is clearly reflected in the European Parliament's December 2020 'Resolution on forced labour and the situation of the Uyghurs in the Xinjiang Uyghur Autonomous Region'.[65] To make matters worse, on 22 March 2021, China imposed sanctions on 10 EU individuals, which included five MEPs.[66] In protest, the European Parliament cancelled a meeting to review the CAI, and the Chairman of the Parliament's Trade Committee reportedly said that: 'There has to be a solution of these sanctions before we come back to ordinary business on this.'[67]

Thus, before China lifts its sanctions on the five parliamentarians, the CAI will not even enter the ratification process. Even if this hurdle is cleared, the aftertaste of such foul play would probably cast a shadow over the minds of many MEPs. Trying to persuade more than 700 parliamentarians will prove to be a much harder task than the dozens of officials in Directorate-General for Trade, especially as these parliamentarians see their roles as much broader than the narrow confines of trade and investment interests.

[61] European Commission (n 2).

[62] ZA Ferenczy, 'Will the EU–China Investment Agreement Survive Parliament's Scrutiny?' (*The Diplomat*, 27 January 2021), https://thediplomat.com/2021/01/will-the-EU–China-investment-agreement-survive-parliaments-scrutiny.

[63] ibid.

[64] ibid.

[65] European Parliament, 'European Parliament Resolution of 17 December 2020 on Forced Labour and the Situation of the Uyghurs in the Xinjiang Uyghur Autonomous Region' (17 December 2020), https://www.europarl.europa.eu/doceo/document/TA-9-2020–0375_EN.html.

[66] 'China Hits Back at EU with Sanctions on 10 People, Four Entities over Xinjiang' (*Reuters* (Beijing), 22March2021),https://www.reuters.com/article/us-EU-China-sanctions-ministry-idUSKBN2BE1WB.

[67] P Blenkinsop, 'EU–China Deal Grinds into Reverse after Tit-for-Tat Sanctions' (*Reuters* (Brussels), 23 March 2021), https://www.reuters.com/article/us-EU-China-trade-idUSKBN2BF276.

V. Conclusion: Strategic Opportunity Meets Strategic Autonomy

In his report at the 16th National Congress of the China Communist Party (CCP) held in November 2002, the then Chinese President and Party General Secretary Jiang Zemin presciently announced that 'the first two decades of the 21st Century will be an important window of strategic opportunity that China must firmly grasp to make great achievements'.[68] Such 'strategic opportunity' was the result of China's accession to the WTO, but it did not really come quite effortlessly at that time. When President George W. Bush came into office in January 2001, he vowed to be 'tough and firm' on China, and labelled it as a 'strategic competitor'.[69] In April of that year, the bilateral relationship reached new low when a US Navy spy plane collided with a Chinese fighter jet.[70] However, 9/11 created a unique opportunity that China quickly seized to turn the tables in its favour. At 8:45 am on 11 September 2001, an American Airlines plane was hijacked by terrorists and crashed into the north tower of the World Trade Center building in New York City.[71] Less than 20 minutes later, another plane crashed into the south tower.[72] At 9.30 am, President Bush addressed the country and called this a 'national tragedy' caused by 'an apparent terrorist attack on our country'.[73] Due to the time difference, it was night-time in Beijing when the attacks happened. Upon watching the news on the attacks, President Jiang immediately called a meeting of the Politburo Standing Committee. At 1.47 am Beijing time, or just five hours after the first attack, President Jiang called President Bush to condemn the attacks and send condolences to American people.[74] On 18 October 2001, President Bush visited Shanghai in his first overseas trip since 9/11, where he met President Jiang and agreed that the US and China should develop 'a constructive and cooperative relationship'.[75] Such a warm relationship in turn cleared the way for China's WTO accession at the WTO Ministerial Conference held in Doha, Qatar, the following month.

[68] 江泽民同志在党的十六大上所作报告全文,全面建设小康社会，开创中国特色社会主义事业新局面, 18 November 2002, https://www.fmprc.gov.cn/web/ziliao_674904/zyjh_674906/t10855.shtml.

[69] R Baum, 'From "Strategic Partners" to "Strategic Competitors": George W. Bush and the Politics of U.S. China Policy' (2001) 1(2) *Journal of East Asian Studies* 191, 192.

[70] 'US Plane in China after it Collides with Chinese Jet' *New York Times* (2 April 2001), https://www.nytimes.com/2001/04/02/world/us-plane-in-china-after-it-collides-with-chinese-jet.html.

[71] 'Flight Path Study – American Airlines Flight 11' (*National Transportation Safety Board*, 19 February 2002), https://nsarchive2.gwu.edu/NSAEBB/NSAEBB196/doc01.pdf.

[72] National Transportation Safety Board, 'Flight Path Study – United Airlines Flight 175' (19 February 2002), www.gwu.edu/~nsarchiv/NSAEBB/NSAEBB196/doc03.pdf.

[73] The White House, 'Remarks by the President after Two Planes Crash into World Trade Center' (11 September 2001), https://georgewbush-whitehouse.archives.gov/news/releases/2001/09/20010911.html.

[74] 吴建民, 中国对'9·1 1 事件'的快速反应, 《中外书摘》 2008年 第06期, https://www.xiaoshuo.online/zhongwaiwz/zwsz2008/zwsz20080614-1.html.

[75] President GW Bush and President J Zemin, 'US, China Stand against Terrorism, Remarks during Press Availability', Western Suburb Guest House, Shanghai, People's Republic of China, 19 October 2001, https://2001–2009.state.gov/s/ct/rls/rm/2001/5461.htm.

Ten days after meeting President Bush, President Jiang gave a speech to the Chinese military, in which he used the China–US relationship as the example that China should actively 'create advantageous strategic situation at the international level'.[76] When he met the drafting group for the 16th Party Congress Report in January 2002, President Jiang first used the expression 'the first two decades of the 21st Century will be an important window of strategic opportunity that China must firmly grasp to make great achievements', which was subsequently duly copied into the Report.

Leveraging on the 'window of strategic opportunity' created by the WTO accession, China was able to grow its trade and economy exponentially, and emerged as the largest trader and second-largest economy in the world. However, as the second decade of the twenty-first century was drawing to a close, it seems that the window of opportunity was closing fast, as evidenced by the refusal by the major Western countries to recognise China's market economy status and the subsequent trade war launched by the US against China. Reflecting on the issue in his Report at the 19th Party Congress in 2017, President Xi made the political judgement that 'while there are deep and complex changes both domestically and internationally, China's development is still in an important window of strategic opportunity'.[77] The 5th Plenum of the 19th Party Congress held in October 2020 repeated this by stating that 'for now and the period afterwards, China's development is still in an important window of strategic opportunity, but there are new developments and changes in both the opportunities and challenges'.[78] The same language was also copied into the CCP Central Committee's Recommendations on Making the 14th Five-Year Plan and the 2035 Vision that was adopted on the same day, which recommends that China shall 'actively seek change' and try to 'promote international cooperation by taking advantage of China's huge market'.[79]

On the other hand, the EU was also moving towards its own 'strategic autonomy'. The concept started as an idea of the French, when they published their 1994 White Paper on defence.[80] Gradually, however, it was accepted by all of the big three EU Member States: Germany, France and Italy.[81] The concept was adopted by the

[76] 营造有利战略态势，增强国家战略能力，二〇〇一年十月三十一日，江泽民文选，第三卷，, 352–53.

[77] 决胜全面建成小康社会, 夺取新时代中国特色社会主义伟大胜利-在中国共产党第十九次全国代表大会上的报告，（2017年10月18日）, www.gov.cn/zhuanti/2017-10/27/content_5234876.htm.

[78] 中国共产党第十九届中央委员会第五次全体会议公报， （2020年10月29日中国共产党第十九届中央委员会第五次全体会议通过）, www.12371.cn/2020/10/29/ARTI1603964233795881.shtml.

[79] 中共中央关于制定国民经济和社会发展第十四个五年规划和二〇三五年远景目标的建议，（2020年10月29日中国共产党第十九届中央委员会第五次全体会议通过）,www.12371.cn/2020/11/03/ARTI1604398127413120.shtml.

[80] 'Livre Blanc sur la défense et la Sécurité Nationale' (1994), www.livreblancdefenseetsecurite.gouv.fr/pdf/le-livre-blanc-sur-la-defense-1994.pdf.

[81] U Franke and T Varma, 'Independence Play: Europe's Pursuit of Strategic Autonomy' (*European Council on Foreign Relations*, 18 July 2019), https://ecfr.eu/special/independence_play_europes_pursuit_of_strategic_autonomy.

EU in 2016 when it unveiled its Global Strategy, which was supposed to 'nurture the ambition of strategic autonomy' for the EU.[82] Following Trump's election as US President and Brexit, the concept started to take off among the governments of EU Member States.[83] While there was some ambiguity on the exact content of the concept, the bigger EU Member States typically perceive it as referring to decision-making autonomy.[84] This is recently confirmed by the new trade strategy paper issued in February 2001, in which the EU further refined it as a concept of 'open strategic autonomy' which emphasises 'the EU's ability to make its own choices and shape the world around it through leadership and engagement, reflecting its strategic interests and values'.[85]

Against such a background, we can see that the CAI is what you get when China's 'strategic opportunity' meets with EU's 'strategic autonomy'. This also seems to be the official views of both the EU and China. For example, the EU's new trade strategy paper explicitly recognises the CAI as part of the efforts of 'open strategic autonomy' with 'a combination of active engagement, both at bilateral and multilateral level, and of parallel development and implementation of autonomous instruments necessary to protect the EU's essential interests and values – in full compliance with its international commitments'.[86] When President Xi Jinping talked to German Chancellor Angela Merkel on 7 April 2021, he emphasised that 'China-Europe relations are facing new development opportunities and various challenges. The key is to firmly grasp the general direction and main tone of the development of China-Europe relations from a strategic height, have mutual respect and dispel distractions. China's development is an opportunity for the EU, and we hope that the EU will make a correct judgment independently and truly achieve strategic autonomy'.[87] The same message was also repeated at the virtual summit between Xi, Merkel and French President Emmanuel Macron held later that month.[88]

In conclusion, it was the conflation of strategic considerations that gave birth to the CAI, but this, paradoxically, also means that the CAI comes with unique birth defects. When the geopolitical forces shift, as we have seen over the past few years, the fate of this major investment deal might also be cast into doubt, especially

[82] 'Shared Vision, Common Action: A Stronger Europe. A Global Strategy for the European Union's Foreign and Security Policy' (*European Union Global Strategy*, June 2016), https://eeas.europa.eu/archives/docs/top_stories/pdf/eugs_review_web.pdf.

[83] Franke and Varma (n 81) 7.

[84] Franke and Varma (n 81) 10–11.

[85] European Commission, 'Trade Policy Review – An Open, Sustainable and Assertive Trade Policy' (April 2021), https://trade.ec.europa.eu/doclib/docs/2021/april/tradoc_159541.0270_EN_05.pdf.

[86] Franke and Varma (n 81) 9.

[87] 习近平同德国总理默克尔通电话, www.xinhuanet.com/politics/leaders/2021-04/07/c_1127304170.htm.

[88] 习近平同法国德国领导人举行视频峰会， www.xinhuanet.com/politics/leaders/2021-04/16/c_1127339605.htm.

as it is now entering the most political part of the process – ratification by the European Parliament. In order to make the ratification happen, the parties should be trying to insulate it from geopolitical tensions rather than further entangling it in geopolitical and strategic considerations, so as to usher in a new beginning in EU–China relations.

PART 3

Sustainability Law

10

Land and the Legal Language of Decolonisation

Examples from Indonesia

KEEBET VON BENDA-BECKMANN

I. Introduction

Indonesia has a unique way of dealing with its colonial past compared to other former colonies, where decolonisation and the role of law have been prominent political and academic issues. For one thing, the kind of decolonisation debates that are so prominent in these post-colonies seem to be lacking in Indonesia, even though the expanding plantation industry has greatly exacerbated the problems of dispossession and displacement. There is a broad consensus among post-colonies that colonial laws are still affecting current social relations. However, the issues that each of them has foregrounded have assumed very different forms and degrees of intensity.[1] The debates share the proposition that coloniality remains an integral part of modernity, even after independence. De Sousa Santos argues that 'the three main modes of modern domination are capitalism, colonialism, and patriarchy', adding that '[c]olonialism and patriarchy … are premised on the ontological degradation of the worker, be it the racialised worker or the sexualised worker'.[2] In a similar vein, but with a focus on relations to land, Mignolo argues that 'the 'colonial matrix of power concerns the coloniality of political, economic, and military power' in connection with 'the three pillars of being in the world: racism, sexism, and the naturalization of life and the permanent regeneration of the living (e.g., the invention of nature)'.[3] The current discussions are part of a long history

[1] U Baxi, 'Postcolonial Legality: A Postscript from India' (2012) 45(2) *Verfassung und Recht in Übersee/Law and Politics in Africa, Asia and Latin America* 178, https://www.jstor.org/stable/43256851.

[2] B de Sousa Santos, 'Postface as Disquietude' in B de Sousa Santos (ed), *Toward a New Legal Common Sense: Law, Globalization, and Emancipation*, 3rd edn (Cambridge, Cambridge University Press, 2020) 590–91.

[3] W Mignolo and CE Walsh, *On Decoloniality: Concepts, Analytics, and Praxis* (Durham, NC, Duke University Press, 2018) 10.

of critical interventions against dispossession, displacement and misconceiving of local laws. One important episode in this history was the criticism of the making of customary law in the 1980s, to which Francis Snyder provided an important contribution.[4]

The kinds of resistance that emerge against the colonial heritage, how social movements get involved, the continued influence of colonial law and the idioms in which resistance is formulated are very diverse. Discussions on these topics, and the call for autonomy vis-a-vis a dominant White population, are most prominent in former settler colonies, where Indigenous populations were forcefully driven from their lands, if not murdered.[5] For instance, Indigenous groups in Latin America are calling for autonomy against the domination of a population of mixed Spanish and Indigenous descent. Russian 'annexation colonialism' used (and uses once again) colonial techniques to conquer 'Asian hordes' who differed in culture and customs from Russians.[6] But though Russian colonisers stayed on in the colonised regions after the end of the Soviet Union, they do not occupy the same privileged position as, for instance, settlers in North America, Australia and New Zealand. Elsewhere, White colonists – who made up the colonial administration, governed and taxed the subjugated Indigenous population, controlled trade, and ran the plantation and extraction economy – left the country upon independence. Yet here, too, the colonial legacies left their imprint on the current legal system, accounting for serious problems of inequality. In India, where an important part of the decolonisation literature focuses on ontological and epistemic legacies and criticism about the Western (mainly English) categories and understandings by which India's history and social reality are described, analysed and misunderstood, the rigid distinction between religious tenets – resulting in the discrimination of non-Hindus – is considered to be a lasting result of colonial law. This has also been at the root of lively media debates, where strong voices have emerged to demand

[4] F Snyder, 'Colonialism and Legal Form: The Creation of 'Customary Law' in Senegal' (1981) 19 *Journal of Legal Pluralism and Unofficial Law* 49, https://commission-on-legal-pluralism.com/system/commission-on-legal-pluralism/volumes/19/snyder-art.pdf.

[5] S Xavier et al (eds), *Decolonizing Law: Indigenous, Third World and Settler Perspectives* (Abingdon, Routledge, 2021).

[6] KD Kernig, *Lenins Reich in Trümmern: Schatten Über Russlands Zukunft* (Munich, Deutsche Verlags Anstalt, 2000) 345. Kerning distinguishes five types of colonialism: (1) mixing colonialism (*Vermischungskolonilimus*), in which the colonial and indigenous populations mixed freely; (2) colonialism with a White class of administration and leaders that discouraged to mix with the indigenous population (*Überschichtskolonialsmus*); (3) extinction colonialism (*Ausrottungskolonialismus*), in which the indigenous population was killed or extremely marginalised; (4) apartheid colonialism (*Apartheidskolonialismus*), in which White settlers remained in the former colony and created distinctive social spheres; (5) annexation colonialism (*Annexionskolonialismus*), by which adjacent captured territories were incorporated into the state. Mignolo and Walsh ((n 3) 16) distinguish between colonialism (which they associate with settler colonies) and empire (colonies intended for control for political and economic purposes). Mitchell and others speak of 'extractive imperialism': T Mitchell et al, 'The Right to Free, Prior, and Informed Consent (FPIC): Reflections on Experiences of Two Indigenous Communities in Northern Regions of Canada and Chile' in Xavier et al (n 5).

that the legal system be decolonised by abolishing English as the main judicial language and simplifying laws and court judgments.[7]

In striking contrast to other states where the White colonisers left after the declaration of independence, in Indonesia, the question of the decolonisation of law was explicitly debated only briefly, namely immediately after independence and no longer after the rise of the authoritarian Suharto regime. Yet some of the thorniest issues that haunted Suharto's authoritarian regime are rooted in colonial law and are a direct continuation of that legal regime. They include: claims to land and forest, calls for autonomy, and redress for marginalised Indigenous groups that are dominated by Indonesian economic and administrative elites. Even within Indonesia, the debates and the legal language used show remarkable diversity. Whereas in some regions, claims resemble those made by marginalised groups in the Americas, Australia and New Zealand in many respects, in other regions, other legal idioms are brought into play – for instance, when making land claims.

This chapter attempts to shed light on the puzzling absence of a decolonisation debate in Indonesian legal discourse. It also discusses some major reasons for the remarkable diversity in the legal idioms used to claim land and autonomy during the so-called *Reformasi*, the period of reform since the fall of the Suharto regime. The chapter is structured as follows. Section II lays out the legal foundation for carrying out dispossessions in the plantation and extraction economy of the Dutch Indies. This is followed in section II by an overview of criticisms of colonial land policies, which, in some ways, might be seen as precursors of decolonisation. Section IV is devoted to Indonesian discussions of legal decolonisation immediately after independence and the reasons for the ensuing disconnection from the Dutch legal developments, as well as the continuing dispossessions under the Suharto regime based on the colonial legal structure. Section V explains how three legal idioms (international human rights, environmental protection and *adat*/*adat* law/customary law) are mobilised against land dispossession.

II. The Plantation and Extraction Economy and its Legal Foundations

Up until the late eighteenth century, the Dutch East India Company was mainly centred in port cities, from where it traded goods produced by local populations. When the emphasis of the Company began to shift from mercantilism to a plantation economy, controlling the main ports was no longer sufficient. The Dutch began to expand into the interior to secure access to land for its plantations and

[7] See, for example, Chief Justice NV Ramana, 'Indianisation of Our Legal System is Need of the Hour' (*Times of India*, 18 September 2021), https://timesofindia.indiatimes.com/india/indianisation-of-our-legal-system-is-need-of-the-hour-chief-justice-of-india/articleshow/86316597.cms.

to control the population outside the small port societies. Land and minerals – as well as labourers – were turned into commodities to be put to use for a capitalist economy. Treaties with local rulers – with the promise to recognise local laws and not to interfere in the internal affairs of the local population – secured their allegiance. These promises would be broken on a regular basis in order to cater to the needs of the colonial economy. It would not be until the beginning of the twentieth century before the whole archipelago would be brought under Dutch rule.

At the turn to the nineteenth century, the Napoleonic Wars also affected the Dutch East Indies. The French occupation of the Dutch Republic until 1816 allowed the British to take over the Dutch East Indies. During this time, Sir Thomas Stamford Raffles introduced a system of land rent based on British law, according to which the British Empire would own all land, which it would give out to the farmers, extracting from them a certain percentage of their crops – sometimes as much as half – or a land rent of the same value. This system was continued after the Dutch regained possession of their colony. However, it did not work to the satisfaction of the government, owing to problems collecting the money; more importantly, this system was not conducive to producing export crops in large quantities. The Java War that ravaged central Java from 1825 to 1830, killing 200,000 Javanese, brought the colony to near-bankruptcy. To ensure a steady income for the government, Governor-General van den Bosch introduced a new system of 'forced cultivation' (*cultuurstelsel* or further Cultivation System),[8] again making the government the sole land owner.[9] Farmers were required to sell approximately 20 per cent of their land crops (such as sugar, coffee, tea and indigo) exclusively to the government at prices set by the government, and village heads were made responsible for the delivery of these products. The government then sold these products at a great profit on the global market. In addition, the local population had to provide unpaid services of various kinds for up to 100 days. As wet rice fields (*sawah*) were used for sugar cultivation, the local population faced the consequences of severely diminished rice production. Besides, the thriving practices of systemic corruption and extortion exacerbated the problem of severe hunger, adding to the heavy burden already shouldered by the local population. Only after this system was deemed to be no longer profitable to the government was the policy repealed. The Agrarian Law of 1870, allowing private entrepreneurs to buy land in order to establish a plantation economy, is basically still in force. Enormous tracts of land were converted into private ownership or long lease and controlled by Dutch/European planters who ran their plantation using enslaved or poorly paid labour, often under abominable working conditions.[10] Mining companies also obtained

[8] C Fasseur, RE Elson and A Kraal, *The Politics of Colonial Exploitation: Java, the Dutch, and the Cultivation System* (Ithaca, NY, Cornell University Press,1992) ch 2.

[9] ibid 31, fn 31; para 62 of the Constitutional Regulations of 1830 and 1836.

[10] See, eg, AL Stoler, *Capitalism and Confrontation in Sumatra's Plantation Belt 1870–1979* (New Haven, Yale University Press, 1985); J Breman, *Koelies, Planters en Koloniale Politiek* (Dordrecht, Foris Publications, 1987).

licences that entailed the appropriation of land. In addition, the Dutch colonial administration took over control of all forests.

This growing plantation and extraction economy resulted in enduring legal conflicts in which two kinds of legal issues were particularly problematic. The first concerned the question of which property regime was applicable: the laws of the colonial government, or local, customary laws. A second, related problem was illegal land occupation – that is, illegal according to both local and colonial law, by means of corruption, forging documents, intimidation or outright violence. This chapter focuses on the former issue.

III. Conflicting Notions of Land Rights

In the 1870s, the colonial government enacted the so-called Domain Declarations (*Domein Declaraties*), according to which a fundamental distinction was made between public and private law, and the state no longer claimed automatic ownership of all land. The Declarations stipulated that all public rights (but not ownership) were to be assumed by the colonial administration, as local rulers had passed on the sovereignty to them.[11] This included all land on which no 'private' rights or rights that resembled private rights rested. Such land could be given out in private ownership – for example, for plantation or mining purposes. Forest land and other public land were governed by the government. The colonial administration set up a system of land registration based on the Dutch property system, in which measured plots of land under *eigendom* (ownership), or its derivatives, were registered in the *kadaster*. This register was to be the material basis for recognising existing 'private' rights to land in the hands of the local population – and thus for title security – but only if these rights resembled private ownership. This clause became particularly problematic because, on that basis, many rights to land that Indigenous people regarded as theirs were converted into private ownership (*eigendom*) or long lease (*erfpacht*), governed by Dutch colonial law. Communal rights – for example, of kin groups – could be registered, but it was incorrectly assumed that all members of common property had equal rights, and that the male representative had full and exclusive rights of distribution, exploitation and management. Yet, in fact, the structure and the entitlements associated with *ulayat* were far more complex than the registers had assumed. As a result, the registers undermined the rights of many of its members. The village commons or land kept in reserve for the community, or rights to collect forest products did not resemble private ownership and therefore did not fall within the ambit of recognition.

[11] This section is largely based on K von Benda-Beckmann, 'Anachronism, Agency, and the Contextualisation of Adat: Van Vollenhoven's Analyses in Light of Struggles over Resources' (2019) 20(5) *Asia Pacific Journal of Anthropology* 397, https://www.tandfonline.com/doi/full/10.1080/14442213.2019.1670242.

Most colonial officers regarded these lands as waste land that could be given out to plantation owners and mining companies.

From the beginning, the Domain Declarations met with strong criticism from among Indonesian citizens, who argued that they violated the promises made in the various treaties with local rulers and communities to recognise existing rights and refrain from internal interference with village communities. These issues continue to haunt land rights to this day. Some colonial officers were also highly critical, if not against colonial rule as such. Eduard Douwes Dekker, a colonial officer, under the pseudonym Multatuli, wrote in 1860 the influential novel *Max Havelaar, of de Koffij-veilingen der Nederlandsche Handelsmaatschappij* (*Max Havelaar or the Coffee Auctions of the Dutch Trading Company*), which was a satirical depiction of colonial abuse and a sharp criticism of colonial corruption. One might say that this constituted a first precursor to decolonisation demands. In West Sumatra, the regional colonial administration, facing resistance from the local population, tried to accommodate some facets of the intricate Minangkabau land rights regime. Kinship and inheritance patterns followed the female line, and women (especially elderly women) held strong rights to family land. However, over time, the position of the male representative of a kin group was strengthened, to the disadvantage of women.[12]

It was not until the beginning of the twentieth century that a serious debate emerged about the recognition of local land rights. Cornelis van Vollenhoven, a Dutch professor of law at Leiden University, undertook a serious study of Indonesian Indigenous laws and became one of the most severe critics of Dutch colonial law, especially its conception of Indigenous land rights, which he deemed to be misconceived. In local laws, relationships to land, water and forest were understood in terms that differed fundamentally from Dutch law and could not be 'squeezed into' Dutch legal conceptions. For example, no Indigenous legal system in the archipelago made a public/private distinction, which was the very foundation of the Dutch property regime. Private ownership in the Dutch sense was unknown in most Indigenous legal orders. Recognition of existing legal orders had to include village commons and other forms of common property. Dutch expropriation of such land was illegal and in disregard (Dutch *miskenning*) of the local land rights.[13] In the dominant colonial legal perspective, *adat* – a generic term to denote 'the way of life' – was misunderstood as 'mere customs' and could therefore be set aside in the state's interests. Van Vollenhoven argued that Indonesians had law – *adatrecht* (*adat* law), a part of *adat* that could not be equated with customs

[12] K von Benda-Beckmann, 'Development, Law and Gender-Skewing: An Examination of the Impact of Development on the Socio-Legal Position of Indonesian Women, with Special Reference to Minangkabau' (1990–91) 30–31 *Journal of Legal Pluralism and Unofficial Law* 87, 100, https://commission-on-legal-pluralism.com/system/commission-on-legal-pluralism/volumes/30-31/bendabeckmann-art.pdf.

[13] C van Vollenhoven, *Miskenningen van Het Adatrecht* (Leiden, EJ Brill, 1909).

as it had legal characteristics.[14] Importantly, it was subject to change in line with social and economic developments. Thus, land to be acquired for plantations or mining had to be based on contracts with local title holders and properly compensated for. In 1919 he published *De Indonesiër en zijn grond* (*The Indonesian and His Land*), a concise analysis of Indigenous relations to land, which included obligations to protect the land. He criticised the government for misunderstanding and disregarding these laws, for underestimating the potential for development and for illegally expropriating land on which Indigenous people had rights.

Van Vollenhoven was by no means against colonialism in general. Yet, he radically condemned the debasing treatment of Indonesians as second-class citizens, depriving so many rural people of their land. For this critical stance, his work can be seen as a precursor to the decolonisation debate. What made his work unique at the time, and particularly relevant for today's decolonisation debates, is the generic concepts that he developed to capture the characteristics of Indonesian *adat* laws. He realised that *adat* had lost its influence in most urban areas and in large parts of Java, and began to collect descriptions of *adatrecht* from places all over the Indonesian archipelago, including the Philippines and Madagascar, where *adat* was still in force. A body of highly diverse data, the *Adatrechtbundels*, formed the basis for his analysis and systematisation.[15] Van Vollenhoven's work demonstrated that many Indonesian systems used specific procedures to prevent conflicts. For this, he proposed two more analytic concepts: first, *gesteunde naleving* (attested observance), which entailed the use of specific witnesses at important transactions to attest their legitimacy; and, second, as most legal orders had institutionalised mechanisms to prevent conflicts, he called this *preventieve rechtszorg* (preventive law care).[16]

With regard to relationships to village territory, van Vollenhoven showed that Dutch legal concepts differed fundamentally from local concepts. To underscore this difference, he designed the concepts of *adatrechtsgemeenschap* (*adat* jural communities) and *beschikkingsrecht* (the right of avail or control) of a local polity.[17] Such a polity could be territorially defined or based on other principles (mostly kinship). These relationships were not to be equated with European conceptions of civil communal rights, or associated with equality, as they represented highly differentiated structures of rights, obligations and procedures that could include spiritual relationships. He also found that rights that Europeans tended to gloss over as communal rights were, in fact, either held by the entire village or by kin groups of various genealogical links. The term *ulayat*, commonly used by the West Sumatran Minangkabau, was given a more generic meaning to capture a range of such communal rights.

[14] Christiaan Snouck Hurgronje introduced the terms *adat* and *adatrecht* as generic terms in 1893: C Snouck Hurgronje, *De Atjèhers*, vols 1 and 2 (Leiden, EJ Brill, 1893/1894).

[15] C van Vollenhoven, *Het Adatrecht Van Nederlandsch-Indië*, vol I (Leiden, EJ Brill, 1918).

[16] See also HWJ Sonius, 'Introduction' in JF Holleman (ed), *Van Vollenhoven on Indonesian Adat Law* (The Hague, Martinus Nijhoff, 1981).

[17] See also Fasseur, Elson and Kraal (n 8) 28.

The common opinion within the colonial administration – that the *adat* law in general, but especially the communal land governed by *adat* was unsuitable for economic progress – was highly cynical, because that very colonial government issued a series of regulations prohibiting the interlocal trade of agricultural products that had flourished throughout the archipelago. The toxic combination of an utter disregard for this characteristic of local property rights to land and the suffocating restrictions on trade, access to credit, and disposition of land under *adat* rule precluded an economic development based on *adat* communal rights. The colonial government felt justified in setting aside local 'customs' for its own interest and expropriate land to further its plantation and extracting economy.[18] Van Vollenhoven's criticism could not change these colonial policies. As a result, local people were dispossessed of their land and forest on a large scale.

IV. Independence and the Continuation of Dutch Colonial Law: Continuing Dispossession

After independence, the question was what legal order would be appropriate for the new state. Until the late 1950s, the process of constitution making was discussed in terms of decolonisation,[19] in adopting the Dutch colonial civil and criminal codes, which in turn were based on the Napoleonic Code. But over time, interest in legal developments in the Netherlands declined, and the Civil Code came to function more or less as a mere example which judges could set aside when it did not fit the social realities. Besides, over the years, the volume of administrative law enacted, often borrowed from common law systems, sharply increased. More importantly, after independence, Bahasa Indonesia replaced Dutch as the official language. As a result, lawyers' capacity to read Dutch slowly faded. When Franz von Benda-Beckmann and I conducted our first fieldwork in 1974–75, elderly academics, judges and lawyers were still fluent in Dutch, but younger lawyers and lay judges had no command of Dutch. Today, law students learn select Dutch legal terminology, but are unable to follow the developments in the Dutch legal literature. This is fundamental different compared to some former British colonies, where lawyers retained their ability to read English and keep up with legal developments within the Commonwealth. By contrast, the Indonesian legal system – which became increasingly separated from Dutch legal developments – is composed of a mixture of various legal traditions, which has led to a fragmentation of Indonesia's

[18] S Gautama and RN Hornick, *An Introduction to Indonesian Law: Unity in Diversity* (Bandung, Alumni, 1974) 83; F von Benda-Beckmann, *Property in Social Continuity: Continuity and Change in the Maintenance of Property Relationships through Time in Minangkabau, West Sumatra* (The Hague, Martinus Nijhoff, 1979) 211.

[19] HP Wiratraman and DAH Shah, 'Indonesia's Constitutional Responses to Plurality' in JL Neo and S Ngon (eds), *Pluralist Constitutions in Southeast Asia* (Oxford, Hart Publishing, 2019) 118.

legal system. Not only is it no longer conducive to more fundamental questions of decolonisation of law, but, as Bedner and Vel argue, it has also created the serious problem of a lack of communication between the judiciary, the legislative, the bar and academia.[20] Thus, paradoxically, even as Indonesian law was 'decolonised' to a greater extent than in other countries, much of this occurred without a 'decolonisation debate'. However, perhaps the most important reason for the absence of a decolonisation debate is the competing demand for overcoming the legacies of Sukarno and especially of Suharto's authoritarian and corrupt 'New Order', which many consider to be far more urgent than discussing the legacy of the colonial regime.

Arguably, the most controversial issue concerned the position of *adat*, especially in relation to land rights.[21] The Constitution of 1945 recognised the existence of *adat* law communities (*masyarakat hukum adat*), but under restricted conditions. The Basic Agrarian Law of 1960, which had drawn on van Vollenhoven's terminology and recognised *adat* land rights to some extent, should have put an end to the controversies. However, the law was highly partial to a system of ownership rather than to *adat* titles, so that communal land rights could be registered only under the title of the male head of the kin group. At the same time, even as the law offered the possibility of converting *adat* titles into ownership to cater to a land market, the right of avail (*hak ulayat*) was severely curtailed. Bedner and Arizona have reasoned that the Indonesian Communist Party was influential in the early years after independence and supported the interests of poor peasants and land labourers, without restoring a strong role for *adat*, which they associated with feudalism.[22] To strengthen the rights of peasants who had occupied colonial plantation land, they favoured large-scale land reform and redistribution of plantation land and forests. The Sukarno government, too, had little interest in *adat* land titles. It wanted to nationalise Dutch companies to exert maximal state control over land and forests. Titles of existing concessions were to be exchanged for long lease (*hak guna usaha* (HGU)), usually 25 years, after which the land would automatically revert to the state. Under this rule, many *adat* claims were virtually wiped out. The rights of concession holders were privileged over *adat* rights. At the same time, producing the kind of evidence for other claims to land titles that would be acceptable in the state legal system was extremely complex, expensive and time-consuming. Material objects, such as contracts, registration and other documents, and maps, were always privileged over other means of place making and forms of evidence of land title. The Indonesian legal system therefore continued with an interpretation

[20] A Bedner and J Vel, 'Legal Education in Indonesia' (2021) 1(1) *Indonesian Journal of Socio-Legal Studies* 1, https://scholarhub.ui.ac.id/cgi/viewcontent.cgi?article=1007&context=ijsls.

[21] A Bedner and Y Arizona, '*Adat* in Indonesian Land Law: A Promise for the Future or a Dead End?' (2019) 20(5) *Asia Pacific Journal of Anthropology* 416, 418–19, https://www.tandfonline.com/doi/epub/10.1080/14442213.2019.1670246?needAccess=true.

[22] ibid 419.

of *adat* that had little to do with the understandings of local people – a process that Francis Snyder and others had criticised in respect of other regions in the world.[23] However, local interpretations of *adat* continued to exist at the same time. Arizona concludes that the law in fact destabilised customary titles.[24]

When President Suharto came into power in 1965, his New Order opted for capitalist development under the strict control of the regime. Logging, mineral extraction and oil plantations expanded rapidly – ruthlessly encroaching on village property and other communal land. Deforestation, displacement and dispossession were rampant and had intergenerational effects.[25] The regulation that land under HGU title would fall to the state after the expiry of the concessions was maintained. Many companies fell into the hands of high-ranking military officers and persons from among a small circle of Suharto's allies. His authoritarian regime created a dreaded system of control – supported by the armed forces, semi-military groups and thugs – to deter serious criticism. Critics risked being accused of communist inclinations and imprisonment. Nonetheless, the policies met with increasing resistance. An idiom drawing on class differences, common under Sukarno's previous regime, was unacceptable under the New Order of Suharto. So was the idiom of decolonisation, for Suharto feared that this would bring to the fore the atrocities committed by the Indonesian army towards communists during the War of Independence.[26] The legal idioms used from the early 1980s onwards derived from international human rights and the environmental protection laws of the early 1990s.[27] Though *adat* was primarily associated with backwardness and feudalism, and *adat* rights to village land had lost traction for most Indonesians, non-governmental organisations (NGOs) discovered a connection of *adat* rights with international human rights. They began to use this idiom to mobilise against dispossession and displacement.

[23] Snyder (n 4); K von Benda-Beckmann and B Turner, 'Anthropological Roots of Global Legal Pluralism' in P Schiff Berman (ed), *Oxford Handbook on Global Legal Pluralism* (Oxford, Oxford University Press, 2020); L Salaymeh and R Michaels, 'Decolonizing Comparative Law: A Conceptual Beginning' (2022) 86(1) *Rabel Journal of Comparative and International Private Law* 166, 178, https://papers.ssrn.com/sol3/papers.cfm?abstract_id=4014459.

[24] Y Arizona, 'Rethinking *Adat* Strategies: The Politics of State Recognition of Customary Land Rights in Indonesia' (PhD thesis, Leiden University, 2022) 88. See also A Lucas and C Warren, 'The Land, the Law, and the People' in A Lucas and C Warren (eds), *Land for the People: The State and Agrarian Conflict in Indonesia* (Athens, OH, Ohio University Press, 2013). This is exactly the opposite of 'destabilising the authority of the coloniser's law so that we are able to analyse the relationship between power, knowledge and the construction of "truth" in legal discourses' that is called for to decolonise Australian justice. See I Nursoo, 'Indigenous Law, Colonial Injustice and the Jurisprudence of Hybridity' (2018) 50(1) *Journal of Legal Pluralism and Unofficial Law* 56, 62 https://www.tandfonline.com/doi/abs/10.1080/07329113.2018.1433118?journalCode=rjlp20.

[25] T Murray Li, 'Intergenerational Displacement in Indonesia's Oil Palm Plantation Zone' (2017) 44(6) *Journal of Peasant Studies* 1158, https://www.tandfonline.com/doi/abs/10.1080/03066150.2017.1308353.

[26] For more on the civil war during Indonesian's War of Independence, see HA Poeze and H Schulte Nordholt, *Merdeka: De Strijd om de Indonesische Onafhankelijkheid en de Ongewisse Opkomst van de Republiek 1945–1950* (Zutphen, Walburg Pers, 2022).

[27] Bedner and Arizona (n 21) 421.

V. International Human Rights, Environmental Protection and *Adat*

When Suharto was forced to step down, the country embarked on large-scale constitutional reforms that would be known as *Reformasi*. As Wiratraman and Shah argue, this had to be understood in the context of 'the country's experiences with authoritarianism and the move toward democratization and decentralization',[28] and to that extent, it did not address decolonisation. Coming to terms with Suharto's legacy therefore partially eclipsed the ongoing decolonisation process. The problem of land dispossession from the colonial era was exacerbated by large-scale expropriations under the Suharto regime. Throughout Indonesia, resistance surfaced in diverse political constellations, whereby the legal idioms mobilised to regain control over dispossessed land were not uniform. Legislation had not resulted in solace. The decentralisation laws and forestry laws provided for the recognition of *adat* rights, but were not devoid of the same restrictions as before, and the Constitutional Court established in 2003 upheld these restrictions.[29] Besides, despite decentralisation, the state retained control over forests. Issuing concessions was now a complex decision-making process involving the national state, provinces, and districts, and led to much conflict.[30] In this struggle, *adat* would figure large in all cases, but in different connotations and in combination with a diverse set of legal idioms.

A. International Human Rights, Indigeneity, Environmental Protection and *Adat*

From the mid-1980s onwards, national and international development projects, as well as the state and plantation concession holders, were criticised for violating human rights under international human rights law. The main issues were land dispossession, workers' rights, and discrimination against women and the urban poor.[31] In the 1990s, when calls for the protection of Indigenous peoples in the former settler colonies gained international prominence – forcing the United Nations (UN) to deal seriously with these issues, Indonesian NGOs saw an opportunity to use the legal idiom of human rights to put dispossession on the Indonesian agenda. These NGOs worked primarily in Kalimantan and Sulawesi – regions with former sultanates, histories of voluntary and forced migration, and

[28] Wiratraman and Shah (n 19) 118.
[29] Arizona (n 24) 94–108.
[30] Arizona (n 24).
[31] Bedner and Arizona (n 21) 421. See also T Murray Li, '*Adat* in Central Sulawesi: Contemporary Deployments' in JS Davidson and D Henley (eds), *The Revival of Tradition in Indonesian Politics. The Deployment of Adat from Colonialism to Indigenism* (New York, Routledge, 2007).

resulting mixed populations – where the forest was being used in various ways and on the basis of a range of local land titles.

In this international discourse, indigeneity became associated with a second powerful discourse – namely, that of environmental protection. Indigenous groups were said to have an age-old tradition of protecting their environment due to their traditional, isolated way of life and mode of production, and to have practised their customary law since time immemorial. In this discourse, Indigenous became synonymous with the premodern, isolated forest dwellers who protected their environment, notwithstanding histories of their involvement in long-distance trade – long before colonisation and the notion of *adat* as being affixed to an unknown, idealised past.[32] If the aim of the Suharto administration's response was to support these 'isolated communities', educate them and guide them towards 'modern life', it also continued expanding the plantation economy deep into the forests and life-world of Indigenous people.

A series of land occupations that occurred during the Suharto regime on the basis of Indigenous and environmentalist arguments, some of which were successful, led to disputes with concession holders, who rejected the rights of such occupants. Indigenous organisations, together with a variety of environmental and human rights NGOs, offered support in these disputes. They acted as mediators between local groups, state agencies and companies. They used participatory mapping techniques with the use of geographic information system (GIS) technology to measure land. By 'stealing the master's tools',[33] they could provide evidence for traditional land use and encroachment on their *adat* land – evidence that would be acceptable to the state administration and courts.[34] They used an *adat* framework in combination with the materiality of modern techniques to accommodate their land claims within the state legal system. However, this process of 'translation' happened at the expense of the original meaning of land and land titles, and of the community that held titles.[35]

Among the prominent NGOs was, Aliansi Masyarakat Adat Nusantara (AMAN: Alliance of *Adat* Communities of the Archipelago). This Indonesia-wide

[32] T Murray Li, 'Masyarakat Adat, Difference, and the Limits of Recognition in Indonesia's Forest Zone' (2001) 35(3) *Modern Asian Studies* 645, https://www.jstor.org/stable/313184; Li (n 31); B Hauser-Schäublin, *Adat and Indigeneity in Indonesia: Culture and Entitlements between Heteronomy and Self-Ascription* (Göttingen, Göttingen University, 2013); AL Tsing, 'Becoming a Tribal Elder, and Other Green Development Fantasies' in T Murray Li (ed), *Transforming the Indonesian Uplands: Marginality, Power and Production* (Amsterdam, Harwood Academic Publishers, 1999).

[33] A Lowenhaupt Tsing, PJ Brosius and C Zerner, 'Introduction: Raising Questions about Community Conservation' in PJ Brosius, A Lowenhaupt Tsing and C Zerner (eds), *Communities and Conservation: Histories and Politics of Community-Based Naturlas Resource Management* (Lanham, MD, Rowman Altamira, 2005), as cited in MH Sanmukri, 'Mobilities of Indigeneity: Intermediary NGOs and Indigenous Peoples in Indonesia' in Hauser-Schäublin (n 32) 123.

[34] Sanmukri (n 33) 124.

[35] For the concept of translation, see A Behrends, S-J Park and R Rottenburg, 'Travelling Models: Introducing an Analytical Concept to Globalisation Studies' in A Behrends, S-J Park and R Rottenburg (eds), *Travelling Models in African Conflict Management Translating Technologies of Social Ordering* (Leiden, Brill, 2014).

organisation was founded in 1999, the year following the end of the Suharto regime, by activists who had supported land claims in Kalimantan and Sulawesi. AMAN became a powerful ally for locally based organisations in the movement of land claims. They combined the legal idiom of indigeneity with *adat* to identify local groups as tribes, or Indigenous people, using the term *masyarakat adat* – Originally coined by van Vollenhoven, the term is translated in this context to connote 'Indigenous' as defined in the UN Declaration.

B. *Adat*, Ethnicity and Social Stratification

Claims for recognition of *adat* also had some very problematic aspects. *Adat* has been mobilised to strengthen or even create ethnic identities and boundaries – often by groups that had not defined themselves as an ethnic group in the past. This occurred especially in regions with a highly mixed population of groups that had entered the region at different times in the past. Here, the register of *adat* not only served to reclaim land from companies, but also as an argument to exclude 'newcomers' from 'their' territories. These newcomers were poor peasants from different backgrounds who had migrated at some stage in the past. Some had arrived in the context of transmigration programmes, by which the government relocated poor people from densely populated to sparsely populated areas.[36] Others had come on their own. Usually they were leading an equally precarious life as those claiming indigeneity. In parts of Kalimantan and Sulawesi, this had at times led to violent fights and killings.[37]

In regions with an aristocratic past, heirs of former rulers tried to re-establish the old sultanates and principalities. By mobilising *adat*, descendants of rulers saw an opportunity to acquire control over expropriated land. The argument of royal control could even be used against the existence of *adat*, in the sense of local customary law. The control they were seeking would therefore be much more

[36] Li (n 25) 1164; JF McCarthy, 'Tenure and Transformation in Central Kalimantan: After the "Million Hectare" Project' in Lucas and Warren (n 24). See also Tsing (n 32) 196, who argued in this context that the concept 'tribe', which had been banned as a descriptive term in scholarly discourses, has been rehabilitated in a political context, where it forms the basis of fantasies for those who find themselves caught in particular political dilemmas. She urged analysts to take these processes seriously in order to understand how the complex situation in South Kalimantan (and elsewhere) became codified and simplified.

[37] JS Davidson, *From Rebellion to Riots: Collective Violence on Indonesian Borneo* (Madison, University of Wisconsin Press, 2008); NL Peluso, 'Rubber Erasures, Rubber Producing Rights: Making Racialized Territories in West Kalimantan, Indonesia' (2009) 40(1) *Development and Change* 47, https://onlinelibrary.wiley.com/toc/14677660/2009/40/1; JF McCarthy, 'Processes of Inclusion and Adverse Incorporation: Oil Palm and Agrarian Change in Sumatra, Indonesia' (2010) 37(4) *Journal of Peasant Studies* 821, https://www.tandfonline.com/doi/abs/10.1080/03066150.2010.512460?journalCode=fjps20; Li (n 25); WE van der Muur, 'Land Rights and the Forces of *Adat* in Democratiying Indonesia: Continuous Conflict between Plantations, Farmers and Forests in South Sulawesi' (PhD thesis, Leiden University 2019).

comprehensive than in the past and would be at the expense of the local population that were also trying to regain their rights to the land.[38] Apart from the claims of old ruling families, village elites could deploy the idiom of *adat* to monopolise fallow or swidden land.[39] The 'return of the sultans' met with much opposition from local peasants, forest dwellers and citizens trying to re-establish democracy alike. They had no wish to return to the rule of despotic aristocrats.[40]

C. Indigenous But No *Adat*

Some regions do not have a long history of settlement and have no recourse to the legal idiom of *adat*. For example, in a region of West Kalimantan that borders Malaysia, people only shifted in the early twentieth century from fishing and maritime trade to rice and rubber cultivation. They now have to defend their land claims against large rubber companies that expand their plantations to what the companies deem to be waste, empty land. In addition, the concessions often overlap with local land uses, and many plantations illegally exceed the territory of their concession.[41] The increased pressure on land due to expanding plantations forces the local population to secure land titles in ways that offer tangible material evidence of their land use in the form of documents and maps. Some have registered their land as private ownership. Those who have no formal title use a variety of modern tools to secure their rights to land. Territorialisation, counter-mapping (counter to the companies) with the use of GIS technologies and homemade drones, and spatial village-level planning and participatory techniques are being used to express claims, garner public support and negotiate with state agencies that regard the land as state land, and rubber companies that encroach upon their land. In this situation, local people define themselves as 'Indigenous', in the sense of being prior settlers of different backgrounds and ethnicities who have the right to exclude others from what they consider to be their land. But they certainly do not regard themselves as premodern and backward, as implied by the provisions of international law on Indigenous peoples. They claim rights to the land they use and have local ways of dealing with such claims, based on 'a combination of Islamic law, state law, and customs that have been developed and maintained

[38] L Bakker, 'The Sultan's Map: Arguing One's Land in Pasir' in F von Benda-Beckmann, K von Benda-Beckmann and A Griffiths (eds), *Spatializing Law: An Anthropological Geography of Law in Society* (Farnham, Ashgate 2009); Arizona (n 24) 113.

[39] Li (n 31) 338–42; McCarthy (n 36).

[40] G van Klinken, 'Return of the Sultans: The Communitarian Turn in Local Politics' in Davidson and Henley (n 31).

[41] R de Vos, 'Counter-mapping against Oil Palm Plantations: Reclaiming Village Territory in Indonesia with the 2014 Village Law' (2018) 50(4) *Critical Asian Studies* 615, https://www.tandfonline.com/doi/full/10.1080/14672715.2018.1522595; R de Vos, 'Oil Palms in the Rice Field: An Ethnography of Large-Scale Land Acquisition for Oil Palm Plantation Development in West Kalimantan' (PhD thesis, Wageningen University, 2019).

through generations', but which they do not understand as *adat*.[42] They do not define themselves as an *adat* community because they cannot claim long-term precolonial occupation, as the settlement goes back only a few generations.

D. *Adat* But Not Indigenous

In the Province of West Sumatra, *adat* also became a powerful idiom for claiming rights to land, and here, too, *adat* was not associated with the connotation of indigeneity of international law.[43] This region has a comparatively homogeneous population of ethnic Minangkabau, who are well known for being devout Muslims and for their elaborate principles of matrilineal kinship and property. Before colonisation, the central region was settled in relatively autonomous village polities called *nagari*, with a low degree of hierarchy that had loose connections with the main kingdom. When the colonial administration introduced its land registration system, most people in rural areas refused to register common property because it did not pay sufficient attention to the internal structure of common property. Women were particularly opposed to registration due to fears that they would lose their rights to their family land.

In contrast to other regions where land claims against plantation companies have dominated since the reforms of 1999, the main issues in West Sumatra concerned the reorganisation of village government and control over the exploitation of village territory, epitomised as the 'return to the *nagari*' (the village structure that went back to precolonial times). There was a general consensus among the population of West Sumatra that the village structure should be based on *adat*. However, there was disagreement about the way in which *adat* should govern village government. Some wanted to re-establish the position of lineage leaders and referred back to the 1970s, or even to an unspecified precolonial era, when *adat* was still in force. Among the highly educated, transmigrant communities, and descendants of slaves, many supported the use of *adat* only for regaining control over village territory and favoured a democratically elected village government. The combinations of principles that villages opted for varied widely. However, on one point there was no disagreement: being highly educated and well integrated into the global economy, the Minangkabau were adamant not to identify as Indigenous, which they associated with backwardness. The related environmental legal idiom also had little traction in this region.

The discussions about the role of *adat* were also relevant for land claims against the government (which had declared village and lineage forest as state

[42] De Vos, 'Oil Palms in the Rice Field' (n 41) 150.

[43] See F von Benda-Beckmann and K von Benda-Beckmann, *Political and Legal Transformations of an Indonesian Polity: The Nagari from Colonisation to Decentralisation* (Cambridge, Cambridge University Press, 2013).

forest) and against plantation owners. Oil palm plantations, which had been established in the coastal areas during colonial times, underwent a major expansion that began under Suharto and became dominant in the far south and in coastal areas of the province. In contrast to other regions in Indonesia, it was officially understood that *adat* land titles of villages and kin groups were to be recognised, albeit according to the state's interpretation and not local interpretations. Most plantations had negotiated the transfer of customary land with representatives of villages and kin groups. However, corruption – among state officials, local politicians, traditional rulers and heads of lineages – had rendered the land titles and the territory of plantations, villages and lineages unclear. The ensuing conflicts between local populations and plantation owners and among lineage heads, kin groups and local governments were carried out in terms of Minangkabau *adat* law. However, courts and officials held on to the state interpretation of *adat* law. Besides, in order to provide evidence that would be acceptable in court and in official negotiations, they had to rely on measuring techniques and documents such as contracts and land registration. The very procedures by which they might regain their land rights rendered these land rights simplified.[44]

VI. Conclusion

For an answer to the puzzling question as to why the decolonisation of law in Indonesia disappeared from public debate relatively soon after independence and has not resurfaced as it has in other former colonies, we have identified two main factors. Because the Dutch language had fallen into disuse, the Indonesian legal system, although based on Dutch colonial law, lost its connection with Dutch legal developments. New legislation based on other legal traditions, combined with the lack of coherence within the judicial system and poor legal training, accelerated this disconnection, thereby decolonising the law without much reflection. Second, the repressive Suharto regime suppressed debates about decolonisation. With *Reformasi*, public debate turned to the legacies of the Suharto regime.

One precursor of the decolonisation of law – Cornelis van Vollenhoven – has had a lasting influence because of his conceptual framework of *adat* designed to capture the specificities of Indonesian Indigenous legal orders. It found its way into the Constitution and the agrarian and forestry legislation, and has also recently been used for land claims. A range of NGOs have translated *adat* and *adat* law community as Indigenous law and Indigenous people, referring to the idiom of the international law of Indigenous peoples. In this legal idiom, *adat* also became associated with the legal idiom of environmental protection, one of the few issues on which the Suharto regime allowed some discussion. While this gained traction

[44] Afrizal, 'Oil Palm Plantations, Customary Rights, and Local Protests: A West Sumatran Case Study' in Lucas and Warren (n 24).

in the major plantation regions of Kalimantan and Sulawesi in West Sumatra, the focus remained on the concept of *adat* that was not connected with the Indigenous legal idiom. There was no need there to demonstrate that they had a specific legal order. And in some parts of Indonesia, communities without a precolonial history claimed indigeneity – albeit not in the sense of forest dwellers – and did not consider the legal idiom of *adat* to be appropriate for their situation. *Adat* proved to be most conducive for land claims in regions with a relatively homogeneous population and low levels of hierarchy. Where hierarchical structures are pronounced and under conditions of a mixed population, reliance on *adat* has problematic effects, leading to exclusion and violence. This is especially the case in regions with a powerful plantation industry and a population that depends on the forest.

The high hopes placed on *adat* have disappeared and have given way to the sobering insight that the problems of land dispossession and displacement founded in colonial law have not yet been solved. Indeed, the devastating effects of the combination of colonialism, capitalism and modernity have continued since independence, especially under Suharto's New Order. Corruption and collusion, extreme power differences, weak land titles, registration, and the materiality of providing evidence for land titles and to demonstrate illegal expansion of territories under concession of plantations have been formidable obstacles. And, where successful, land claims have led to very restricted titles that do not do justice to the meaning people actually attach to their land. The system of land registration has forced local communities to use modern techniques to prove their rights and to register land titles that do not do justice to the way in which they understand their relationships to land and the forest. Under these circumstances, the very concepts that van Vollenhoven designed to demonstrate flexibility and diversity now appear as fixed, undifferentiated and homogeneous *adat* titles within the state legal system.

Many now call for a reform of the recognition procedures in place, mainly to make them shorter, cheaper and less complex. They also call for more flexible plantation and forestry schemes to allow co-management.[45] Today, there is some debate on whether an idiom of democracy and justice might not be a sounder basis for just land titles. From this perspective, not only *adat* titles but also a range of other use rights that cannot be labelled *adat* would be eligible for registration.[46] This might solve the problems of exclusion and inter-ethnic violence, but it is doubtful whether it will stop state- and company-induced forms of dispossession and displacement.

[45] Arizona (n 24) 220.

[46] Bedner and Arizona (n 21) 429.

11

The Incorporation of the Principle of Sustainable Development into Chinese Environmental Law

YING SONG

I. Introduction

The principle of sustainable development is an important concept or principle in environmental law. It is important because human society would accomplish the ideal relationship between human development and the environment when it is fully translated into practice and reality. It is a concept or principle because the legal status of sustainable development is still in debate at both the international and domestic levels. In spite of this, it attracts the author's interest because it is like a piece of sponge – it looks simple, flexible and limited on the outside, but is capable of absorbing and retaining much water inside. From the political and legal perspectives, it is one of the most iconic concepts[1] or principle in the history of environmental policies and laws. It has had a substantial influence on the making and changing of environment development policies and laws in many countries. China incorporated this principle into its domestic environmental policies and laws in the mid-1990s. From the perspective of transnational law, the introduction and evolution of sustainable development in China provides an appropriate case to study, following the scholarship of Francis Snyder on the legal pluralism and sites of governance, especially in relation to the domestic legal regulation of food safety, which shares certain similarities with environmental regulation in China.[2] This chapter aims to explore the following issues: the concept and evolution of the

[1] V Heyvaert, *Transnational Environmental Regulation and Governance: Purpose, Strategies and Principles* (Cambridge, Cambridge University Press, 2019) 247.

[2] F Snyder, *Food Safety Law in China: Making Transnational Law* (Leiden/Boston, Brill, 2015); F Snyder, 'Understanding the Regulation of Ecological Food in China: Regulatory Intermediation, Path Dependence and Legal Pluralism' in BC Goh and R Price (eds), *Regulatory Issues in Organic Food Safety in the Asia Pacific* (Singapore, Springer, 2020).

sustainable development principle, when, how and why the principle is incorporated into Chinese environmental policy and law, and how it is interpreted and applied in practice. Such an investigation will hopefully reflect certain features of the evolution of Chinese environmental law and, more generally, of the rise and development of China.

II. The Concept and Evolution of Sustainable Development

The history of exploiting and conserving natural living resources goes as far back as the history of humankind, because the sustainability of natural living resources provides food, medicine, clothing and shelter for the survival and development of humans. In the ancient law of Qin Dynasty (221–206 BCE, *Tian Lű*) of China, it was expressly prohibited to cut down trees and hunt animals in the early springtime, because this was the time for their reproduction for sustainable use. Similarly, at the domestic level, there exists a long history of various policy and legal measures for the conservation of natural resources. However, at the international level, the collective legal protection and conservation came much later. The case of the *Bering Fur Seal Arbitration* (1892) was one of the early well-known cases that concerned the conservation of the fur seal in the high seas beyond the national jurisdiction, although the motivation behind the conservation claims at that time was considered to be mainly to protect the economic interests of the US.[3] Apart from this arbitration, there were also a number of bilateral and regional treaties or arrangements on conservation measures. The creation of the United Nations (UN) opened up a new avenue of collective efforts for the environment at the international level. The 1972 Declaration of the United Nations Conference on the Human Environment (hereinafter the 'Stockholm Declaration') was adopted at the first UN conference (the 1972 Stockholm Conference) on the environment. Apart from the focus on pollution control, it called for conservation of natural resources for sustainable use. For example, Principle 2 states that the natural resources of the earth – including the air, water, land, flora and fauna, and especially representative samples of natural ecosystems – must be safeguarded for the benefit of present and future generations through careful planning or management, as appropriate. Principles 3–5 go on to call upon states and people to protect and appropriately manage renewable and non-renewable resources, wildlife and its habitats, and the natural ecosystems. Principle 14 expressly endorses this rational planning as an essential tool for reconciling the conflict between the needs of development and the needs to protect and improve the environment. Although the Stockholm Declaration did not expressly proclaim the principle of sustainable development,

[3] N Schrijver, *The Evolution of Sustainable Development in International Law: Inception, Meaning and Status* (Leiden, Martinus Nijhoff Publishers, 2008) 33.

relevant elements were already inserted into these principles and paved the way towards the sustainable development principle.

The 1980s witnessed the process of decolonisation, and urgent needs for economic independence and development by the newly independent states. The tension between the environment and development became more acute, and was pushed high on the agenda of the UN. The notion was that a new and practical development model has to be formulated and recommended to the newly independent members of the UN to adopt. This was because of the assumption that if the developing states imitated the conventional model of the developed states – particularly the model of high dependence and consumption energy generated by non-renewable resources – then the natural resources on the earth would not be able sustain these developing states long enough to reach the same level of improved living standards of the developed states. In December 1983, the UN General Assembly appointed the World Commission on the Environment and Development, later known as the Brundtland Commission, to propose new long-term strategies to achieve sustainable development by 2000 and thereafter. The Brundtland Commission published the report *Our Common Future* in 1987.

The report touched upon a wide range of issues: from population and human resources to food security, species and ecosystems, from energy to industry, from managing the commons to proposals for institutional and legal change etc. It analysed the common concerns, common challenges and common endeavours, and proposed 22 legal principles for environmental protection and sustainable development, which laid down the theoretical and practical foundation for the 1992 Rio Declaration on the Environment and Development (Rio Declaration) and Agenda 21. In the report, sustainable development was defined as 'development that meets the needs of the present without compromising the ability of future generations to meet their own needs'. It called for concerted efforts towards building an inclusive, sustainable and resilient future for people and the planet. In order to achieve sustainable development, it was crucial to harmonise three inter-related core goals: economic growth, social inclusion and environmental protection.[4]

The report emphasised the limits of environment on human development needs. On the one hand, sustainable development requires meeting the basic needs of all and extending to all the opportunity to satisfy their aspirations for a better life. On the other hand, living standards that go beyond the basic minimum are sustainable only if consumption standards everywhere have regard for long-term sustainability. It was a moderate limit. Our perceived needs are socially

[4] The above definition and elements remain unchanged even today. See UN Environment Programme (UNEP), 'Frequent Asked Questions – What is Sustainable Development?', www.unep.org/explore-topics/sustainable-development-goals/why-do-sustainable-development-goals-matter/frequently.

and culturally determined, and sustainable development requires the promotion of values that encourage consumption standards that are within the bounds of the ecological possibility, and to which all can reasonably aspire. Therefore, sustainable development is a process of change in which the exploitation of resources, the direction of investments, and the orientation of technological development and institutional change are all in harmony, and enhance both current and future potential to meet human needs and aspirations. The need for the integration of economic development, the management and protection of natural resources, and social equity and inclusion was introduced for the first time by the report, and was central in framing the discussions at the 1992 UN Conference on Environment and Development (UNCED or the 'Rio Conference'), also known as the Earth Summit.

The 1992 Rio Conference, in comparison with the 1972 Stockholm Conference, put more emphasis on economic and social development at the request of developing states. The Rio Declaration endorsed 27 principles, some of which include recognising both the right to a healthy and productive environment, and the right to development for the present and future generations of humankind (Principles 1 and 3), and sovereignty over natural resources (Principle 2). The Declaration further stated that in order to achieve sustainable development, environmental protection will constitute an integral part of the development process and cannot be considered in isolation from it (Principle 4). This principle echoed the position of many developing states, including China: that environmental pollution was an inevitable problem in the process of development and could only be solved in the process of development. As Indira Gandhi said at the Stockholm Conference, the environment could not be improved in conditions of poverty.[5] Several Rio principles, including that on sustainable development, were incorporated into the UN Framework Convention on Climate Change (UNFCCC), the Convention on Biological Diversity (CBD) and Agenda 21, which was a comprehensive international programme of actions for the twenty-first century. These three documents were all adopted at the Rio Conference. The principles and treaty provisions clearly grew from the roots planted in the Brundtland Report. In 1993 the UN General Assembly established the Commission on Sustainable Development (CSD) as the UN high-level political body entrusted with the monitoring and promotion of the implementation of the Rio outcomes, including Agenda 21.

The 2000 Millennium Development Goals (MDGs) adopted at the UN Millennium Meeting of the General Assembly declared several development objectives for the new century. Once again, it put the emphasis on development and eradication of poverty, with eight goals for the following 15 years. It was considered a global project for poverty eradication, but it lacked sufficient

[5] JE Viñuales, 'Sustainable Development' in L Rajamani and J Peel (eds), *The Oxford Handbook of International Environmental Law*, 2nd edn (Oxford, Oxford University Press, 2021) 286.

practical mechanisms for implementation. The 2002 Johannesburg Declaration on Sustainable Development put sustainable development back on the agenda. The participating states committed to act together – united by a common determination to save the planet, promote human development and achieve universal prosperity and peace – to expedite the achievement of the time-bound socio-economic and environmental targets.[6]

In 2012 at the Rio+20 Conference, the international community decided to establish a High-Level Political Forum on Sustainable Development, to replace the UN Commission on Sustainable Development, which had previously been the main body taking care of sustainable development within the UN framework. At the Rio+20 Conference, the UN Member States decided to launch a new process to develop a set of Sustainable Development Goals (SDGs), which were to build upon the MDGs and converge with the post-2015 development agenda. Unlike the MDGs and the Johannesburg Declaration, the UN 2030 Agenda for Sustainable Development (2015, hereinafter the '2030 SDGs Agenda') substantially broadened the scope of sustainable development, and engaged both developing states and developed states. It proclaimed 17 SDGs with 169 associated targets. This agenda provided more explicit and concrete goals and targets. The 17 goals cover a wide range of areas, from ending poverty to achieving gender equality, and promoting sustained, inclusive and sustainable economic growth. The SDGs provided more practical provisions and means for financial resources, capacity building, technological transfer and innovation, and also a framework for evaluation and review. Monitoring here is the key basis for effective implementation. Progress has been made in terms of the availability of internationally comparable data for monitoring of SDGs: the number of indicators included in the global SDGs database increased from 115 in 2016 to 217 in 2022.[7] As of August 2022, 187 UN Member States had already submitted 292 Voluntary National Reviews (VNRs) since the reporting began in 2016, as mandated by the General Assembly and the 2030 SDGs Agenda (Resolutions 67/290 and 70/1). China submitted two VNRs in 2016 and 2021, respectively.[8]

From the 1987 *Our Common Future* report to the 2030 SDGs Agenda, the concept, elements and scope of sustainable development have been growing and expanding. In the 30 years after the 1992 Rio Conference, many global and regional intergovernmental organisations, states, non-governmental organisations etc have contributed to the evolution of sustainable development through their political, legal, judicial and academic activities. For the purposes of discussing the main theme of this chapter, the above description only serves as a brief note on the UN political and legal documents.

[6] U Beyerlin and M Reichard, 'The Johannesburg Summit: Outcome and Overall Assessment' (2002) 63(2) *Heidelberg Journal of International Law* 213, www.zaoerv.de/63_2003/63_2003_2_a_213_238.pdf.

[7] UN, *The Sustainable Development Goals Report* 2022, 4, https://unstats.un.org/sdgs/report/2022.

[8] UN, 'Voluntary National Reviews', hlpf.un.org/vnrs.

From the historical perspective, first, when the term of sustainability appeared in early international documents before the 1987 Brundtland Report, it mainly referred to the sustainable use of living natural resources, especially marine living resources,[9] and the scope was later extended to cover non-living resources. At present, the term of sustainability is used almost everywhere to cover the aspect of peace, anti-corruption, human rights etc. Second, the three core goals of sustainable development, as it was then systematically defined in the 1987 Brundtland Report, included economic growth, social inclusion and environmental protection. However, the 2030 SDGs Agenda expanded the elements to cover most of the development goals and targets. The 17 goals with 169 targets cover almost all realms – economic, social, political, environmental, educational, cultural, health, technology development etc. They encompass all the present economic, social, environmental, political and cultural strategies and goals of the state and the international community. These goals and targets are designed to influence and guide states in terms of adopting their national sustainable development objectives, strategies, policies, plans and laws in consonance with global sustainable development agendas. Thus, at present, the sponge of sustainable development is still absorbing more water and is still in flexible shape. The COVID-19 pandemic and the global responses to it provide a good opportunity to observe how the SDGs deal with emerging new challenges to SD by assisting in the channelling of resources to fight the pandemic.

In spite of the flexible concept and expanding scope of sustainable development, its key elements include the following: (1) the need to preserve natural resources and a healthy environmental status for the benefit of future generations (intergenerational equity); (2) the need for a state to also take into consideration the needs of other states while using natural resources (intragenerational equity); (3) the aim of exploiting natural resources in a manner which is sustainable, prudent, rational and appropriate (sustainable use); and (4) the need to integrate environmental considerations into economic and social development strategies, plans, programmes and projects (the principle of integration). These four key elements are closely related and often used in combination, though different authors presented them in different ways.[10]

Among the different interpretations of the ethical and economic foundations of sustainability, two versions are noteworthy; the weak version (weak sustainability) and the strong version (strong sustainability). The differences between them, from the economic perspective, derives from contrasting assumptions about the substitutability of natural capital (resources). According to weak

[9] P Sands et al, *Principles of International Environmental Law*, 4th edn (Cambridge, Cambridge University Press, 2018) 222.

[10] Sands et al (n 9) 219; U Beyerlin, 'Sustainable Development' (2013) *Max Planck Encyclopaedia of Public International Law*, opil.ouplaw.com/view/10.1093/law:epil/9780199231690/law-9780199231690-e1609?rskey=gLrc1V&result=1&prd=MPIL; Viñuales (n 5) 286–88; E Holden et al, *The Imperatives of Sustainable Development: Needs, Justice and Limits* (Abingdon, Routledge, 2018) 11–20.

sustainability, natural capital is abundant and substitutable, but strong sustainability regards natural capital as fundamentally non-substitutable through other forms of capital.[11] The legal implication of such differences may be reflected in the extent of limits on human activities. Principle 1 of the Rio Declaration states that human beings are at the centre of sustainable development. They are entitled to a healthy and productive life in harmony with nature. This is obviously an anthropocentric version, so the limits on human activities are comparatively weak. The strong version puts more emphasis on the ecologically sustainable development, in which justice extends to the entire global community and future generations. It is ecocentrism and places stronger limits on human activities, and hence is called strong sustainability.[12] For example, in comparison to the 1992 UNFCCC, the 2015 Paris Agreement (Article 2) puts explicit and stronger limits on the increase in the global average temperature to below 2°C above pre-industrial levels and pursuing efforts to limit the temperature increase to 1.5°C above pre-industrial levels, recognising that this would significantly reduce the risks and impacts of climate change. Therefore, the Paris Agreement comparatively adopts the strong version with a clear target to achieve and a series of measures to take. The differences between the two versions also exist at the domestic level. A country like China, as indicated in the following section, adopted the weak version at first and then, as time passed and following economic and social development, it switched to the strong version in some areas.

III. The Incorporation of the Sustainable Development in China

A. The Introduction of Sustainable Development in China

The concept of SD was introduced in China after the 1992 Rio Conference. In March 1994, the State Council approved and published the China Agenda 21 – the White Paper on the Population, Environment and Development of China in the Twenty-First Century – after two years' preparation by a team of over 300 government officials, consultants and academics, with technical assistance from the United Nations Development Programme (UNDP). Almost all the relevant government ministries, agencies and institutions participated in the work. It was one of the earliest national Agenda 21s published by any UN Member State. It established the strategic framework and main targets in the relevant policy areas

[11] E Neumayer, *Weak versus Strong Sustainability: Exploring the Limits of Two Opposing Paradigms*, 4th edn (Cheltenham, Edward Elgar, 2013); J Pelenc, 'Weak Sustainability versus Strong Sustainability' (2015), sustainabledevelopment.un.org/content/documents/6569122-Pelenc-Weak%20Sustainability%20versus%20Strong%20Sustainability.pdf.

[12] Beyerlin (n 10).

for achieving sustainable development in China. In this document, four objectives for achieving sustainable development were proposed for the period up to 2000: first, whilst maintaining rapid economic growth, to improve the quality of development by improving the scientific and technological progress and the quality of the working force; second, to improve comprehensive social progress which would lay down the social foundations for sustainable development; third, to prevent and control environmental pollution and to improve the ecological environment, which would lay down the material foundations for sustainable development; and, fourth, to gradually establish the policy and legal system for sustainable development, which would lay down the decision-making and coordination framework and mechanism for sustainable development. These four objectives clearly incorporated the core elements of sustainable development into the document.

In September 1995, the Fifth Session of the Fourteenth Party Assembly of the Chinese Communist Party (CCP) adopted the recommendations for drafting the Ninth Five-Year Plan (FYP) of National Economic and Social Development. This document stated that comprehensive social development must occupy an important strategic position, and that coordination between economy, society and sustainable development must be achieved. This is the first time that sustainable development appeared in the document of the party's session. In 1996, the premier's annual report (by Peng Li) to the annual Plenary Session of the National People's Congress (NPC) made sustainable development a national development strategy. This is the first time that sustainable development appeared in the premier's annual report.[13] The appearance and frequency of a term in the important party and government documents, like the above two documents, has important political implications in the Chinese context. This also marked the beginning of sustainable development as a national development strategy[14] established in China. The 1996 premier's report announced two national development strategies: the first was the education, scientific and technological development strategy, while the second was the sustainable development strategy. In order to achieve economic and social progress in the subsequent 15 years, the report stated that it was important to speed up the progress of education, scientific and technological development: to adopt family planning, to rationally exploit natural resources, to protect the environment, and to achieve coordinated and sustainable economic and social development. One year later in 1997, the Report of the Fifteenth Party Assembly

[13] 1996 premier's report (by LI Peng), www.gov.cn/test/2006-02/16/content_201115.htm. Following the author's research, the term 'sustainable development strategy' continuously appeared in the premier's annual reports from 1996 until 2011. However, from 2012 to 2015, the term disappeared from the reports; instead, the terms 'scientific development' (*kexu fazhanguan*), 'continuous and healthy economic development' and 'harmonious social stability' (*shehui hexie wending*) were used in these reports. After the UN 2030 SDGs Agenda, the term 'sustainable development strategy' appeared again in the 2016, 2017, 2021 and 2022 premier's annual reports.

[14] The sustainable development strategy still stood as a national development strategy in the 2021 premier's annual report (by LI Keqiang), www.gov.cn/premier/2021-03/05/content_5590519.htm#7.

of the CCP once again endorsed these two strategies. This marked the first time that sustainable development was endorsed by the CCP's assembly document.[15]

This is when and how sustainable development was introduced into China and established as a national development strategy in the political realm. The sequence and interaction among the above four documents needs more exploration. The first document is the China Agenda 21. The second and the fourth are party documents of the CCP, but the difference is that the second document is a session document, while the fourth is an assembly document which is an important political document on the national policies and government administration for a five-year period. The third document is the premier's annual report, which is a comprehensive administrative document of the year, informing the public what the government has done in the previous year and what it is going to do next year. By being integrated into the premier's annual report, sustainable development took root in government policies and strategies, and obtained resources for its implementation in practical terms.

The interaction between the party's document, the government policy and the law is an important factor in understanding the policies and laws of China. First, the party document adopted at the assembly reflects the party's internal consensus, which provides the prime political guidance and guarantee for the government policies, strategies and laws in China. This is another good example that confirms the observation by Francis Snyder on the predominant role of the party's political line, norms and policies in China.[16] Second – particularly in the environmental field – there is a close interaction between the party's consensus, the government policies and laws. By reviewing the party's documents and the premier's annual report, it becomes easier to understand the reasons behind the making, amending, revising or even abolishing of environmental policies, strategies and laws. It reflects the shift in major concerns in environmental strategies, policies and laws by both the party and the government. Since the Eighteenth Assembly, the party's role of leading and guiding has been increasingly strengthened compared to before. The most important environmental policy documents were usually jointly adopted by

[15] 1997 Report of the Fifteenth Party Assembly of the CCP (by Zemin Jiang): https://fuwu.12371.cn/2012/09/27/ARTI1348726215537612.shtml. Following the author's research, the Fifteenth Assembly of 1997, the Sixteenth Assembly of 2002, the Seventeenth Assembly of the 2007, the Eighteenth Assembly of the 2012 and the Nineteenth Assembly of the 2017 all endorsed the sustainable development strategy. In the reports of the Seventeenth and the Eighteenth assemblies, two adjectives were added before the term 'sustainable development': comprehensive (*quanmian*) and coordinated (*xietiao*). Moreover, several related terms were also added, including sustainability (*kechixu fazhan nengli*). In the Nineteenth Assembly report, the strategy of sustainable development was still retained, but the rationale of the new development (*xin fazhan linian*), ecological civilisation (*shengtai wenming*), green development (*lüse fazhan*) and the term 'human community with a shared future' (*renlei mingyun gongtongti*) were added and given more emphasis in dealing with the relationship among the environment, the economy and society.

[16] F Snyder, Hu Zhouke and Ni Lili, 'Transnational Law in the Pacific Century: Mapping Pesticide Regulation in China' in P Zumbansen (ed), *The Many Lives of Transnational Law: Critical Engagements with Jessup's Bold Proposal* (Cambridge, Cambridge University Press, 2020) 153, 183.

the Central Committee of the CCP and the State Council. The separation of powers between the party and the government adopted in the 1990s is yesterday's story. Further integration of the party and government functions is being made after the 2022 Twentieth Assembly. This joint actions and joint responsibilities are not limited to the policy making, but also extend to the phase of implementation and enforcement – for example, holding local party and governmental officials personally responsible for their failure to implement the policies, strategies and laws. A Central Ecology and Environment Supervision Office[17] was established in 2015 and as of July 2022 had conducted two supervisions of 31 provinces/autonomous regions, two entities under the State Council and six state-owned enterprises. The effect was very impressive. Over 95 per cent of the 3,294 cases have been settled in the first supervision, while the same is true of over half of the cases in the second supervision. The public sent about 287,000 letters of petition to the office and over 285,000 have been settled.[18]

Third, the constitutional basis for environmental matters is so defined in China. In the 2018 amended Constitution, there are three 'environmental' provisions. The first is a sentence in the preface, which states that the Chinese people of all nationalities, under the leadership of the CCP, shall promote the coordinated development of material, political, spiritual, social and ecological civilisations to build China into a great modern socialist country. It establishes the goal for the environmental matters – ie, ecological civilisation – which will be discussed in more detail below. The second is Article 26, which defines the power of the state on environmental matters. It notes that the state protects and improves the living environment of the people and the ecological environment. The state prevents and controls pollution and other public hazards. This provision is interpreted as conferring legislative powers upon the National People's Congress (NPC) and its Standing Committee to adopt laws to protect the environment, and prevent pollution and ecological damage. The third is Article 89, which explicitly delegates relevant competence to the State Council. The State Council shall have the competence 'to direct and administer economic affairs, urban and rural development, and development of ecological civilisation'. The above provisions provide the constitutional basis of environmental law making

[17] In accordance with the 2019 Working Rules, www.mee.gov.cn/zcwj/zyygwj/201906/t20190618_706922.shtml and the 2021 Supervision Measures, www.mee.gov.cn/xxgk2018/xxgk/sthjbsh/202105/t20210517_833112.html jointly issued by the Central Committee of the CCP and State Council, a leading supervision group was established, including the officials from the Central Committee of the CCP (General Office, Personnel Department, Communication Department) and the State Council (General Office, Ministry of Justice, Ministry of Environment and Ecology, National Audit Office and the Supreme Procuratorate). This composition means that the consequences of violation or failure to fulfil the obligation could be serious.

[18] J Kou and Y Liu, 'Consolidate the Responsibility of Ecological Civilization Construction and Promote High-Quality Development: An Exclusive Interview with the Relevant Person in Charge of the Central Ecological and Environmental Protection Supervision Office' (Key Environmental News, Ministry of Ecology and Environment of the People's Republic of China, 29 July 2022), www.mee.gov.cn/ywdt/hjywnews/202207/t20220729_990337.shtml.

in China, which also reveals that the nature of Chinese environmental laws is predominately administrative law.

Another related constitutional issue in relation to Chinese environmental law is the public ownership (*quanmin suoyou*) of natural resources established by the Constitution. Article 9 provides that all mineral resources, waters, forests, mountains, grasslands, unclaimed land, beaches and other natural resources are owned by the state – that is, by the whole people – with the exception of the forests, mountains, grasslands, unclaimed land and beaches that are owned by collectives in accordance with the law. The state ensures the rational use of natural resources and protects rare animals and plants. The appropriation or damaging of natural resources by any organisation or individual by whatever means is prohibited. This provision is interpreted as defining the economic aspect of the environmental laws on natural resources, such as water, forest, grassland and mineral resources. Both administrative laws and economic laws are public laws in China.[19] Therefore, the public ownership of natural resources in China reinforces the predominant role of the government in relation to environmental matters. The principal legal tools of Chinese environmental law are public law tools and rather than private law tools. This is why the integration of sustainable development into the key party and government documents is an important step in its development in China.

After the UN 2030 SDGs Agenda was adopted in 2015, China revitalised its actions on sustainable development. At the G20 Summit in Hangzhou in September 2016, the G20 Action Plan on the 2030 SDGs Agenda was issued. At the same time, China published its National Plan on the Implementation of the 2030 SDGs Agenda. In December 2016, the State Council announced that China would designate 10 demonstration regions within the framework of the 2030 SDGs Agenda.[20] As of July 2022, all 10 regions had been approved by the State Council as demonstration models. In 2017, 2019 and 2021, China issued three progress reports respectively on the implementation of the 2030 SDGs Agenda. The 2021 report systematically reviewed progress in the eradication of poverty, continuous economic growth, personal income improvement, improvement in ecological environment, and the development of the Belt and Road and its synergies with the 2030 SDGs Agenda.[21]

[19] See the Chinese law appendix in State Council Information Office, *China's Efforts and Achievements in Promoting the Rule of Law* (2008), http://www.gov.cn/zhengce/2008-02/28/content_2615764.htm.

[20] State Council, 'Notice of the State Council on Printing and Distributing China's Implementation of the 2030 Sustainable Development Agenda Innovation Demonstration Zone Construction Plan' (3 December 2016) Guofa (2016) No 69, www.gov.cn/zhengce/content/2016-12/13/content_5147412.htm.

[21] Ministry of Foreign Affairs, 'China's VNR Report on Implementation of the 2030 Agenda for Sustainable Development' (2021), sustainabledevelopment.un.org/content/documents/280812021_VNR_Report_China_English.pdf. The Chinese government proposed building a 'Silk Road Economic Belt' and a '21st Century Maritime Silk Road' in cooperation with related countries along the Belt and Road. It was announced by Chinese President Xi Jinping during his visits to Central and Southeast Asia in September and October 2013. It is often referred to as the 'Belt and Road Initiative'.

As described above, China sincerely embraced the principle of sustainable development and has made it a national development strategy since the mid-1990s. An interesting question is why China embraced it from the very beginning. Connecting to the international track (*yu guoji jiegui*) has been a consistent approach employed since the late 1970s in order to modernise China and open it up to the outside world. Is this the only reason? This is just one reason out of many. There may be other considerations for such a choice. First, the key word of the concept of sustainable development is development. 'Development is the hard truth' (*fazhan shi yingdaoli*), as the then paramount leader, Deng Xiaoping, often said. With such a large population, but with limited natural resources and comparatively low levels of economic and social development at that time, the improvement of the national GDP and people's living standards all depended on development. Sustainable development matched China's urgent need for development since the late 1970s. Second, sustainable development recognised the finite limits of the environment and natural resources on human development, and proposed means and approaches to coordinate the development of the economy, society and the environment. It satisfied the need of China to search for means and approaches in response to the same challenges after over a decade of whole-hearted economic development practice. Third, by not only connecting China to the international track, but also by integrating it into the global endeavour for sustainable development, China would have benefited and also contributed to the UN sustainable development goals and targets.[22] The timing was right for incorporating sustainable development into China.

B. The Incorporation of Sustainable Development into Chinese Environmental Laws

The issue of incorporating sustainable development into Chinese environmental laws may be addressed from the following perspectives. First, the scope of environmental law has to be defined. The list of Chinese laws promulgated by the NPC and the Standing Committee includes nearly 300 laws in 2022.[23] Some of these laws are directly relevant to the environment, such as pollution prevention laws, while others are indirectly relevant, such as the Agriculture Law. A selection is necessary. The list of selected Chinese environmental laws given in the Appendix at the end of this chapter is the author's selection, taking into consideration their relevance to the environment and particularly to the main theme of this chapter. Second, it has to define what it means by the incorporation of sustainable development into

[22] J Huang, 'China's Sustainable Development Strategy Implementation Process Review' (2019) Z2 *China Sustainability Tribune* 14, 15.

[23] ZX Yang, '50 Years of China's Environmental Legislation: Inter-generational Evolution from Environmental Law Version 1.0 to 3.0' (2022) 3 *Journal of Beijing Institute of Technology (Social Science Edition)* 88.

the law. Section IV below will explore the issue from the following two aspects: the perspective of legislative objective in environmental laws and the perspective of legal tools or mechanism in the area of water protection. The legislative objective in the given law is usually brief and explicit, stating the aim and purposes of the law. The legal tools, on the other hand, are the instruments or mechanisms designed to fulfil legislative objectives, usually in more than one provision. The identification of such tools by the author is to examine both the intention and the effect of the law on the limits put on human activities for the protection of the environment and natural resources.

i. Sustainable Development as a Legislative Objective

The legislative objective is like a compass; stating the aim, purpose, key values and interests of the law. The objectives of environmental laws are mainly to protect the environment and human health. Apart from this, do environmental laws also protect other values and interests? Different states may have different approaches. Even within one state, the legislative objectives of a law may be changed in the process of amendments and revision. This is the feature of Chinese environmental laws.

The legislative objectives are usually provided by Article 1 of the Chinese environmental laws. Nearly half of the environmental laws in the list were first adopted in the 1980s, when the economic development or growth was the top priority. When the Air Pollution Prevention and Control Law was adopted in 1987, the objectives were 'to prevent and control air pollution, to protect and improve living environment and ecological environment, to protect human health and *to promote the construction and development of the socialist modernisation*'. It is remarkable that an environmental law, apart from the environmental objectives, was for modernisation, which mainly meant economic development at that time. When the law was amended in 1995, no change was made to this article, even when the China Agenda 21 had already been adopted a year earlier. However, a change did come in 2000 when the first major revision was made. The objectives were amended in order 'to prevent and control air pollution, to protect and improve living environment and ecological environment, to protect human health and to promote *economic and social sustainable development*' (Article 1). The sustainable development replaced the modernisation (economic development etc) as one of the objectives. Though this law was further revised in 2015 and amended in 2018, this article remains unchanged. The evolution of the legislative objectives of this law is not an isolated example in Chinese environmental law; a similar pattern can also be seen with the Land Administration Law, the Environmental Protection Law, the Solid Waste Pollution Prevention and Control Law, the Water and Soil Conservation Law and the Energy Conservation Law. Another example is the Environmental Protection Law, in which the objectives were almost identical to those of the 1987 Air Pollution Prevention and Control Law. However, after the 2014 revision, the objectives are now 'to protect and improve the environment, to prevent and control pollution and other public hazards, to safeguard public health, to promote *the construction of ecological civilisation*, and to improve the *economic and social sustainable development*'. Up to now, of the 33 environmental laws in the Appendix, 23 incorporated sustainable development into their legislative objectives.[24] The above two examples demonstrate that the objectives and priorities of environmental law have already shifted from modernisation (especially economic development) to sustainable development and ecological civilisation, which will be dealt with in the next section.

What is more revealing of such a shift is the integration clause (Article 4) of the Environmental Protection Law of 1989, in which it required that the environmental plans should be integrated into the national economic and social development plans, and that environmental protection must be *in harmony with the economic construction and social development*. In other words, the master plan was the economic and social plans – and the environmental plan was meant to be subordinate to or at least not in conflict with master plan. But the revised 2014 revised law turns the order upside down. Article 4 of the 2014 revised law states that it is the fundamental state strategy to protect the environment. The state adopts economic and technological policies and measures on energy conservation, renewable resources, protection and improvement of the environment, improving the harmony between humankind and nature, *making the economic and social development in harmony with the protection of the environment*. It took about 25 years for the objectives to have been changed in this way.

Moreover, since 2015, sustainable development in Chinese laws is not only a development issue but also a national security issue. In accordance with the 2015 National Security Law, sustainable development is a component of national security. Article 3 states that the national security means a status in which the regime, sovereignty, unity, territorial integrity, welfare of the people, *sustainable economic and social development*, and other major interests of the state, along with the capability to maintain a *sustained security* status, are not faced with any danger and not threatened internally or externally. Article 30 in particular stipulates what the state shall do to maintain national security. It provides that the state shall improve the rules and system for environmental protection, strengthen ecological construction and environmental protection, determine the red line for ecological protection, reinforce the early warning, prevention and control of ecological risks, properly handle environmental emergencies, protect the atmosphere, water, soil, and other natural environment and conditions indispensable for the people's living and development against threat and destruction, and promote the harmonious development of human and nature. Therefore, sustainable development has been further upgraded to the level of national security.

[24] Three of the 33 laws in the Appendix to this chapter incorporated ecological civilisation into their objectives.

ii. Ecological Civilisation as a Legislative Objective

The discussion on ecological civilisation could be traced back to the theoretical discussions by Japanese, German, Soviet and Chinese academics in the mid-1980s.[25] The term 'ecological civilisation' first appeared in the book *General Introduction to the China's Sustainable Development Strategy of Forestry*[26] edited and published by the State Forestry Agency in 2002. The 2003 'Decisions to Expedite the Forestry Development'[27] jointly issued by the Central Committee of the CCP and the State Council formally used the term 'ecologically civilised society'. The document called upon the government to construct a beautiful society of ecological civilisation. In 2007, the term 'ecological civilisation' appeared in the report of the Seventeenth Party Assembly for the first time.[28] It proposed it as a goal in realising moderate prosperity (or a moderately well-off society, *xiaokang*) in 2020 by achieving the accomplishments of the production structure, economic growth pattern and consumption pattern along with energy conservation and environmental protection. From then on, the notion of ecological civilisation started to take root in the key party assembly documents. From 2008, ecological civilisation started to be incorporated into the Premier's Annual Report to the NPC.[29] It called on the whole society to strengthen the notion of ecological civilisation, to mobilise the people to establish an energy conservation and environmentally friendly society, and to push forward the establishment of economic, political, cultural, social and ecological construction. In 2012, the Eighteenth Party Assembly report put forward the Five-in-One general strategy, which refers to the synergy of economic development, political development, cultural development, social development and ecological civilisation. In 2015 the Central Committee of the CCP and State Council jointly adopted the Opinion Paper on Speeding up the Construction of Ecological Civilisation. In September 2015, the Politburo of the CCP reviewed and approved the Ecological Civilisation Construction Action Plan. These two documents elaborated the notion and provided the basis and guidance for its implementation. In May 2016, China announced the China

[25] Yang (n 23) 97; 'Ecological civilization' (Wikipedia, 16 August 2022) en.wikipedia.org/wiki/Ecological_civilization#:~:text=Ecological%20civilization%20is%20the%20hypothetical,reform%20within%20a%20given%20society.

[26] Team of China's Sustainable Development Strategy of Forestry, *General Introduction to China's Sustainable Development Strategy of Forestry* (Beijing, China Forestry Publishing, 2002).

[27] Central Committee of the Chinese Communist Party (CCP) and State Council, 'Decision to Speed up the Forestry Development' (25 June 2003), www.gov.cn/test/2005-07/04/content_11993.htm.

[28] The term 'ecological civilisation' appeared twice in the report by HU Jintao at the Seventeenth Assembly of 2007 (fuwu.12371.cn/2012/06/11/ARTI1339412115437623.shtml), 27 times in the report by HU Jintao at the Eighteenth Assembly of 2012 (www.12371.cn/2012/11/17/ARTI1353154601465336.shtml), 12 times in the report by XI Jinping at the Nineteenth Assembly of 2017 (www.12371.cn/2017/10/27/ARTI1509103656574313.shtml) and twice in the report by XI Jinping at the Twentieth Assembly of 2022 (www.12371.cn/2022/10/25/ARTI1666705047474465.shtml).

[29] 2008 premier's annual report by J Wen, www.gov.cn/test/2009-03/16/content_1260198.htm The term 'ecological civilisation' appeared eight times in the premier's reports by Wen from 2008 to 2013. It appeared 21 times in the premier's reports by LI Keqiang from 2014 to 2022.

Ecological Civilisation Strategy and Actions at the Second Session of the UNEP Environmental Assembly. Thereafter, ecological civilisation has been integrated into the state strategies, action plans and laws of China. As mentioned earlier in this chapter, the 2018 revised Constitution formally incorporated the ecological civilisation in the preface and Article 89 on the competence of the State Council. The Chinese government has indicated that ecological civilisation is to be in place as the essential basis for a modern China by 2035.

From the legal perspective, ecological civilisation has been incorporated as legislative objectives in Chinese environmental laws. The revised 2014 Environmental Protection Law, as mentioned earlier, incorporated ecological civilisation in the legislative objectives of Article 1, apart from the sustainable development. The other environmental laws that embedded ecological civilisation as a legislative objective include the 2017 amended Water Pollution Prevention and Control Law, the 2018 Soil Pollution Prevention and Control Law, the 2020 revised Solid Waste Pollution Prevention and Control Law, the 2021 Noise Pollution Prevention and Control Law, and the 2021 Wetland Protection Law. These laws incorporated both sustainable development and ecological civilisation as the legislative objectives. However, in the Environmental Tax Law of 2016, the Yangtze River Protection Law of 2020 and the Wetland Protection Law of 2021, the ecological civilisation and coexistence between humankind and nature replaced sustainable development as a legislative objective.

What does the term 'ecological civilisation' mean? There are many definitions, descriptions and interpretations that are similar to the term 'sustainable development'. It may refer to the following things at least. First, it is a development of civilisation. Humankind has experienced primitive civilisation, agricultural civilisation and industrial civilisation. Now in the face of unprecedented ecological challenges, such as climate change, a new form of civilisation is needed to accommodate nature and not to conquer it, focusing particularly on the harmony between humans and nature. That is ecological civilisation. The central elements are a good environment, balanced ecology, sustainable natural resources, high-quality economic and social development, improved quality of life etc. Second, for China, it is a set of values and development concepts enshrined in the 2018 revised Constitution, and a key driver towards a high-quality development of a 'New Era'. It is simultaneously a philosophy, vision and compass for a green and prosperous future. One of the most important features of ecological civilisation is that it acts as a catalyst for bringing together related components needed for green development.[30] The construction of ecological civilisation is a great plan for the sustainable development of the Chinese nation. Third, the implication of

[30] The term 'green development' is used in a generic sense to cover all the environment-related issues as one of the 15 major tasks of the CCP in the next five years in the Twentieth Assembly report of 2022, though the term 'sustainable development' still appeared once in the report in connection with the achievements of the previous 10 years.

ecological civilisation on Chinese environmental law is profound. It transformed the environmental legislative objectives, legal systems, arrangements, mechanism and tools etc. The legal tools to be discussed in the following section are just the beginning of this transformation. This is the reason why Chinese environmental law is changing from pollution control law to ecology law. Fourth, China still adheres to sustainable development, but the focus or priority has been changed. The focus of sustainable development is development. This is the reason why it was appealing to developing states and welcomed by developing states at the Rio Conference of 1992. Thirty years later, China is different, and so is the world. The focus and priority are still the development, but no longer economic development alone – it is the Five-in-One development or green development. The importance of sustainability of the ecology is increased to a very high level – the level of civilisation.

At the Fifth Session of the Eighteenth Assembly of the CCP in October 2015, a new development notion was adopted; of which the core is the innovation, coordination, being green, opening up and sharing. The innovation not only includes technological innovation, but also includes the innovation in theories, systems and culture etc. The coordination refers to the proper relationship between urban and rural development, economic and social development and other aspects which are important for China, such as the new industrialisation, information and urbanisation. The green development particularly refers to sustainable development. XI Jinping made it clear in plain language that the lucid water and lush mountains are invaluable assets and China should never have to sacrifice environment and ecology for the temporal economic gains. In May 2018, ecological civilisation was confirmed as the fundamental strategy for the Chinese people.[31] Ecological civilisation is an upgraded version of sustainable development with Chinese characteristics.[32]

IV. Incorporation of the Sustainable Development in Chinese Environmental Law: Protection of the Freshwater and Marine Water

Water resources are one the most important valuable natural resources on the earth. Air and water are the basis for human survival. This is even more true for China, when the necessity of feeding a population of 1.4 billion and providing

[31] China Environment News, 'High Standard! What Important Information Did This National Ecological Environmental Protection Conference Reveal?' (9 May 2018). A series of news reports, analysis and comments are also available on the website of the Ministry of Ecology and Environment.

[32] A Hanson, 'Ecological Civilization in the People's Republic of China: Values, Actions, and Future Needs' (2019) *ADB East Asia Working Paper Series* 21/2019, www.adb.org/sites/default/files/publication/545291/eawp-021-ecological-civilization-prc.pdf.

them with drinking water is taken into consideration. The legal protection of the water resources in China is also a good example to explore the establishment and evolution of Chinese environmental legal framework in relation to sustainable development. The following section will concentrate on the incorporation of sustainable development into the specific legal framework for the protection of water resources, including freshwater and marine water.

A. Legal Framework for Water Protection

The legal framework for the protection of water resources in China may be divided into two sub-sections: freshwater and marine water. Within each of these, the discussion will be further divided into two sections – economic laws regulating the exploitation of the resources and administrative laws regulating pollution prevention and control.

i. Freshwater

The administrative measures for freshwater resources started from early 1950s, soon after the People's Republic of China was founded in October 1949. The Hygiene Standards of Drinking Water (trial application) and the Water Quality Standards of Fishing Water (trial application) were made during this initial period of time.

For the exploitation of water resources, a challenging issue is the fair allocation of freshwater resources in the river basins and among different administrative regions (provinces, municipalities and counties, and even villages). This is regulated by the Water Law (brought into effect in 1988 and amended in 2016). Moreover, the legal responses to water and soil erosion are regulated separately by the Water & Soil Conservation Law (brought into effect in 1991 and revised in 2010). The implementation and enforcement of these laws fell within the competence of the Ministry of Water Resources, while the issue of water pollution fell within the then Ministry of Environmental Protection (MEP, now the Ministry of Ecology and Environment (MEE)). For the issue of water pollution prevention and control, the Water Pollution Prevention and Control Law (WPPCL) was promulgated by the Standing Committee of the NPC on 11 May 1984 (it was amended in 2017). Based on this law, the Implementation Measures were made in 1989 (which were abolished in 2018), and the then National Environmental Protection Administration (NEPA, now the MEE) adopted a series of related water quality standards and discharge standards. Moreover, the Flood Prevention Law was promulgated in 1997 (it was last amended in 2016), the Yangtze River Protection Law was promulgated in 2020 and the Yellow River Protection Law was promulgated on 30 October 2022. The national legal regime for the protection of freshwater resources was thus established, consisting of several laws and administered by several ministries and agencies.

ii. Marine Water

On 4 September 1958, soon after the first UN Conference on the Law of the Sea, China issued the Declaration of the Territorial Sea, in which it declared the breadth of the territorial sea was, and still is, 12 nautical miles. After the Declaration, the legal framework on marine water has been divided into two parts. The first part mainly relates to the external legal aspect, which includes the 1992 Law of the Territorial Seas and Contiguous Zones, the 1996 Declaration on the Baseline of the Territorial Sea and the 1998 Law of the Continental Shelf. The second part mainly relates to the internal aspect, chiefly for the protection of the marine environment and exploitation of marine resources. In 2016, the Law of Exploration and Exploitation of the Resources in Deep Seabed Areas was adopted, which has both external and internal aspects.

China began legally protecting the marine environment in the 1970s. In 1974 (still during the Cultural Revolution), the State Council adopted the first legal document to prevent and control marine pollution: the Interim Rules for the Prevention of Costal Water Pollution. Some provisions of this document were incorporated into the first environmental law: the Environmental Protection Law (trial implementation) of 1979. In 1982, the Marine Environmental Protection Law (1982 MEPL) was promulgated by the Standing Committee of the NPC, so the national legal framework for the protection of marine environment was established. The 1982 MEPL was the first piece of environmental law in China and belongs to the first generation of Chinese environmental laws; which means its major goal was to establish a legal framework in the first instance, and its provisions were usually general and abstract, without sufficient and detailed substantive and procedural rules for effective implementation and enforcement – more or less like policy guidelines. This law was subsequently amended in 1999, 2013 and 2016, following China's participation in the 1982 UN Convention on the Law of the Sea.

Other relevant laws in this area include the Administrative Law on the Utilisation of Marine Areas (2001) and the Law on the Protection of Islands (2009). In relation to the protection of fishery resources, the Fishery Law (brought into effect in 1986 and last amended in 2013) applies to both inland water fisheries and marine fisheries.

B. Sustainable Development as the Legislative Objective

When the Marine Environmental Protection Law was adopted in 1982, its objectives were 'to protect the marine environment and resources, to prevent pollution damage, to protect ecological balance, to protect human health and to promote the development of the marine cause'. Like the Environmental Protection Law of 1989, the objectives of the other environmental laws adopted during the 1980s and early 1990s often included phrases like promoting or contributing to the economic development/construction, the relevant business/cause, socialist modernisation, etc. Two years later in 1984, when the Water Pollution Prevention and Control Law was adopted, the objectives were 'to prevent and control water pollution, to protect and improve the environment, to protect human health to safeguard the effective utilisation of water resources and to promote the development of socialist modernisation'. A similar formulation was also followed by the 1986 Fishery Law, the Water Law of 1988 and the 1991 Water and Soil Conservation Law.

Sustainable development was incorporated into these laws when the revision and amendment was made after their integration into the policies and strategies in 1997. The first environmental law to incorporate sustainable development as its objective was the 1998 revised Land Administration Law. The second was the 1999 revised Marine Environmental Protection Law, in which the phrase 'to promote the development of marine cause' was replaced by the phrase 'to promote the economic and social sustainable development'. This was a clear change of objectives in this law. Similarly, in the 2008 amendment of the Water Pollution Prevention and Control Law (WPCL), the phrase 'to promote the development of socialist moderation' in both the 1984 law and the 1996 amended laws was replaced by 'to promote comprehensive and harmonious economic and social sustainable development'. The 2017 amendment of the law made two further changes to the objectives: first, deleting the two adjectives of 'comprehensive' (*quanmian*) and 'harmonious' (*xietiao*) before sustainable development; and, second, inserting the phrase 'to promote the construction of ecological civilisation'. In the 2010 revised Water and Soil Conservation Law, the phrase 'to safeguard economic and social sustainable development' replaced the phrase 'promote production' in the 1991 law and the 2009 amended law.

Another relevant term incorporated into these laws is 'sustainable use' (*kechixu liyong*) in this area. In the 2001 Administrative Law on the Utilisation of Marine Areas, one of the objectives is to 'promote rational exploitation and sustainable use of the marine area'. Similarly, in the 2002 revised Water Law, one of the objectives is 'to achieve the sustainable use of water resources'. In the 2016 Law of Exploration and Exploitation of the Resources in Deep Seabed Areas, the objectives include to 'promote the sustainable use of the resources in the deep seabed areas'. The sustainable use of natural resources is one of the components of the sustainable development. In these three laws, sustainable use of the relevant resources has been singled out and has replaced the emphasis on sustainable development in a more general sense.

Another noticeable phenomenon is that instead of the use of the term 'sustainable development', in the 2020 Conservation Law of the Yangtze River, the objectives are defined as to 'strengthen the conservation and restoration of the ecological environment of the Yangtze River basin, to promote reasonable and effective use of the resources, to safeguard ecological safety, to achieve the harmony between the human and the nature, to achieve perpetual development of the Chinese people'. Similarly, the 2021 Conservation Law on the Wetland also defines it in this way – that is, to 'strengthen the protection of the wetland, to conserve the ecological function and biological diversity, to safeguard ecological safety, to promote the construction of ecological civilisation and to achieve the harmony between the human and the nature'. The 2022 Yellow River Protection Law also incorporated 'to achieve the harmony between the human and the nature, to achieve perpetual development of the Chinese people' in its legislative objectives. As discussed above, ecological civilisation is more emphasised, although sustainable (or perpetual) development is still mentioned, indicating the changing priorities of environmental laws and policies in China.

C. Sustainable Development as a Specific Tool and Mechanism

The incorporation of sustainable development into the legislative objectives is only the first step. In order to achieve the designated objectives, practical tools or mechanisms have to be established and developed in the given law. Among many tools and mechanisms of environmental law, two are particularly important for achieving the objective of sustainable development and ecological civilisation: the ecological protection red line and the discharge permit.

i. The Ecological Protection Red Line

The tool of red lines may be used in many places, indicating certain limits for recommended safety. It first originated from urban planning. It required that development projects or buildings not transcend the area enclosed by the red line. Later, it was incorporated into environmental laws. The ecological protection red line means to set up the minimum ecological area limits for ecological security reasons. The ecological protection red line is now a national security issue in China – the state shall reinforce the early warning, prevention and control ecological risk etc (Article 30 of the National Security Law). In the 2014 revised Environmental Protection Law, Article 29 requires that the state shall set up the red line for strict ecological protection in the important ecologically functional zones, ecological sensitive zones and fragile zones. In 2015, the MEE issued the Technical Guidance to the Designation of the Ecological Protection Red line, which is applicable to the designation of the red lines in China. In the amended 2017 Marine Environmental Protection Law, Article 3 provides that the state shall set up the red line for strict ecological protection in the important marine functional zones, ecologically sensitive zones and fragile zone etc. In the 2017 revised Water Pollution Prevention and Control Law, Article 29 requires that those who conduct development construction activities shall take effective measures to protect the ecological functions of the river basin and strictly adhere to the ecological protection red line. Article 19 of the Yangtze River Protection Law provides that the zoning plan of the Yangtze

River basin shall incorporate the red line and basic agricultural land. The Yellow River Protection Law also incorporated the ecological protection red line in Articles 22 and 26.

In February 2018, the State Council approved the plans of ecological protection red lines of 15 provinces and municipalities, including Beijing, Tianjin, Hebei, Ningxia and 11 provinces along the Yangtze River basin. According to the plans of these 15 provinces and municipalities, about 610,000 km^2 of the area was to be covered by the red line, which was about a quarter of the land area of these 15 provinces and municipalities. They included 291 counties of national key ecological functions areas in seven categories.[33]

In August 2022, the Ministry of Natural Resources, the Ministry of Ecology and Environment, the State Forestry Agency and the Grassland Agency jointly issued a notice on strengthening the administration of the ecological protection red line. First, it states that the red line is an important control limit of the territorial space plan. It requests to strengthen control over human activities, so that damage to the ecological function is not generated. It requires putting necessary measures and regimes in place to protect the red line. Second, it provides that the red line will be used to regulate the application and approval of the use of land, water and islands. Third, it requires to strengthen the monitoring of the ecological protection red line. From the perspective of limits on human activities, it is a strong sustainable development tool.

The limits on human activities in the area enclosed by the red line triggered disputes concerning land leasing contracts. In a case involving a contract dispute, a county court of Sichuan Province invalidated a contract relating to processing sands and rocks which was located within the area designated by the ecological protection red line, following Article 29 of the 2014 Environmental Protection Law.[34] Also in Sichuan Province, a solid brick factory was constructed in 2009 in the area which was later designated as a natural reserve for waterfowl and wetlands enclosed by the ecological protection red line; as a result, the factory was shut down and the production facilities were dismantled by the county government. The applicant sued the county government and requested compensation for the loss. The county court justified the government act of shutting down the factory and dismantling the facilities, but the county government was ordered to pay compensation for the loss incurred by the factory owner.[35]

[33] Ministry of Environmental Protection, 'The State Council Approved the Plans of Ecological Protection of Beijing and 14 Provinces' (Ministry of Ecology and Environment of the People's Republic of China, 12 February 2018), www.mee.gov.cn/gkml/sthjbgw/qt/201802/t20180212_431371.htm.

[34] Civil Judgment on the Case Concerning the 'Processing Contract between HE and XU', Qiangzu Autonomous County Court (2021) Chuan 0726 Civil First Instance 421, 2 June 2021, www.pkulaw.com/pfnl/95b2ca8d4055fce10f9bf7517cc839d68ac0866697b50de4bdfb.html?articleFbm=CLI.C.419043026.

[35] Civil Judgment on the Case Concerning the 'Xingfu Bricks Factory v Santai Natural Resource Agency and County Government for Compensation' (2019) Chuan 0723 Administrative Compensation First Instance 1, 13 December 2019, www.pkulaw.com/pfnl/a6bdb3332ec0adc438602d112dd11809a2cb32c520c7bf7abdfb.html?articleFbm=CLI.C.105822087.

Does the red line constitute a fundamental change of circumstances of a contract? Another land leasing contract dispute was appealed to the Jinan Intermediate Court of Shandong province. In January 2013, a real estate company concluded a contract with a village in Jinan suburb over the land lease of 786 *mu* (about 52.4 hectares) for 50 years. Then the real estate company had a contract with a tour operator to develop tourist holiday villas during the period 2015–20 for RMB 1.5 million. However, during this period the area was enclosed by the red line. In order to reduce the loss, the tour operator took the real estate company to court to plead for fundamental changes of circumstances of the contract. The court of first instance supported the plea and held that the tour operator could pay less to the real estate company. However, the case was appealed to the Jinan Intermediate Court, which rejected the argument of fundamental change. The court ruled that the area before enclosed by the red line was already a natural reserve where the villa construction projects was not permitted. As such, the tour operator should have foreseen the legal risk when the contract was concluded. The loss was not caused by the red line, so the tour operator could not plead to change or nullify the contract on the basis fundamental changes of circumstance in the case.[36]

ii. Discharge Permits

Unlike the ecological protection red line which focused on control of an area, discharge permits target point sources of water pollution. It is an important tool for preventing, reducing and controlling water pollution, which is widely used in the environmental laws of many states. However, it did take considerable time for China to establish the legal system of permits in environmental law.

Article 45 of the 2014 Environmental Protection Law provides that the state shall implement the system of discharge permit in accordance with the law. These enterprises, units or other business entities that discharge pollutants in the operation are requested to discharge pollutants according to the permit. It is prohibited to discharge pollutants without a permit. This was the first time that Chinese environmental legislation provided for the requirement of discharge permits. According to Article 21 of the 2017 revised Water Pollution Prevention and Control Law, those who directly or indirectly discharge industrial waste water or medical waste water and other pollutants into the water shall apply and obtain the discharge permit first and then discharge the pollutants in accordance with the permit. The requirement of discharge permit also applied to the business operators of urban sewage treatment facilities. The State Council shall make implementation measures on the discharge permit. In December 2020, the State Council adopted the Regulation of Administration of the Discharge Permit, which entered into

[36] Case Concerning the Lease Contract between 'Shandong X Tour Operator v Jinan X Real Estate Company', in 'Ten Environment and Resources Cases of the Jinan Intermediate Court', 2 June 2022, www.pkulaw.com/lar/759da476b61947894faf38cffc7e6e68bdfb.html?way=listView.

force in March 2021. The legal regime for discharge permits was thus established. With this Regulation, the MEE publicly announced that 85 iron and steel smelting enterprises (out of 871 enterprises nationally) were not able to extend the validity period of their discharge permits and 152 enterprises did not submit their permit report in due course. They were given a period of time to correct their failure.[37] The permits became an effective monitoring and supervision tool. By the end of 2020, 337,700 discharge/emission permits had been issued nationally.[38]

In the marine water area, Article 38 of the 1982 Marine Environmental Protection Law provided dumping permits, requiring that those units in dumping business shall apply and obtain dumping permit before carrying out ocean dumping activities. This provision is the Article 55 of the 2017 revised law. The difference of the 2017 revised law from that of the 1982 law is that the application for the dumping permit shall be in written form. The requirement of written form was inserted by the first revision in 1999, and the 2017 law remains the same.

The evolution of discharge permit in Chinese environmental law, particularly in the WPPCL, is an interesting case to study. Article 14 of the 1984 WPPCL required polluting units to register with the local environmental protection agency (EPA) the treatment facilities, categories, quantity and density of the pollutants to be discharged. Prior approval should be obtained from the local EPA if the treatment facilities are to be dismantled or laid off. However, the house had only been half-built; mere registration and permission or approval were not required before discharging pollutants. It was the intention of the drafting group to complete matters by formally establishing the discharge permit legal system. However, the result was just the opposite; even the registration requirement was deleted altogether from the 1996 revised law. But that was not the end of the story. In the 2000 Detailed Rules on the Implementation of the WPPCL adopted by the State Council, Article 10 provided that a discharge permit was still required and Article 44 provided the penalties for violation of the provisions of permit. No one challenged the legal basis for the 2000 detailed rules in court. In the 2008 amended law, the permit was again inserted by Article 20, without more elaborated rules. In the 2017 revised law, the permit system is finally established.

The discharge permit system may have different characteristics in different countries; however, it is an effective tool for implementing environmental law. It defines the discharging source's legal obligation in objective and unambiguous terms. Based on the monitoring data, the source, the government authorities and the public can readily determine whether the source complies with the rules or not. In addition, the total loadings from all sources on a given water body can

[37] General Office, 'Circular on Issues Related to the Failure to Extend the Validity Period of the Pollutant Discharge Permit in the Iron and Steel Smelting Industry and the Failure to Submit an Enforcement Report as Required' (Ministry of Ecology and Environment of the People's Republic of China, 3 September 2021), www.mee.gov.cn/xxgk2018/xxgk/xxgk06/202109/t20210903_897669.html.

[38] '2020 China Eco-Environmental Statistical Annual Report' (18 February 2022), www.mee.gov.cn/hjzl/sthjzk/sthjtjnb.

readily be determined. If it is an effective legal tool, why it was deleted in the revision of 1996? One possible answer was that the legislator at that time preferred to give more leeway to enterprises in relation to their economic development. Another possible answer may be that the application of a permit system would automatically increase the administrative cost of the enterprises and the government as well. The deletion of the permit system might reduce unnecessary costs for the enterprises. In the end, the interests of the enterprises were prioritised over environmental interests. As was mentioned earlier in this chapter, the legislative objectives of the 1996 amended WPPCL included promoting the development of socialist modernisation. In comparison with the legislative objectives of sustainable development since 1998 and more recent ecological civilisation, the amendment and revision of the WPPCL show where Chinese environmental laws started, their process of evolution and how they arrived at the current position today.

V. Conclusion

The incorporation of sustainable development into Chinese environmental law provides an example demonstrating how an international concept or principle made its way into the domestic political and legal framework of China. Its introduction and incorporation were made possible by both internal and external factors. Such a process explained the tension and shifts of priorities in political and legal decision making on economic, social and environmental issues during the rise of China over the past 30 years, especially by examining the changes in the legislative objectives in Chinese environmental law. At the same time, it may also serve as an example of transnational law defined by Philip Jessup in 1956 as 'all law which regulates actions or events that transcend national frontiers'.[39] Sustainable development not only horizontally regulated actions or even those that transcend national frontiers, but also vertically penetrated into the domestic political and legal boundaries of the state and had a profound impact within China. From the *Our Common Future* report to Agenda 21, the 2030 SDGs Agenda and the multilateral environmental treaties in which China participated, and from the CCP party documents and Chinese premiers' annual reports to the national environmental laws and case law of local courts, it confirmed Francis Snyder's findings in his academic contribution to transnational law from the perspective of legal pluralism and sites of governance on the regulation of food safety and pesticides in China.[40] Besides, the incorporation of sustainable development also demonstrated the close link and unique interaction in the party–state relationship, especially the predominant role of the CCP's political line, norms and policies, which is very different from the idealised versions of Western countries.[41]

[39] P Jessup, *Transnational Law* (New Haven, Yale University Press, 1956) 2.
[40] Snyder, *Food Safety Law in China* (n 2); Snyder, Zhouke and Lili (n 16).
[41] Snyder, Zhouke and Lili (n 16) 183.

Sustainable development, after being incorporated into Chinese environmental law, is not just a political statement for China – it is a legislative objective, supplemented and supported by concrete legal tools and mechanisms which were applied in disputes at the local courts. Akin to the process of incorporation of sustainable development, the incorporation of ecological civilisation experienced a similar process – from a party policy initiative to policy implementation and finally to legal provisions in the law. The term 'civilisation' is a generic term; however, it has special meaning and implication in this chapter: as a symbol of the change or shift in national strategies and priorities in China. When China started its reform and opening-up strategy, the CCP emphasised the material civilisation in 1978 Third Session of the Eleventh Assembly. In 1982, the Twelfth Assembly report endorsed two civilisations: material and spiritual civilisations. In 1997, a third civilisation – political civilisation – was inserted into the Fifteenth Assembly report. The Seventeenth Assembly report added the fourth civilisation: social civilisation in 2007. Finally, as mentioned earlier in this chapter, the fifth civilisation – ecological civilisation – was inserted into the Eighteenth Assembly report in 2012. This process produced an important impact on the development of the Chinese environmental legal framework. It is interesting to note that China rose from material civilisation in the late 1970s to ecological civilisation in the twenty-first century. With the 2022 CCP Twentieth Assembly report, ecological civilisation was perceived as a major achievement in the past 10 years, while green development was designated as a main task for the next five years until 2027. Therefore, sustainable development, with Chinese characteristics, is expected to continue its route in China. A continued observation on Chinese practice of sustainable development is necessary on the new phase of green development.

Appendix: Select Chinese Environmental Laws

No	Title of the Law	Date of adoption	Date of implementation	Amendment (A) or Revision (R) information
1	Marine Environmental Protection Law	23 August 1982	1 March 1983	25 December 1999 (R); 28 December 2013 (A); 7 November 2016 (A); 4 November 2017 (A)
2	Water Pollution Prevention and Control Law	11 May 1984	1 November 1984	15 May 1996 (A); 28 February 2008 (R); 27 June 2017 (A)
3	Forest Law	20 September 1984	1 January 1985	29 April 1998(A); 27 August 2009 (A); 28 December 2019 (R)

(continued)

(Continued)

No	Title of the Law	Date of adoption	Date of implementation	Amendment (A) or Revision (R) information
4	Grassland Law	18 June 1985	1 October 1985	28 December 2002 (R); 27 August 2009 (A); 29 June 2013 (A); 29 April 2021 (A)
5	Fishery Law	20 January 1986	1 July 1986	31 October 2000 (A); 28 August 2004 (A); 27 August 2009 (A); 28 December 2013 (A)
6	Mineral Resources Law	19 March 1986	1 October 1986	29 August 1996 (A); 27 August 2009 (A)
7	Land Administration Law	25 June 1986	1 January 1987	29 December 1988 (A); 29 August 1998 (R); 28 August 2004 (A); 26 August 2019 (A)
8	Air Pollution Prevention and Control Law	5 September 1987	1 June 1988	29 August 1995 (A); 29 April 2000 (R); 29 August 2015 (R); 26 October 2018 (A)
9	Water Law	21 January 1988	1 July 1988	29 August 2002 (R); 27 August 2009 (A); 2 July 2016 (A)
10	Wild Animal Protection Law	8 November 1988	1 March 1989	28 August 2004 (A); 27 August 2009 (A); 2 July 2016 (R); 26 October 2018 (A)
11	Environmental Protection Law	26 December 1989	26 December 1989	24 April 2014 (R)
12	Water and Soil Conservation Law	29 June 1991	29 June 1991	27 August 2009 (A); 25 December 2010 (R)
13	Solid Waste Pollution Prevention and Control Law	30 October 1995	1 April 1996	29 December 2004 (R); 29 June 2013 (A); 24 April 2015 (A); 7 November 2016 (A); 29 April 2020 (R)

(continued)

(Continued)

No	Title of the Law	Date of adoption	Date of implementation	Amendment (A) or Revision (R) information
14	Noise Pollution Prevention and Control Law	24 December 2021	5 June 2022	
15	Energy Conservation Law	1 November 1997	1 January 1998	28 October 2007 (R); 2 July 2016 (A); 26 October 2018 (A)
16	Desert Prevention and Transformation Law	31 August 2001	1 January 2002	26 October 2018 (A)
17	Marine Areas Administration Law	27 October 2001	1 January 2002	
18	Cleaner Production Promotion Law	29 June 2002	1 January 2003	29 February 2012 (A)
19	Environmental Impact Assessment Law	28 October 2002	1 September 2003	2 July 2016 (A); 29 December 2018 (A)
20	Radioactive Pollution Prevention and Control Law	28 June 2003	1 October 2003	
21	Renewable Energy Law	28 February 2005	1 January 2006	26 December 2009 (A)
22	Circular Economy Promotion Law	29 August 2008	1 January 2009	26 October 2018 (A)
23	Island Protection Law	26 December 2009	1 March 2010	
24	Law of Exploration and Exploitation of the Resources in Deep Seabed Areas	26 February 2016	1 May 2016	

(continued)

(Continued)

No	Title of the Law	Date of adoption	Date of implementation	Amendment (A) or Revision (R) information
25	Environmental Protection Tax Law	25 December 2016	1 January 2018	26 October 2018 (A)
26	Nuclear Safety Law	1 September 2017	1 January 2018	
27	Soil Pollution Prevention and Control Law	31 August 2018	1 January 2019	
28	Resources Tax Law	26 August 2019	1 September 2020	
29	Biological Security Law	17 October 2020	15 April 2021	
30	Yangtze River Protection Law	26 December 2020	1 March 2021	
31	Wetland Protection Law	24 December 2021	1 June 2022	
32	Black Soil Protection Law	24 June 2022	1 August 2022	
33	Yellow River Protection Law	30 October 2022	1 April 2023	

12

Trade and Labour Links in Free Trade Agreements

A Critical Assessment of the US–Guatemala Panel Report and its Future Impact

FEDERICO ORTINO

> The Members recognize that unfair labour conditions, particularly in production for export, create difficulties in international trade, and, accordingly, each Member shall take whatever action may be appropriate and feasible to eliminate such conditions within its territory.
>
> Article 7.1 of the Havana Charter, 24 March 1948

I. Introduction

The growth and relevance of transnational law is for everyone to see: 'In many respects, it is easier to identify the numerous varieties of transnational law than it is to pinpoint laws and other norms which remain purely national or regional.'[1] One theme in Professor Snyder's vast scholarship has focused on highlighting the contradictory and conflicting aspects of the relationship between globalisation and economic integration. According to Snyder, economic, political and social differences among countries that aim to integrate economically (often initially through the liberalisation of international trade and foreign investment) are deepened by globalisation making such integration uneven and difficult.[2]

[1] F Snyder and L Yi, 'Transnational Law and the European Union: Reflection from WISH in China' (2013) 19 *European Law Journal* 705.

[2] F Snyder, 'Europeanisation and Globalisation as Friends and Rivals: European Union Law and Global Economic Networks' in F Snyder (ed), *The Europeanisation of Law: Legal Effects of European Integration* (Oxford, Hart Publishing, 2000) 293–320.

This chapter focuses on one common site of transnational governance, the vast and growing network of free trade agreements (FTAs) and the emerging controversial issue that pivot trade liberalisation on the one hand and the protection of labour rights on the other hand. Over the past three decades, several countries have in fact recognised the link between trade and the protection of social values (such as labour standards) and have included specific 'disciplines' (or 'chapters') in their FTAs. The 1992 North America Free Trade Agreement (NAFTA) was the first to contain specific labour disciplines. They were contained in a side agreement to NAFTA, entitled the North American Agreement on Labor Cooperation (NAALC), which, for example, imposed on the contracting parties an obligation to provide for high labour standards as well as obligations concerning the enforcement of domestic labour laws. The NAFTA approach has inspired many subsequent FTAs, including those concluded by the European Union (EU) (which often includes labour disciplines in 'sustainable development' chapters). Labour disciplines in trade agreements have evolved over time, particularly in terms of making reference to a greater number of international labour conventions and expanding the availability of enforcement mechanisms.

In particular, this chapter zooms in on a specific phrase that is often found within these labour disciplines, expressly linking labour standards (or their violation) to trade. For example, in the 2004 Dominican Republic-Central America FTA (CAFTA-DR), Article 16.2.1(a) requires the parties not to fail to effectively enforce their labour laws (through a sustained or recurring course of action or inaction) 'in a manner affecting trade between the Parties'. This specific clause was the object of a dispute brought under the CAFTA-DR FTA by the US against Guatemala. Relying on a relatively narrow interpretation of the relevant phrase – 'in a manner affecting trade' – the Panel concluded that the US had failed to demonstrate the required link between Guatemala's failure to enforce its labour standards effectively and trade between the CAFTA-DR parties.[3]

Was the US-Guatemala Panel correct in its interpretation of the specific language on trade links in Article 16.2.1(a) CAFTA-DR? As many labour obligations in FTAs adopt similar language, answering this question has become crucial in order to assess the strength of labour obligations in trade agreements.[4] The EU has, for one thing, used the same language in its recent FTAs, not only with

[3] 'In the Matter of Guatemala – Issues Relating to the Obligations under Article 16.1.1(a) of the CAFTA-DR (US-Guatemala), Final Report of the Panel' (*International Trade Administration*, 14 June 2017), https://www.trade.gov/sites/default/files/2020-09/Guatemala%20%E2%80%93%20Obligations%20Under%20Article%2016-2-1%28a%29%20of%20the%20CAFTA-DR%20%20June%2014%202017_1_0.pdf (hereinafter 'US-Guatemala Panel Report 2017').

[4] K Claussen, 'Reimagining Trade-Plus Compliance: The Labor Story' (2020) 23 *Journal of International Economic Law* 25, 32.

regard to so-called non-enforcement clauses (such as the one in Article 16.2.1(a) CAFTA-DR), but also with regard to non-derogation clauses.[5] Article 13.7 of the 2010 EU–Korea FTA provides a good example of non-enforcement and non-derogation clauses using the same relevant phrase 'in a manner affecting':

> 1. A Party shall not fail to effectively enforce its environmental and labour laws, through a sustained or recurring course of action or inaction, in a manner affecting trade or investment between the Parties.
> 2. A Party shall not weaken or reduce the environmental or labour protections afforded in its laws to encourage trade or investment, by waiving or otherwise derogating from, or offering to waive or otherwise derogate from, its laws, regulations or standards, in a manner affecting trade or investment between the Parties.

Furthermore, the interpretation given by the US-Guatemala Panel may also influence the future application of labour obligations contained in other FTAs that employ differently worded trade links. One example is the 2016 EU–Canada CETA, which links both non-derogation and non-enforcement clauses to an 'encouragement' test. Article 24.5 of the EU–Canada CETA reads, in relevant part, as follows:

> 2. A Party shall not waive or otherwise derogate from, or offer to waive or otherwise derogate from, its environmental law, to encourage trade or the establishment, acquisition, expansion or retention of an investment in its territory.
>
> 3. A Party shall not, through a sustained or recurring course of action or inaction, fail to effectively enforce its environmental law to encourage trade or investment.

Accordingly, the aim of this chapter is to critically assess the decision of the US-Guatemala Panel with regard to the phrase 'in a manner affecting' and attempt to sketch how similar clauses should be interpreted in future disputes. This chapter puts forward two related arguments. First, while the US-Guatemala decision was correct in focusing its analysis under 'in a manner affecting trade' on the impact of the respondent's conduct on the *conditions of competition in international trade*, it erred in apparently excluding from the link analysis that conduct's *potential* impact on those conditions. Second, an interpretation based on actual and potential effect on the conditions of competition in trade or investment should also be extended to similar link clauses in other FTAs. It is suggested that such interpretation better reflects two of the distinct objectives in many modern FTAs, which are the protection of fair competition between the contracting parties and the protection of labour rights.

[5] See M Bronckers and G Gruni, 'Taking the Enforcement of Labour Standards in the EU's Free Trade Agreements Seriously' (2019) 56 *CML Rev* 1591; I Hallak, 'The Level Playing-Field for Labour and Environment in EU-UK Relations' (*European Parliamentary Research Service*, November 2021), https://www.europarl.europa.eu/thinktank/en/document.html?reference=EPRS_BRI%282021%29690576.

The chapter first describes the US-Guatemala Panel Report with regard to the phrase 'in a manner affecting trade' (see section II). It then offers a critical assessment of the panel's interpretation and application of the specific trade link at issue in the US-Guatemala dispute (see section III) and an examination of the potential impact that the panel report may have on how similar provisions will be interpreted in future disputes or clarified by future trade agreements (see section IV).

II. The US-Guatemala Panel Report

Following a complaint from the American Federation of Labor and Congress of Industrial Organizations (AFL-CIO) and six Guatemalan labour unions in 2008, in 2011 the US requested the establishment of a panel pursuant to Article 20.6.1 of CAFTA-DR to consider whether Guatemala had failed to effectively enforce its labour laws related to the right of association, the right to organise and bargain collectively, and acceptable conditions of work in violation of Article 16.2.1(a) CAFTA-DR.

Article 16.2.1(a) stipulates that '[a] Party shall not fail to effectively enforce its labor laws, through a sustained or recurring course of action or inaction, in a manner affecting trade between the Parties, after the date of entry into force of this Agreement'.

While the Panel identified several interpretive issues, the key issue for the purposes of the present analysis is what a complaint must show in order to establish that a failure to enforce labour laws through a sustained or recurring course of action or inaction is 'in a manner affecting trade between the Parties' (para 107). This section briefly identifies the disputing parties' arguments (see section II.A), and describes in detail both the panel's interpretation of the relevant phrase (see section II.B) and its application to the specific facts of the case (see section II.C).

A. The Disputing Parties' Arguments

Based on its ordinary meaning and relying on the broad interpretation given to a similar term in the context of Article III of the General Agreement on Tariffs and Trade (GATT) and Article I of the General Agreement on Trade in Services (GATS), as well as on the CAFTA-DR Agreement's objective to 'promote conditions of fair competition' in Article 1.2, the US submitted that 'in a manner affecting trade' means 'that has a bearing on, influences or changes cross-border economic activity, including by influencing conditions of competition within and among the CAFTA-DR Parties'.[6] According to the US, a complaining party needs

[6] US-Guatemala Panel Report 2017 (n 3) paras 153–56.

to present evidence demonstrating: (1) that there is trade between the parties; and (2) that, based on the responding party's failure to effectively enforce its labour laws, there has been a modification to the conditions of competition. Crucially, the US pointed out that an econometric analysis of the effects on trade is not required, as there is no need to show 'actual trade effects'. The US added that such a requirement would not be 'reasonable or feasible' in the context of labour disputes under the CAFTA-DR.

On the other hand, Guatemala submitted that Article 16.2.1(a) requires an 'unambiguous showing that the challenged conduct has an effect on trade between the Parties'.[7] In other words, the complainant must prove 'actual trade effect' and that this be shown by a change in prices of or trade flows in particular goods or services.

B. The Panel's Interpretation of the Phrase 'in a Manner Affecting Trade'

The Panel's analysis can be divided into three parts: first, it focused on the meaning of the phrase 'in a manner affecting trade'; second, it dealt with the arguments advanced by the disputing parties; and, finally, it put forward what must be shown by a complaining party in order to satisfy the 'in a manner affecting trade' test.

i. The Meaning of 'in a Manner Affecting Trade': 'Trade-Related' versus 'Affecting Conditions of Competition'

First of all, focusing on the wording of the relevant provision, the Panel excluded an interpretation of 'in a manner affecting trade' as equivalent to 'trade-related'. In other words, in the view of the Panel, a failure to effectively enforce labour laws would not be 'in a manner affecting trade' 'simply because it occurred in a traded sector, or with respect to an enterprise engaged in trade'.[8] Pointing to the 'trade-related' language used in the context of the NAFTA side agreement on labour, the Panel said that if that had been the intention of the CAFTA-DR parties, they could have easily done so using such language.

Second, while the Panel emphasised at least three relevant objectives of the CAFTA-DR – (1) to 'enforce basic worker rights', (2) to 'build on their respective international commitments in labour matters' and (3) to 'promote conditions of fair competition in the free trade area' – the Panel seems to privilege the last of these in its interpretation of Article 16.2.1(a). The Panel noted as follows: 'Addressing failures to effectively enforce labour laws that are not in a manner affecting trade, while perhaps desirable for other reasons, presumably would do

[7] ibid para 157.
[8] ibid para 168.

little if anything to promote conditions of fair competition "in the free trade area".[9] In other words, while requiring effective enforcement of labour laws may respond to the objective of enforcing basic worker rights, it would not per se promote conditions of fair competition in the free trade area. The Panel thus concluded that a failure to enforce through a sustained or recurring course of action or inaction is 'in a manner affecting trade' only if it 'confers some competitive advantage on an employer or employers engaged in trade between the Parties'.[10]

Third, the Panel explains the link between the 'failure to enforce' and the 'effect on trade' in the following three steps:

- first, a failure to effectively enforce labour laws 'may affect costs, risks or potential liabilities associated with production processes';
- second, relieving an employer of such costs or risks 'could provide a competitive advantage to such employer' (for example, enabling the employer or employers in question to make economic gains at the expense of employers who are in compliance with the law and in turn incentivising other employers not to respect the rights in question, weakening their protection by law);[11]
- lastly, these competitive advantages could in turn affect conditions of competition in international trade (ie, affect international trade) as long as the 'advantaged' employer or employers are engaged in export or competing with imports.[12]

In other words, according to the Panel, a failure to effectively enforce labour laws may reduce an employer's costs or risks, which in turn could provide a competitive advantage to such an employer, which in turn could affect conditions of competition in international trade, if the employer is engaged in export or competing with imports.

ii. Addressing the Disputing Parties' Arguments: 'Relatively Narrow' versus 'Relatively Broad' Interpretation

Based on this interpretation, the Panel, first of all, rejected the 'relatively narrow' interpretation advanced by Guatemala. According to the Panel, limiting the ambit of Article 16.2.1(a) to failures that produced effects on prices or quantities sold in international trade, as argued by Guatemala, would exclude certain failures to enforce in a way that would not be consistent with the Agreement's objectives and would often make proof of trade effects almost impossible.[13] Second, the Panel

[9] ibid para 171.
[10] ibid para 190.
[11] ibid para 173.
[12] ibid para 174.
[13] ibid para 176. See also para 179: 'If a Party, for example, fails to effectively enforce its labor laws in a way that lowers cost structures of firms operating within its territory, and competing firms in other CAFTA-DR countries respond by lowering wages sufficiently to maintain their market share, there may be no obvious effects on trade flows, and yet the conduct would have affected trade.'

also rejected the 'relatively broad' interpretation advanced by the US, which had relied on the interpretation of the term 'affecting' in the context of the GATT and the GATS. In that context, the World Trade Organization (WTO) Appellate Body has interpreted the term 'affecting' (in Article III:4 GATT and Article I:1 GATS) to include measures that might 'adversely affect' or 'bear upon' conditions of competition between domestic and imported products/services. However, in the view of the US-Guatemala Panel, the function of the relevant term in Article III:4 GATT and Article I:1 GATS is 'significantly different' from the function of the same term in Article 16.2.1(a) CAFTA-DR: in the former, the term 'affecting' assists in defying the types of measure that fall within the scope of the national treatment obligation (or the GATS), whereas in the latter, the relevant term is used in a phrase that forms an essential part of the obligation itself.[14]

iii. The 'in a Manner Affecting Trade' Test: 'Actual' versus 'Potential' Effects?

Turning to the question of what must be shown by a complaining party to establish that a failure to effectively enforce labour laws 'confers a competitive advantage on a participant or participants in trade between the Parties and thus is in a manner affecting trade', the Panel's analysis seems (eventually) to point to the need for the complainant to show *actual* effects. First, the Panel's acknowledgement that the question of whether any given failure to effectively enforce labour laws affects conditions of competition by creating a competitive advantage is 'a question of fact'[15] seems to point to the need to show actual rather than potential effects. Second, the requirement to show actual effects appears implicit in the Panel's statement that 'we need only determine that a competitive advantage has accrued to a relevant employer to find that there is an effect on conditions of competition'.[16] Even if only with regard to one relevant employer, the Panel seems to imply that an actual effect on the conditions of competition needs to be demonstrated.

In a later section, the Panel confirms its emphasis on actual effects when, in order to determine whether a failure to effectively enforce is 'in a manner affecting trade', the Panel sets out the following three-part test:

> (1) whether at the relevant time the enterprises in question exported to one or more of the CAFTA-DR Parties in a competitive market or competed with imports from one or more of the CAFTA-DR Parties;
> (2) what effects, if any, failures to effectively enforce labor laws had on any of those enterprises; and
> (3) whether these effects are sufficient to confer some competitive advantage on such an enterprise or such enterprises.[17]

[14] ibid paras 185–86.
[15] ibid para 192.
[16] ibid paras 192–95.
[17] ibid para 449.

The use of the past tense ('exported' and 'had') seems to indicate that the Panel requires a complaining party to prove that: (a) the enterprise in question has *actually* been involved in trade; and (b) the failure to effectively enforce labour standards has *actually* conferred some competitive advantage on such an enterprise. In other words, the Panel seems to focus on 'actual' effect rather than just 'potential' effect.

However, all these elements are simply indicia of the purported (strict) test, as the Panel does not expressly state that actual effects are indeed required or that potential effects are not sufficient. In fact, one can even find a potentially contradictory element in the Panel's reasoning when the Panel appears to soften the test being formulated by lowering the standard of proof. The Panel states that: (i) 'for a given set of facts, competitive advantage may be inferred on the basis of likely consequences of a failure or of failures to effectively enforce labour laws, or other aspects of the totality of the circumstances';[18] and (ii) that proving competitive advantage does not require proof of cost or other effects 'with any particular degree of precision'.[19]

In conclusion, while the US-Guatemala Panel's interpretation of the phrase 'in a manner affecting trade' seems to imply the need to show *actual* effects on the conditions of competition in international trade, the Panel does not conclusively clarify this issue.

C. The Panel's Application of the 'in a Manner Affecting Trade' Test

Moving from the Panel's *interpretation* of the phrase 'in a manner affecting trade' to its *application* to the specific case at hand, the US-Guatemala Panel does appear to confirm that the claimant needs to show that the respondent's failure to enforce its labour laws has had actual effects on the conditions of competition in international trade.

Having concluded that Guatemala had failed to 'effectively enforce its labour laws' with respect to 74 workers at eight worksites,[20] the Panel then tackled the relevant question of whether these failures were 'in a manner affecting trade'. While the Panel's analysis involved several companies in three different sectors (shipping, garment manufacturing and rubber plantation), the Panel concluded that the US had indeed managed to prove that Guatemala's failures to effectively enforce labour laws were 'in a manner affecting trade' only with regard to one garment manufacturer (Avandia). The Panel eventually found that Article 16.2.1(a) had not been

[18] ibid para 194.
[19] ibid para 195.
[20] See ibid para 428 'The Panel found that Guatemala had failed to compel compliance with court orders to reinstate and compensate workers who had been unlawfully dismissed in the context of union organising activities and also to impose sanctions for such unlawful dismissals.'

breached, on the ground that the only failure to effectively enforce labour laws that *did* affect trade was not enough to meet the additional requirement imposed by Article 16.2.1(a) that such a failure be 'through a sustained or recurring course of action or inaction'.[21]

However, in order to better understand the nature of the 'in a manner affecting trade' test, it is useful to focus on the Panel's application of the test with regard to all three garment manufacturers considered by the Panel (Fribo, Alianza and Avandia).

Applying the three-part test advanced above to the three garment manufacturers, the Panel first of all quickly found that the employers in question were indeed engaged in CAFTA-DR trade at the relevant time.[22] With regard to the other two components of the test – whether the failures to effectively enforce labour laws had any effect on those enterprises and whether such effects were of sufficient scale and duration to confer a competitive advantage on them – the Panel reached different conclusions depending on two sets of costs at issue. The US had argued that a failure to effectively enforce labour laws with regard to the employers at issue had meant that such employers had avoided both: (a) costs associated with paying wages owed to workers who had not been not reinstated and with paying fines imposed to sanction unlawful dismissals ('compensation and sanction costs'); and (b) costs linked with workers' ability to advocate for better pay and working conditions through the formation of a union ('unionisation costs').

With regard to compensation and sanction costs, while the Panel found that there was evidence establishing that each of the three employers avoided these costs, it could not conclude that the failure to ensure the payment of such compensation and penalties in itself conferred a competitive advantage on the garment manufacturers. It found that there was 'no evidence' with regard to 'the total amounts owed to the workers' and to 'the significance of those amounts in relation to the overall labour costs of each firm'.[23]

With regard to the unionisation costs, the Panel found that the failure to enforce orders remedying reprisals against union leaders *did* confer some competitive advantage upon one of the three employers (Avandia), even if there was 'no direct evidence' of the impacts that the dismissals of the entire provisional executive committee of a union in formation had on workers' attempts to form a union and bargain collectively (para 487). While the Panel reiterated that a complainant will generally be required to introduce evidence of the extent and duration of effects of the failure to effectively enforce labour laws protecting the right to organise or the right to bargain collectively,[24] it also reiterated its willingness to

[21] ibid para 505.
[22] ibid para 468.
[23] ibid para 471.
[24] ibid paras 483–85. The Panel recognised, in principle, 'the possibility that a failure to enforce laws against retaliatory dismissals can place an employer at liberty to use effective intimidation tactics', and that this will in turn 'provide such an employer with a competitive advantage by substantially lowering

soften the complainant's evidentiary standard in certain cases. It noted that there may be circumstances in which 'the consequences of a failure to remedy serious violations would be so evident on the face of the failure that further proof would not be necessary, and a Panel could conclude that the failure was in a manner affecting trade'. Based on the circumstances surrounding the failure to enforce the court orders against Avandia, the Panel was prepared to conclude that such a failure 'necessarily conferred some competitive advantage to Avandia by effectively removing the risk that Avandia's employees would organize or bargain collectively for a substantial period of time'.[25]

On the other hand, the Panel concluded that there was insufficient evidence to prove that: (a) the failures to effectively enforce court orders against the other two employers (Fribo and Alianza) conferred some competitive advantage on them;[26] and (b) the failures with regard to all three garment manufacturers incentivised others to violate the relevant labour provisions.[27] These further conclusions eventually led the Panel to find that Article 16.2.1(a) had *not* been breached as the only failure to effectively enforce labour laws that did affect trade (with regard to Avandia) was not enough to meet the additional requirement imposed by Article 16.2.1(a) that such failure was 'through a sustained or recurring course of action or inaction'.[28]

III. Why the US-Guatemala Panel Interpretation of 'in a Manner Affecting Trade' is Unconvincing

The Panel's interpretation of the 'in a manner affecting trade' language as requiring that complaining party establish that: (1) the enterprise(s) in question has *actually* been involved in trade among the FTA parties; and (2) the failure to effectively enforce labour laws has *actually* conferred some competitive advantage on such enterprise(s) is not convincing because the Panel fails to offer any cogent reason to support its conclusion.

the risk of unionization within its facilities on an ongoing basis' (para 483). However, according to the Panel, 'this does not mean that such consequences necessarily will flow each and every time there is a failure to effectively enforce labor laws in relation to freedom of association and the right to bargain collectively. Whether such a failure substantially impairs the ability of an employer's workforce to exercise such rights is a question of fact to be determined in light of the circumstances of each case. Factual circumstances such as the number of workers dismissed, the timing of their dismissal, whether union leaders were dismissed, and the length of time that failure to enforce legal remedies persists may contribute to the likelihood of the failure to enforce necessarily leading to the hypothesized consequences' (para 484).

[25] ibid para 487.

[26] ibid para 488 'The Panel cannot conclude, without more information, that the delay in enforcing reinstatement orders against Fribo and the failure to enforce payment orders in favor of seven workers necessarily substantially impaired the capacity of its workforce to organize and bargain collectively.'

[27] ibid para 490.

[28] ibid para 505.

A. The Ordinary Meaning does not Support the Imposition of an 'Actual' Trade Effect Condition

The reasons advanced by the Panel to support its textual interpretation of the relevant phrase do not really offer a solid justification for requiring 'actual' trade effects. First, the ordinary (ie, dictionary) meaning of the term 'affecting', which is 'having an effect on' or 'making a difference to', appears to leave open the question of whether the existence of *actual effects on one or more employer(s)* is indeed a necessary condition. The phrase 'in a manner affecting trade between the Parties' neither specifies that the effects (of the failure to effectively enforce labour laws) should have actually materialised nor refers to an effect on any individual employer.

Similarly, the Panel's rejection of an interpretation of the 'in a manner affecting trade' phrase that is equivalent to 'trade-related' (ie, it occurred in a traded sector or with respect to an enterprise engaged in trade) does not on its own justify reading 'affecting' as 'having had *actual* effects on an individual employer' either.

Furthermore, the Panel's rejection of an interpretation based on the 'trade-related' language shows the Panel's heavy reliance on the 'plain meaning' of the term 'affecting', without taking into account other contextual elements. For example, while the Panel pointed to the NAALC choice of 'trade-related' (to show that the CAFTA-DR parties could have 'easily' used that language if they had wanted to), the Panel did not seem to consider the relevance of the history of labour obligations in trade agreements and particularly the role that the NAALC and the US had played as part of that history. As noted above, the NAALC was the first attempt to link labour disciplines in a trade agreement, and since then many other trade agreements have included similar disciplines. What is interesting is that the evolution over the past 30 years has been principally to extend those disciplines (for example, by including more references to international labour conventions) and to make them more effective (for example, through binding provisions and greater availability of enforcement mechanisms). Based on this history and evolution, the US-Guatemala Panel could have inquired whether the CAFTA-DR parties had actually meant to impose a (more demanding) condition on the obligation to effectively enforce their labour laws compared with the condition imposed by the NAALC.

Moreover, it is interesting that, following the US-Guatemala Panel report, the US, Mexico and Canada have actually clarified the term 'in a manner affecting trade' in the new chapter on Labour of the US-Mexico-Canada Agreement (USMCA), which modernises the old NAFTA. Footnote 11 in Article 23.5.1 states as follows:

> For greater certainty, a 'course of action or inaction' is 'in a manner affecting trade or investment between the Parties' if the course involves: (i) a person or industry that produces a good or supplies a service traded between the Parties or has an investment

in the territory of the Party that has failed to comply with this obligation; or (ii) a person or industry that produces a good or supplies a service that competes in the territory of a Party with a good or a service of another Party.[29]

This definition appears to be very similar to the 'trade-related' language that the US-Guatemala Panel had quickly rejected and it thus represents a plausible interpretation of the phrase 'in a manner affecting trade' (see section IV below).

B. CAFTA-DR's Object and Purpose do not Support the Imposition of an 'Actual' Trade Effect Condition

As noted above, the Panel found that CAFTA-DR's relevant objectives include (i) the enforcement of basic worker rights, (ii) building on their respective international commitments in labour matters and (iii) promoting conditions of fair competition in the free trade area. However, none of them appears to support an interpretation of 'in a manner affecting trade' as requiring 'actual trade effects'.

First of all, in its interpretation of the phrase 'in a manner affecting trade', the Panel relies heavily on the objective of promoting conditions of fair competition. However, the Panel's interpretation of 'affecting trade' as meaning 'affecting conditions of competition in international trade' does not seem to require per se showing that a competitive advantage has *actually* been conferred on an *individual employer*. A failure to effectively enforce labour laws that has only the *potential* to modify the conditions of competition in the free trade area should be sufficient. This is what the US had in fact argued for: in order to determine whether a failure to effectively enforce labour laws influences conditions of competition within and among the CAFTA-DR parties, there is no need to carry out an econometric (ie, empirical or quantitative) analysis of the effects on trade of such a failure. However, the Panel rejected the US's argument and instead required *actual* effects.

The only justification advanced by the Panel to require *actual* effects on the conditions of competition in international trade appears to be the rejection of the relevance of the broad interpretation of 'affecting' given in the context of the GATT and the GATS, as argued by the US. As noted above, the Panel judged this relevance to be 'misplaced' because the function of the relevant term in Article III:4 GATT and Article I:1 GATS is 'significantly different' from the function of that same term in Article 16.2.1(a) CAFTA-DR. The Panel reasoned that, in the former two provisions, the term 'affecting' assists in defying the scope of the national treatment obligation and the GATS, respectively, whereas in the latter, the relevant term is used in a phrase that forms an essential part of the obligation itself. However, the Panel failed to explain why the alleged different function justifies a

[29] Moreover, the US-Guatemala Panel Report 2017 (ibid) clarifies that: 'For purposes of dispute settlement, a panel shall presume that a failure is in a manner affecting trade or investment between the Parties, unless the responding Party demonstrates otherwise.'

different interpretation of the same phrase. It is submitted that whether a certain phrase (such as 'affecting trade') assists in defying the subject-matter scope of an obligation (or an agreement) or is used instead as an essential part of the obligation itself should *not* be the basis for a different interpretation of that phrase, unless other contextual elements justify such difference. To follow the Panel's reasoning would lead to the conclusion that a broad interpretation is appropriate when it comes to the 'scope of application' of an obligation, while it would not be appropriate with regard to an essential part of the obligation itself. Such a conclusion would need to be explained and justified, which, however, the Panel did not do.

Moreover, drawing a line between what defines the subject-matter scope of an obligation (or an agreement) and what defines the content of an obligation is not always easy. Imagine that Article 16.2.1(a) had been drafted as follows: 'Any Party's failure to effectively enforce its labour laws, through a sustained or recurring course of action or inaction, in a manner affecting trade between the Parties is prohibited.' In this version of the non-enforcement obligation, is 'in a manner affecting trade' part of the obligation's normative content or scope of application?

More fundamentally, the Panel seems to miss the implication of interpreting the phrase 'affecting trade' on the basis of the CAFTA-DR objective of promoting conditions of fair competition in the free trade area to mean 'affecting conditions of competition in international trade'. Conditions of competition in international trade may be affected by a particular governmental conduct even if there is no actual trade at the time of the conduct itself. Accordingly, while a failure to effectively enforce labour laws that has an 'actual impact' on trade will fall under the notion of a failure 'affecting trade', the same should be said for a failure to effectively enforce labour laws that only has a 'potential' – that is, 'future' – impact on trade. Protecting 'conditions of competition' in international trade is not aimed simply at protecting existing trade flows, but also includes potential trade flows.[30] Accordingly, in the context of Article 16.2.1(a) CAFTA-DR, in which, as correctly stated by the Panel, a relevant treaty objective includes the promotion of conditions of fair competition in the free trade area, the interpretation of 'in a manner affecting trade' should ensure that any failure to effectively enforce labour laws is prohibited when such failures have either an actual (ie, past) or potential (ie, future) impact on the conditions of fair competition of trade (in goods or services) among CAFTA-DR parties.

Second, the Panel's interpretation of 'in a manner affecting trade' that requires actual effects on specific employers also appears to go against the other relevant objective of CAFTA-DR, namely 'enforcing basic worker rights'. As an instrument

[30] Appellate Body Report, *United States – Measures Concerning the Importation, Marketing and Sale of Tuna and Tuna Products* (16 May 2012) WT/DS381/AB/R, para 239. In the context of Art III GATT, the broad reading of the term 'affecting' is linked to the drafters' intention to provide 'equal conditions of competition' to domestic and imported products, and thus includes the protection of 'competitive opportunities' for imported products rather than existing 'trade flows': 'It is well established that WTO rules protect competitive opportunities, not trade flows.'

for enforcing basic workers' rights, Article 16.2.1(a) should be principally seen as addressing 'failures to effectively enforce labour laws'. That is the key object of the provision under review. The provision does limit the prohibition through the reference to 'a sustained or recurring course of action or inaction' and 'in a manner affecting trade between the Parties'; however, a narrow interpretation of those two phrases may excessively limit the key objective of addressing failures to effectively enforce labour laws. Conversely, an interpretation of the phrase 'in a manner affecting trade' that includes both actual and potential impact on trade between CAFTA-DR parties would also be in line with the additional, key objective of enforcing basic labour rights.

C. The Panel's Application of the 'Trade Link' Requirement Remains Ambivalent

Lastly, it may be worth noting that the US-Guatemala Panel itself seems to acknowledge the problematic implications of its emphasis on 'actual' effects by softening the evidentiary standard that its emphasis on 'actual effect on individual employer engaged in CAFTA-DR trade' would otherwise require. As noted above, the Panel admits that there may be circumstances in which 'the consequences of a failure to remedy serious violations would be so evident on the face of the failure that further proof would not be necessary, and a Panel could conclude that the failure was in a manner affecting trade'. The softening of the standard of proof clearly makes a claim based on a failure to enforce labour laws easier. Unsurprisingly, the only instance in which the Panel applied such evidentiary softening (with regard to Avandia, a garment manufacturer) was the only instance in which the Panel found that the failures to effectively enforce labour laws were indeed 'in a manner affecting trade'.[31]

More fundamentally, it is not clear what such softening would entail. If there is no evidence showing that certain failures to enforce labour laws have *actually* conferred some competitive advantage on an enterprise, would a panel be able to rely on certain assumptions similar to those permitted to show *potential* effects? For example, the failure to enforce court orders to reinstate union members may be seen as *necessarily* providing a competitive advantage for the employer who is not abiding by such reinstatement orders simply by assuming that such failure would in principle avoid certain 'unionisation costs', which in turn would affect conditions of competition in international trade (whether existing or future trade). Ultimately, is such softening of the standard of proof capable of de facto transforming the required 'actual' effect test into a 'potential' effect test for the purposes of a claim under Article 16.2.1(a) CAFTA-DR? As these questions remain

[31] The US's claim nevertheless failed because the Panel found that there was no sustained course of action, as there was only *one* failure to effectively enforce labour laws in a manner affecting trade.

unanswered in the US-Guatemala Panel report, the Panel's approach with regard to the meaning of the 'in a manner affecting trade' requirement remains somewhat ambivalent.

IV. Trade (and Investment) Links in Labour Obligations: Where Do We Go from Here?

It is difficult to assess what impact the US-Guatemala Panel Report is going to have on how similar provisions will be interpreted in future disputes (or, for that matter, clarified in future trade agreements). Formally speaking, the US-Guatemala decision does not constitute a binding precedent for future dispute settlement panels, whether interpreting the same language in Article 16.2.1(a) CAFTA-DR or similarly worded provisions in other FTAs, as there is no rule of stare decisis (or binding precedent) in international law.[32] It will, however, have the potential of representing a persuasive precedent which (at least one of) the disputing parties may rely on and which the adjudicator may in turn need at least to consider.[33] Accordingly, the potential impact of the US-Guatemala Panel Report will depend on the perceived strength of its underlying reasoning.

Moreover, while the future relevance of the US-Guatemala Panel Report may also rely on adjudicators' general unwillingness to expressly overrule or contradict past decisions, various judicial techniques exist that make it possible to move past an 'uncomfortable' precedent without expressly acknowledging the conflict. Aside from ignoring it altogether, adjudicators can clarify or reinterpret what the past decision stands for; they can also supplement the earlier decision or distinguish it.[34] Future adjudicators enjoy plenty of leeway in interpreting the same or similar language linking trade with labour law that was at issue in the US-Guatemala dispute. The following sections highlight: (i) how future dispute settlement panels should approach these links, particularly focusing on the lessons learned from the US-Guatemala decision; and (ii) how policy makers have reacted to the US-Guatemala decision, focusing on the United States-Mexico-Canada Agreement (USCMA).

[32] G Acquaviva and F Pocar, 'Stare Decisis' (*Max Planck Encyclopaedia of International Law*, January 2022), https://opil.ouplaw.com/view/10.1093/law:epil/9780199231690/law-9780199231690-e1683?rskey=DYnnN3&result=2&prd=OPIL.

[33] G Guillaume, 'The Use of Precedent by International Judges and Arbitrators' (2011) 2 *Journal of International Dispute Settlement* 5; R Bhala, 'The Myth about Stare Decisis and International Trade Law (Part One of a Trilogy)' (1999) 14(4) *American University International Law Review* 845.

[34] See J Hanna, 'The Role of Precedent in Judicial Decision' (1957) 2(3) *Villanova Law Review* 367, 371. For an example of 'distinguishing' involving the US-Guatemala Panel Report, see J Murray, L Boisson de Chazournes and J Lee, 'Panel of Experts Proceeding constituted under Article 13.15 of the EU-Korea Free Trade Agreement' (*European Commission*, 20 January 2021), paras 90–93, https://trade.ec.europa.eu/doclib/docs/2021/january/tradoc_159358.pdf.

A. 'In a Manner Affecting Trade or Investment'

It is submitted that the interpretation of the phrase 'in a manner affecting trade' in other labour (or sustainable development) chapters of FTAs should focus, as in the US-Guatemala Panel Report, on the effect that the respondent's conduct under review has on the *conditions of competition in international trade* rather than on trade flows. However, the US-Guatemala Panel's apparent reliance on 'actual' effects should be rejected in favour of allowing both *actual* and *potential* effect on the conditions of competition in international trade.

This broader interpretation is in line in particular with the ordinary meaning of the relevant phrase and the object and purpose of the labour disciplines in trade agreements. As noted above, the term 'affecting' (or 'having an effect on') does not limit the relevant effect to 'actual' effects and thus the term could be interpreted to include 'potential' effects too.

The object and purpose of the trade agreement is then key to interpreting the phrase 'affecting trade'. The US-Guatemala Panel was correct in identifying multiple relevant objectives, in particular the 'enforcement of basic worker rights' and the 'promotion of fair competition in the free trade area'. These two objectives are central to understanding the labour disciplines included in many trade agreements (including CAFTA-DR) concluded over the past 30 years and thus they play an important role in interpreting a phrase such as 'in a manner affecting trade'. Accordingly, 'affecting trade' should be interpreted as affecting the conditions of competition in international trade (rather than affecting trade flows), and an effect on conditions of competition should include both actual and potential effects (rather than just actual effects). As noted above, a narrow interpretation (focusing on either trade flows or actual effects on trade only) would undermine the two key objectives of promoting fair competition in the free trade area and enforcing basic worker rights.[35]

An interpretation that focuses on the (actual or potential) impact on the conditions of competition would be valid independently of the specific labour provision to which it is applied. For example, in addition to other non-enforcement provisions similar to Article 16.2.1(a) CAFTA-DR (such as Article 13.7.1 of the EU-Korea FTA), it would also apply to non-derogation provisions requiring a

[35] This conclusion may be strengthened if the parties to the applicable trade agreement have put greater emphasis on the protection and promotion of labour rights. See Murray, Boisson de Chazournes and Lee (n 34) para 93: 'Even if the matters raised before the CAFTA-DR Panel were identical to those in the EU's Panel Request, the Panel notes that there are important differences between the texts of the CAFTA-DR Agreement and the EU-Korea FTA which would require careful examination. Most notably, the CAFTA-DR Agreement's Chapter 16, which contains the provision upon which the United States of America made its complaint against Guatemala, does not have the same contextual setting of sustainable development as the EU-Korea FTA, nor does it refer to the range of multilateral and international agreements and declarations which the Parties have included in the EU-Korea FTA.'

party not to waive or derogate from its labour laws and regulations 'in a manner affecting trade' (such as Article 13.7.2 of the EU-Korea FTA).[36]

What would a complaining party have to prove in order to establish that, for example, a 'derogation from' or 'failure to enforce' its labour laws have an effect on the conditions of competition in international trade? There appear to be two key elements in applying the 'actual or potential effect on conditions of competition' test identified above. First, a complaining party would need to establish that either a derogation from its labour laws or a failure to enforce (through a sustained or recurrent course of action or inaction) such laws has modified the conditions of competition, for example, by reducing the costs of the domestic producers or service providers. For example, in the US-Guatemala dispute, the US had argued that it had demonstrated such modification of the conditions of competition by showing, for example, that Guatemala's failure to compel compliance with court orders for reinstatement had permitted Guatemalan employers to evade the payment of back wages, economic benefits and fines ordered by the domestic labour courts. The focus should be on the conduct under review (ie, the derogation from, or failure to enforce, labour laws) and its ability to affect the conditions of competition.

Second, a complaining party would also need to show that a derogation from, or failure to enforce, labour laws has modified the conditions of competition *on international trade*. If the employer (benefiting from the derogation or failure to enforce labour laws) produces goods or provides services that are exported abroad or that compete with imports, such a second requirement would easily be met.[37] This would arguably also include the case of products and services that are components of products and services that are actually traded as the alleged derogation and failure to enforce labour laws with regard to the components may affect the entire supply chain. Furthermore, it is argued that a derogation from, or failure to enforce, labour laws can also modify the conditions of competition on international trade *even if* the products or services affected have *not* yet been traded (as imports or exports), as long as those products or services could be lawfully traded. For example, a derogation from or failure to enforce labour laws may 'affect trade' simply by (contributing to) preventing the importation of a competing product or service from abroad.

[36] A Mitchell and J Munro, 'No Retreat: An Emerging Principle of Non-regression from Environmental Protections in International Investment Law' (2019) 50 *Georgetown Journal of International Law* 625, 686.

[37] As noted above, this is the definition of 'in a manner affecting trade' that has recently been included in the USMCA: 'For greater certainty, a failure is "in a manner affecting trade or investment between the Parties" if it involves: (i) a person or industry that produces a good or supplies a service traded between the Parties or has an investment in the territory of the Party that has failed to comply with this obligation; or (ii) a person or industry that produces a good or supplies a service that competes in the territory of a Party with a good or a service of another Party.'

B. 'To Encourage Trade or Investment'

In certain trade agreements, labour disciplines employ different terminology in linking trade (and investment) with specific labour obligations, such as non-derogation and non-enforcement provisions. As noted in the introduction, Article 24.5 EU-Canada of the CETA links the parties' obligation not to derogate from, or fail to effectively enforce, their labour laws with the encouragement of trade or investment. For example, Article 24.5.3 EU-Canada of the CETA reads as follows:

> A Party shall not, through a sustained or recurring course of action or inaction, fail to effectively enforce its environmental law to encourage trade or investment.

The origin of this language appears to be the environmental non-derogation clause contained in the investment chapter of NAFTA.[38] The aim was to address so-called 'incentives competition' and avoid a possible 'race to the bottom' by prohibiting a host state from derogating its environmental laws for purposes of attracting a specific foreign investor.[39] The phrase 'to encourage' (or 'as an encouragement') can now be found in labour (or sustainable development) chapters as a substitute for the 'in a manner affecting' language.[40]

Some commentators have suggested that 'encouraging' is narrower than 'affecting'[41] and that it appears to require an 'intent' to affect trade.[42] According to Mitchell and Munro, the prepositions 'to' and 'as' suggest that, in order to fall within the scope of the labour obligation (ie, non-derogation provision), the derogation from labour laws 'must be the mechanism through which the "encouragement" is given effect'.[43] In other words, the 'purpose' or 'intention' of the derogation must be the encouragement of trade (or investment).[44]

It is submitted that future adjudicators should interpret the 'to encourage trade' language in light of the US-Guatemala Panel Report and the ensuing discussion regarding labour (and environmental) disciplines in trade agreements. For example, interpreting the 'to encourage trade' phrase as imposing a requirement

[38] 'A Party should not waive or otherwise derogate from, or offer to waive or otherwise derogate from, such measures as an encouragement for the establishment, acquisition, expansion or retention in its territory of an investment of an investor.' See Article 1114(2) NAFTA.

[39] UNCTAD, *Incentives – UNCTAD Series on Issues in International Investment Agreements* (Geneva, United Nations, (2003), https://unctad.org/webflyer/incentives.

[40] See, for example, the 2019 EU-Mercosur and the 2018 EU-Mexico FTAs, both of which have been agreed in principle.

[41] Mitchell and Munro (n 36) 686.

[42] Bronckers and Gruni (n 5) 1597.

[43] Mitchell and Munro (n 36) 680.

[44] Mitchell and Munro (n 36) refer to a decision of the WTO Appellate Body stating that: 'The word "to" in adverbial relation with the infinitive verb "protect" indicates a purpose or intention. Thus, it establishes a required link between the measure and the protected interest.' See Appellate Body Report, *Australia – Measures Affecting the Importation of Apples from New Zealand* (29 November 2010) WT/DS367/AB/R, para 172.

on the complaining party to establish the responding party's *subjective intention* linking the derogation from, or failure to enforce, labour laws with the encouragement of trade (or investment) should be rejected as too restrictive and not in line with the relevant object and purpose of the trade agreement. A more convincing alternative interpretation would be to focus instead on whether the derogation or failure to enforce *is capable of* encouraging trade (or investment). The analysis should thus focus on the *potential* of the conduct under review (ie, a derogation or failure to enforce labour laws) to encourage trade rather than on the party's intent to do so. In this sense, Bartels has pointed to the WTO Appellate Body's reliance on 'objective intention' in order to interpret the phrase 'so as to afford protection' in the context of Article III GATT,[45] which involves an 'objective analysis of the structure and application of the measure' rather than 'the many reasons legislators or regulators often have for what they do'.[46]

Accordingly, a determination of whether a derogation from, or failure to effectively enforce, labour laws is 'to encourage trade or investment' will involve an examination not dissimilar to the one based on 'in a manner affecting', as suggested above: the adjudicator's key question would be whether the derogation or failure has the *potential* to encourage exports or inward foreign investments by, for example, reducing the costs of manufacturers or service providers (operating in the territory of the responding party) and thus affecting the conditions of competition on trade or investment.

i. 'Material Impacts on Trade or Investment ... Arising as a Result of Significant Divergences' in the EU-UK Trade and Cooperation Agreement

While the discussion linked with the US-Guatemala Panel Report can certainly be instructive in the interpretation of other relevant links between labour and trade – as, for example, in the novel 'rebalancing' provision of the EU-UK Trade and Cooperation Agreement (TCA) (Article 411 or 9.4) – future adjudicators should also be mindful of any relevant textual and contextual differences.

The rebalancing provision in the EU-UK TCA requires that a significant divergence in labour laws has 'material impacts on trade or investment'. It is submitted that, similar to the link clauses in the more traditional labour disciplines examined above, the rebalancing provision in the EU-UK TCA focuses on whether a significant divergence in labour laws has an impact *on the conditions of competition* on

[45] L Bartels, 'Human Rights, Labour Standards, and Environmental Standards in CETA' in S Griller, W Obwexer and E Vranes (eds), *Mega-Regional Trade Agreements: CETA, TTIP, and TiSA: New Orientations for EU External Economic Relations* (Oxford, Oxford University Press, 2017) 206; L Bartels, 'Social Issues: Labour, Environment and Human Rights' in S Lester, B Mercurio and L Bartels (eds), *Bilateral and Regional Trade Agreements: Commentary and Analysis*, 2nd edn (Cambridge, Cambridge University Press, 2016) 364.

[46] Appellate Body Report, *Japan Alcoholic Beverages II* (4 October 1996) WT/DS8/AB/R, 27 and 29.

trade or investment between the two parties. However, unlike the link clauses in more traditional labour disciplines, the rebalancing provision in the EU-UK TCA specifies that the impact be 'material' (that is, 'significant'), and that it be 'based on reliable evidence and not merely on conjecture or remote possibility' (Article 9.4.2 EU-UK TCA). These two additional requirements seem to impose a higher threshold for establishing the required link between 'impact on trade or investment' and 'regulatory divergence' compared with the 'affecting' or 'encouraging' language examined above. However, it is submitted that the nature of the analysis is not fundamentally different. Even the express reference to 'reliable evidence' and rejection of 'conjecture' do not appear to exclude reliance on the *potential* impact on trade or investment stemming from such regulatory divergence.

ii. Policy Makers' Options Going Forward: Two Examples from the USMCA

The recent NAFTA update, the USMCA, provides an interesting case study of how policy makers may react to the US-Guatemala decision or, more broadly, to the challenges of labour disciplines in trade agreements. The section focuses on: (i) the clarification of the phrase 'in a manner affecting trade'; and (ii) the introduction of the labour value content (LVC) rule for automotive trade.

a. Clarification of the Phrase 'in a Manner Affecting Trade'

As noted above, following the US-Guatemala Panel report, the US, Mexico and Canada have clarified the term 'in a manner affecting trade' in the USMCA non-enforcement provision with the addition, in a footnote, of the following text:

> For greater certainty, a 'course of action or inaction' is 'in a manner affecting trade or investment between the Parties' if the course involves: (i) a person or industry that produces a good or supplies a service traded between the Parties or has an investment in the territory of the Party that has failed to comply with this obligation; or (ii) a person or industry that produces a good or supplies a service that competes in the territory of a Party with a good or a service of another Party. (Article 23.5.1, footnote 11)[47]

The new USMCA language clearly challenges the strict interpretation given to 'in a manner affecting trade' by the US-Guatemala Panel,[48] and appears to adopt a broader understanding of the required link between the responding party's conduct (ie, the failure to effectively enforce labour laws) and trade between the parties. In particular, the choice of the verb 'to involve' seems to exclude the need to demonstrate an *actual* impact on trade (as required by the US-Guatemala Panel)

[47] Same clarification has also been added in other labour obligations in the USMCA, such as the non-derogation provision in Article 23.4.

[48] R Zandvliet, 'Trade, Investment and Labour: Interactions in International Law' (doctoral thesis, University of Leiden, 2019) 221.

and to point instead to conduct that may more simply 'concern' or 'relate to' trade. Furthermore, the new language also clarifies the meaning of 'trade between the parties' by specifying that the relevant conduct under review involves 'a person or industry producing a good or supplying a service that is traded between the Parties' or is 'in competition with a good or service of another Party'.

While not altogether clear, a reading of the new language does not seem to require that the employer benefiting from the responding party's failure to effectively enforce its labour laws be *directly* involved in international trade. However, a failure to enforce labour laws taking place along the supply chain (whether upstream or downstream) could be said to be *indirectly* involving a person or industry producing a good or supplying a service that is traded or in competition with a good/service of another party.

The USMCA also makes it easier for the complaining party to satisfy the trade link requirement by establishing a presumption in favour of an effect on trade in the following terms:

> For purposes of dispute settlement, a panel shall presume that a failure is in a manner affecting trade or investment between the Parties, unless the responding Party demonstrates otherwise. (Article 23.5.1, footnote 12)

b. The Labour Value Content Rule

The new LVC rule introduced by the USMCA provides a second interesting example of possible reactions to the frustration, following the US-Guatemala decision, of ensuring the protection of labour rights and fair competition through traditional labour disciplines in trade agreements. The new LVC rule basically requires that, in order to enjoy the preferential tariff treatment of the USMCA (zero tariff), a minimum of 40 per cent of the value of a vehicle's content must be produced by workers earning at least US$16 per hour. In other words, the new LVC rule is a 'rule of origin' based on a non-product-related (NPR) process and production method (PPM).[49]

In theory, the new LVC rule will either push wages up in the automotive sector (particularly in Mexico, where the current average wage in manufacturing appears to be one-third of the US$16 per hour rate set in the USMCA) or increase demand for automotive parts produced in USMCA parties with already high wages (like the US). While the actual impact of the new rule of origin for the automotive sector remains unclear, it seems that, from the perspective of the 'protection of labour rights' and the 'improvement of working conditions' (see the preamble to the USMCA), the impact is, even in the best-case scenario, limited in important ways. Besides the fact that the new LVC rule applies only to the automotive sector,

[49] See C Conrad, *Process and Production Methods in WTO Law: Interfacing Trade and Social Goals* (Cambridge, Cambridge University Press, 2014).

the rule has an inherently strong trade link feature as it functions only as a condition for preferential tariff treatment. In other words, the LVC rule will push up automotive workers' wages only to the extent that the relevant vehicle is exported and the preferential tariff treatment (for example, US most-favoured nation (MFN) tariff for passenger cars is 2.5 per cent ad valorem) outweighs the higher costs of production.

V. Conclusion

The US-Guatemala Panel report clearly highlights the importance and controversy of the trade and labour link in trade agreements. Specifically, many (but not all) of the labour obligations included in trade agreements are subject to a more or less specific trade link requirement. Such a trade link requirement seems to be justified on the basis that labour disciplines in trade agreements respond to two distinct objectives: the protection of labour rights on the one hand and the protection of fair competition between the contracting parties on the other hand. However, the language used to capture the trade link requirement often lacks precision (and differs from provision to provision and from trade agreement to trade agreement) and thus needs to be interpreted by a dispute settlement panel in case a dispute arises. As the US-Guatemala dispute shows, the interpretation of the specific trade link requirement may play a crucial role in enforcing labour disciplines in trade agreements. In the chapter, it has been submitted that, while the US-Guatemala decision was correct in focusing its analysis under 'in a manner affecting trade' on the impact of the respondent's conduct on the *conditions of competition in international trade*, it erred in apparently excluding from the link analysis the conduct's *potential* impact on those conditions. Such exclusion has clear implications for the relevance of labour disciplines in FTAs as well as, more fundamentally, the protection of labour rights and fair competition between the contracting parties of the FTA.

Looking forward, this chapter has also argued that future dispute settlement panels should interpret similar link clauses by focusing on the actual or potential impact of the respondent's conduct on the conditions of competition in trade or investment. However, policy makers should consider two options, which do not rely on the dispute settlement panels adopting the correct interpretation of the required link between labour rights and trade. The first option is to clarify the meaning of the trade link, as the US, Mexico and Canada have attempted to do in the context of the USMCA. The clarification could of course go in different directions, either tightening or loosening the link. The second option is to eliminate any specific trade link for labour obligations in trade agreements, thus strengthening such disciplines. As confirmed by the Panel of Experts in the EU-Korea FTA, there already exist labour provisions in trade agreements that do not require such a link (this is particularly the case for those provisions requiring that the contracting parties implement certain multilateral labour obligations, such as Article 13.4 of the EU-Korea FTA or Article 23.3 of the EU-Canada CETA).[50] If the parallel demands for more labour rights protection and fair competition among countries continue to grow, one should not be surprised if future trade agreements start to go for the latter option. This latter approach may not always be politically feasible but, if adopted, it would have the benefit of addressing head-on the potential conflicts between greater liberalisation of trade and investment and differences in the economic, political and social fabric of any participating countries.

[50] Report of the Panel of Experts EU-Korea FTA 2021 (n 34).

13

Precaution: China's Authorisation of Genetically Modified Crops

ZINING JIN

I. Introduction

It is an honour to be asked to contribute to this *Liber Amicorum* in honour of Professor Francis Snyder, not only because he is a distinguished scholar with a large number of publications – he is so very well known and highly acknowledged as an expert on EU–China relations and China's food law that he was invited by the Chinese Central Government in 2013 to serve as lead foreign expert on reform of food safety system in China – but also because I had the pleasure of working with him as a colleague from 2012 to 2015 at the School of Transnational Law of Peking University (Shenzhen campus) and I have been deeply grateful for his guidance and support over the years.

As Professor Snyder has highlighted: 'Health, shelter, and food are essential human needs.' However, 'we have seen increased risks throughout the world concerning food security (do people have enough to eat?), food safety (is our food safe to eat?), and food quality (is our food nutritious?)', and related researches (and teaching) shall 'contribute to safeguarding the present and ensuring a future that it is ecologically sound and environmentally sustainable'.[1] Therefore, the topic of this chapter is to take up Professor Snyder's thoughts on China's food safety and agriculture law,[2] along with making use of what I have learnt from sitting in on his classes on EU law at the School of Transnational Law of Peking University.

Genetic modification, also known as genome engineering, is one of the most exciting modern technologies enabling scientists make changes to DNA. The first genome engineering technologies were developed in the late 1900s, and now

[1] F Snyder, 'Bio of Faculty', https://stl.pku.edu.cn/cn/info/1070/2135.htm.
[2] F Snyder, *Food Safety Law in China: Making Transnational Law* (Leiden, Brill, 2016).

scientists can remove, add or replace the DNA of many organisms, including plants, bacteria and animals, either within or across species. As a controversial application of genome engineering technologies,[3] genetically modified (GM) crops are plants used in agriculture, whose DNA has been modified to induce desired new traits, such as improved resistance to disease/pests/herbicides, increased yields and nutrients, and enhanced quality and taste.

It is widely believed that the application of genetic modification technology is going to reap tremendous benefits, although it is also accompanied by huge risks. Heated debates have been sparked repeatedly across the globe on using biotechnology in agriculture, especially in the case of GM crops.[4] It is important to establish or maintain means to regulate, manage or control the risks associated with the use of genetically modified organisms (GMOs), while many countries, including China, have been struggling with issues involving competing factors regarding GM crops, such as safety and acceptance.

The legal implications of sustainable development should be placed in specific contexts. In the case of GM crops, there are two sides of the same coin. On the one side, China must grow food for nearly one-fifth of the world's population, with access to limited natural resources such as freshwater and arable land, which cannot be substantially improved in the near future. Hence, it has been claimed that 'China cannot afford to turn its back' on genetic modification, given the potential of the technology 'to produce more food with less pollution'.[5] On the other hand, the ban on employing gene technology in any major food product in China has been welcomed as a 'decision to put the interests of the Chinese people before the interest of transnational biotech companies', and investment in gene technology instead of 'ecological agriculture' has been criticised as 'a big obstacle for the development of modern sustainable agriculture in China'.[6]

This chapter is an essay in understanding risk regulation concerning GM crops in China. Section II provides a brief introduction presenting China's existing system regulating GM crops, including the historical evolution of practices and the normative framework. Section III turns to the precautionary principle and identifies features of China's authorisation of GM crops compared to the US and the European Union (EU). The remainder of the chapter explores possible suggestions to improve China's regulation of GM crops by examining the implications of the precautionary principle, especially how to structure the precautionary principle under scientific uncertainties.

[3] Another highly controversial application is human genome editing, especially for reproductive purposes.

[4] US-NAS Committee, *Genetically Engineered Crops: Experiences and Prospects* (Washington DC, National Academies Press, 2016).

[5] Q Wang, 'China's Scientists Must Engage the Public on GM' (2015) 519 *Nature* 7.

[6] 'Greenpeace Welcomes China's Courageous Stand on GM Crops', www.greenpeace.org.au/news/greenpeace-welcomes-chinas-courageous-stand-on-gm-crops.

II. China's Authorisation of GM Crops: Practice and Regulatory System

A. The Practice of Authorising GM Crops in China

China was among the first countries to grow GM crops commercially (starting with virus-resistant tobacco plants).[7] In the 1990s, China seemed to embrace biotechnology farming by authorising genetically modified plants, such as Bt cotton, tomatoes, sweet peppers and petunias, to be grown domestically with no discernible objections from the public, even though the technology of genetically modifying has been controversial in the world ever since DNA combination in the 1970s.[8] In those early days, beside the desired new traits of GM crops which have direct benefits to producers or consumers, other potential advantages have also been stressed in China, such as increasing food security (due to increased yield), helping environmental protection (through deceasing the need to use pesticides), serving the needs of sustainable development (as to conservation of soil, water and energy) etc.

Events took a dramatic turn in China at the beginning of the twenty-first century and what turned up with surprising frequency was concern that GMOs might endanger human health and ecosystems.[9] This turn was so clear that it was impossible to be ignored, especially after two GM rice varieties (Huahui-1 and Xianyou63), for the first time in China, were granted biosafety certificates in 2009, which was considered an important step in order for the crops to be commercialised. Contrary to the expectation that China would be the first nation to commercialise GM rice with no strong public objections,[10] campaigns against GMOs propagated through social media[11] have greatly swayed public perceptions to anti-GMOs. Surveys showed that at the beginning of the twenty-first century, Chinese consumers' acceptance level of GM foods in China – ranging from 57 per cent to 88 per cent – was very high compared with many other countries that have been reported in the literature,[12] whereas it was reported that the acceptance level declined sharply a decade later and consumers who perceived GM food to be unsafe increased from 13 per cent in 2002 to 45 per cent in 2012.[13]

[7] Which was removed from production because of international pressure.

[8] P Berg et al, 'Potential Biohazards of Recombinant DNA Molecules' (1974) 185 *Science* 303.

[9] Why this turn happened is still to be explored, while one of the obviously influential factors was China's signing of the Cartagena Protocol on Biosafety to the Convention on Biological Diversity in 2000 (approved by the State Council in 2005).

[10] X Lei, 'China Could Be First Nation to Approve Sale of GM Rice' (2004) 306 *Science* 1458.

[11] Z Xiao and WA Kerr, 'Biotechnology in China: Regulation, Investment, and Delayed Commercialization (2022) 13(1) *GM Crops & Food* 86.

[12] J Huang, H Qiu, J Bai and C Pray, 'Awareness, Acceptance of and Willingness to Buy Genetically Modified Foods in Urban China' (2006) 46 *Appetite* 144.

[13] J-K Huan and B-W Peng, 'Consumers' Perceptions on GM Food Safety in Urban China' (2015) 14 *Journal of Integrative Agriculture* 2391.

The government had been obviously stalled in issuing approvals for GMOs ever since the turn of the twenty-first century. In the case of GM crops, the government had been silent in authorising GM crops for a decade ever since 2009. When China finally resumed the issuing of biosafety certificates to domestically developed maize and soybean varieties in 2019, none of them has achieved commercialisation. In fact, no genetically modified rice varieties have ever successfully attained permits for commercial cultivation in China up to the present day, and Bt cotton is still the only GM crop that is widely grown in China,[14] which received approval from the government in 1997.

B. China's Legal System of Authorising GM Crops

If we examine closely the different languages used to articulate legislative purposes of related decrees issued by the Chinese government, indications of the turn of the century mentioned above had already showed before the strong opposition to authorisation of GM crops manifested in the public media. *Measures for the Safety Administration of Genetic Engineering*[15] promulgated in 1993, which was the first formal national administrative rule for genetic engineering in China, states that its purposes are 'to promote the research and development of agricultural genetically modified technology', followed by 'safety', 'the public and workers' health' and environment protection. By contrast, by 2001, the Regulation on Administration of Agricultural GMOs Safety[16] (see also below) states its purposes as 'to protect human health and secure biosafety', followed by 'promote the research and development of agricultural genetically modified technology'. The legislative purposes listed in those two decrees are similar, while the priorities varied: the latter placed more emphasis on safety in contrast to the former, which placed more on the development of technology.

All in all, considering both pro-technology and biosafety, China has established a regulatory regime for agricultural GMOs, including GM crops, over decades. Even though there are a few general provisions concerning GM plants included in several national laws, such as the Seed Law (种子法) passed by the National People's Congress (NPC) in 2000,[17] the Agriculture Law (农业法) amended by the NPC in 2002,[18] and the Environmental Protection Law 环境保护法) amended by the NPC in 2014,[19] authorising GM crops in China has long been based on the

[14] Another GM crop, papaya, is limited to Gunagdong Province.

[15] Issued by the State Science and Technology Commission of the People's Republic of China, which has been reorganised as the Ministry of Science and Technology in 1998 《基因工程安全管理办法》.

[16] 《农业转基因生物安全管理条例》.

[17] Article 14 (which became Article 7 when the law was revised in 2013, 2015 and 2021).

[18] Article 64(2), which was revised in 2009 and 2012.

[19] Article 30(2).

so-called 'one regulation & four rules', which provided more specific requirements in relation to standards and procedures of the approval of GM crops.

'One regulation' refers to the Regulation on Administration of Agricultural GMOs Safety[20] promulgated by the State Council in 2001, which states that the Ministry of Agriculture (MOA) is in charge of the administration of national agricultural GMOs. According to this regulation, agricultural GMOs are divided into classes I, II, III and V, depending on the nature of their potential risk to humans, animals, plants and micro-organisms, and each class has its own requirements for safety assessment. To implement this 'one regulation', three administrative rules[21] were issued in 2002 by the MOA, which regulate biosafety evaluation, administration for imports and labelling of GMOs respectively. The last administrative rule of the 'four rules' refers to a rule issued by the MOA in 2006[22] regulating processing of GMOs.

'One regulation and four rules' set out the biosafety evaluation system of agricultural GMOs. The evaluation system aims to detect the dangers or potential risks that may be caused by agricultural GMOs to humans, animals, plants and micro-organisms, and the environment. Before commercialisation, an applicant must go through each step of the whole approval procedures of research: from study in laboratories and small-scale experiments under controlled conditions (intermediate experiments) to release to environment and trial production, the applicant can only move to the next step after passing the safety evaluation. It should be noted that although safety evaluation is conducted by the Committee for Biosafety of Agricultural GMOs, which is organised and overseen by the MOA according to the 'one regulation', it is the MOA that has the legal power to issue biosafety certificates based on biosafety assessment. For genetically modified crop seed, a biosafety certificate from the MOA is also required for the new variety's examination and approval.

Under the legal framework of 'one regulation and four rules', when the research of GMOs is done and a biosafety certificate is granted, permits from the MOA are still required to produce, process, sell or import/export GMOs. Moreover, GMOs shall be labelled if listed in the particular catalogue issued by the MOA, and the GMOs label must be 'prominent' (醒目) and using specific language provided by the rules, otherwise the products will not be sold in China.

Figure 13.1 Key steps required for governmental approval for commercialised GM crops in China

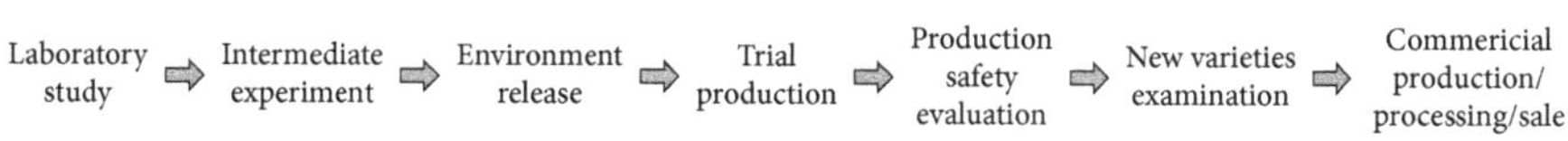

[20] 《农业转基因生物安全管理条例》.

[21] Amended in 2004, 2016, 2017 and 2022, respectively. 《农业转基因生物安全评价管理办法》、《农业转基因生物进口安全管理办法》、《农业转基因生物标识管理办法》.

[22] Amended in 2019. 《农业转基因生物加工审批办法》.

III. Precaution: Comparing China to the EU and the US

The most astounding thing about gene modification is that, unlike making changes to objects without life, this technology changes living creatures. This means that its products are no longer something like cold machines, but 'living' lives that can grow, breed and adapt to changes. While they are alive, they interact with other lives (including but not limited to human beings) as vital components of the functioning ecosystem; hence, they have the potential to change the ecosystem fundamentally. Therefore, the particular consequences are difficult, if not impossible, for scientists to predict.

Accordingly, unique concerns about GM crops have been raised. Besides worries about the adverse impacts of GM food which are not evident immediately, there are also other concerns, including the unintended transfer of modified genes through cross-pollination (gene flow/gene drift), creating 'super weeds' or 'super pests', which will be immune to common control methods, accidental harm to non-target organisms, and loss of flora and fauna biodiversity, especially the long-term impact of gene fusion of different species on human health and ecological systems. These disadvantages are mostly not conclusive, and a lot more research is required to better understand them. To cut a long story short, due to the limitations of the existing scientific knowledge, even scientists with expertise cannot be completely certain about the potential risks of GM crops. Thereby, the precautionary principle is invoked to acknowledge the limits of science as a basis for policy.[23]

Broadly speaking, the precautionary principle indicates that the 'lack of full scientific certainty' should not delay the adoption of measures to control-related risks.[24] It is difficult to give a common formulation of the precautionary principle,[25] though there is no doubt that the regulation of GM crops is one of the typical circumstances where the principle could be applied – if we agree that the precautionary principle is relevant where risk regulation is about to be carried out in cases of scientific uncertainties.[26] As the saying goes, 'better safe than sorry'.

A. The EU Model Versus the US Model

The Maastricht Treaty 1992 recognised the precautionary principle as a guiding principle of EU environmental law.[27] EU measures governing GM crops explicitly

[23] L Levidow, 'Precautionary Uncertainty: Regulating GM Crops in Europe' (2001) 6 *Social Studies of Science* 842.

[24] Principle 15 of the Rio Declaration on Environment and Development (18 December 1992).

[25] Some researchers even argue that there is no such thing as 'the' precautionary principle because there are so many different versions of the principle. CD Stone, 'Is There a Precautionary Principle?' (2001) 31 *Environmental Law Reporter* 10790.

[26] E Fisher, 'Precaution, Precaution Everywhere: Developing a Common Understanding of the Precautionary Principle in the European Community' (2002) 9(1) *Maastricht Journal of European and Comparative Law* 7.

[27] Treaty on European Union [1992] OJ C191/1, Article 174(2).

refer to the precautionary principle, such as Directive 2001/18[28] on the deliberate release into the environment of GMOs and Regulation 1830/2003[29] concerning the traceability and labelling of GMOs and the traceability of food and feed products produced from GMOs. Based on those decrees, the EU's practice on regulating GM crops is taken as a model of a system with explicit recognition of the precautionary principle, grounded in a key assumption as genetic engineering (as newly developed technologies revolutionising the agriculture), is fundamentally different from conventional breeding technologies and thus requires special oversight, and the process, as well as the product, should be regulated.

Typically, the EU's regulation such as Directive 2001/18[30] not only imposes stringent standards for the risk assessment of potential adverse effects on human health and the environment, but also requires traceability and labelling of GMOs at all steps of production and trade. Notably, a full environmental risk assessment, which must address direct, indirect, immediate or delayed effects on human health and the environment,[31] is required for experimental release or field trials[32] and for placing GM products on the market.

With the risk of oversimplification, the so-called US model, in contrast with the EU model, refers to a system governing GM crops and their products with no explicit reference to the precautionary principle. It has been based on a key assumption as genetic engineering is not fundamentally different from conventional breeding technologies (as the latter also involve changing the genes of organisms); hence, the product, rather than the method of production, should be regulated.[33] Typically, when the US Food and Drug Administration (USFDA) states[34] that most GM foods are substantially equivalent to their traditional counterparts, it is suggested that special treatments, including but not limited to more stringent risk assessment and management, are unnecessary. Hence, in the US, there is no such legislation specifically governing GMOs, and different agencies carry out the responsibilities regulating GM crops by implementing the sectoral legislation relating to agriculture, the environment and human health etc.

However, this does not mean that the US takes no precautionary measures concerning GM crops. For example, under the Plant Protection Act,[35] although GM plants that do not present novel risks can be tested without a permit, this can only be done after notification to the authorities; for the new GM crop with higher risks, a permit from the US Department of Agriculture (USDA) is required. And

[28] Directive 2001/18 [2001] OJ L106/1.
[29] Regulation 1830/2003 (amending Directive 2001/18) [2003] OJ L268/24.
[30] Directive 2001/18, 2001 OJ L106/1..
[31] ibid Annex 11.
[32] For some low-risk field trials, fast-track procedures allow the applicant to skip the full environment risk assessment.
[33] Coordinated Framework tor Regulation of Biotechnology, 51 Fed Reg 23,302 (26 June 1986), at 23,304.
[34] FDA, 'Statement of Policy: Foods Derived from New Plant Varieties' (1992) 57 *Federal Register* 22984, 22992.
[35] 7 USC §§ 7701–72.

before a permit of field trial is issued, the USDA shall prepare an environmental assessment (or an environmental impact statement). In the stage of environment release, field trials shall be conducted in isolated areas and all experimental materials used must be completely destroyed when the trails are done to control the potential risks of gene flow/drifting. Moreover, before a new GM crop can be commercialised, the developer shall file a petition for the USDA's determination of 'non-regulated status' based on extensive data and scientific assessment, and the petition will be granted only if that crop is 'unlikely to pose a greater plant pest risk than the unmodified organism from which it was derived'.[36]

In summary, if we agree that 'explicit reference to precaution or the precautionary principle is not a prerequisite for taking precaution[s]',[37] then we shall agree that both the US and the EU implement precautions in the protection of the environment and public health in authorising GM crops, only in different approaches.

B. Where is China on the Spectrum of Precautions?

China has made a significant research and development investment in biotechnology over the last few decades.[38] Even in the decade of inaction on authorising the commercialisation of GM crops, the government's investment into research and development on agricultural technology continued,[39] primarily because food security is a deep-rooted concern of China, given its large and still-growing population. However, as of today, China has commercialised no major crops, despite the fact that Chinese scientists have successfully developed many GM crop varieties, and China turned into a net food importer in 2003 and the import-export gap has been increasing ever since.[40] Putting all the pieces together, it is suggested that China has also taken a precautionary approach regarding GM crops, which is in common with the approaches taken in the US and the EU, although it seems different in certain aspects from both the US and the EU.

i. Like/Unlike the EU

As far as biosafety is concerned, the EU has established a high level of protection by establishing a general obligation 'to avoid adverse effects on human health and the environment which might arise from the deliberate release or the placing on the market of GMOs'.[41] Accordingly, GMOs with any potential adverse effect on

[36] 7 CFR 340.6(c).

[37] H Tegner Anker and M Rosso Grossman, 'Authorisation of Genetically Modified Organisms: Precaution in US and EC Law' (2009) 4(1) *European Food and Feed Law Review* 3.

[38] J Huang, S Rozelle, C Pray and Q Wang, 'Plant Biotechnology in China' (2002) 295 *Science* 674.

[39] 夏冠男、于文静：《中央一号文件九年六提转基因透露了什么信号》,www.gov.cn/xinwen/2015-02/03/content_2814049.htm.

[40] FAOSTAT, 'Data', www.fao.org/faostat/en/#data/QCL.

[41] Directive 2001/18, Article 4(I).

human health or the environment should not be authorised. Essentially, the EU model has predetermined human health and the environment as the top priority, which is helpful to improving public trust in the regulatory agencies. By contrast, the US model can be far more flexible about priorities, which mostly depend on cost-benefit analysis. In this regard, China's normative framework of authorising GM crops, as described above, is much closer to the EU than to the US.

In spite of highly conflicting views about the merits of GM crops, the main concern of the public in China has always been the safety of agricultural GMOs. Actually, China's legal requirements regulating GM crops in terms of some particular contents is even stricter compared to the EU system. For example, some specific requirements of biosafety evaluation in China were considered as too cautious, even unnecessarily cumbersome,[42] such as basing the case-by-case evaluation on verity instead of 'event' or 'convert' (which means an applicant had to apply several biosafety certificates for different genetic modified varieties based on one convert);[43] limiting the legal effect of a biosafety certificate to a specific province (which means an applicant had to apply for several biosafety certificates in order for one GM variety to be grown in several provinces).

Another significant example is China" GMO labelling requirements, which are process- based, as are those of the EU. While labelling in China is mandatory for all GMO products listed in the official catalogue and all GM food (either listed in the catalogue or not),[44] with no exceptions, by contrast, in the EU the mandatory labelling could be exempted as long as the GM ingredients mixed into food or feed are unintentional or technically unavoidable and the GM content does not exceed 0.9 per cent. However, the enforcement of mandatory labelling requirements in China is relatively weak, due to many factors including not incorporating specific traceability requirements as the EU does.[45]

ii. Unlike/Like the US

There is no explicit reference to the precautionary principle in China's related decrees, as is also the case in the US. However, the inaction on authorising the commercialisation of GM crops in practice, together with normative requirements even stricter than those in the EU, are obvious factors that make China distinct from the US. A very strong example for this difference is that after 10 years of efforts in relation to commercialisation failed in China, the GM rice variety Huahui-1, developed by Chinese scientists, has been declared by the USFDA

[42] These two requirements were changed in early 2022 (see below).

[43] 王琴芳：《转基因作物生物安全性评价与监管体系的分析与对策》中国农业科学院2008博士论文.

[44] This was a newly added requirement (art 69) when China's Food Safety Law (食品安全法) was revised in 2015.

[45] X Zhu et al, 'Genetically Modified Food Labelling in China: In Pursuit of a Rational Path' (2016) 71(1) *Food and Drug Law Journal* 30.

in 2018 such that it 'does not raise issues that would require premarket review or approval by [the] FDA'.[46]

The US was among the first countries to introduce GMOs and has remained the biggest grower of GM crops ever since the 1990s. Because of 'a core premise of the American legal culture that requires an extensive factual record to justify government regulatory action',[47] the US model predetermines that the enterprises have the freedom to produce and sell GMOs unless there is evidence that hazards exist. Typically, there are 'no pre-market reviews of approvals required of foods'; instead, 'manufacturers or distributors bear the burden of ensuring that any finished food placed on the market meets the safety levels.[48] As a result, the US model is very favourable for the development of gene technology.

It is interesting to note that the Chinese government has echoed the US model in terms of attaching much importance to technology innovation: the official policy statements of China's government have been clearly pro-biotechnology.[49] Notably, the MOA of China declares to the public repeatedly and consistently that GMO products passing its evaluation are safe;[50] this kind of rhetoric is regarded as showing a tendency towards the adoption of GMOs, because it serves to downplay the scientific uncertainties about potential risks, thus justifying the approval of the commercialisation of GM crops.

This tendency of the MOA of China did not stop at talking. At the start of 2022, the MOA has taken several actual actions to reduce the burden on GM crop developers. On 21 January 2022, the MOA amended its administrative rule on the biosafety evaluation of GM crops[51] by changing the basis of its evaluation to 'convert' (instead of variety), and the provisions limiting biosafety certification to one province have also been revised. On 24 January 2022, the MOA issued the Guide for Safety Evaluation of Gene Edited Plants[52] to regulate GM crops applying non-transgenic technologies (such as cisgenesis, intra-genesis and genome editing) for the first time in China's history. Based on the analysis that gene editing regulated in this Guide, unlike transgenic technologies, does not evolve introducing foreign gene(s), there are no related worries about crossing species boundaries; the Guide simplifies the application process and shortens the approval time compared to previous requirements on GM crops. Those moves are expected to speed up the commercialisation of GM crops in China – in other words, moving closer towards the US model.

[46] USFDA, 'Biotechnology Consultation Agency Response Letter BNF-156', https://www.fda.gov/media/110390/download.

[47] G Charnley and E Elliott, 'Risk versus Precaution: Environmental Law and Public Health Protection' (2002) 32 *Environmental Law Reporter News & Analysis* 10363, 10364.

[48] E Marden, 'Risk and Regulation: US Regulatory Policy on Genetically Modified Food and Agriculture' (2003) 44(3) *Boston College Law Review* 733.

[49] 夏冠男、于文静：《中央一号文件九年六提转基因透露了什么信号》, www.gov.cn/xinwen/2015-02/03/content_2814049.htm.

[50] 农业部：《转基因权威关注》https://www.moa.gov.cn/ztzl/zjyqwgz/kpxc.

[51] 《农业转基因生物安全评价管理办法》.

[52] 《农业用基因编辑植物安全评价指南》.

IV. What's Next? Suggestions for Improvement

In this chapter, when I compare China with the EU and US models, I am not saying that China should have to choose one of those two models to follow. Nonetheless, comparison does help people not only see themelves more clearly, but also to see how complicated are the actual issues faced.

In China, there is an obvious tension between the government's tendency to pro-technology and the public's concern about safety, and it seems to have reached a deadlock: although the scientific establishment has been largely supportive,[53] and 'critics and proponents of GMOs alike agree that genetically modified foods have failed to produce any untoward health effects',[54] doubts and objections surrounding GM crops persist.

Simply labelling this deadlock as 'conflict between scientific and social rationality', or even stigmatising the public's objection as 'irrational fear', as some observers did,[55] has not been very helpful in finding a way out of it. A better understanding of the public's concern needs to be developed before we can break the deadlock.

A. The Crux of the Matter: Uncertainties

Before a genuine and respectful dialogue over GM crops in China can begin, it is crucial to understand that: due to the limitations of existing scientific knowledge, even experts are not fully certain about the risks associated with the application of genetic modification as a new technology. When GMO products are required to pass the safety assessment before they are put on the market, doubts are still there because such safety assessment is based on the 'existing' knowledge and technology, following standards (eg, 'substantial equivalence') derived from the 'existing' theory/experience and depending on the 'existing' feasible methods/tools, which cannot address the concern that genetic modification, as a 'new' technology, may have implications beyond the 'old' experience and 'current' safety standards.

In other words, when proponents claim that a specific GM technology is safe, they are just announcing that the particular GM technology meets the 'best available' safety standards, which are developed in light of past experience and existing theory. However, those who claim that GM technology is unsafe are not based on existing specific safety standards at all, but on the basis of the 'potential' consequences of genetic modification as a new technology, which is mostly something about which we are currently ignorant. The result is that it is impossible for the proponents to 'scientifically prove' that GMOs are certain to be harmless, and for

[53] European Commission, *A Decade of EU-Funded GMO Research 2001–2010* (Luxembourg, EU, 2010).

[54] L DeFrancesco, 'How Safe Does Transgenic Food Need to Be?' (2013) 31 *Natural Biotechnology* 9794.

[55] Q Wang, 'China's Scientists Must Engage the Public on GM' (2015) 519 *Nature* 7.

the opponents to 'scientifically prove' that GMOs are certain to be harmful. In this case, what has caused the public's concern is a specific kind of uncertainty defined as 'Don't know what we don't know',[56] and therefore fundamentally cannot be addressed by using existing scientific knowledge.

The development of human knowledge is a process of dynamic iteration, and what looks obvious in hindsight may not have been at all obvious at the time. Hence, it is unfair to criticise decision makers who had already done their best with the limited knowledge available at the time if it is only in hindsight that we can really see they had made bad calls.[57] In other words, regarding risk regulation, what we really need is not to expect decision makers to square the circle with limited extant knowledge and information, but to clarify that it is risky to make a decision as to whether or not to put some particular technology like genetic modification into use before it is fully understood. 'Better safe than sorry.'

As was shown earlier, there are various precautionary approaches, while each of them deals with the uncertainties in its own way. To be precise, as general principle instead of specific rules, the precautionary principle regulates only 'the reasons for a decision and the process by which a decision is make' and 'it can only be substantively defined in the context that it is operating'.[58] In particular, what the principle requires is that the decision makers simply take into account the limitations of available knowledge and information and the uncertainties brought about by the limit, not specific decisions such as regulation or non-regulation, or the specific type of regulation – those choices will be made by the decision makers after considering uncertainties and other factors. 'In this sense, as long as uncertainties are raised and considered in the decision-making process, the precautionary principle has played its part.'[59]

B. Improving the Process of Decision Making under Uncertainty

Since 'the crux of the matter' is rooted in scientific uncertainties, it is easy to think of improving the scientific assessment of risk, trying to reduce disputes through decreasing the vagueness and indeterminacy of existing knowledge and information as far as possible. Proposals have been put forward to improve the decision-making process in relation to GM crops, including ideas such as risks should be 'adequately flagged'[60] and assessment should respond to significant

[56] B Wynne, 'Uncertainty and Environmental Learning: Reconceiving Science and Policy in the Preventative Paradigm' (1992) 2 *Global Environmental Change* 111.

[57] J Zining, 'Introducing the Precautionary Principle into Administrative Law' (2016) 19 *Academia Sinica Law Journal* 53.

[58] E Fisher, *Risk Regulation and Administrative Constitutionalism* (Oxford, Hart Publishing, 2007) 40. 中译可见：费雪：《风险规制与行政宪政主义》，沈岿译，法律出版社2012年版，第54页.

[59] 金自宁：《科技不确定性与风险预防原则的制度化》，载《中外法学》2022年第2期.

[60] 金自宁：《风险评估内在不确定的法律规制》，载《中国法律评论》2022年第2期.

counter-evidence etc. These are valuable suggestions, and the MOA of China has actually done a lot of work to analyse counter evidence on its official website[61] in terms of explaining why claims that GM food is unsafe are wrong.

However, when the limitations of human knowledge are reached, 'there are no experts at risks'.[62] Now things are different because no one could claim his or her judgement is more 'scientifically rational' than that of others, such as the general public, who are laypeople. Consequently, the focus no longer falls on how to make the 'right' risk decision according to the scientific rationality, which is impossible, but how to make the 'fair' risk decision according to social justice.[63] In other words, when the 'right' answer is not available, the purpose of improving the process of decision making shall not be confined to scientific issues as to the 'right' answer, but rather shall reduce possible objections as to the 'fair' answer. In this respect, especially referring to China's experience of authorisation of GM crops, particular emphasis shall be placed on public involvement.

Public participation is not explicitly mandated in the 'one regulation and four rules', while there are general decrees requiring public participation in the administrative process in China, such as the Administrative Licence Law (行政许可法) and the Regulation on Disclosure of Government Information (政府信息公开条例), that apply to agricultural GMOs regulation. Nevertheless, in view of due process and social justice, it is only fair to ensure that those affected or likely to be affected by a particular decision can participate in the decision-making process.

For decisions under uncertainty it is even more important to involve those affected or potentially affected in the decision-making process. To be precise, what matters here is not just including the general public in the decision-making process, but rather that those affected or potentially affected shall be the decision makers in a substantive sense. In other words, all the affected or potentially affected should collectively decide through deliberation and negotiation what kind of risk and what level of risk should be taken: 'By doing so, if the results of our decisions turn out to be good, we can thank ourselves; if the results of our decisions turn out to be bad, we'll have nobody to blame but ourselves.'[64] As such, those affected, not someone else, would be responsible for their own future.

Here, a reference to Luhmann's distinction between 'risk' and 'danger'[65] would be helpful. 'Risk' used by Luhmann refers to the adverse consequences of one's own decisions, while 'danger' refers to the adverse effects of someone else's decisions on others. With this distinction, we can easily see that the decision that causes 'risk' to ourselves is acceptable in principle, whereas the decision that brings 'danger'

[61] 农业部：国外转基因"事件"有哪些, https://www.moa.gov.cn/ztzl/zjyqwgz/kpxc/201304/t20130427_3446865.htm.

[62] 乌尔里希.贝克：《风险社会》，何博闻译，译林出版社2004年版，第17页.

[63] Zining (n 57).

[64] ibid.

[65] N Luhmann, *Risk: A Sociological Theory* (translated by R Barrett) (Berlin, Walter de Gruyter, 1993).

to others is usually unacceptable. A baseline as to fairness and justice involved in a risky decision has thus been revealed: it is unfair and unjust that one person's 'risky' decision becomes the source of 'danger' to others. In other words, the separation of decision makers and those affected or potentially affected by the decision is problematic.

In the case of GM crops, the following questions will also be raised: regarding the acceptable level of risk, who is the decision maker and who will be affected by the decision? For the former, the answer in Chinese practice is the government, with some help from scientific knowledge provided by experts; for the latter, the answer is the general public, including but not limited to consumers and farmers. From this perspective, the general public in China has been involved in the debate about GM crops, mostly as a result of a natural reaction 'to refuse to become the victims of others risky decision';[66] therefore, what is controversial here has been beyond the issue of science and technology. One typical example is the so-called 'golden rice event 2012' in China. It has been found[67] that better awareness of food derived from GM crops was achieved during the event due to more information and knowledge provided; however, this improved level of awareness did not improve the public's acceptance of GM food in China. This finding has supported that the general public was furious with this event, not out of ignorance or prejudice against genetic technology itself, but with the indignation created by the fact that Chinese children had become unwitting subjects in an experiment involving GM rice.

It is understandable that people would be angry when they neither have access to critical information nor any chance to express their preferences, whereas they have to bear the consequences of the decisions of others. In a world where we have to live with risks and where the acceptable level of risk has to be decided, the most important implication of reflecting on the separation of decision makers and those affected or potentially affected in practice is to change the unexamined existing model of authorising GM crops and to empower those affected and potentially affected, otherwise the resistance of the unwitting subject or the victim of the 'risky' decision made by others will be inevitable.

In China, the general public's concern about genetic modification is related not only to the risks presented by the technology itself, but also to the particular way in which the technology risks are assessed and managed. In 2009, China's MOA actually endorsed two GM rice varieties by granting safety certificates to them. However, this endorsement apparently provoked a reaction against GM crops rather than reassuring the public about the safety of GM crops. This reflects the public's distrust in China, which can be increased if the uncertainties that come with genetic modification as a new technology are downplayed. As far as the

[66] ibid.

[67] 靳明、靳涛：《从黄金大米事件进展透析公众的态度与认知变化 - - 基于新浪微博的内容分析》，载《商业经济与管理》2013年第11期.

government is concerned, only transparency can build trust, so in order to address this, the promotion of transparency of government is undoubtedly important. Nevertheless, from the point of view of this chapter, China's model of authorising GM crops would still be fundamentally flawed if the problem caused by the current separation of decision makers and those affected or potentially affected by the risky decision is not dealt with.

V. Conclusion

China has been slow in its adoption of GMOs in the past two decades and now looks like it is taking tentative steps to facilitate the commercialisation of GM crops. Are GM crops safe or not? For the purposes of sustainable development, should China ease (or tighten) the restrictions on the domestic cultivation of GM crops? These questions are ones that trouble both the general public and the government in China. Nevertheless, these are not questions for this chapter to answer. From the perspective of the precautionary principle, it is the process of decision making, instead of the specific content of the decision itself, that matters. Therefore, suggestions for improvement will focus on the process of decision making under uncertainty.

To improve the of decision-making process in relation to GM crops, it is crucial to concretely shape the meaning of sustainable development in China. As a developing country with a vast population, in the past few decades China has witnessed both rapid economic growth and the environmental cost that has come with this. During this process, decision makers have been repeatedly challenged by fierce social controversies with competing interests and values. In terms of risky decisions regarding the development of a new technology such as genetic modification, scientific uncertainties add another layer of complexity to sustainable decision making in China. These factors all need to be taken into consideration in the of decision-making process on GM crops, as it is difficult not to lose focus.

It has been argued in this chapter that China has taken a precautionary approach regarding GM crops, which is in common with the US and EU models. Even though China's legal requirements regulating GM crops in relation to some particular contents concerning biosafety is even stricter than the EU system, China's government has echoed the US model in terms of attaching considerable importance to technology innovation. A prickly deadlock has been reached in the tension between biosafety and pro-technology in China. Actually, it appears that this deadlock resulted in – or has even caused – China's practice on authorising GM crops taking a dramatic turn in the twenty-first century and even been largely silent until recent years.

The regulation of GM crops has generated and will continue to generate controversy, and related legal issues are inextricably linked with economics and politics in the context of multilevel governance, civil society, international trade and environmental liability.[68] However, it is argued here that in order to break the specific deadlock in China, the key is to recognise that a specific kind of uncertainty exists in the public's concerns – that is, a kind of worry about something we don't yet know. As such, it is crucial to change the former practice in China of separating decision makers from those affected or potentially affected by those decisions, and substantially including the latter group in the decision-making process in line with the precautionary principle.

[68] L Bodiguel and M Cardwell (eds), *The Regulation of Genetically Modified Organisms: Comparative Approaches* (Oxford, Oxford University Press, 2010).

14

China as the Next Global Data Regulator?

Assessing China's Global Data Security Initiative as a Site of Governance

QIANLAN WU

I. Introduction

Since launching its 'Go Digital' development strategy in 2005, China has taken pride in its rapid domestic digitalisation in all aspects of society and has vowed to influence the global data governance framework. On 8 September 2020, China launched the Global Initiative on Data Security.[1] This initiative calls for states and private parties to bear comprehensive obligations on data security within domestic and global digital spaces. It is China's formal exportation of its national security-based regulation model to the pluralistic legal space on data regulation.

In the digital era, big data and machine learning can automate the collation of unstructured data flows. Backed with algorithm technology, such as intensive analysis of datasets on past behaviour, big data could provide wide-ranging and accurate predictive analysis for any society.[2] Globalisation has facilitated the cross-border data flow, which could pose risks to national security if it is exploited or used unlawfully.

Against this backdrop, China and other global trade powers, such as the US and the European Union (EU), have converged to strengthen respective regulatory autonomy in the global data flow.[3] However, China has adopted a national security-based regulation approach as part of its security-led development model

[1] China's Global Digital Security Initiative (in Chinese and English), www.china.org.cn/chinese/2020-09/15/content_76704524.htm.

[2] M Chi, 'Big Data in National Security', Australian Strategic Policy Institute Report 2017, https://www.aspistrategist.org.au/big-data-national-security.

[3] S, Yakovleva, 'Three Data Realms: Convergence or Competition', Amsterdam Law School Research Paper No 2022-58 (7 February2022), http://dx.doi.org/10.2139/ssrn.4028668.

in this field.[4] According to Chinese scholars, China is committed to economic development through digitalisation, which is subject to the protection of significant national interests in the political, social and economic spheres.[5] Such an approach departs from the EU's digital sovereignty-based data regulatory model, which is rooted in fundamental rights protection,[6] and from the US's economic benefits-oriented regulation for data flow restrictions.[7]

What implications can be derived from China's national security-based data regulation to the transnational law development in the global digital space? This chapter aims to answer this question by assessing China's data security regulation as a site of governance. The Sites of Governance and Legal Pluralism Theory by Professor Francis Snyder argues that globalisation is governed by the totality of strategically determined, situationally specific and often episodic conjunctions of a multiplicity of sites throughout the world. Each site of governance has both a structural dimension (consisting of institutions, norms and dispute resolution processes) and a relational dimension –(comprising its relations with other sites of governance). The totality of sites of governance constitutes a new form of global legal pluralism. Strategic actors such as companies and governments use the law, are shaped by it and are fundamental in determining the creation and survival of sites.[8]

By applying Snyder's Sites of Governance and Legal Pluralism Theory, this chapter examines China's institutional structure, dispute settlement and normative basis as a site for data security regulation. It illustrates that China's regulatory structure reflects its market regulation path dependence while imposing comprehensive and nuanced control over undertakings in the form of *ex ante* self-assessment, centralised review and post-regulation monitoring. The site's dispute settlement design confirms tightened control over undertakings with limited judicial oversight. The site's normative basis centres on China's conceptualisation of data security as a sustainable, state-centric capacity building, which the protection of personal information as a tort-based personality right supports. This chapter argues that the institutional aspect, normative basis and dispute settlement of China as a site have a dialectical relationship with the site's external relations. Hence, while China actively projects its national security-based data regulation model into the transnational legal space, it will face tests from global businesses, stakeholders

[4] J Tianshu and W Ziyue, 'Data Security Governance and China's Strategy in the Digital Economy' (2022) 1 *International Security Studies* 130.

[5] P Yuan, 'Strategic Thinking on the Path of National Security with Chinese Characteristics' (2022) 31(5) *Contemporary International Relations* 1.

[6] L Floridi, 'The Fight for Digital Sovereignty: What it is, and Why it Matters, Especially for the EU' (2020) 33 *Philosophy & Technology* 369.

[7] World Trade Organization, 'The Economic Benefits of Cross-Border Data Flows', Communication from the United States, S /C/W/382, 17 June 2019.

[8] F Snyder, *The EU, China, and the WTO: Legal Pluralism and International Trade Regulation* (London, Bloomsbury Publishing, 2010) 32. See also F Snyder, 'Economic Globalisation and the Law in the 21st Century' in A Sarat (ed), *The Blackwell Companion to Law and Society* (Oxford, Blackwell) 624–40.

and trade partners, in terms of the effectiveness and transparency of its structure, values underpinning the normative basis and the fairness of the dispute settlement mechanism. Such tests would feed back to China's site development. This dynamic process would have a far-reaching impact on the transnational norms making on global data regulation.

II. China as a Site of Governance for Data Security

China started its market-oriented reform in 1978 and achieved economic upsurge by benefiting from foreign investment, international trade and globalisation, among other factors.[9] In 2005, it started building up the national innovation system as part of its economic development upgrade strategy.[10] The Chinese information technology sector has, as a result, seen an intensive and nationwide upgrade in infrastructure and booming business activities, driven by continuous government policy support.[11]

In parallel, the Chinese Communist Party (CCP) has emphasised China's national security discourse building. National security formally appeared in the CCP's 14th Party Congress Report in 1992, which primarily concerned national defence and military capacity building.[12] In the CCP's 18th Party Congress third Plenary Session in 2013, national security was expanded beyond traditional national defence to include non-traditional security – for example, security in the economic and financial sectors and ecological protection.[13] In the same year, the National Security Commission of the Communist Party of China was established beneath the CCP standing committee and was headed by President Xi Jingping.[14] During the National Security Commission's first meeting on 15 April 2014, President Xi delivered a report on developing an overall national security outlook for China.[15] According to the report, the overall national security outlook refers to international security (peace, collaboration and win-win situations among states) and domestic security (development, reform and stability). The report clearly

[9] Communist Party of China (CPC), 11th Party Congress third Plenary Session Report to start the market oriented reform, http://cpc.people.com.cn/GB/33837/2535013.html. See also L Brandt and TG Rawski, *China's Great Economic Transformation* (Cambridge, Cambridge University Press, 2010) 1–26.

[10] China's State Council (Central Government) White Paper Report on Peaceful Development Pathway December 2005, www.gov.cn/zwgk/2005-12/22/content_134060.htm.

[11] China's State Council (Central Government) Notice on the Planning to Improve China Autonomous Innovation Capability Issued on 15 January 2013, www.gov.cn/zhengce/content/2013-05/30/content_5186.htm.

[12] The CPC Report on the 14th CPC National Congress, www.gov.cn/test/2007-08/29/content_730511.htm.

[13] The CPC Decision on Significant Issues to Deepen the Reform, Report adopted at the CPC 18th Party Congress, Third Plenary Session 2013, www.ce.cn/xwzx/gnsz/szyw/201311/18/t20131118_1767104.shtml.

[14] https://news.sohu.com/20170217/n481030722.shtml.

[15] Xi Jingping Report to the First Meeting of National Security Commission April 2014, www.gov.cn/xinwen/2014-04/15/content_2659641.htm.

delineated national security to include not only traditional definitions such as military and territorial security, but also political security, cultural security, social security, technology security, information security, ecological security, resources security and nuclear security.[16] It signals China's shifting from a GDP-focused economic growth path to a more China-centric security-based trajectory for its development.

On 18 November 2021, the Political Bureau of the CCP Standing Committee issued China's National Security Strategy (hereinafter 'the Strategy').[17] The Strategy continues to strengthen security governance in all domestic areas, including the areas of cyber-security, data security and Artificial Intelligence (AI), and to adopt a collaborative stance on international front of national security regulation. However, it designates political and ideological security as the priority in the national security strategy.[18] More importantly, it expanded the normative basis of China's national security regulation to include the protection of China's independence and autonomy, state key interests and national dignity in international relations.[19] In April 2022, China published its Overall National Security Outlook Studies Outline, which marks the periodical completion of its discourse building on national security.[20]

Against this backdrop, China published its Global Initiative on Data Security in 2020.[21] This initiative shows China's effort to lead the transnational law making on cross-border data flows by exporting its national security-based regulatory approach. First, by depoliticising data security regulation, it in essence calls for a state responsibility and right to data security regulation, based on a state-centred sovereignty concept in the global digital space. To this end, it calls for positive and negative obligations on states in order to safeguard 'the openness, security and stability of the global supply chain of information and technology products and services'.[22] Such obligations include the following: states should oppose conduct which damages key infrastructure or steals important data from information technology in other countries, and should oppose conduct that will endanger other countries' national security and public interests; states should commit to adopt measures to prevent and stop undertakings from carrying out conduct which infringes personal data by using information technology; states should oppose the large-scale surveillance and unlawful collection of personal data of citizens in other countries by abusing information technology; states should require

[16] ibid.
[17] www.gov.cn/xinwen/2021-11/18/content_5651753.htm.
[18] Z Yu, 'The Political Bureau of the Central Committee of the Communist Party of China reviewed the 'National Security Strategy 2021-2025' *Xinhua News Agency* (18 November 2018), www.gov.cn/xinwen/2021-11/18/content_5651753.htm.
[19] ibid.
[20] China's National Security Commission Office, *Overall National Security Outlook Study Outline* (Beijing, People's Publishing House, 2022).
[21] Global Data Security Initiative (in Chinese and English), www.china.org.cn/chinese/2020-09/15/content_76704524.htm.
[22] ibid.

undertakings to abide by laws and regulations of the state where the undertakings operate; and states should not require their own business enterprises to store data acquired overseas within their territory. While the initiative recognises bilateral and multilateral cooperation regarding cross-border data flows, such cooperation is restricted, for example, to combating crime and is subject to the respect of state sovereignty and jurisdiction, and the state's right to regulate data security.

The Initiative also calls for obligations on undertakings, particularly information and communication technology (ICT) products and services providers, regarding the acquisition of data, business conduct and remedy provision. First, it calls for an obligation on ICT providers to not install back doors with the aim of illegally obtaining users' data, or controlling or manipulating users' systems and devices. Second, it calls for ICT companies not to abuse their market power by taking advantage of users' dependence on their products and not to force users to upgrade their systems and devices. Further, it calls for ICT product providers to bear the responsibility to notify their business partner and users on serious vulnerabilities in their products in a timely fashion and offer remedies in the event of malfunction.[23]

China's Global Data Security Initiative stems from its Overall Outlook on National Security and confirms data security serving as a sub-element of its national security development strategy. This reflects China's long -stablished state-centric outlook on state sovereignty in international relations. The advocated obligations on the states and private undertakings reflects the fact that China, which aspires to be a global digital space power, draws upon its own strategic interests, international relationship principles and market regulatory practices to exert its impact on the norms making of global cross-border data flow regulation. While the implications of such an initiative remain to be seen, it is vital to understand why China has developed such an initiative by analysing its data security regulation as a site of governance in global digital space.

A. The Institutional Structure for Data Security Regulation

Since 2011, China has established an institutionalised regulatory framework for data security, which is applicable to data processing and data flows within and outside Chinese territory, as well as cross-border.

The Cyberspace Administration of China (CAC) is the leading regulator, through which the CCP channels cyberspace policies to the state apparatus. Set up as a lower office under the Information and News Office of the State Council (Central Government of China) in 2011, the CAC was originally tasked with overseeing news and propaganda in the digital sector. Then followed China's digitalisation development strategy, and the office was elevated to a ministerial office for cyber-governance and data security in China. Within China's party-state political system,

[23] ibid.

the CAC was formally merged with the CCP Internet and Informationalization Office, following China's central government reshuffle in 2018.[24]

The CAC's competence is threefold. First, it leads, coordinates and monitors sectoral regulators to implement the party-state's policies on strengthening and cooperating internet content and cyber-security regulation. Second, it oversees the internet infrastructure's technical regulation. It directs sectoral regulators to monitor the telecommunication business entity, monitor IP address assignment, website registration and others. It also leads the sectoral regulators to set data security standardisation,[25] advocates data security awareness,[26] and issues templates for cross-border data flow agreements.[27] Third, it has the competence to enforce administrative penalties against business undertakings – for example, against companies controlling websites and platforms, when the latter are found to have breached relevant laws and regulations.[28] However, it relies on sectoral regulators for the enforcement of its decision and post-regulation monitoring. Hence, despite its leading position, the CAC is in a more consultative and coordinative partnership with the sectoral regulators.

China's data security legal framework is composed of primary legislations, legally binding sectoral ministerial regulations, rules and non-legally binding soft laws. Key primary legislation includes the National Security Law 2015,[29] the Cybersecurity Law 2016,[30] the Data Security Law 2021,[31] the Personal Data Protection Law 2021[32] and the Key Information Infrastructure Security Protection Regulation 2021.[33] Soft law tools include ministerial notices and opinions – for example, on the standardisation of security criteria[34] and the Supreme People's Court legal interpretations on cyber-security, data security and others.[35]

[24] State Council of the People's Republic of China, 'Notice of the State Council on Institutional Setup', www.gov.cn/zhengce/content/2018-03/24/content_5277121.htm.

[25] Cybersecurity Law, art 15.

[26] ibid arts 19 and 20.

[27] Personal Information Protection Law, art 38.

[28] State Council of the People's Republic of China, 'Notice of the State Council on Authorizing the Cyberspace Administration of China to Be Responsible for the Management of Internet Information Content', www.gov.cn/zhengce/content/2014-08/28/content_9056.htm.

[29] National Security Law of the People's Republic of China (2015).

[30] Cybersecurity Law of the People's Republic of China (2016).

[31] Data Security Law 2021 of the People's Republic of China (2021).

[32] Personal Information Protection Law of the People's Republic of China (2021).

[33] Key Information Infrastructure Security Protection Regulations (2021).

[34] The standardisation settings include, for example: 'Information security technology – Risk assessment specification for information security' (GB/T 20984-2007 National Standard of People's Republic of China, General Administration of Quality Supervision, Inspection and Quarantine; Standardisation Administration of PRC 2007); 'Information security technology – Personal information security specification' (GB/T 35273-2020, National Standard of People's Republic of China, State Administration for Market Regulation; Standardisation Administration of PRC 2020); 'Information security technology – Guidance for personal information security impact assessment' (GB/T 39335-2020, National Standard of People's Republic of China, State Administration for Market Regulation; Standardisation Administration of PRC 2020), among others.

[35] 'The Supreme People's Court's Provisions on Several Issues Related to Trial of Cases by the Internet Courts' (SPC Interpretation 6/9/2018, Supreme People's Court 2018).

Within the regulatory framework, the undertakings face legally provided *ex ante* obligations, centralised review and post-regulation monitoring. First, undertakings bear legally provided obligations to comply with data security standardisation and undertake *ex ante* risk evaluation, based on security and personal data protection laws. Second, certain undertakings face compulsory and centralised cyber-security review. This is applicable to the key information infrastructure (KII) in the purchase of key products and services, and qualified platforms (platforms process 1 million and above personal information) in its overseas Initial Public Offering (IPO). Third, certain qualified undertakings (for example, KII and qualified platforms) face compulsory data exportation security review in cross-border data flows. Both national security review and data exportation security review are *ex ante*. Fourth, all undertakings, including the KII and qualified platforms, are subject to continuous post-regulation monitoring by the respective sectoral regulators and the public.[36]

B. The *Ex Ante* Obligations of Undertakings

Within China's data security regulatory framework, the undertaking's legal obligation lies mainly in the field of cyber-security and personal data protection. With respect to cyber-security, the undertakings are required to: adopt internal cyber-security management systems and appoint a cyber-security contact person; put in place measures to prevent and combat cyber-attacks; monitor and record relevant data operation for a minimum of six months; and categorise data and protect data confidentiality.[37] The undertakings are required to install a cyber-security contingency plan, which would be triggered by cyber-attacks.[38] Undertakings are required to satisfy the cyber-security standardisation requirement, set out by the CAC, as a prerequisite to sell products or provide services on the market.[39]

With respect to personal data protection, the undertakings are obligated to install user information protection systems.[40] The data collection should be lawful, just, necessary, transparent and based on user consent.[41] The transfer of personal data should also be based on consent from users.[42] The operator is required to set up and provide an effective complaint mechanism for users on personal data protection.[43]

[36] Compatible with China's government administrative system, the cyber-security review is led by the Cybersecurity Review Office located at the CAC, in coordination with another 12 central government regulators including the National Development and Reform Commission (NDRC), the Ministry of Police, the Ministry of National Security, Mofcom, the State Administration of Market Regulation and others. Under the Cybersecurity Law, the key information infrastructure operators are those which purchase internet products and services, and platforms which execute data processing, which impact or potentially can impact national security are required to submit for cyber-security review.

[37] Cybersecurity Law, art 21.

[38] ibid art 25.

[39] ibid art 23.

[40] ibid art 40.

[41] ibid art 41.

[42] ibid art 43.

[43] ibid art 49.

KII is defined as sectors covering public telecommunication, information service, energy, transport, water supply, finance, public service, e-government and other sectors. These are the sectors whose damage will endanger national security, people's welfare and the public interest.[44] KII sectors are subject to more stringent legal obligations and scrutiny in China's data security regulation. They are not only subject to a specific security plan, led and set out by sectoral regulators,[45] but are also under obligations to safeguard cyber-security. This includes for KII to undertake background checks for the contact person in charge of cyber-security, set up a dedicated cyber-security office, provide regular cyber-security education, training and appraisal, provide disaster recovery back-up for key systems and databases, and make contingency plans for a potential cyber-security incident and provide regular rehearsals.[46]

C. Cyber-security Review

In November 2021, the CAC, along with 12 other central government regulators, issued the Method on Cyber-security Review as a secondary ministerial rule to enforce the Cybersecurity Law, the Data Security Law and the Regulation of KII Security.[47] The Method came into force in February 2022.

The Cyber-security Review is applicable to any KII undertaking purchasing key digital products and services. The key goods and services here are defined as core cyber-equipment, computers and servers, storage, large databases, cyber-security equipment and other products and services with a significant impact on KII, cyber-security and data security. Any platforms with over one million users are required to obtain cyber-security clearance, prior to their IPO overseas.[48]

The Method requires any KII undertaking to first pre-assess potential risks to be incurred by the application of a product or a service on national security. This pre-assessment exercise largely transfers the burden from the regulator to the KII undertaking, in terms of ensuring the compliance of provider/seller of products and services with China's cyber-security reviews, including commitments not to unlawfully acquire data using their leverage as goods or service providers, not to unlawfully control users' equipment, and not to stop supplying goods or essential technological support without justifiable reasons.[49] The KII undertaking should submit to the CAC for cyber-security review if it concludes that the goods

[44] ibid art 31.

[45] ibid art 32.

[46] ibid art 34.

[47] 'Network Security Measures 2021', www.gov.cn/zhengce/zhengceku/2022-01/04/content_5666430.htm.

[48] Cybersecurity Law, art 7. The key goods and services here are defined as core cyber-equipment, computers and servers, storage, large databases, cyber-security equipment and other products and services with a significant impact on KII security, cyber-security and data security (art 21).

[49] ibid art 6.

or services pose actual, or potential, dangers for national security. However, the Method does not provide such discretion to the qualified platform, and requires the latter to submit for cyber-security review once it satisfies the user number threshold and plans for overseas listing.

Following the pre-assessment, the undertakings are required to submit the cyber-security application form, its evaluation report on the actual and potential impact on national security, any procurement contract agreement, or documents for IPO overseas, among other documents.[50]

With respect to the substantive review, the CAC considers the risk of unlawful control, disruption or damage to the key information infrastructure; the danger to the key information infrastructure by the lack of supply of goods and services; the risk arising from the security, transparency and reliability of goods and services; the risks of supply shortage due to political, diplomatic and trade factors; the legal compliance of Chinese law, regulation and ministerial rules by the providers of goods and services; the risks resulting from leakage, damage or theft of core data, key data or significant amounts of personal data; the risk of key information infrastructure, core data, significant data being influenced, controlled or maliciously used by foreign governments during the IPO process overseas and other factors.[51]

The CAC Cyber-security Office (CSO) confirms with the undertaking in question whether a review is necessary within 10 working days of receiving the application. If the CAC CSO decides that a national security review is necessary, the review will then comprise two phases. The CAC CSO should complete the preliminary review (Phase One) within 30 working days. Its preliminary conclusion will be sent to all joint regulators for comment. The 30-day deadline can be extended for another 15 working days, depending on the complexity of the case.[52] The consulted regulators should reply, with comments, within 15 working days. Phase One lasts at least 45 days and can, potentially, be 60 working days or longer. If by the end of the Phase One review, the joint regulators cannot reach a consensus, the review will then move into the special investigation phase (Phase Two). The Phase Two investigation should be completed within 90 working days, although this can be extended on a case-by-case basis.[53]

D. Security Review for Data Exportation

Article 37 of China's Cybersecurity Law states that key data and personal data, collected and created by the KII undertakings within China's territory, should be stored within China.[54] Undertakings should submit themselves for a data

[50] ibid art 8.
[51] ibid art 10.
[52] ibid art 11.
[53] ibid art 14.
[54] ibid art 37.

exportation security review when they export data for business reasons.[55] In May 2022, the CAC itself adopted the Method on Security Review for Data Exportation, which becomes effective in September 2022.[56]

Pursuant to the Method, a data processor is required to submit for exportation security review if any of the following criteria is satisfied. The first criterion concerns whether the data processor exports key data. Key data is defined as data which, once modified, damaged, leaked, unlawfully acquired or unlawfully employed, will endanger national security, the economy, social stability, public health and security.[57] The second criterion concerns whether any KII sector or data processor processes one million or more pieces of personal information when exporting data. The third criterion is whether the data processor has provided over 100,000 pieces of personal information or 10,000 pieces of sensitive personal information since 1 January of the previous year. Article 4 of the Method provides that there can be further criteria to be set out by the CAC.[58]

When compared with the cyber-security review, the data exportation security review casts a wider net; where not only the KII sector and qualified platforms but also any data processor satisfying certain user number thresholds are subject to review. Further, the security review for data exportation scrutinises risks beyond cyber-security and includes risks for endangering national security, the public interest, and for infringing lawful interests arising from personal information protection.

Like the cyber-security review, an undertaking is required to complete a self-assessment prior to submitting the data exportation security review. It is then subject to compulsory notification and application for clearance. In the self-assessment, the undertaking should review the sphere, the categories and the sensitivity level of the data to be exported; check the overseas data processor commitment and legal obligation; check the management and technological measures in place to enforce the obligations to ensure data exportation security; assess the risk during and after exportation, including the risk of data being modified, damaged, leaked, lost, transferred or unlawfully acquired and used; assess if the channel of personal data protection is smooth; and assess if contracts for data exportation or legal documents have sufficient safeguards regarding the legal obligations on data security, and other matters.[59]

Following the self-assessment, the undertaking is required to submit the data exportation security review form, the self-assessment report on the risks of data exportation, and the draft legal documents between the data processor and the overseas receiving data processor for review.[60] The documents are submitted to

[55] ibid.
[56] CAC Order No 11, 'The Method on Security Review for Data Exportation', adopted on 7 July 2022, www.gov.cn/zhengce/zhengceku/2022-07/08/content_5699851.htm.
[57] ibid art 19.
[58] ibid art 4.
[59] ibid.
[60] ibid art 6.

provincial CAC offices for a preliminary check and, once they are satisfied, the documents are submitted to the CAC for formal review.[61] The CAC should issue a notice, in writing, to confirm the start of the formal review within seven days of receiving the documents from the provincial CAC.[62] The CAC will then undertake consultation with other key regulators in the joint scheme.[63] However, the key regulators seem to have less veto power in the exportation review in comparison to the cyber-security review. The CAC will decide on the review within 45 working days from the day it issues the notice of review.[64]

Unlike the cyber-security review, the data exportation security review has a validation period of two years. The undertaking is under an obligation to apply for a new data exportation security review if either of the following conditions is satisfied: when the methods of exporting data, or the purpose, method, sphere and categories of data exported have changed, which impact on exportation data security; when the personal information and key data storage period overseas has been extended; when there is a material change in the legal framework or cyber-security environment in the data receiving jurisdiction; when the actual control of the data processor or receiver data has changed; and when legal documents have changed which impact on data security in exportation.[65]

In the substantive review, the CAC reviews the risks in both the data exportation process and in the legal documents supporting the exportation. First, it scrutinises the lawfulness, legitimacy and necessity of the purpose, sphere and method of data exportation. Second, it considers whether the receiver's data security policy, law and the cyber-security environment and the receiver's data protection standards have reached the level provided by the law, policy and compulsory standards of China. Third, it is concerned with the scale, sphere, categories and sensitivities of the exported data, the risks of the data being modified, damaged, leaked, lost, transferred, or unlawfully acquired or used during and after exportation. Fourth, it considers whether the data security and personal information will be sufficiently protected; whether the data processor and the receiver's legal documents are sufficiently sound on the obligations regarding data security; and whether the receivers are in compliance with Chinese law, administrative regulations and rules, and other criteria set out by the CAC.[66]

The CAC sets out the minimum requirements and the template of the legal documents involved in data exportation. In the contract, the parties (the data exporter and the data receiver) are required to provide the following: the purpose of the exportation, the method of exportation of the data, the sphere of the data, the use and methods of data processing by the receiver, the storage venue, the

[61] ibid art 7.
[62] ibid art 7.
[63] ibid art 10.
[64] ibid art 12.
[65] ibid art 14.
[66] ibid art 8.

duration of the data overseas, measures applicable after the storage duration has expired, the purpose to be achieved, the legal documents that have been implemented, information on the retransfer of data to a third party after the data is exported, security measures when there is a change of control of the receiving data processor, business sphere or change in the cyber-security environment; law and policy or *force majeure* and the dispute settlement for the contract enforcement, remedies and breaches of contract; and a contingency plan for ensuring access to remedies by private parties when data are modified, damaged, leaked, transferred or lost in the exportation.[67]

E. Post-regulation Monitoring

The CAC has emphasised the importance of post-regulation monitoring for both national security review and security review for data exportation. Chinese market regulators, led by the CAC, have made a few high-profile decisions to increase societal awareness of the security review, including imposing the fine of over US$10 billion on Didi as a result of cyber-security review.[68] Since 2021, leading platforms including Alibaba, Didi and Meituan have issued public pledges in the media regarding their commitment to complying with all Chinese laws and regulations applicable to the digital economy.[69] While the public pledge remains non-legally binding, they serve as high-profile social events, putting pressure on the undertakings for compliance. The Method for National Security Review and the Method for Security Review of Data Exportation have provided the legal basis for any individual to report unlawful data processing activities to the CAC.[70]

The regulatory framework has imposed an obligation on the undertakings regarding post-regulation monitoring. Following the cyber-security review, undertakings bear the responsibility of monitoring the suppliers of goods and services in order to implement the commitment they have made during the cyber-security application.[71] Undertakings which obtained clearance in the data exportation security review continue to face scrutiny. If the CAC discovers that data processing breaches data security, despite being cleared in the security review for exportation, it will order the undertaking to cease activity, in writing, and will demand the latter reform and submit itself for review again.[72] The Chinese administrative

[67] ibid art 9.

[68] China Netcom, 'The Cyberspace Administration of China's Decision to Impose Administrative Penalties on Didi Global Co. Ltd. In Accordance with the Law for Cybersecurity Review' (Office of the Central Cyberspace Affairs Commission, 21 July 2022), www.cac.gov.cn/2022-07/21/c_1660021534306352.htm.

[69] L Jiwei, '34 Internet Platform Companies Promise to Operate in Compliance with Laws and Regulations' (Xinhuanet, 15 April 2021), www.xinhuanet.com/tech/2021-04/15/c_1127332031.htm.

[70] Data Exit Security Assessment Measures, art 16.

[71] Network Security Review Measures, art 19.

[72] Data Exit Security Assessment Measures, art 17.

system has long provided soft law instruments for market regulation: meeting with market operators, education, warnings etc.[73] Such tools continue to be used in combination with hard law instruments in post-security review monitoring.

The institutional aspect of China as a site for data security governance reflects its path dependence on its unitary administrative system. First, in line with China's market regulatory practice, both the cyber-security review and the exportation security review are composed of the compulsory self-assessment by undertakings, the centralised review by the regulators and long-term post-regulation monitoring by the regulators and the public.

However, the regulatory framework has not only imposed comprehensive obligations on the undertakings, but has also conferred the latter with regulatory power, making the undertakings both a gatekeeper and a rule maker. Articles 47 and 48 of the Cybersecurity Law empower the undertaking to stop transmitting information once it discovers that the information is unlawful and requires the undertaking to keep a record and subsequently report to regulators. Any undertaking providing an email or software service has a security management obligation and is empowered to cease providing the service, erase the relevant service, keep records and report to regulators if unlawful content and activities are discovered. The KII sector is provided with the competence to make pre-assessment guidance for other undertakings in the sector. As a result, the CAC and regulators rely on the undertakings to generate economic welfare, and to act as gatekeeper in relation to internet content and the virtual space. The undertakings, in turn, have a certain level of bargaining power in the decision-making process.

Second, the CAC and sectoral regulators are equipped with overwhelming power, but with limited judicial oversight. The regulators are provided with extendable timeframes to complete the reviews. During the investigation, the applicants are required to employ measures required by the security review regulators to mitigate and prevent risks to cyber-security prior to the adoption of the final review decision. The undertakings are not provided with the option of proposing commitments with the purpose of pre-empting or mitigating actual or potential risks to security during the data exportation. The result of the Cyber-security Review and Data Exportation Security Review are final and are not subject to judicial review.

However, China's data security institutional framework involves strategic actors with plural interests, including the CAC, sectoral regulators, the organisations and users to name but a few. The sectoral regulators have de facto veto power in the cyber-security review, which could determine whether or not an application can be closed in Phase One or an application must enter into the Phase Two review. Consequently, this gives the sectoral regulators a certain level of leveraging power in the decision-making process. Hence, while the CAC wields strong power in the regulatory framework, the undertakings act as gatekeepers and quasi-sectoral regulators. The undertakings' communication and negotiation with the CAC also shape the outcome of the regulation.

[73] Law of the People's Republic of China on Administrative Penalty, art 5.

III. Is there a Normative Basis?

A. National, Cyber and Data Security as Capacity

While China's statement on the national security strategy remains vague, it confirms the start of China's era of security-based economic development. What, then, constitutes significant national interests, which must be safeguarded in China's cyber-security and data security exportation review? This question remains unanswered. However, such interests have been put under the umbrella of security, as reflected in national security, cyber-security and data security, which run through the threads of China's data regulation framework.

The concepts of national security, cyber-security and data security have been consistently conceptualised as capabilities held by China, which should be developed, trained, strengthened and maintained on a continuous basis. Article 2 of the National Security Law defines national security as a capacity which safeguards the integrity of the political system, sovereignty and territorial unity, safeguards the welfare of the population, the sustainable development of society and the economy, and ensures that other key state interests are not at risk or subject to internal or external threats.[74] Article 76 of the Cybersecurity Law defines cyber-security as the capability to use necessary measures to prevent the attack, invasion, disturbance, damage and unlawful usage of cyberspace; the capability to ensure the internet has steady and reliable functioning; and the capability to safeguard the integrity, confidentiality and applicability of data in cyberspace.[75] Data security is defined as the capability to ensure data is under effective protection and lawful exploitation. It also involves the capability to ensure security on a sustainable basis.[76]

In China, this capacity is predominantly contained within the Chinese state. However, this capacity cannot be sustainably achieved without training and strengthening the organisation's and the public's capacities. In building up the capacity, the state aims at striking a balance between strengthening its capacity and not supressing the innovation-led economic development in the digital sector. Cyber-security and data security are integral parts of national security and sub-elements of the overall capability China aims at building, which serve as the building blocks of China's data governance normative framework.

B. Rights-Based Personal Data Protection?

Any actual or potential harm to an individual or an organisation's lawful interests is the other main risk scrutinised in the data exportation security review. While the CAC has not clarified what such lawful rights and interests refer to, its substantive

[74] National Security Law, art 2.
[75] Cybersecurity Law, art 76.
[76] Data Security Law, art 3.

assessment indicates that such risk is based on the protection of personal data and any lawful interests arising out of it.[77]

In China, the normative basis for personal data protection is rooted in the personality rights provided under section IV of the Civil Code.[78] The term 'personality rights' refers to the rights based on personal freedom and human dignity. It includes a group of rights, namely the right to life, the right to body, the right to health, the right to name, the right to image, the right to honour and the right to privacy, among others. Privacy in the Civil Code is defined as the right of a natural person to have a private and peaceful life, which includes, for example, the private space, activities and information. The infringement of the right to privacy – for example, the invasion of other people's private life with texts, messages, emails etc – is prohibited under the Civil Code. The right to privacy constitutes one part of the normative framework for China's protection of personal data. Hence, personal data under protection goes beyond the data centred on people's private and peaceful life; and is defined as information used exclusively, or in combination with other information, to identify a specific natural person, either in the digital form or any other. Examples of such data include names, birthdates, personal ID numbers, biological information, addresses, telephone numbers, email addresses, health information and travel histories.

The Personal Data Protection Law (ie, China's General Data Protection Regulation (GDPR) categorises personal data into general personal data and sensitive personal data. Sensitive personal data refers to data that, once abused or leaked, are likely to injure the personal dignity of a natural person, or harm their personal or financial security.[79] Such data are subject to more stringent protection; for example, the data processing of such information can be subject to a government licensing requirement.[80]

When it comes to the protection of the lawful interests of individuals and organisations, based on personal data protection, China's approach departs from that of Western liberal democratic societies such as the EU. First, the protection provided by personality rights is conceptualised as an economic tort, the remedy of which serves to provide corrective justice to the victim of the wrong mainly in the form of compensation. Consequently, potential claimants bear the burden of proving the causal relationship between the wrong suffered and the organisation's alleged conduct. The organisation in question is provided with a defence based on reasonable and rational grounds. Hence, the Civil Code has restricted its protection to personal data which can be identified for specific natural persona. It has not provided protection for anonymised information. The Civil Code waives the data processor's legal liability in the following cases: when the data processing is agreed and consented to by the natural person in question; when processing

[77] CAC Order No 11 (n 56).
[78] Civil Code of the People's Republic of China (2020), s IV.
[79] Personal Data Protection Law, art 28.
[80] ibid arts 29, 30 and 31.

information is publicised by the person, or information is already available in the public domain, unless such processing is rejected by the person in question or harms the person's significant interests; and when such processing serves to protect the public interest or protects the lawful interests of the natural person.

Second, the right to privacy, now defined as part of the personality rights, has been non-justiciable before the Chinese courts as a human right.[81] Third, and more importantly, faced with the overwhelming accumulation of power by the digital economy, certain jurisdictions such as the EU refer heavily to the human rights framework, with the aim of promoting the self-determination and autonomy of individuals.[82] Such a rationale is not echoed in China; instead, China perceives the challenges from the powerful digital players in the borderless digital economy as threats to its status quo. To this end, organisations have a legal obligation to the state to mitigate and prevent any risk to cyber and data security. They also face tortious liability towards individuals for infringing the latter's rights subject to a reasonable defence. However, the legal obligations of undertakings to the state is likely to prevail over their tortious liability to victims when conflict arises between the two.

IV. Dispute Settlement Mechanisms in the Site

The dispute settlement process of China's data security governance comprises three channels which can overlap with each other. These channels include, first, the complaint and dispute settlement provided internally by undertakings, for example, platforms as part of their legal obligation; second, private parties' access to court to seek remedies for contractual disputes, tortious liabilities against third parties or public bodies;[83] and, third, private parties' resort to the review of regulators decisions within the government administrative system.[84]

As required by the Cybersecurity Law, undertakings – especially the key infrastructure data processor and platforms – bear the obligation to install in place an effective complaint system and dispute settlement mechanism.[85] The undertakings set out internally applicable rules on complaints and dispute settlement, and act as the arbitrator for dispute settlement, in addition to the obligation to undertake pre-assessment on security risks, and obtaining data security clearance. The dispute settlement offered by the undertaking often becomes the first choice of dispute settlement of affected parties. This is mainly due to the low cost and

[81] G Greenleaf, *Asian Data Privacy Laws: Trade and Human Rights Perspective* (Oxford, Oxford University Press, 2014) 191–225.

[82] Case C-311/18 *Data Protection Commissioner v Facebook Ireland Ltd and Maximillian Schrems*, 16 July 2020; Case C-362/14 *Maximillian Schrems v Data Protection Commissioner*, 6 October 2015.

[83] Tort Law of the PR China 2010; arts 1 and 2 of the Administrative Litigation Law 1989, 2014, 2017.

[84] Law of the People's Republic of China on Administrative Reconsideration (1999).

[85] Cybersecurity Law, art 49.

Figure 14.1 China's cyberspace governance dispute settlement

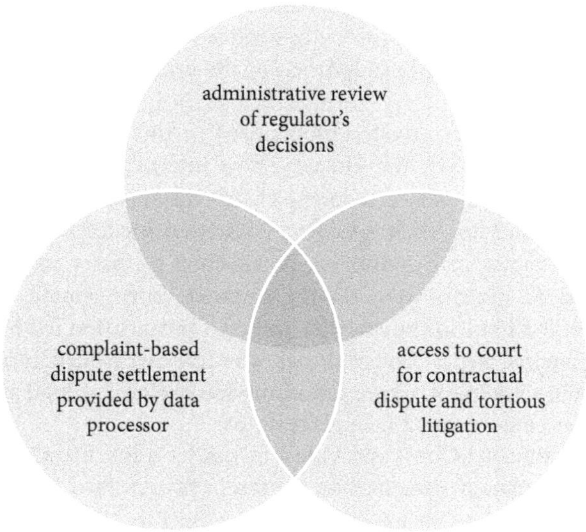

the accessibility of the mechanism, along with the power held by the undertaking due to the undertaking's control of the algorithm. However, the dispute settlement mechanism offered by the undertaking remains voluntary and does not pre-empt parties' resort to the court or investigation by the regulator.

Private parties can bring legal actions to seek remedies for contractual disputes or the infringement of rights provided by Cybersecurity Law, the Data Security Law and the Personal Data Protection Law, as well as for disputes with public authorities before the Chinese courts.[86] In Chinese law, the breach of personal data security is mainly a tortious liability, and private parties as claimants face financial and technical barriers to successfully establishing the liability of the defending undertaking.[87] In order to enhance private parties' access to the courts, China has shifted the burden of proof to undertakings in the proceeding. For instance, Article 69 of the Personal Data Protection Law has provided that once a claimant has filed the legal proceeding, it is for the alleged undertaking to prove that it has not caused actual or potential risks to the data security of the claimant, and has not infringed the claimant's lawful rights and interests arising from personal data.[88] Further, both the Data Security Law and the Personal Data Protection Law provide for civil prosecution-led class action to seek remedy for private parties.

[86] ibid art 74; Data Security Law, art 52; Personal Data Protection Law, arts 69–70; SPC Interpretation 6/9/2018 (see n 35).

[87] Note that art 71 of the Personal Data Protection Law provides that the infringement can incur criminal sanctions. Article 67 of the Personal Data Protection Law sets out that undertakings caught by the law can be recorded in the government credit rating system as an administrative penalty.

[88] Personal Data Protection Law, art 69.

Under both laws, the people's procurator (prosecutor) and civil organisations – including consumer protection organisations and any organisation dedicated by the CAC – can act as the civil prosecutor against the undertaking data processor when a class of persons have been harmed by the undertaking conduct regarding data protection.[89]

In order to strengthen private enforcement in this field, China created the Hang Zhou Internet Court, the Guang Zhou Internet Court and the Beijing Internet Court in 2018 as regional courts of first instances to adjudicate disputes arising from the internet. Their specific jurisdiction includes but is not limited to contractual disputes in e-commerce, intellectual property rights disputes for work published or disseminated on the internet, infringement of personality rights or property rights on the internet and civil prosecution led by the Chinese Procuratorate against digital undertakings. The Internet Courts function as platforms for dispute settlement, where the admission of the case, trial and delivery of the judgment and enforcement take place online.[90]

Whereas the Internet Courts provide a forum for administrative disputes, the CAC and joint regulators' decisions on cybersecurity review for data is final, and decisions on data security for exportation are subject to government administrative review only rather than judicial review.[91] However, the situation becomes more tricky when the CAC has cleared the security review for an undertaking's data exportation on the grounds of national and data security and protection of lawful interests from personal data, and a third party wishes to bring legal proceedings against the undertaking on potential or actual infringement of personality rights. The question remains as to what extent the CAC decision would impact the case admission, and to what extent the decision can be relied upon by the undertaking as a valid defence.

In relation to the private enforcement of data security laws, China provides private parties with enhanced access and a lower burden in seeking remedies before the Chinese court system by shifting the burden of proof. It has empowered prosecutors and government bodies to act as civil prosecutors to seek remedies on behalf of private parties; the establishment of Chinese Internet Courts, as institutional development, is a significant and innovative step forward in terms of providing accessible dispute settlement in relation to disputes arising from the internet. This has de facto equipped private parties and civil prosecutors with stronger powers to bring undertakings within the ambit of judicial oversight. In the meantime, undertakings are faced with regulators' state-centric security-based regulatory power with limited judicial review. Hence, corrective justice-based enhanced private enforcement by the Chinese court system and socially mobilised public monitoring work in tandem with the administrative regulatory power to subject undertakings to comprehensive scrutiny.

[89] ibid arts 70 and 80.
[90] SPC Interpretation 6/9/2018 (see n 35).
[91] Data Exit Security Assessment Measures, art 13.

V. Relationship with Other Sites

China's data security governance has not developed in a vacuum. At the unilateral level, it has strategically referred to norms and tools used by external sites and has socialised them into the Chinese context to serve its own interests. At the bilateral and multilateral levels, it has attempted to influence global norms making and be a norms exporter in the field.

First, China has referred primarily to the US practice and extended extra-territorial jurisdiction of its multiple data security laws. Article 2 of the Data Security Law provides that data processing activities which have had a detriment effect on national security, the public interest or the lawful rights and interests of citizens and organisations will be prosecuted.[92] Article 3 of the Personal Data Protection Law provides that the law is applicable to data processing of natural persons within Chinese territory when the data processing serves to provide products or services to natural persons in China, when it serves to analyse or evaluate the conduct of the natural persons in China, or when the activity is proscribed by other laws and regulations.[93] While both laws require the regulators to comply with confidentiality protection for undertakings in the extra-territorial application where needed, the lack of judicial oversight on the extra-territorial application of the laws means that the regulators may have undefined discretion for the global digital market. It also creates challenges for China's regulators regarding the local enforcement of its extra-territorial enforcement and highlights the importance of bilateral and multilateral dialogue and collaboration.

At the bilateral level, China has been in continuous bilateral dialogues and cooperation with external sites on data security governance. For example, the EU and China have engaged with each other on information technology since 2009.[94] The 'EU-China 2020 Strategic Agenda for Cooperation' was adopted with a focus on the internet and the information society.[95] For cyber-security, the EU and China have set up the China-EU Digital Economy and Cybersecurity Expert Group. However, the bilateral dialogues focus on discussing technical exchanges at the bilateral level.[96]

At the multilateral level, China ratified the Regional Comprehensive and Economic Partnership (RCEP), which became effective in January 2022. The RCEP aims to promote cross-country data governance within the framework of trade liberalisation. However, it deviates from the US approach of prohibiting

[92] Data Security Law, art 2.

[93] Personal Data Protection Law, art 3.

[94] 'EU-China Hold First High-Level Digital Dialogue', press release, 10 September 2020, https://ec.europa.eu/commission/presscorner/detail/en/ip_20_1600.

[95] 'China-EU Strategic Agenda for Cooperation Released at 16th China-EU Summit', https://www.fmprc.gov.cn/mfa_eng/wjdt_665385/2649_665393/201311/t20131123_679356.html.

[96] A Mogni and A Goethals, 'Perspectives on an EU Dialogue with China on Digitalization' (Policy Brief, July 2020), https://www.eias.org/wp-content/uploads/2019/07/Policy-Brief-5G_Mogni_Goethals_EU-CN-Dialogue-Digitalization.pdf.

trade-restrictive data measures on the grounds of arbitrariness and discrimination, and makes it possible for parties to restrict cross-border data trade on the grounds of legitimate public policy and essential security interests. Article 12.14 sets out that no party shall require a covered person to use or locate computing facilities in that party's territory, as a condition for conducting business, unless either of the following grounds of exemption are satisfied: namely, when the measure is considered to be necessary to achieve a legitimate public policy objective, and such a measure is not applied in an arbitrary or unjustifiably discriminatory manner or as a disguised trade restriction,[97] and when such a restriction is considered by a party to be necessary for protecting essential security interests, the definition of which shall not be disputed by other parties under the RCEP.[98] When it comes to the definition of legitimate public policy and essential security interests, and the evaluation of the extent to which such measures are necessary for achieving such public policy goals and security interests, Article 12.4 leaves the definition and evaluation entirely to individual parties and accords each party the final say on it.

Article 12.8 is concerned with online personal information protection and sets out the legal obligation for each party to put a legal framework in place for such protection. Each party, when creating such a framework, should refer to the standards, principles, guidelines and criteria of international bodies. Such protection should include legally imposed responsibilities for businesses and remedies for consumers.[99] Article 12.8 requires all parties to cooperate on the protection of transferred information among parties, to the greatest extent possible.[100] However, the RCEP deviates from the human rights-based approach when it comes to personal information protection, and sets out a minimum requirement for personal information to be protected by law – where consumers should have access for remedies for the harm suffered from contractual or tortious liability. Further, the RCEP has remained silent on the level and adequacy of protection and has left it for the parties to decide.

The RCEP's design on data security protection and trade liberalisation reflects China's strategic interests in its security-led development strategy, as it has created the legal basis for cross-border data flow restrictions to be justified on state-centric security grounds. It is compatible with China's regulatory approach, as the non-disputability of the parties' own definition of essential security interests and the consultative nature in dispute settlement in this field mean that parties are subject to as little as possible external scrutiny, whether from judicial oversight or from the international community. However, China's future interaction with the parties in the RCEP forum, and its relationship with other external sites (for example the CPTPP) remains to be seen, which could, potentially, have an impact on China as a site for data security governance.

[97] Regional Comprehensive Economic Partnership (2022), art 12.14 (a).
[98] ibid art 12.114(b).
[99] ibid art 12.8.
[100] ibid art 12.8.

VI. Conclusion

The challenges raised by the digital economy to human societies have provided an opportunity for China to develop and institutionalise its state-centric national security regulatory model over the digital space. The analysis of the institutional aspect, the normative basis and the dispute settlement mechanism of China's data security regulation reveals the following features.

First, China has established a national security-led regulatory framework for domestic and cross-border data flow. The framework is led by the party-state's National Security Commission, overseen by the CAC and supported by sectoral regulators at the central government level with a similar structure at the local government level. Within the framework, qualified undertakings, though not necessarily Chinese, will be subject to continuous regulatory scrutiny through pre-review assessment, centralised review and post-review monitoring. The regulators can employ soft law instruments – for example, requested meetings with the regulators or warnings in the process. These tools, combined, enable regulators to achieve regulatory goals with flexibility and innovation. However, with limited judicial and external oversight, the structure poses potential risks of legal certainty and transparency to undertakings.

Second, maintaining and strengthening the Chinese state's capacity to handle the risks generated by the digital economy to its political, economic and social systems constitute the cornerstone of the normative basis of China's digital governance. The protection of personal data and lawful interests is one element of the normative basis and goes beyond protecting the right to privacy as a personality right. However, the value underpinning the normative basis lies in strengthening the state vis-a-vis the power held by the digital economy and the digital market players. This feature significantly differentiates China's value trade-off in the substantive assessment of data security from the self-autonomy-based EU approach and the economic welfare-based US approach.

Third, dispute settlement within the site comprises the internal resolution mechanism provided by the undertaking and the private enforcement of contractual disputes or economic torts before the Chinese courts. Institutional innovation (for example, the regional internet courts) and procedural innovation (for example, shifting the burden of proof to defending undertakings) have been installed to increase parties' access to justice. However, the economic tort-based lawful interests of personal data is determined on a case-by-case basis, and such protection gives way to the state-centred security interests in the hierarchy of interests protected by China's cyber-security governance.

Fourth, China's influence in the RCEP and the launch of China's Global Data Security Initiative serve as examples of its efforts to lead the norms making on global data flows. Such efforts in the international setting are largely shaped by and reflect the features of China as a site of governance on data security regulation. Meanwhile, they provide fora for China to communicate, understand and even clash with other sites of governance, which feed back to China's site building. The development of China as a global data security site of governance illustrates how the site's institutional aspect, normative basis and dispute settlement mechanism, on the one hand, and its external relations, on the other hand, are in a dialectic and dynamic relationship.

With the digital economy advancing under globalisation, the question of how we should regulate data can hardly remain entirely domestic. Global actors have strived to project respective regulatory approaches into the global digital space, hoping to influence and lead relevant transnational law making. Fundamentally, the effectiveness and transparency of the institutional structure, the values underpinning the normative basis and the accessibility and credibility of each site of governance, and the approach that the site uses to work with the rest of the world would interact with each other and contribute to the sites' influence in the pluralistic legal field and shape the outcome of transnational law making.

INDEX

www.ingramcontent.com/pod-product-compliance
Ingram Content Group UK Ltd.
Pitfield, Milton Keynes, MK11 3LW, UK
UKHW020236290926
15470UKWH00002B/569

9 781509 964499